THE REVOLT IN CENTRAL INDIA, 1857-59

THE REVOLT IN CENTRAL INDIA, 1857-59

REGINALD GEORGE BURTON

GYAN

Published by

Gyan Publishing House
5, Ansari Road
Daryaganj, New Delhi-110002
Phone: 011-47034999, 9811692060
E-mail: books@gyanbooks.com

Distribution Network
gyanbooks.com
India, USA, Canada, UK, Australia

ISBN: 978-93-7225-179-1 (PB)

First Published, 1908

2nd Impression 2026

Printed at: Gyan Press, Delhi.

THE REVOLT IN CENTRAL INDIA, 1857-59
Author: REGINALD GEORGE BURTON

THE REVOLT IN CENTRAL INDIA

1857–59

COMPILED IN THE

INTELLIGENCE BRANCH

DIVISION OF THE CHIEF OF THE STAFF

ARMY HEAD QUARTERS

INDIA.

SIMLA:

PRINTED AT THE GOVERNMENT MONOTYPE PRESS.

1908.

PREFACE.

General Sir Archibald Hunter, K.C.B., D.S.O., when inspecting the Jhansi Brigade in the winter of 1906-07, suggested that "all officers should be made acquainted with the details of the operations within the Brigade area, 'specially those leading to the capture of Jhansi,' and that 'these operations might form the basis for manœuvres and staff rides'."

To enable this suggestion to be carried out, the history of the Revolt in Central India has been compiled from the original despatches and reports of those engaged in the events narrated by Major R. G. Burton, 94th Russell's Infantry.

Lord Esher, referring to the volcanic forces of insurrection, which must always exist, even though they slumber, in an Empire such as ours, recently said :—"British Officers of every rank, and of all ages, may be suddenly called upon to take responsibilities, upon which many of them have never pondered, and to decide issues, big with the fate of their countrymen and women, which, perhaps, a few months of careful historical study in time of peace would enable them to solve with conspicuous success." The truth of this observation is exemplified in this history. The facts related further serve to emphasise the conspicuous loyalty of, and the active support rendered by, some of the great Native Princes of India in the time of stress and trouble with which this book deals.

In this narrative the term "Central India" is used in its wider geographical sense, and includes Rajputana and part of the country now known as the Central Provinces, in fact, the whole tract between the Jumna and Narbada rivers, a far greater area than the region comprised under that designation for political and administrative purposes.

It has been found impossible to show in the pocket map, which is necessarily of small scale, all the places named in the text of this volume. The principal physical features, towns and villages are, however, indicated, and no difficulty will be experienced in tracing the march of the various columns and the routes pursued by the enemy during the operations. Every place mentioned can be found in the larger scale maps prepared by the Survey of India.

It is particularly requested that any errors or important omissions may be brought to the notice of the Division of the Chief of the Staff, Intelligence Branch.

W. MALLESON, Lieut.-Colonel,

Simla;	*Assistant Quarter Master General,*
21*st March* 1908.	*Division of the Chief of the Staff.*

CONTENTS.

CHRONOLOGICAL TABLE OF EVENTS.

INTRODUCTION.

CHAPTER I.

CENTRAL INDIA.

CHAPTER II

JHANSI AND BUNDELKHAND.

CHAPTER III.

THE SAUGOR AND NARBADA TERRITORIES.

CHAPTER IV.

THE MUTINIES IN RAJPUTANA.

CHAPTER V.

CHAPTER VI.

OPERATIONS OF THE MALWA FIELD FORCE.

CHAPTER VII.

SIR HUGH ROSE'S CAMPAIGN IN CENTRAL INDIA.

CHAPTER VIII.

SIR HUGH ROSE'S CAMPAIGN IN CENTRAL INDIA—(*continued*).

CHAPTER IX.

THE GWALIOR CAMPAIGN

CHAPTER X.

GENERAL WHITLOCK'S OPERATIONS AND THE PACIFICATION OF BUNDELKHAND.

CHAPTER XI.

THE CAMPAIGN IN RAJPUTANA.

CHAPTER XII.

THE PURSUIT OF TANTIA TOPI.

MAPS.

Chronological table of events during the revolt in Central India.

Date.	Central India.	Rajputana.	Jhansi, Bundelkhand, Saugor, and Narbada.	Remarks.
1857 May				
28th ..	....	Mutiny at Nasirabad.	....	May 10th, outbreak of the mutiny at Meerut. May 16th, mutiny at Delhi. May 20th, revolt at Aligarh.
June 3rd ..	....	Mutiny at Neemuch	....	....
6th ..	....	....	Mutiny at Jhansi	June 4th, outbreak at Cawnpore.
8th ..	....	....	Massacre at Jhansi	....
9th ..	....	....	Mutiny at Nowgong.	June 27th, massacre at Cawn ore.
" ..	Mutiny of the Malwa Contingent Cavalry.	....	....	....
12th ..	....	....	Mutiny at Lalitpur	....
13th ..	....	....	Mutiny at Hamirpur.	....
14th ..	Rising at Gwalior	....	Outbreak at Banda	....
" ..	Mutiny at Sipri ..	....	....	....
25th ..	....	....	Mutiny at Malthone.	....
" ..	....	Sack of Deoli ..	....	....
July 1st ..	Attack on the Indore Residency.	....	Mutiny at Saugor	....
" ..	Mutiny at Mhow	....	....	....
3rd ..	....	....	Mutiny at Damoh	July 4th, mutiny of the Kotah Contingent at Agra. July 16th, second massacre at Cawnpore. July 17th, battle of Cawnpore.
9th ..	Abandonment of Sehore.	....		....
17th ..	....	....	March of the Nagpore Moveable Column.	....

Chronological table of events during the revolt in Central India—contd.

Date.	Central India.	Rajputana.	Jhansi, Bundelkhand, Saugor, and Narbada.	REMARKS.
JULY—*contd.*				
18th ..	....	....	Action at Benaika	....
AUGUST				
2nd ..	Relief of Mhow ..	....	....	....
10th ..	....	Second outbreak at Nasirabad.	....	....
12th ..	....	Second outbreak at Neemuch.	....	....
21st ..	....	Attack on Mount Abu.	....	....
23rd ..	....	Mutiny at Erinpura.	....	....
26th ..	Insurrection at Mandesar.	....	....	....
31st ..	Seizure of Dhar by the rebels.	....	....	....
SEPTR.				
1st ..	....	....	Capture of Balakot	September 14th, storm of Delhi.
8th ..	....	Attack on Neemuch by rebels.	....	....
" ..	....	Defeat of Jodhpur army by rebels at Awah.	....	....
17th ..	....	....	Destruction of rebels at Narsingarh.	....
18th ..	....	Abortive attack on rebels at Awah.	....	....
" ..	....	Seizure of Nimbahera by British Agent.	Mutiny at Jubbulpore.	....
" ..	....	....	Mutiny at Nagode	....
21st ..	....	....	Abandonment of Damoh.	September 27th, first relief of Lucknow.
27th ..	....	....	Action at Katangi	....

Chronological table of events during the revolt in Central India—(contd.)

Date.	Central India.	Rajputana.	Jhansi, Bundelkhand, Saugor, and Narbada.	Remarks.
Octr.				
2nd	...	...	Capture of Rehli	...
8th	...	...	Action at Hindia	...
10th	...	Rebel attack on Bhopawar and Sirdarpur	...	....
15th	...	Outbreak at Kotah	...	...
17th	...	...	Defeat of rebels at Piplia.	....
21st	....	...	Sack of Patan ...	...
22nd	Action at Dhar ..	...	...	...
23rd	...	British repulse at Jhiran.	...	...
31st	Capture of Dhar	...	...	...
Novr.				
4th	...	...	Rout of Bijiraghugarh rebels.	...
8th	Mutiny at Mehidpur	...	...	....
12th	Combat of Rawal	...	...	November 16th, second relief of Lucknow.
14th	...	...	Fight at Katangi...	November 17th, defeat of the Jodhpur Legion.
23rd	...	...	Destruction of rebels on the Narbada.	....
"	Battle of Mandesar	...	...	...
24th	Storming of Goraria.	...	...	...
Decr.				
14th	Entry of British into Indore.	...	...	...
26th	....	....	Fight at Koni Pass	...

Chronological table of events during the revolt in Central India—(contd.)

Date.	Central India.	Rajputana.	Jhansi, Bundelkhand, Saugor, and Narbada.	REMARKS.
1858. JANY.				
5th ..	....	British capture Sirohi.	....	....
6th ..	Advance of the Central India Field Force.	....	....	....
19th ..	....	Awah captured by the British.	....	....
29th ..	....	....	Capture of Rahatgarh.	....
31st ..	....	....	Action at Barodia	....
FEBY.				
3rd ..	....	....	Relief of Saugor	....
8th ..	....	....	Capture of Sanoda	....
11th ..	....	....	Fall of Garhakota	....
26th ..	....	....	Whitlock relieves Damoh.	
27th ..	....	....	Advance of Sir H. Rose from Saugor.	....
MARCH				
3rd ..	....	....	Battle of Madanpur Pass.	....
4th ..	....	....	Capture of Surahi and Maraura.	March 14th, storming of Lucknow.
17th ..	....	....	Sir H. Rose's 1st Brigade captures Chanderi.	....
21st ..	....	....	Sir H. Rose arrives before Jhansi.	....
23rd ..	....	....	Investment of Jhansi.	....
30th ..	....	Capture of Kotah by the Rajputana Field Force.	....	....
31st ..	....	....	Battle of Betwa River.	....

Chronological table of events during the revolt in Central India—(concld.)

Date.	Central India.	Rajputana.	Jhansi, Bundelkhand, Saugor, and Narbada.	Remarks.
April				
3rd ..	....	....	Capture of Jhansi	....
11th ..	....	....	Action at Jhigan	....
18th ..	....	....	Battle of Banda ..	....
25th ..	....	....	Sir H. Rose advances from Jhansi.	....
May				
2nd ..	....	....	Capture of Lohari	....
7th ..	....	....	Battle of Kunch.	....
22nd ..	....	....	Battle of Kalpi.	....
31st ..	....	....	Combat of Bilayan	....
" ..	Capture of Gwalior by the rebels.	....	....	....
June				
6th ..	Advance of Sir H. Rose from Kalpi.	....	Capture of Kirwi (1st).	....
16th ..	Battle of Morar ..	....	....	....
17th ..	Battle of Kotah-ki-Serai.	....	....	....
19th ..	Capture of Gwalior	....	....	....
" ..	Battle of Jaora, Alipur.	....	....	....
June to December			Pacification of Bundelkhand.	....
	Pursuit of Tantia Topi, August 1858 to March 1859.			

INTRODUCTION.

The Indian Mutiny.

The history of the events which occurred south of the river Jumna during the Indian Mutiny is less generally known than that of the rising in Oudh and the North-West. Perhaps it is that all eyes were then turned towards Delhi and Lucknow, where the more dramatic events of this great tragedy took place, which no doubt possessed more political and military importance, and on which public attention was, therefore, and has since been, concentrated. But, if the events in Central India possess less dramatic interest, their general bearing on the situation throughout the whole of India was of the first importance, whilst the military episodes of Sir Hugh Rose's march from the Narbada to the Jumna reflect no less glory on the British arms than do those on which the light of history has cast a deeper glamour. To the military student in particular the study of that campaign in which no mistake was made, and which was brought to a triumphant conclusion by the skill, energy, and courage of one of the greatest of British Generals, and by the valour of his troops, is of lasting interest and utility.

Political influences.

In 1856 Lord Dalhousie resigned to Lord Canning the Viceroyalty of India, after a term of office marked by strenuous activity, and by an extensive policy of annexation. This policy was largely rendered necessary, as in the case of Oudh, by the misgovernment of native rulers; but in many instances it was characterised by a disregard of native custom; such were the cases of succession of the Nana of Bithur and of the Rani of Jhansi, who were not permitted to succeed respectively to the emoluments and estates, the one of his adoptive father, the deposed Peshwa Baji Rao, and the other of her deceased husband, the Raja of Jhansi. These two disappointed suitors became the bitterest and most cruel enemies of the British. From Oudh, a dissolute and incompetent King was removed, and his territories were annexed to the British dominions. This was a severe shock to the susceptibilities of the feudal nobles of Oudh; and it must be remembered that the Bengal Army was largely recruited from that Province.

There were thus political causes of disaffection in India; there were Princes and States ripe for rebellion; while on the Delhi throne there sat the shadow of a monarch whom tradition and the greatness of a name caused to be venerated by Musalmans throughout India; and in the Bengal Army political agitators found a fertile soil for planting the seed of corruption.

The infantry of that army had in its ranks a great majority of Oudh sepoys; while men of the same class formed the bulk of forces such as the Gwalior Contingent, maintained by Native States under the terms of treaties with the British Government. A small percentage of Muhammadans of Hindustan was also to be found in the Bengal Native Infantry, while they supplied the greater part of the Cavalry* of that Presidency. It will thus be understood that in both arms there was a dangerous preponderance of one class, facilitating and extending combination on the part of the disaffected.

The Native Army.

It was, however, different in the armies of the other Presidencies, where men of every caste and creed were mingled in the ranks. This obviated the likelihood of combination among men ever wont to be suspicious of one another. There were, moreover, in the Madras Army, family ties to keep the men true to their salt. In that Presidency the sepoy had in almost every instance a large number of relatives, sometimes of several generations, living with him in the lines. He was not likely to abandon these relations to their fate, and mutiny against the Government he served. But the Oudh sepoy left his belongings in his native village when he enlisted, and the Bengal Army was practically a bachelor army.

While the susceptibilities of the Oudh sepoy had been touched by the annexation of his country, the Muhammadans still held in veneration the puppet who occupied the throne of the Great Mughals, and cherished the recollection of former glory and power. They had also the influence of a fanatical religion to incite them to a holy war against the Christians. Their combination with the hated Hindus is, however, somewhat remarkable, and the causes which brought these antagonistic peoples into alliance must be sought for elsewhere than in political influences. That there were leaders such as Nana Sahib, the Maulvi of Fyzabad, the Rani of Jhansi, and others who made use of the native army for purposes of intrigue and rebellion has already been indicated. But the army would not mutiny merely at the instigation of a few political intriguers and agitators. The native of India is not greatly influenced by politics. The smooth course of rural life has undergone little alteration in its main characteristics by the changes of a thousand years. Whether living under the rule of Buddhist, Hindu, Musalman, or European, the agricultural class from which the sepoys were drawn pursued their peaceful avocations comparatively undisturbed. The passage of fire and sword over the land in the hands of Mughal, Mahratta, or Pindari only disturbed the surface of village life, and, from a political point of view, the peasant sank back again after such irruptions into the slumber

Leaders of sedition.

* In 1853, however, half the Bengal Irregular Cavalry was composed of Hindus.

of an uneventful existence. It mattered but little to him under what King he served, so long as he was able to earn his daily bread and his religion was undisturbed.

The seeds of disaffection had long been at work in the Bengal Army. The disasters of the Afghan War had taught the sepoy that his European comrade was not invincible. It had, in fact, shaken that prestige by which alone the few can rule the many. And the proportion of native to British soldiers in India was far too great. For, as Bacon says, "as for mercenary forces (which is the help in this case) all examples show that, whatsoever estate, or prince, doth rest upon them, he may spread his feathers for a time, but he will mew them soon after." Our Indian Empire in those days rested too largely on mercenary forces.* There were in the country only some 38,000 European soldiers, while the native troops numbered 200,000 men, not including the levies of independent or semi-independent Princes. A great establishment of native artillery had grown up, although the Court of Directors had recognised it as a danger so far back as in 1813 and had then characterised it as "an arm which it ought to be our policy not to extend the knowledge of it to the natives."

Mercenary forces.

The Bengal sepoy had cause for discontent. His allowances had been more than once interfered with, while he thought he had reason for dreading an attempt to destroy his caste and subvert his religion; the points on which he was most sensitive. Ill-advised measures of the military authorities, combined with political intrigue, caused the mutiny of the Madras troops at Vellore in 1806. That outbreak was, indeed, typical of the greater tragedy which took place fifty-one years later. It had in it elements, both as regards its cause and its suppression, which may be fitly compared with those which characterised the greater disaster.

In the fort of Vellore in 1806 were confined the sons of Tipu Sultan of Mysore, whose kingdom had been overthrown and himself slain in 1799. Here these descendants of the most fanatical enemy of the British in India were permitted to maintain a large body of adherents and an almost regal state. Naturally they intrigued. The soldiers had grievances. The military authorities introduced a new fashion of turban which, owing to its resemblance to the head-dress worn by the East Indian drummers, gave rise to a rumour that this measure was preparatory to forcible conversion to Christianity. About the same time an order was issued directing that "a native soldier shall not mark his face to denote his caste, or wear earrings when dressed in his uniform; it is further directed that at all

Lessons of history.

* "Ancient Rome and Sparta were free and strong for many ages, thanks to their armies drawn from the people. The primary cause of the fall of Rome was the inclusion in the army of the mercenary Goths."—*The Art of War*.—Machiavelli.

parades and on all duties every soldier shall be clean-shaved on the chin. It is directed also that uniformity shall, as far as is practicable, be preserved in regard to the quantity and shape of the hair on the upper lip.'' It is not surprising that such inconsiderate orders, prejudicial to the religion and sentiment of both Hindus and Musalmans, should cause the smouldering discontent already existing to break out into open mutiny. There were other signs and portents typical of the events of 1857. The officers had become estranged from their men, and lived too much apart from them, while they were in most cases ever striving to get away from regimental duty. In the native army, where personal influence is of the first importance, and is in fact the mainspring of all efficiency in the soldier, this was disastrous. As in 1857 signs of the coming storm were disregarded.

At Vellore the native troops suddenly broke into open mutiny and killed the majority of the European officers and soldiers quartered in the fort, while the striped flag of Mysore was raised upon the ramparts. But if the parallel so far is close, the method of dealing with the outbreak in 1806 diverges from the weakness displayed at Meerut in 1857. In 1806 there was happily at the neighbouring station of Arcot a soldier of energy, decision, and courage, both moral and physical. Colonel Gillespie with the 19th Dragoons and galloper guns came down upon the mutineers like a hurricane ; blew open the gates of the fort, destroyed the majority of the sepoys, and in the course of a few hours suppressed the rebellion. This stern retribution struck terror into the hearts of other would-be mutineers ; and disaffection, which was rife throughout the Madras Army, did not elsewhere find active expression.

In 1857 similar measures at the o set might have had similar results. Gillespie was killed in the Nepal War in 1814, and buried at Meerut, and "by the irony of fate, on the 10th May 1857, the first shots of the great Sepoy Mutiny were fired within a mile of the monument over his grave, and were the beginning of events that at one time threatened to involve British Power in the East in ruin, and that have changed the whole course of Indian history. If that gallant spirit was still permitted to take interest in the events of that day, how it must have chafed at the exhibition of incapacity and indecision that led to such disastrous consequences. In view of what happened at Vellore, it is allowable to believe that the great Mutiny of 1857 would never have assumed the proportions it did, had the first outbreak been met by the same display of energy and resolution as was shown, under similar circumstances, fifty-one years earlier." *

Assuredly the past contains valuable lessons both for the statesman and the soldier which may well be remembered with profit when the day of action comes !

* *The Nineteenth and their times.* By Colonel John Biddulph.

In 1850 an Indian Army Officer of long experience wrote that the reserved and exclusive habits of the European officers were gaining ground

British Officers.

The generality of officers took but little interest in their men, who, on their part, ceased to feel either love or reverence for superiors who were virtually strangers to them, and powerless, besides, either to reward or punish. This want of sympathy between the European officers and their men appeared to the author* as fraught with impending peril, and there could be no doubt of its impairing the efficiency of any regiment. He deeply regretted the unprofessional eagerness manifested by officers of all ranks to get away from their regimental duties:† nor did he regard with less apprehension the paucity of officers doing duty with each native corps. This led to frequent changes, so that the men were seldom commanded by officers whom they knew, and who knew them, the one thing above others needful for the native army, the men of which are more easily guided by loyalty to the person than to the State.

There was, moreover, too much centralization of power in the hands of the military authorities at Army Head-Quarters, who to the sepoy were mere phantoms living among the clouds of the Himalayas. Thus Commanding

Immediate causes of mutiny.

Officers lost power and prestige. The proselytising spirit was also abroad, and amiable but fanatical Christian Commanding Officers preached their religion about the country. Then came the crucial question of the greased cartridges. With a great deal of reason, the sepoys complained of the new cartridge, the paper of which was greased with animal fat, which, whether truly or otherwise, was said to be that of swine and oxen. Here was a handle for the political agitator to lay hold of. Then reports were spread that the flour sold to the native troops in the bazaar was mixed with bone dust, with a view to destroying their caste. Sugar was refined with the blood of oxen.‡ In fact all kinds of rumours, easily manipulated by astute agitators, and as readily believed by a credulous and simple-minded people, were spread broadcast throughout the land.

Nor were signs of the coming storm wanting. Some old and experienced officers tendered solemn warnings, others, even with a life-long experience of the native people, were blind to all possibility of disaffection. The Governor-General was surrounded by counsellors who had spent their service in Government Offices; the military authorities were said to have been out of touch with the native army, with which most of them had served but little, and that not for many years.

* Brigadier J. S. Hodgson, late commanding the Punjab Irregular Force.

† Seeing, however, that extra regimental employment was the only way to advancement, the blame cannot apply only to the officers.

‡ It is perhaps not remarkable that similar reports were spread by seditious agitators in 1907.

The mysterious *chapathis* were circulated, and, while their significance was realised by some, it was ignored by the majority. The Nana visited Kalpi, Lucknow, and Delhi, no doubt tampering with the troops at those places, but his mission was unsuspected. Native newspapers and native demagogues preached sedition.

Signs and portents.

The introduction of the new cartridge* for the Enfield rifle in January 1857 caused widespread alarm. At Barhampore the 19th Bengal Infantry mutinied, and was marched into Barrackpore, where the regiment was disbanded on the 31st March. In February General J. B. Hearsey, who commanded at Barrackpore, wrote—"We have been dwelling upon a mine ready for explosion. I have been watching the feelings of the sepoys here for some time. Their minds have been misled by some designing scoundrels, who have managed to make them believe that their religious prejudices, their caste, is to be interfered with by Government; that they are to be forced to become Christians."

Mangal Pande.

On the 29th March sepoy Mangal Pande, of the 34th Bengal Infantry at Barrackpore, attacked and wounded the Adjutant and Sergeant-Major of his regiment. His comrades sympathised with him; some of the guard who were near taking an active part in the affray, while other sepoys whose sympathy was passive looked on with indifference. Mangal Pande and the Jemadar of the Guard were hanged, and eventally the 34th Bengal Infantry was disbanded. Meanwhile alarm occurred at Umballa and other stations, the greased cartridge being the ostensible, if not the real, cause. Disaffection found vent in incendiarism, the almost invariable precursor of mutiny, as will be seen from the ensuing narrative.

The outbreak at Meerut.

At Meerut on the 24th April eighty-five men of the 3rd Bengal Cavalry refused to take the new cartridge. They were tried and sentenced to ten years' imprisonment, their sentence being announced and fetters put on on parade on the 9th May. This degradation was the spark which fired the mutiny.† Next evening the native troops in Meerut rose, killed every European they met, released their comrades in the gaol, and went off to Delhi. It is unfortunate that at Meerut there was no senior officer capable of meeting the crisis. There were in garrison two batteries of British Field Artillery, as well as one of

* In those days the paper ends of the cartridges were bitten off by the soldier when loading.

† It is said that the end of the British Raj had been predicted to take place on the 23rd June, 1857, the centenary of the battle of Plassey. Elsewhere it is stated that this outbreak was premature, and that a concerted rising had been arranged for the 31st May. This may be doubted. In most corps the mutiny appears to have been entirely unpremeditated

the finest cavalry regiments in the British Army—the Carabineers, and a battalion of Rifles. But there was no Gillespie to wield the weapon thus ready to hand. A fatal inaction characterised the Europeans. Where the charge of a Squadron and a few rounds of grape might have arrested the mutiny at its outbreak, nothing was done, and the mutinous soldiery marched unmolested to Delhi.

Delhi.

Delhi is the historic capital of India. Upon its time-worn walls rests the prestige of a thousand years of Empire. Here the effete descendant of the Great Mughal Emperors sat in tinsel state in the palace of his fathers. The streets had often run red with blood when the hosts of Taimur, of Nadir Shah, and of Ahmad Shah Durani had made their triumphant entry into the capital of Hindustan, and in former times the possession of Delhi meant the possession of the Empire; indeed the same may be said of Delhi fifty years ago. The prestige involved in its possession was felt throughout the length and breadth of India.

Yet Delhi was held for the British by a few regiments of mercenary soldiers!

Early on the 11th May some of the mutinous troopers from Meerut arrived at Delhi. Here the troops soon followed suit, murdered some of their officers, while others escaped, and a number of Europeans were massacred in the palace and in the streets. A few heroic men blew up the magazine. Some fifty Christians, held captive in the palace for five days, were then inhumanly slaughtered in the courtyard, and their bodies thrown into the Jumna.

An army was at once organised for the recovery of Delhi, while forces were collected in the Punjab for the same purpose. The columns under General Barnard, having defeated the rebels who opposed them at Badli-ki-Sarai, arrived before Delhi on the 8th June, and commenced the long siege which terminated with the capture of the city in the middle of September.

Cawnpore.

Meanwhile the mutiny had spread to other corps of the Bengal Army. The native troops at Cawnpore rose on the 4th June, massacred the Europeans of the garrison who surrendered on the 27th, while the women and children who had been captured were butchered under circumstances of unspeakable horror on the 15th July, the day before Havelock's relieving column defeated the Nana and entered Cawnpore.

Spread of the mutiny.

There was also mutiny at many other places during this period, not only at Azimgarh, Allahabad, Agra, Jaunpur, and other stations north of the Jumna, but in Central India and the adjoining territories, as related in this volume. In the Punjab risings occurred in several places, but in many instances were quickly put down or averted by strong men and strong measures, while the Sikhs remained loyal, and rendered great service to the State.

Lucknow.

On the 30th May the troops at Lucknow rose, and there commenced the long and glorious defence of the Residency by the beleaguered garrison, who were first relieved on the 27th September, although the rebel hold on the defenders was not relinquished until Sir Colin Campbell advanced and drove off the mutineers with terrible slaughter two months later.

After the relief of Lucknow, Sir Colin Campbell marched to Cawnpore, where General Wyndham had been driven into the intrenchments and was with difficulty holding his own against the Gwalior Contingent under Tantia Topi. On the 6th December Cawnpore was relieved, and Tantia Topi retired on Kalpi with the defeated remnants of his army, where we shall meet with him again in the course of this narrative.

Oudh, Rohilkhand, and Central India.

So far we have dealt principally with the mutiny of the Bengal Army. But the people in many parts of the country rose also. The whole of Oudh and Rohilkhand were in revolt, while Central India from the Jumna to the Narbada was in a state of rebellion. It is with this latter region that the ensuing narrative deals, and it will be seen that while the mutiny had been put down in many places in Oudh and the North-West, while Delhi had fallen, Lucknow had been twice relieved, and the Nana had been driven from Cawnpore and his followers dispersed before the end of 1857, no general movement for the suppression of rebellion in Central India took place until early in 1858.

It must not be supposed, however, that Sir Hugh Rose, who commanded the Central India Field Force, had an easy task before him. In 1858 Oudh was still a seething mass of revolt; the besiegers of Lucknow were not finally defeated until March of that year, by which time Sir Hugh Rose had relieved Saugor and was advancing against the rebels at Jhansi under the Rani.

Strategical combinations.

From this it will be understood that the various events were connected, that they were in some measure interdependent, and that from a strategical point of view the operations both north and south of the Jumna were directed towards one common object. The Commander-in-Chief said in his order of the 26th June, 1858, when congratulating Major-General Sir Hugh Rose on the successful result of his advance on Gwalior:—

"It must not be forgotten that the advance of the Central India Field Force formed part of a large combination, and was rendered possible by the movement of Major-General Roberts, of the Bombay Army, into Rajputana, on the one side, and of Major-General Whitlock, of the Madras Army, on the other, and by the support they, respectively, gave to Major-General Sir Hugh Rose as he moved onwards in obedience to his instructions."

How far Sir Hugh Rose's advance was assisted by the halting operations and dilatory proceedings of Major-General Whitlock will be gathered from a study of the ensuing pages. The flanks of the Central India Field Force were to some extent protected by the advance of the columns through Rajputana and Eastern Bundelkhand, but those columns exerted but little influence on the general course of the war. Perhaps with more reason the Commander-in-Chief might have referred to the assistance which Sir Hugh Rose rendered Sir Colin Campbell in the pacification of Oudh by the containing power of the Central India Field Force which, manœuvred by the greatest commander of those times, held and finally defeated and destroyed thee rebel army south of the Jumna.

THE REVOLT IN CENTRAL INDIA.

CHAPTER I.

CENTRAL INDIA.

The theatre of operations.

The revolt of the sepoy army in Hindustan in 1857 spread rapidly towards the south, threatening at one time to engulf the whole of India in the flames of rebellion. But, except for sporadic outbreaks, it was practically checked on the line of the Narbada by the vigorous measures undertaken to prevent its further extension outwards.

The country included in the theatre of military operations to the south of the line Cawnpore-Agra comprised Central India,* including Gwalior, Western Malwa, Indore, and Bundelkhand, as well as Jhansi and a portion of the Central Provinces then known as the Saugor and Narbada Territories, whilst part of Rajputana was also in the area of rebellion.

This extensive region comprised the great table-land of Malwa, a highly cultivated country, varied with small conical and flat-topped hills and low ridges, watered by many rivers, including the Banas, Chambal, Sindh, and Betwa, draining into the Jumna on the north; and the Narbada with its tributaries on the south.

A large portion of the country is covered with forests, especially in the more hilly regions which have not been brought under cultivation. The plains are generally characterised by a dark alluvial surface known as black cotton soil, which is highly fertile.

The climate of Central India is generally equable, the year being divided, as elsewhere in the central part of the peninsula, into seasons influenced by the prevalence of the monsoon. In the hot weather, from April to July, the heat is intense; this season is followed by some three months of heavy rain, succeeded by a cold weather during which the thermometer ranges from 70° to below freezing point.

The country is inhabited by peoples of many races and many tongues—Pathans, Mahrattas, and Rajputs represent the civilization of the Orient; aboriginal Bhils and Gonds share with savage beasts the fastnesses of forest and mountain. It is interesting to note that a large portion of the region of revolt had been the scene of operations during the great Mahratta and Pindari War of 1817, after which the Confederacy of the nation founded by Sivaji had been broken up and the territories of the Peshwa had been annexed.

* Central India and Bundelkhand comprised many States, of which the principal were Dhar, Orchha, Samthar, Panna, Charkhari, Rewah, Nagode, Gwalior, Indore, Bhopal, Jaora, Rutlam and others.

The Peshwa Baji Rao, whose overthrow took place in the war of 1817, had not been forgotten in Central India and the Deccan, whilst his adopted son, the infamous Nana Sahib of Cawnpore, who in 1854 succeeded to his legacy of wealth and hatred towards the British, aspired to sovereignty and was recognised by the Mahrattas as their legitimate chief. The spark of nationality still glowed in the heart of the Mahratta people of the Deccan, and required but little encouragement to kindle into a blaze that would have fired the whole country from the Jumna to the Krishna and Tungabhadra. But it was quenched for ever by the suppression of the rebellion in Central India. The two great Mahratta Chiefs, Sindhia and Holkar, had their capitals, respectively, at Indore and Gwalior, and their attitude and that of their people during the crisis was important, and at the same time that of the latter was uncertain. At Jhansi the British had a bitter enemy in the Rani. Early in 1857 the Nana paid a visit to Kalpi on the bank of the Jumna, while his agents had been at work in every part of the Mahratta country. The outbreak at Meerut on the 10th May, 1857, was followed by the revolt of regiments stationed in other parts of the country, including Agra and Aligarh, which were in dangerous proximity to Gwalior. After the war of 1843, Lord Ellenborough had restored Gwalior to Sindhia. He disbanded the Maharaja's Army, and in its place raised a subsidiary force, known as the Gwalior Contingent, under British Officers, while a Resident was placed at the Court of Sindhia. The Maharaja, then a minor, grew up a staunch adherent of British rule, and on the outbreak of the Mutiny loyally adopted the cause of the Suzerain Power, and, on the request of the Lieutenant-Governor of the North-West Provinces, sent troops to his assistance at Agra and Aligarh.

The Mahratta country.

Gwalior.

Gwalior was within 70 miles of Agra; the Contingent was composed of 2 regiments of cavalry, 4 field batteries, a small siege train, and 7 infantry battalions, a total of 8,318 men under Brigadier Ramsay; there were outposts at Sipri, Agra, Goona, Agar, and other places, and we find troops of the Gwalior Contingent as far south as Mehidpur, Neemuch, and Asirgarh. The men of which it was composed were drawn from the same sources as the Bengal Army. On hearing of the revolt of the 9th Bengal Infantry at Aligarh, detachments of that regiment at Bulandshahr, Mainpuri, and Etawah, all near the Gwalior frontier, also mutinied.

When the news of the mutiny at Meerut and Delhi reached Indore, it was feared by Colonel Durand, the Officiating Agent to the Governor-General, that no dependence could be placed on the native troops of the regular army in Central India; but he had hopes that several local corps and Political Contingents at his disposal were not tainted with any feeling of disloyalty. To form a counterpoise at Indore to men of the 23rd Bengal Infantry and of the 1st Light Cavalry, who were stationed at Mhow, he sent for a detachment of the Bhopal Contingent from Sehore and for the Malwa Bhil Corps from Sirdarpur. To these were added some troops and guns furnished by the Maharaja Holkar.

Indore.

At Gwalior the emissaries of rebellion were actively poisoning the minds of the people with reports that the bones of pigs and cows had been pulverized by the British and mixed with the flour and sugar which were sold all over the country. Sindhia was much oppressed with anxiety. He had information that the men of the Gwalior Contingent and some of his own troops, who were natives of our provinces, held nightly meetings and had pledged themselves on the Ganges water to exterminate the Christians; and he warned Major Macpherson, the Political Agent, that no dependence could be placed on the sepoys. Brigadier Ramsay, however, who commanded the troops, as well as the rest of the officers of the Contingent, held a different opinion. The Lieutenant-Governor at Agra shared in some measure this feeling of confidence; and at his requisition the 1st Cavalry Regiment of the Contingent and a battery were sent to him, and the 1st Infantry Regiment to Etawah. At the same time, to mark in an unmistakeable manner that he had identified the British cause with his own, Sindhia sent his body-guard to the Lieutenant-Governor and a troop of Mahratta Horse to Etawah.

Disaffection at Gwalior.

On the 23rd May the first overt act of mutiny in the Gwalior Contingent was committed at Hathras by 100 men of the 1st Cavalry who, raising the war-cry of Islam, went off to Delhi. On May 27th, the symptoms of disaffection having become stronger at Gwalior, Major Macpherson, at Sindhia's suggestion, removed the men of the Contingent who were guarding the Residency, and allowed their places to be filled by the Maharaja's own troops. Sindhia himself carefully posted his guards. Some of the ladies and children took shelter there; but the families of the officers of the Contingent remained in their own houses, as Brigadier Ramsay considered it inexpedient that any want of confidence in his men should be manifested. On the following day, however, all the ladies living in cantonments fled to the Residency; and Major Macpherson received a message from the Brigadier that the troops were expected to rise that night. But the sun had not gone down when Brigadier Ramsay's confidence in his men revived; and he and his officers slept in the lines at Morar, some five miles distant from Gwalior.

The sepoys loudly declared that their honour was touched when the guard of the Contingent was removed from the Residency, that the imputation on their fidelity was intolerable, and that they would not permit the smallest amount of treasure to pass from their hands into those of Sindhia's troops. The 4th Infantry, moreover, volunteered to serve against the rebels. Similar offers were made about the same time by the troops at Mhow, at Bhopal, at Lalitpur, and in other parts of Central India.

On the 29th May, by the advice of Sindhia, who began to fear that a feeling of hostility towards the British prevailed more extensively among his own troops than he had at first suspected, Major Macpherson took the ladies and children from the Residency to the palace, in the Maharaja's carriages. But on the next day (Brigadier Ramsay becoming more confident in his men) several ladies returned to cantonments.

Early in the month of June the wave of revolt reached Central India. The cavalry of the United Malwa Contingent, who were marching from Mehidpur to Neemuch, mutinied on the road, and murdered Captain Brodie, their Commanding Officer, and Lieutenant Hunt, their Adjutant. At Neemuch* the 7th Infantry of the Gwalior Contingent and other troops mutinied on the 3rd June. Captain Carter, commanding the 5th Infantry of the Contingent, who had been ordered to move from Agar to Mandesar, hearing of these occurrences, and fearing that a dash would be made by the mutineers upon Agar, made a counter-march to that station.

Mutiny of the Malwa Contingent Cavalry.

Neemuch.

When Holkar heard of the revolt of the cavalry of the Malwa Contingent he was much troubled. He informed Colonel Durand † that there was a strong sympathy between those mutineers and his own cavalry, that they were "as one," and that he had no longer any confidence in the latter. A troop of the Malwa Contingent Cavalry being at the time on escort duty at Indore, Colonel Durand ordered it at once to proceed to Mehidpur, and promised rewards to the men if they would lend loyal assistance to Major Timins, the Commandant of the Contingent.

Trouble at Indore.

On the 7th June the rising occurred at Jhansi, and on hearing of the massacre there, Captain Murray, who had been sent from Gwalior to Jhansi with a wing of the 4th Regiment Infantry and a battery, retraced his steps, and reached Gwalior on the 13th June. On the same day a wing of the 6th Regiment of the Contingent mutinied at Lalitpur.

The news of the Jhansi massacre stirred the capital of Sindhia to its inmost depths. All believed that the foundations of the British Empire in India were crumbling into dust. On the morning of the 14th June the Mess House at Morar and a bungalow were burnt down; but nothing further occurred until night, when, between the hours of 9 and 11, the sky was reddened by the blaze of all the bungalows in cantonments, and amid cries that the Europeans were down upon the sepoys, the troops of the Contingent shot down as many Christians as they could find. Six officers, a clergyman, six non-commissioned officers, three women, and three children perished by their hands. Some managed to escape to the palace or the Residency, and two officers rode off at once to Dholpur and Agra. The conduct of a few of the sepoys deserves notice. Three men of the 2nd Infantry escorted Lieutenant Pierson and his wife to the Residency, carrying Mrs. Pierson in a litter a distance of seven miles. A guard of the 1st Regiment protected the family of their absent Commandant; and the rear-guard of the 4th Regiment defended Captains Murray and Meade and their families against an attacking party of the 2nd Regiment.

Rising at Gwalior.

*For particulars of the Neemuch mutiny see page 54.

† Colonel H. M. Durand was Officiating Agent to the Governor-General in Central India, the permanent incumbent, Sir Robert Hamilton, Bart., being on leave in England. Indore was made subsidiary to the British Government after the defeat of Holkar at the battle of Mehidpur in 1817.

On hearing of the outbreak Major Macpherson got into a carriage, with a lady of his family and an officer who had escaped, and proceeded to join Sindhia, escorted by some Muhammadans and forty Mahratta horsemen. On the way they were met by a number of *ghazis* who vehemently demanded that the Christians should be given up to them; but on learning from the Mahratta who commanded the escort that by Sindhia's order he was carrying Major Macpherson as a prisoner to the palace, the fanatics allowed the party to proceed. On arriving at the palace, Major Macpherson found Brigadier Ramsay and several officers and their families assembled there. Sindhia was much agitated. He declared that it was out of his power to protect the Christians for even one hour. It was, therefore, necessary that they should fly towards Agra, and he had conveyances and an escort of his body-guard ready for them. Their flight was at first attended with great danger, for 200 *ghazis* were thirsting for their blood on the road to the Chambal river, and at a most critical moment the body-guard deserted their charge. Fortunately a Thakur, Baldeo Singh,* the head of a tribe who were indebted to Major Macpherson's mediation for some favours which they had received from Sindhia, unexpectedly made his appearance on the scene with a body of armed men, and offered to show his gratitude by defending the fugitives with his life.

Flight of the British to Agra.

Conducting them by by-paths so as to avoid the *ghazis*, the Thakur escorted them safely to the banks of the Chambal, on the opposite side of which some troops of the Dholpur State were waiting with elephants to escort them to their master. The Rana gave them an escort to Agra, which they reached in safety on the 17th June. A few days after their arrival a second party of fugitives, mostly women and children, whom the mutineers, after subjecting them to very insulting treatment, had sent to Sindhia, reached Agra in safety under an escort from Dholpur.

The outbreak at Gwalior was immediately followed by the mutiny of the 1st Infantry of the Gwalior Contingent at Etawah, and of the 3rd Infantry and 3rd Battery at Sipri. At the latter station reports had been circulated that ground bones were mixed with the flour sold in the bazaar. To allay the apprehensions thus raised, one *bunniah* was placed on his trial before a court composed of native officers, who acquitted the man, and publicly expressed their conviction that the purchasers of the flour inspected by them had themselves polluted it. To satisfy the sepoys, however, the members of the court applied for and obtained permission to inflict a fine upon the *bunniah*. But the disaffected did not desist from their efforts to bring matters to a crisis. The men of the 3rd Battery charged their Commanding Officer, Captain Lemarchand, with attempting to destroy their caste. A sentry snapped his musket at Sergeant Callan. Some of the men of the artillery and

Mutiny at Etawah and Sipri.

*With Baldeo Singh was his son, Gopal Singh, who afterwards joined the Central India Horse, with a troop of his followers, and eventually became Risaldar-Major, Sirdar Bahadur, A. D. C. to the Viceroy. He was a man of fine physique and great intellectual qualities. The tribe were Danotia Thakurs, Brahmins by caste, expert swimmers, and known in the Regiment as the "Chambal Horse." Gopal Singh and his men greatly distinguished themselves in crossing the Kabul River in flood near Jalalabad on the 23rd May 1880. (Official History of the 2nd Afghan War, page 445.)

four sepoys of the infantry entered into a plot to blow Major Macpherson out of his verandah in which he used to sleep, but their treachery was exposed by the native officers. Volunteers being required to march to the relief of Jhansi, only 147 men stepped out of the ranks, the rest refusing to march against their brethren of the 12th Bengal Infantry, and taunting those who had volunteered. On the 18th June the pay of the 3rd Regiment arrived from Gwalior, and with it came the news that the sepoys at that place had mutinied.

The troops at Sipri became wild with excitement; and Major Macpherson was informed that ten men had been told off from each company to murder the officers that night. Arrangements were instantly made for flight; and with the exception of two non-commissioned officers, all the Christians escaped to Agar.

Indore.

At Indore the attitude of Holkar caused great anxiety. His dominions lay to the south of and adjacent to those of Sindhia; on the west was the independent State of Dhar, and the territory was in part surrounded by Rajputana, while the States of Jaora and Bhopal were also adjacent. Matters were rapidly coming to a crisis. For some days before the outbreak took place the Sikh sowars of the Bhopal Contingent observed that the three guns which Holkar had placed at the disposal of Colonel Durand, and which had been posted at the entrance to the city bazaar, were shifted about at night and pointed at the stable-square of the Residency, where the Sikhs were stationed, so as to rake it diagonally. Captain Ludlow, the Superintending Engineer of the Saugor and Narbada territories, and Captain Cobbe, the Executive Engineer at Mhow, advised Colonel Durand to remove the guns to the Residency where they would be more under control. They also asked permission to entrench the Residency; but he did not consider it advisable to accede to either of these proposals.

Attack on the Indore Residency.

On the 27th June religious mendicants made their appearance among the troops. On the morning of the 1st July the Maharaja's guns were suddenly unlimbered, and, after being fired in the direction of the stable-square, were quickly moved up to a position close to the Residency, on which they opened with grape.†

They were answered by two guns of the Bhopal Contingent, worked by Captain Cobbe and a European Sergeant, with the aid of the native gunners, who remained faithful and did their duty well. One of Holkar's guns was dismounted, but Captain Cobbe, who had been seriously ill, fainted from his exertions, and the Sergeant received a severe contusion. In the meantime Colonel Travers, Commandant of the Bhopal Contingent, having with much difficulty collected about 25 of the Sikh sowars, charged the Maharaja's guns; but he was followed by only five men, his horse was wounded, and he was obliged to retreat, having cut down a few of the gunners. At the same time Captain F. L. Magniac, who had ridden

* This report proved false.

† The Residency was struck by only one shot, the mark of which was preserved for some years. Among those who charged the guns with Colonel Travers were Nehal Singh and Harsa Singh, both of whom received the Order of Merit, and served many years in the Central India Horse.

up to the Infantry of the Bhopal and Malwa Contingents for the purpose of taking them into the Residency, returned and reported that they also were mutinous. The men of the Bhil Corps were then placed in the upper storey of the Residency; but they seemed panic-stricken and did not remain steadily at their posts. The European battery at Mhow had been previously sent for, and was expected momentarily; but the arrival of some more of Holkar's guns, and a report* that the Maharaja had himself set out, at the head of his forces, to attack the Residency induced Colonel Durand to decide upon retreating to Simrol. The Bhopal Contingent guns were moved to the back of the Residency, the ladies and children were placed on the ammunition waggons and in two or three bullock carts, and the retreat commenced at 10 A.M., the Sikh sowars forming the advanced guard, and the Bhils bringing up the rear. On reaching the ghat leading to the valley of the Narbada, the Sikhs insisted on going to Sehore instead of to Simrol, as they said that a party of Holkar's horse was lying in wait for them on the road to the latter place. Colonel Durand was, therefore, obliged to alter his route.

Retreat of the British from Indore.

As soon as the Indore Residency had been abandoned, the rebel sowars galloped through the bazaar, and, entering the houses of the European and Eurasian clerks, put to the sword 28 men, women, and children. The bodies of the slain were buried four days afterwards by Holkar's orders.

Mhow.

The troops at Mhow, a dozen miles to the south, had evinced a mutinous disposition. The garrison consisted of the 23rd Bengal Native Infantry, a wing of the 1st Bengal Cavalry,* and a battery of Bengal Artillery with European gunners and native drivers. On the evening of the same day, 1st July, the native troops broke into open mutiny; but they revelled in their work of blood and destruction only until the guns of Captain Hungerford's Company of European Artillery opened on them with grape and round shot. That officer had, from the beginning of the mutinies, advised Colonel Platt, who commanded the station, to prepare for the storm which he foresaw would sweep over Central India. In the month of May he suggested that a party of his Europeans should replace the company of sepoys guarding the gateway of the fort or fortified square at Mhow, which contained many heavy guns and a large quantity of ammunition and valuable stores of various kinds. But Colonel Platt feared the effects of showing a want of confidence in the sepoys. He permitted Captain Hungerford, however, to dismount and disable the heavy guns. On the 6th June, when the news of the Neemuch mutiny reached Mhow, Captain Hungerford, in a letter to Colonel Platt, expressed his anxiety to take his guns out of their sheds, which were at a distance of 200 yards from the barracks, and to keep them ready for use at short notice. Colonel Platt permitted him to do what he recommended, but desired him to wait two days. An opportunity, however, offering itself, Captain Hungerford turned out his guns that very day, and parked

* The other wing of this regiment (less one troop at Kherwara) mutinied at Neemuch on the 3rd June.

them in front of the barracks; and every night after that the horses stood ready harnessed and the men were on the alert. This prompt demonstration had a good effect on the sepoys at the time. Colonel Durand was of opinion that it prevented them from rising when they heard of the mutiny at Neemuch.* But as they appeared to many to be ripe for revolt, Colonel Platt was urged to provide for the safety of the women and children at the station. He contented himself with placing a guard of sepoys of the 23rd every night over the houses of the officers of that regiment. On the morning of the 1st July the firing of guns was heard in the direction of Indore, and shortly after a note was received from Colonel Durand containing these words:—"Send the European Battery as fast as you can. We are attacked by Holkar." The battery was immediately turned out; and for an escort two men were told off to each gun and waggon, and were armed with muskets and mounted on the limber boxes. Half-way to Indore, at Rao, Captain Hungerford was met by a horseman bearing a pencil note from Colonel Travers,† which briefly stated that the officers and ladies of the Residency were retreating on Simrol. The sowar added that Colonel Durand had not retired to Mhow, because he expected that it would be attacked by Holkar. The road from Rao to Simrol being narrow and cut up with ruts, Captain Hungerford returned to Mhow. Immediately on his arrival there he asked Colonel Platt to let him take the battery into the fort, as the artillery barracks, in which the families of all the officers and men had taken refuge, could not be easily defended; but he did not obtain permission to do so until late in the evening when he had made a more urgent application. The sepoy guard at the gateway was at the same time increased. At nightfall the troops broke out into mutiny. Colonel Platt had been so completely deceived by the behaviour of his men that he had just commenced a letter to Colonel Durand with the words: "All right, both cavalry and infantry very *khoosh* and willing," when he was interrupted by a sudden uproar without, the firing of shots, and the crackling of burning timber. He hastened to the fort, ordered out the battery, and then rode with his adjutant, Captain Fagan, straight to the quarter-guard of his regiment, where they were both instantly shot. Major Harris of the 1st Light Cavalry was at the same time cut down by his own men.

Mutiny at Mhow.

Captain Hungerford, after disarming the sepoys at the fort gate, took his battery to the parade ground, which was lit up by the blaze of the burning bungalows, and was apparently deserted. Being fired upon, however, by unseen hands, he unlimbered and sent grape and round shot into the lines. Groans and a rushing noise were heard; but in a few minutes everything was perfectly quiet. Captain Hungerford was afterwards informed that, on his opening fire, the whole of the cavalry, in regular files, had left their lines at a hard trot, and had taken the

*The troops at Neemuch mutinied on the 3rd June.

† Afterwards General Travers, V.C. The horseman with Travers' note was Harsa Singh, who cut his way through more than one party of rebels. For many years he was head Shikari in the Central India Horse, and was killed by a tiger in the Goona jungles in 1884. Sir M. Gerard built a *bund* at Goona and on it a monument to the memory of Harsa Singh, by whose name the tank is still known.

road to Indore, and that the infantry had fled from their huts in great disorder. Muskets and coats were found lying scattered about the lines.

Most of the officers escaped to the fort. Captain Brooks and Lieutenants Martin and Chapman, who were on foot, were pursued by troops to within a few hundred yards of the fort, and were drawn in over the walls of one of the bastions.

Captain Hungerford at Mhow.

Early the following morning active preparations were commenced for strengthening the fort and restoring order in and around Mhow. In a week's time Captain Hungerford, who had assumed command, was ready to repel the attack of a native army. The artillerymen, under the direction of Lieutenant Mallock, worked laboriously, throwing up entrenchments, mounting the heavy guns and howitzers on their carriages, placing light pieces on the four corner bastions, and erecting batteries and breastworks outside the fort to protect the north and south gates. Ammunition was made up for the heavy guns by Mr. Postance, the Deputy Commissary of Ordnance, and supplies for men and horses for six months were laid in by Mr. Madras, the Commissariat Officer. The officers, road sergeants, and clerks who had escaped were formed in to a body of horsemen, and placed in two divisions under the command of Captain Brooks of the 1st Light Cavalry and of Captain Trower, 23rd Native Infantry, for employment as flanking parties whenever it was necessary to move the guns out of the fort. They had also to serve as sentries at night, when the artillerymen had rest. For three or four days regularly a portion of Captain Hungerford's battery, accompanied by a proper escort, turned out and did much service. Several villages in which mutineers were hiding were destroyed, and some sepoys and sowars were hunted down and killed; the bodies of missing officers, much mutilated, were buried; a number of muskets and other articles were recovered; and the magazines of the cavalry and infantry, which were full of ammunition, were blown up. The civil duties were chiefly conducted by Captain Elliot of the Thagi Department, whose local knowledge enabled him to be very useful.

Action of Holkar.

On the 5th July Holkar deputed two of his principal officers and Captain Fenwick, an East Indian in his service, to Mhow, with a letter, in which he expressed deep regret at what had occurred and offered to co-operate with Captain Hungerford in maintaining order. The mutineers, it appeared, had carried off nine *lakhs* of treasure from the Residency, some of Holkar's guns, and as many horses, camels, and bullock-carts as they could lay their hands on.

The money remaining in the Treasury, amounting to Rupees 4,16,690, and Government Securities to the amount of twenty-three lakhs and a half, were sent by the Maharaja to the fort of Mhow. He also provided thirteen elephants for the column which was advancing under General Woodburn. On the 9th July he sent in two Muhammadan sepoys of the 23rd, who were tried and hanged. Their surrender caused much excitement among his troops, and an anonymous letter was found in the Durbar hall accusing him of being under the influence of ministers who were in reality Christians. Holkar's tributaries, finding that he was not hostile to the British, as they had at first supposed, exerted themselves to suppress disturbances; and the country speedily wore a tranquil appearance. The report that he had arrayed himself against the Paramount Power caused the Maharaja much perturbation; and when intelligence was received that two columns were advancing from Bombay, he was with difficulty prevented by Captain Hungerford from leaving Indore for the purpose of personally offering an explanation to Lord Elphinstone, Governor of that Presidency.

Postal communication with Bombay was re-opened chiefly by the exertions of Lieutenant W. G. Cumming, Deputy Bhil Agent. That officer had been in an isolated position at Manpur, with a Naik and four sepoys of the Gwalior Contingent, a Havildar and four sepoys of the Bhopal Contingent, and twenty *Najibs* of the Thagi Department. On hearing of the outbreak at Indore he retired to the hills with a few men on whom he could rely, but, after communicating with the officers at the fort of Mhow, he returned to Manpur, and employed himself in making postal arrangements, and threatening with punishment those who attempted to stop the *dâk* runners. During his absence the guard of the Gwalior Contingent had remained at their posts, and had saved his bungalow from being plundered, but the guard of the Bhopal Contingent had left the place, the Havildar being compelled by the sepoys to walk off at the point of the bayonet. The *Najibs* had also absconded after plundering the public money under their charge.

Agar.

On the 4th July the 5th Infantry, Gwalior Contingent, which had received emissaries from the Indore rebels, mutinied at Agar. Hearing a great tumult in the morning Lieutenant O'Dowda, the Adjutant, whose horse was saddled, rode to the lines and was immediately shot. Captain Carter, the Commanding Officer, was riding in the same direction when he was stopped by four sepoys, who with uplifted hands entreated him not to advance further, or he would be killed. He returned, therefore, to his bungalow and made arrangements for flight. Conveyances were procured, and with the exception of Dr. and Mrs. James, who were shot just as they had mounted their horses for a morning ride, the whole of the officers and ladies, including those who had fled from Sipri on the 18th June, left the station safely. They wandered in the jungles for twelve days, exposed to the insults of the villagers along their path, until they reached Hoshangabad.*

Sehore.

While Colonel Durand was at Sehore, he was informed by the Regent of Bhopal, the Sikander Begum, that the *Maulvis* in her city were preaching a religious war, and that her Muhammadan soldiery, chiefly Afghans of the Khyber Pass, were daily becoming more turbulent, and threatening her, and that the proximity of the small party of Europeans at Sehore caused her much embarrassment. Major Richards, the Political Agent at Bhopal, on hearing of the mutiny at Indore, had commenced making a stockade round the Sehore Agency, hoping to be aided by the Bhopal

* The Agar fugitives went first to Kanar, 11 miles N. E. of Agar, where they were harboured by one Lalji, a Jemadar of the Gwalior police of the Nalkhara District. He took them through the jungle to Hoshangabad, hiding by day and travelling by night. Lalji is still (1908) alive, nearly 100 years old and frequently visits the officers at Agar.

Contingent. But it soon became apparent that no reliance could be placed upon those troops. The three companies of infantry which had taken part in the mutiny at Indore returned to Sehore on the 7th July, rich with the plunder of the treasury. The Commandant was forced to temporize with them, and to receive them as if they had not misbehaved at all; and immediately the rest of the Contingent became disaffected, and were ready to join in any local insurrection. When, therefore, the Regent's communications were received, both Colonel Durand and Major Richards were of opinion that, when the pressure of circumstances should become too great, the British officers should retire from Sehore, and that the troops of the Contingent should be informed at the last moment that the British could not maintain their position in a friendly foreign State "against the will and wish of the ruler, if, by persisting in so doing, danger or difficulty ensued to the country or those who governed it." Colonel Travers, however, immediately made known the result of this deliberation to the native officers, and the little discipline and order that remained among the troops vanished.

Sehore abandoned.

In these circumstances Major Richards felt it his duty to provide for the safety of the European Officers and their families (23 persons) who were with him.

Accordingly the station and treasury were made over to an officer of rank, deputed from Bhopal for the purpose, on the 9th July, and the Europeans retired to Hoshangabad. Colonel Travers had at the same time placed the Contingent temporarily under the orders of the Begum. But they were only nominally under her control for the first two or three months, until the worst characters were expelled from the station. The troops refused to obey her orders when she required them to march on Bersia, where Sujawat Khan, Pindari, a political pensioner, had murdered the Superintendent, Babu Subh Rao, plundered the treasury, and burnt the Government bungalows. A good portion of the Contingent, however, and especially the Sikhs and the gunners, were disposed to behave well; but they were rendered powerless on the 6th of August, when a Risaldar raised the Muhammadan standard, and, aided by the cavalry and infantry, seized the guns. After the Begum had got rid of those who were mutinous, she sent a detachment of the Contingent against the rebel Fazil Muhammad Khan of Ambapani. They took his fort and razed it to the ground, although the rebel himself escaped for the time to Rahatgarh. Some of the mutineers from Sehore made their way to Cawnpore and fought under the Nana. The loyal sowars of the cavalry, together with a portion of the 2nd Cavalry of the Gwalior Contingent, were ultimately placed under charge of Captain H. O. Mayne, and served as the nucleus of a body of irregular horse which that officer had been ordered to organise for employment in Central India.*

Sindhia and the Gwalior Mutineers.

At Gwalior Sindhia maintained a difficult struggle with the mutineers of the Gwalior Contingent. They had demanded that he should give them money and carriage and lead them to Agra; and they had threatened to plunder his city and his treasury if he refused to comply with their wishes. His own troops being of the same leaven, he had to rely mainly on the resources of his own skill and ingenuity to control the mutineers, and to prevent them from marching either to Agra or Delhi. By turns he bribed

* Now the Central India Horse.

and cajoled them. He gave them a donation of three months' pay and promised to take them into his service. He sent his emissaries among them and sowed dissension between Hindus and Muhammadans. He bribed many of their officers and priests. The artillery officers being mostly natives of Gwalior, he acted on them through their village interests. He summoned his feudal aristocracy to the capital, and they placed a levy of 11,000 men at his disposal. He ordered the removal of wheels of all carts and sent them on elephants and camels to distant jungles, and swept the Chambal of its boats. In these efforts he had the valuable advice and co-operation of his Dewan, Dankar Rao, who rendered himself so obnoxious to the sepoys that they styled him "the son of the Company."*

On the 20th July the hopes of the mutineers were brought to a very low ebb. The wing of the 6th Regiment of the Gwalior Contingent, which had mutinied at Lalitpur, and had joined the Nana at Bithur, came back to Gwalior on that date, greatly thinned by General Havelock's fire, and averred that it was madness to face Europeans. The rebel officers now sought to secure Sindhia's intercession with the British in case of need. On the 31st July, however, the 23rd Native Infantry, a wing of the 1st Cavalry, 600 of Holkar's troops, and 1,000 *ghazis*, with 7 guns, from Indore and Mhow, entered Gwalior, and the embers of rebellion were rekindled in the Morar Cantonments. All along their line of march these miscreants had plundered villages, dishonoured women, destroyed the telegraph wires and posts, and burnt the staging bungalows and post offices; and their mutinous brethren at Gwalior saw them gorged with plunder. A trooper who was killed in a dispute had gold *mohurs* to the value of 8,000 rupees about his person.

During the month of August Sindhia had to contend with the new elements of confusion that had risen around him. The mutineers set up a pretender whom they called a prince of the Imperial House of Delhi, and honoured him with a salute of 22 guns. Sindhia was required to do homage to this phantom; but he replied evasively that his predecessors had so often been deceived that he would wait until the King of Delhi should himself honour Gwalior with his presence. This excuse did not deceive the Indore and Mhow mutineers; and as the Maharaja was not pliant to their wishes in any other matter, they procured boats, and on the 7th September, accompanied by 800 of his Muhammadan horse, a portion of the Gwalior Contingent, and a large body of fanatics, crossed the Chambal, and entered Dholpur.

Immediately on their departure the mutineers at Morar raised a cry that Sindhia had deceived them, and made preparations to attack him, while the greater portion of his own troops seemed ready to join them. But the Maharaja's energies rose with his danger. He had every bugle taken to his palace and every gun watched by men on whom he could rely; and having passed the night in sleepless anxiety, at daybreak he paraded his troops, and made a feeling appeal to them, corps by corps. Would they permit the mutineers to insult him, their own Maharaja, and to threaten him with coercion? Their sense of honour was touched and they gave up twenty of their comrades who had instigated them to rebellion. To secure more completely the fidelity of his troops, he promised them daily allowances. At the same time he increased his Thakur levies; † and hearing that the rebels had planted

* The British East India Company.

† Levies raised under the prevailing feudal system by Thakurs, or minor chiefs.

batteries against the city and palace, he moved out his whole force, and himself placed his batteries and picquets. He then cut off the supplies of the mutineers, and increased his guards on the Chambal to prevent the Indore and Mhow rebels from returning to Gwalior. Moreover, his emissaries sowed fresh dissensions among the sepoys. The 5th Regiment of Infantry, with which the rest were at variance, because the men had put to death the native officers who had incited them to mutiny at Agar, and the 6th which had fled from General Havelock's force, offered to range themselves under the Maharaja's banners. The enemy became disheartened and withdrew their guns.

The excitement had nearly subsided, when it blazed up again on the appearance at Gwalior of the agents of the Jhansi Rani and the Nana, who bid high for the services of the mutineers. They made their election to fight for the Nana; and Sindhia, being unable to restrain them, affected to approve of their determination. He, moreover, promised to pay them well if, on their way, they would suppress the disturbances at Jhansi and Jalaun; and further to please them he distributed military titles among them with a lavish hand. About the same time the news of the fall of Delhi, which was followed soon after by that of the defeat of the Indore and Mhow rebels by Colonel Greathed's column at Agra on the 10th October, greatly strengthened Sindhia's position. On the 15th October the mutineers of the Contingent, led by Tantia Topi, marched for Cawnpore, burning with hatred against Sindhia, which they manifested by cutting down all the trees in the Cantonments at Morar, laying waste the country on their route, and denouncing him as their greatest enemy. They took possession of Jalaun and Kuchwahagar in the Nana's name, extorted money from the Chief of Gursarai, by destroying his son's eyes with boiling oil, and leaving detachments at Jalaun and Kalpi, they crossed the Jumna on the 15th November, and reached Cawnpore on 1st December. Being reinforced from Oudh and Banda they pressed General Windham until, on the 10th December, they were signally defeated by Sir Colin Campbell.

Insurrection at Mandesar.

While these events were occurring at Gwalior, a formidable insurrection had broken out at Mandesar,* in Sindhia's territory, and had spread itself very rapidly over a great portion of Central India. The elements of conflagration had been rife in the country, but they were scattered until a person styling himself the Shahzada Humayun or Feroz Shah, and wearing the garb of a pilgrim from Mecca, made his appearance and called on the Faithful to join him in a war of extermination against the infidels. On his approaching Mandesar with a few followers on the 26th August, a detachment of Sindhia's troops stationed there, joined by a large body of Afghans, Makranis, and other foreign mercenaries, who had no employment, hailed his advent eagerly, and, raising the standard of Islam, went out to meet him with drums beating. Having brought him into the town, they took him with great pomp to the palace, and installed him on the *masnad*. *Nuzzurs* were presented; *parwanas* were issued, and guns, shot, lead, and small arms were dug up in the fort of Mandesar.

* The treaty under which Indore became subsidiary to the British Government was concluded at Mandesar on the 6th January, 1818.

Turbulent characters in all parts of Central India girded on their swords and hastened to join the Shahzada. The Dhar State also, without applying for the permission of the British Government, and the Raja of Amjhera, who had openly placed himself on the side of rebellion, enlisted a number of *Walayatis* * and Makranis. In a short time the insurgents were nearly in a position to sever the line of communication between Mhow and Bombay, and by attacking Mandesar, to get into communication with the rebels at Satwas and thus isolate Mhow. About the same time the Bhils were committing depredations and plundering the mails on the Bombay road, and their leader Bhima Naik checked the advance of Lieutenant Kennedy of the Khandesh Bhil Corps, who had been sent with a hundred men to keep the road open.

Dhar.

On the 28th August the insurgents of Mandesar defeated a body of Sindhia's troops which had been sent to chastise them. On the 31st August the *Walayatis* and Makranis, who had been taken into the service of the Dhar State, seized the fort of that place, and the treasure, guns, and stores of grain which were in it. The faithful chiefs of Jaora, Rutlam, Sailana, and Sita Mhow were in jeopardy, and repeatedly applied to Colonel Durand for help.

On the 3rd October the Shahzada sent 1,200 men and three guns to Sita Mhow and demanded tribute and a lakh and a half of rupees from the chief, who was obliged to conciliate him. On the 10th October the *Walayatis* of Dhar and Amjhera attacked Bhopawar and Sirdarpur, the latter being the headquarters of the Malwa Bhil Corps and the former the civil station. At Bhopawar they met with slight opposition from some of the troops of Indore and Rutlam which had been placed there by the Bhil Agent for its protection, and some *Sibandis* (country militia) from Dhar, who had also been posted there with two guns, fraternized with the rebels. At Sirdarpur the cantonments were defended for three hours by Subadar Guptar and one hundred and thirty men of the Bhil Corps, who, after their ammunition had been expended, maintained a hand-to-hand fight with their swords and carbines until they were attacked in rear by a fresh party of *Walayatis* from Rajgarh, when the Subadar called out to the men to disperse and save their lives. He himself, with twenty-five men, retired fighting. The *Walayatis* then plundered and burnt the place, killed several women and children, and took away the two mountain guns of the Bhil Corps to Dhar. They also cut down the flag-staff at the Bhopawar Agency.

Bhopawar.

Defence of Sirdarpur.

On the 17th October, the Mewatis and Kukus at Satwas having set up the standard of Islam and menaced the Nimawar Panch Mahal, Colonel Durand directed Major Orr to proceed with the Hyderabad Contingent Field Force through Nimawar to attack and disperse the rebels wherever he might find them, and to ascend into Malwa by Unchod, Piplia, and Raghugarh. Major Orr found the insurgents at Piplia on the 27th October, attacked and took the fort, and captured some forty-five prisoners, thus quelling the rising at Satwas. He then proceeded to join the Malwa Field Force, which had marched from Mhow against Dhar on the 20th October.

Major Orr at Piplia.

* Afghans.

CHAPTER II.

JHANSI AND BUNDELKHAND.

Bundelkhand.

Bundelkhand is a great plain diversified by a series of mountains and hills, with numerous streams flowing into the Jumna, among which the principal are the Pahuj, Betwa, Dhasan, Barma, Ken, and Paisuni. A great number of lakes has also been formed by damming the valleys. In the hills the country is generally wild, rugged, and overgrown with jungle, but the plains, though arid during the hot weather, are well cultivated. The most powerful people of Bundelkhand are the Bundelas, a tribe of Rajputs who established themselves on the right bank of the Jumna in the 14th century.

The British acquired a considerable portion of Bundelkhand from Baji Rao Peshwa, under the terms of the treaty of Bassein in 1802, and, on the extinction of the Peshwa's independence, in the Mahratta War of 1817, that potentate's sovereign rights passed into British hands.* The principal Bundelkhand States in 1857 were Jalaun, Jhansi, Jaitpur, Banda, Shahgarh, Banpur,† Orchha, Samthar, Charkhari, and many minor chiefships. Some of these were confiscated owing to the part taken by their rulers in the rebellion of 1857, as will be seen from the ensuing narrative.

Jhansi forms a portion of the hill-country of Bundelkhand sloping from the Vindhya mountains to the Jumna on the north. The rocky crests of the hills are bare and exposed, as elsewhere in this region, but their sides are clad with bush, and thick forests cluster round their bases. The northern portion of the district has a surface of black cotton soil, which becomes almost impassable after heavy rain, but in the summer is baked hard by the heat of the sun, and cracks into innumerable fissures. This soil is characteristic of the whole of the plain country from the Jumna to the south of the Tapti river.

Jhansi, the capital of a province, lay 142 miles south of Agra. In 1854, in the absence of an heir to the deceased Raja Gangadhar Rao, Jhansi was declared by Lord Dalhousie to have lapsed to the British Government, and together with the Jalaun and Chanderi Districts, was formed into the Jhansi Superintendency under Captain Skene.

The Rani of Jhansi.

The widow of the deceased Raja protested in vain, but ultimately agreed to receive a pension of Rs. 5,000 a month, out of which she was obliged to pay her late husband's debts. She considered herself seriously aggrieved in not being allowed to adopt a son to

* Baji Rao was given a pension and estate at Bithur, near Cawnpore, where he died in 1854; his adopted son Nana Sahib perpetrated the Cawnpore massacres in 1857.

† Banpur was made over to Sindhia in 1860.

succeed Gangadhar Rao as Raja, appealed against the arrangements made for her support, and sent an agent to England to plead her cause, but without effect. Other grievances combined to render her hostile to British rule. Prior to November 1854, the slaughter of cattle was not permitted in Jhansi. On the country coming under British rule this restriction was of course removed, upon which the Rani and inhabitants petitioned against the practice. The matter was referred to Government, and the slaughter of cattle was authoritatively allowed.

The temple of Lachmi, situated outside the walls to the east of Jhansi, had long been supported by the native rulers of the country, and an ancestor of Gangadhar Rao had made over the revenue of two villages for its support. When he died, Captain F. Gordon, Deputy Commissioner, recommended that this arrangement should continue, but it was ordered that the villages should be resumed. This was strongly objected to by the Rani, and the case again referred to Government with the same result. But before the resumption order could be carried out, the outbreak at Jhansi took place.

The Rani was thus ready to take any opportunity of gratifying her revenge, and being, like many other Mahratta women of rank, possessed of a masculine spirit, she was well fitted to carry out her designs, and was ripe for rebellion when the outbreak occurred in 1857.

The garrison of Jhansi was composed entirely of native troops, consisting of a detachment of artillery, a wing of the 12th Bengal Infantry, and a wing of the 14th Irregular Cavalry.

Disaffection.

In May 1857, a report was spread in Jhansi, as in many other places in India, that Government had caused ground bones to be mixed in the flour sold in the bazaars, that cow's and pig's fat had been used in making up the cartridges served out to the troops, and that two regiments of sepoys had been blown away from guns in Calcutta.

About this time Captain F. Gordon was informed that an adherent of the Rani named Bolanath used to hold long private conferences with the native officers of the Jhansi troops, who frequently visited the Rani's palace, and that some treachery was intended. No reliance, however, seems to have been placed on this information, and, shortly afterwards, the troops having used the "greased" cartridges without demur, confidence in the sepoys appears to have been restored for a time among the civil and military officers.

However, Mr. Scott, head writer in the Deputy Commissioner's office, who lived near the lines and mixed much with natives, had much better information of what was going on, and placed his property in the keeping of a loyal native in the town of Jhansi. He persisted in avowing that he had good reason to know that a mutiny was intended, and that the Rani and the troops were one. His assertions appear to have had some weight, as great endeavours were made by the civil and military officers to ascertain the true feelings of the sepoys, who of course made great professions of loyalty, notwithstanding which a feeling of uneasiness arose, and three clerks of the civil establishment fled towards Saugor, but were ordered back and returned to Jhansi. At the same time the Rani obtained permission to entertain a number of armed men, as she said for her protection.

Whilst this was the state of affairs at Jhansi, the Chanderi District was fast getting into disorder.

About 250 years ago the Bundelas appear to have succeeded in overthrowing the Musalman authority in that part of the country. The first Raja was Ramsahai. In the time of the 9th Raja, Ramchand, in 1764, the Peshwa wrested from the Chanderi State the districts of Surahi, Dukrani, and Balabahat, and in 1802 Raja Ramchand, being incapacitated by age and ill health, went on a pilgrimage and made over the country to his eldest son, Pirji Pal, who was murdered the following year and succeeded by his brother Raja Mor Pahlad. This prince was a debauched sot, and the Bundela Thakurs did what they liked and possessed themselves of the greater portion of the kingdom. Continued acts of aggression on the neighbouring State of Gwalior, for which no redress could be obtained, at last stirred up Daulat Rao Sindhia to hostilities, and his army under Jean Baptiste Filose took the fort of Talbahat. Raja Mor Pahlad, who was hated and despised, fled to Jhansi in 1812, and a negotiation was opened with Gwalior, and at first Mor Pahlad was allowed Rupees 25,000 a year, but subsequently, in 1831, Jean Baptiste Filose, with the approval of the British Resident at Gwalior, gave two shares of the former Chanderi State to Sindhia and one to Mor Pahlad, who was henceforth styled the Raja of Banpur, from a town in his share. Mor Pahlad then proceeded to take possession of all independent *jagirs* in his share, which so exasperated the Thakurs of Pali, Jakhlaun, Nanakpur and others, that they rose in a body, devastated the country, and then preferred their complaint to Sindhia, who decided that Mor Pahlad's one share should be divided into three, two of which were to be given to Mor Pahlad, and one to the Thakurs. In 1843 the worthless Raja died, leaving the remnant of his kingdom to his son Mardan Singh.

The Chanderi District.

In 1844 Sindhia's portion of the Chanderi State was ceded to the British as part security for the payment of the Gwalior Contingent, and a Deputy Superintendent was appointed who also had criminal jurisdiction in the Banpur State. About April, 1857, Thakur Jhujar Singh of Nanakpur died, and his tenure was resumed by Government, and a settlement made with his heirs, instead of the third part being given to the Raja of Banpur, as appears to have been the custom according to the original agreement. Upon this Raja Mardan Singh of Banpur sent for his heir, Jowahir Singh, invested him with a *pagri*, and advised him to collect his relations and retainers and rebel, as the surest way to induce Government to restore his tenure, on the same terms as his father held it. It also appears that the Raja was irritated by being refused certain honours to which he considered himself entitled. It will thus be seen that, like the Rani of Jhansi, the Raja of Banpur had injuries to be redressed, and no doubt he had also the hope of regaining, on the expected overthrow of the British, the entire kingdom of Chanderi, the ancient possession of his ancestors.

The Raja of Banpur.

During April and part of May 1857, the Chanderi District was in temporary charge of Zainulabdin Khan, Deputy Magistrate and Deputy Collector, a man of lazy and feeble character and unfit for any post of responsibility. Early in May 1857, Ganeshji, son of Jowahir Singh, Thakur of Nanakpur, presented a petition to Zainulabdin Khan, stating that his father was about to rebel, but the Deputy Magistrate, with inconceivable folly, refused to receive the petition because it was not written on stamped paper. Ganeshji remained two or three days about Zainulabdin's Court, endeavouring to get a hearing, but in vain. A few days after, Jowahir Singh and other Thakurs rebelled and commenced plundering. Lieutenant Hamilton took charge of the District on the 24th May 1857, and Captain A. C. Gordon, who relieved him on the 7th June, found the country in great disorder.

The outbreak at Jhansi.

On the 30th or 31st May the two Mr. Andrews at Jhansi went to Captain F. D. Gordon and recommended that precautionary measures should be taken regarding the fort and magazine, as they were convinced the troops would mutiny. Captain Gordon told them that he had represented this to Captain Skene, who was of opinion that any move of the kind would bring on the mutiny at once, if it had to take place.

Jhansi is a town commanded by a large stone fort, with cantonments at a short distance, and a smaller fort known as the Star Fort.

Occupation of the Fort.

On the 1st or 2nd June, about 4 P.M., two bungalows in the cantonments were set on fire and destroyed. No trace of the incendiaries could be found, but the occurrence tended to increase the uneasy feeling regarding the disposition of the sepoys. On the 5th June, at about 3 or 4 P.M., firing suddenly took place at the Star Fort, in which were kept the magazine and treasure. Upon this, with the exception of Captain Dunlop, Lieutenants Taylor and Campbell, Lieutenant Turnbull, attached to the Survey, Quartermaster-Sergeant Newton and family, and Conductor Reilly, all the Europeans and Anglo-Indians proceeded to the fort to place their families in safety. Captain F. Gordon ordered the police to garrison the fort, which they did. Shortly afterwards twelve sowars of the Irregular Cavalry came to the fort, with a message from Captain Dunlop to the effect that only thirty-five of the sepoys had mutinied, and that those in the fort might return to their houses. This, however, was not done. Captain Gordon then sent two orderly Jemadars to the *vakils* of the Tehri and Datia States, desiring them to write to their respective governments for help. At about 8 P.M. another letter was sent by Captain Dunlop to Captain Gordon, upon receiving which Captains Skene and Gordon and Doctor MacEgan returned to the cantonments, where Captain Dunlop was, and found that thirty-five men of the 12th Bengal Cavalry were in open mutiny, and held possession of the Star Fort, which contained the magazine and treasure. Upon this they returned to the fort at about 11 P.M.

On the morning of the 6th June Captains Skene and F. Gordon again visited Captain Dunlop in the lines, but what passed between them is unknown. Captain

Skene then returned to the fort, as also did Captain Gordon, after breakfasting in his own house, and writing letters to the Tehri and Datia States, and to the Rao of Gursarai for assistance. To none of these applications was any answer sent, although the Tehri and Datia States, being close at hand, might easily have afforded it. Captain Gordon also wrote to different Thakurs to make arrangements for holding Pachor, and to the Tehsildar of Jhansi to raise men, which the latter did, and twenty-four were posted at the gates of the fort. About 2 P.M. a note was received in the fort from Captain Dunlop, stating that he required some powder and cannon balls; that the mutiny of his men was only partial, and that he could quell it with the men who remained faithful. Captain F. Gordon refused to send any cannon ammunition, and the result proved he was right in doing so, for it would afterwards have been used by the mutineers against the Jhansi fort. In the meantime Mr. Robert Andrews, Deputy Collector, who had been sent to the jail to bring the ammunition there into the fort, returned with only a small quantity, as the jail guard, headed by Bakhshish Ali, Jail Daroga, having joined with the mutineers, refused to allow him to remove more.

Mutiny of the troops.

About this time a great number of people, amongst whom were the Rani's principal adherents, bearing two flags, proceeded from the town of Jhansi towards cantonments, and on their arrival at the lines one Ahsan Ali called all the Musalmans to prayers and the troops mutinied. Two Havildars* of the 12th Bengal Infantry alone remained true, and stood by Captain Dunlop and Lieutenants Campbell and Turnbull. A body of mutineers advanced against this small party, which defended itself, but ultimately all (including the faithful Havildars) were shot down, except Lieutenant Taylor, who escaped, severely wounded, on horseback to the fort. On his arrival the fort gates were shut and the walls were manned by the Europeans, East Indians, some sepoys of the Thakur of Karehra, and a few *barkandazes* who had not joined the mutineers. Conductor Reilly, who was in cantonments, escaped to Barwa Sagar, and ultimately to the North-Western Provinces.

Attack on the fort.

After this the mutineers released the prisoners from the jail, and being joined by them and by the jail guard headed by Bakhshish Ali, set fire to the *Kutcherry* and some of the bungalows in cantonments. They then entered the town, and seized all the adherents of the British Government, including Ahmed Husain, the Tehsildar, who had rendered the Europeans every assistance in his power. Taking with them a gun, they then proceeded to attack the fort. Firing went on until the 6th June, when the insurgents drew off, leaving a strong party of the Rani's followers to surround the place until morning.

During the night of the 6th June a meeting was held by the mutineer officers and the *Kamdars* of the Rani to settle as to whom the government of the country of Jhansi was to be made over, and what was to be done with the

* The names of these brave and faithful men are unknown.

European officers and others in the fort. Some were for letting them go, but this was overruled by Bakhshish Ali, and their death was decided on. The question of the government of the country was not settled, as the Rani and mutineers could not come to terms. The latter, therefore, invited over from Unao—a village about twelve miles from Jhansi—Sadasheo Rao Narayan Parolawala, a relative of the late Raja of Jhansi and a claimant to the *raj*, with a view to setting him up in opposition to the Rani. He reached Jhansi on the 8th June and encamped in the mutineer lines close to the Star Fort.

Between the night of the 6th and morning of the 7th June, the *Barkandazes* and Thakurs who were with the Europeans deserted, either through fear or disaffection. A few servants and others remained. The garrison proposed to escape from the fort during the night, but daylight approaching the attempt was abandoned.

Murder of Europeans.

On the morning of the 7th June Mr. Scott and the two Purcells were sent by Captain Skene to the Rani to request protection. On their arrival outside the fort they were met by the Rani's troops and taken to her palace, from whence she sent them to the lines of the mutineers, where they were put to death. Subsequently Mr. Andrews, having left the fort, was seized and killed by the Rani's own servants at the palace door. In the meantime Risaldar Faiz Ali of the 14th Irregular Cavalry wrote to the garrison to say that if they left the fort they would not be injured, but no notice was taken of this communication. Various letters were also exchanged between the Rani and Captains Skene and F. Gordon, but to what effect cannot be ascertained.

Renewed attack.

About 2 P.M. an attack was again made on the fort, which lasted until evening. None of the garrison was hurt, but some rebels were killed. During the night the Rani gave the insurgents some guns, and the fort was again attacked on the morning of the 8th June. An attempted escalade failed, the assailants being shot down by the garrison. The mutineers continued their attack, and towards afternoon got possession of the lower works of the fort. Upon this some of the natives who still remained inside attempted to open one of the gates to admit the enemy. Those most prominent in this treachery, who belonged to the Survey Department, were immediately shot or cut down by Captains Gordon and Burgess, but not before they had mortally wounded Lieutenant Powis. Shortly after, an irreparable misfortune befel the garrison in the death of Captain Francis Gordon, who was shot through the head while looking towards the rebels through a small window over the fort gate. He had from the first been the life and soul of the garrison, and his loss had a very injurious effect on the survivors.

Captain Skene having made a sign that the garrison wished to treat, the rebels collected near the gate, and promised by the most sacred oaths, through the medium of Saleh Muhammad, native Doctor, that the garrison would be allowed to depart in safety on the condition of vacating the fort and laying down their arms. These terms were unhappily agreed to, and the gates being thrown open, the garrison left the fort and were immediately made prisoners, and bound. The whole party were then taken through the town towards the Star Fort, but on reaching the Jokan Bagh, just outside the city walls, some sowars brought a message from the Risaldar, ordering that all were to be put to death. A general massacre then took place. Bakhshish Ali first cut down Captain Skene. Mrs. McEgan, attempting to save her husband, threw her arms round him, but was beaten and pushed aside, and Dr. McEgan was cut down and killed. Mrs. McEgan cast herself on his body and was there killed also. Miss Browne fell on her knees before a sepoy, and begged for life, but was immediately cut down by him. There are no particulars as to the death of the remainder, but all the men, their wives and children,* were cruelly slaughtered, except Mrs. Mutlow, who had concealed herself in the town, disguised in native apparel, and was subsequently rescued on the taking of Jhansi. Mr. Crawford, an East Indian clerk, escaped out of the fort during the night of the 7th June, and made his way to the Samthar State, and thence to Cawnpore.

Surrender of the fort.

Massacre of the Europeans.

The bodies were left exposed for three days on the high road where they were murdered, and were then thrown into gravel pits and covered over. On the evening of the massacre the proclamation was made—" The people are God's ; the country is the King's ; and the two religions govern."

In the meantime the detachment at Karehra had also mutinied and joined their comrades at Jhansi. Lieutenant Ryves, who was in command, escaped to Gwalior. On the 11th June the Jhansi mutineers left for Delhi. The Rani sent agents to the Nana Sahib, levied troops, established a mint, and began strengthening the fortifications of Jhansi.

The Jalaun District.

While these events were taking place affairs were rapidly approaching a crisis in the Jalaun District. On the 6th June an express was received by the officer commanding the two companies of the 53rd Bengal Infantry at Orai with news of the outbreak. At this time these two companies were about to be relieved by two companies of the 56th from Cawnpore, regarding which regiment there were grave suspicions. The Deputy Commissioner, Captain Browne, therefore sent off the bulk of his treasure to Gwalior with a guard of a hundred men of the 53rd under Lieutenant Tomkinson, called in two companies of the 1st Gwalior Regiment from Etawah which, with some Mahratta Horse, reached Orai at 1 A.M. on the 7th June ; and directed the officer commanding the two companies of the 56th Bengal Infantry to retrace his steps to Cawnpore, which he did, and reached Kalpi that night (6th). The same night intelligence was received of the outbreak at Cawnpore.

Captain Browne about this time received a note from Shivpershad, Deputy Collector at Kalpi, expressing a desire to desert his post. As Kalpi was a most important point of communication over the Jumna, Lieutenant Lamb, Assistant

* For list of people massacred, see Appendix II.

Commissioner, was sent there, and at the same time an express was despatched to the Brigadier at Gwalior to send aid to Jhansi.

On Captain Cosseratt's detachment from Etawah joining him, Captain Browne intended to proceed with it and some Samthar troops and guns to the relief of the Europeans at Jhansi, leaving the police at Orai; but this intention was abandoned on receipt of news on the 9th of the massacre at Jhansi. The same day the men of the 53rd Bengal Infantry at Orai deserted their officers; the *Barkandazes* of the Customs Department mutinied; and Captain Cosseratt, who was at Kunch, received orders from his commanding officer to return to Etawah. On the 10th June the two sons of the Gursarai Chief, whose proffered aid had been accepted by Captain Browne, arrived at Jalaun with a force of several hundred men, and a few guns, and on the same day Captain Browne and Lieutenant Lamb arrived at that place.

Captain Browne and Lieutenant Lamb and Captain Cosseratt's party left Jalaun on the 11th or 12th June and proceeded to Etawah, the district being left in charge of Mr. Passanah, Deputy Collector, who remained at Orai.

March of the Jhansi mutineers.

The Jhansi mutineers left for Delhi on the 11th June, and reached Moth, 35 miles north-east of Jhansi, on the 13th, where they plundered the treasury, and took away as a prisoner Niaz Ali, the Deputy Collector. On the 15th their advanced guard of six or eight sowars reached Orai, and Messrs. Passanah and Griffiths, Deputy Collectors, left in the night and passed through Jalaun, where they met Shiuram Tatia, eldest son of the Gursarai Chief, who shortly afterwards assumed authority over the entire district. From Jalaun the two Deputy Collectors made for Gwalior,* but on the 17th June they fell in with the hundred men of the 53rd who had taken the Jalaun treasure to Gwalior. These men plundered the two gentlemen, made them prisoners, and marched to Jalaun, where the mutineers were cordially received by Shiuram Tatia, who bought the plundered horses and guns. On the 21st Messrs. Passanah and Griffiths were released at Orai, and the mutineers proceeded to Cawnpore. They remained at Orai, and after many adventures, during which they were kindly treated and protected by the Gursarai Chief, Keshu Rao, the latter after the defeat of the Nana at Bithur, sent them to Cawnpore on the 2nd September, where they arrived in safety.

Adventures of Messrs. Passanah and Griffiths.

The Gursarai Chief made his head-quarters at Jalaun. On the 29th October, however, Tantia Topi and the Gwalior mutineers arrived there, and were received by the chief. But the latter and his sons were thrown into prison, severely chastised, and plundered of all their wealth, an infant grandson' of the former Chief of Jalaun being installed on the *gadi* by Tantia.

In the meantime Kour Singh of Jagdespur and the 40th Bengal Infantry had reached Kalpi on the 19th October. They were in communication with the

* Mr. Passanah was accompanied by his family, but his mother, being unable to travel, was left at Orai and cruelly murdered there by the Jhansi mutineers on the 17th June, as were Sub-Assistant Surgeon Heming, Mr. Double, head clerk of the Jalaun Office, and his family.

Gwalior mutineers at Jalaun, and on the 3rd November seized and imprisoned Shiuram Tatia, and on the 7th were joined by the mutineers from Gwalior, and marched to attack Cawnpore.

The Chanderi District.

The news of the outbreak at Jhansi was soon known at Lalitpur, and the Chanderi District rapidly fell into greater disorder than ever. The Thakurs rose in every direction and commenced plundering, collecting in large bodies, principally at Chanderi and Talbahat and around Lalitpur, and the Banpur Raja, who had been invited to Lalitpur by Captain Gordon's predecessor, played a double game; for while ostensibly professing loyalty to Government he was in reality at the head of the rising, and by the 11th and 12th June had occupied the passes about Malthone with strong parties of his matchlockmen.

He also tried to demoralize the sepoys of the wing of the 6th Gwalior Regiment and opened a private camel *dâk* to Jhansi. On being ordered to Banpur by Captain Gordon, the Raja left Lalitpur and took up a position in his fort of Maraura, where he had collected a strong force of Bundelas and some guns, and then sent a force towards Chanderi.

On the morning of the 12th June Captain Gordon, in consultation with Captain Sale, the Officer Commanding, determined that the detachment, having no guns, could not hold Lalitpur, and decided to fall back on Gwalior territory towards Isagarh. The police had deserted their posts, and the only hope was in the sepoys, who were showing a mutinous disposition to which they had been incited by forty sowars of the 14th Irregular Cavalry who had just arrived from Nowgong.

Mutiny at Lalitpur.

The native officers were made acquainted with the plan of falling back on Gwalior; the twenty-five thousand rupees in the Treasury were distributed among the sepoys, to confirm waverers and as compensation for their abandoned property; and the detachment was to start on the afternoon of the 12th June; and as the Raja's men had rushed on to the bazaar, in order to prevent plunder Captain Gordon made over the district to the Raja, who still professed friendship.

On proceeding to the lines the officers found two bodies of men collected, but without native officers; these were the bad men of the regiment, the remainder kept out of the way. Captain Sale and Dr. O'Brien went to one party, Captains Irwin and A. C. Gordon to the other. The men broke into open mutiny, saying "We are servants of the King of Delhi, not a man of us will go with you; however, we won't take your lives, but you must be off." The whole party* then proceeded by the Saugor road, but when at the end of the bazaar they were taken by some of the Raja's men to Maraura.

* Captain A. C. Gordon, Deputy Commissioner; Captain Sale, commanding 6th Regiment, Gwalior Infantry; Captain Irwin, 6th Regiment, Gwalior Infantry; Mrs. Irwin and 2 children; Doctor O'Brien, 6th Regiment, Gwalior Infantry; the Sergeant-Major and his wife; Mr. Verrier, Customs Department; Captain Gordon's two Madras servants.

On the 13th June the Raja moved into Lalitpur with a large force and some guns, and the officers and ladies were kept in the fort of Maraura as prisoners, although well treated in other respects. On the 15th June the party were sent to Banpur, and were visited on the 16th, when they arrived, by the Raja's *Mukhtiar*, Muhammad Ali, who was in disgrace owing to his opposition to his master's rebellious schemes. At 2 A.M. on the 17th they were forwarded to Tehri, where they took up their quarters in the house of Prem Narayan, tutor of the young Raja, where they remained until the 2nd July, and were well treated. The Tehri authorities promised to send them in to Saugor, and on the 2nd July they started under a guard for Shahgarh, deserted by all except Captain Gordon's Madras servants. On the 5th July they arrived at Shahgarh and were hospitably received by the Raja of that place. On the 7th they made preparations to proceed to Saugor, when news arrived of the mutiny there. On the 10th some of the mutineers arrived, accompanied by the Raja, whom they met at Kataura, where he had gone to join his troops, and compelled to go with them. The rest of the Saugor mutineers arrived in the course of the day, and the Europeans were sent for safety to a garden house of the Raja, and moved about from village to village until the mutineers left, when they returned to Shahgarh.

The Lalitpur prisoners.

By this time the Raja of Shahgarh had invaded Saugor territory, and was a rebel and in correspondence with the Raja of Banpur, but continued his professions of loyalty to Captain Gordon. On the evening of the 18th July he fired a salute for the supposed fall of Delhi, and next morning the Europeans were told that they were to start at once for Saugor. Henceforth they received nothing but ill-treatment in place of the kindness hitherto experienced. They were hurried off without seeing the Raja, and made over as prisoners to a guard under his brother Diwan Lachman Singh. Shortly after, the latter left to attack the British troops at Benaika,* where he was defeated, lost a gun, and was severely wounded. The prisoners were then sent to Papit, confined in a cow-shed, and insulted in every way.

On the 25th July Captain Gordon was sent for by the Shahgarh Raja, who stated that his troops had attacked the British forces contrary to his orders, and that he was anxious to be an ally if the Garhakota District were given to him; otherwise he would join the rebels.

On the morning of the 27th July the party started for the town of Benaika in the Saugor District, the Raja having promised to send them direct to Saugor,† but they were taken back to Papit by their guard, and at Zalimpur a sowar drove his spear into the cheek-bone of Mr. Verrier, inflicting a severe wound. Captain Gordon stated that all through the Banpur, Tehri, and Shahgarh States the people were bitterly hostile to the Salt Department.

On the 29th July the party were moved to Baretta, a fort in the middle of the jungle, and were informed that the Raja could not send them to Saugor owing to

* See page 37.
† See page 38

the disturbed state of the country. Here they remained, badly treated and half-starved, until their release. On the 12th September they left Baretta and reached Saugor on the 14th, the Raja being induced to set them free by his alarm at the advance of Colonel Millar's Nagpore Moveable Column.*

Hostilities between Bundelas and mutineers.

At Lalitpur, where the Raja of Banpur and his troops had gone on the 13th June, a quarrel arose between him and the 6th Regiment, Gwalior mutineers, and sowars, the Raja demanding a share of the treasure which Captain Gordon had distributed. The mutineers marched from Lalitpur in the evening, and were immediately attacked by the Raja's followers and other Bundelas, but beat them off with heavy loss. These attacks were continued by the Bundelas until they crossed the Betwa river, north of Talbahat, into Jhansi territory, the Bundelas always being worsted. The mutineers passed through Jhansi, where they were well received and feasted for three days by the Rani in the Jokan Bagh; they reached Orai on the 21st June, and thence proceeded to join the other mutineers at Kalpi.

The Raja of Banpur established his authority in the Chanderi District and remained in possession of the northern part of the Saugor district until Sir Hugh Rose's advance in January, 1858.

Orchha and Jhansi.

Although the Rani of Jhansi established her authority throughout that district she did not remain in undisputed possession. The Tehri or Orchha State had in former times possessed a great part of Jhansi territory, and conceived that a favourable opportunity had arisen for aggrandisement and plunder. On the 10th August a Tehri force took Mau Ranipur, overran the country between the Betwa and Dhasan rivers, burned villages, and captured cattle. They then took Barwa Sagar, and besieged Jhansi from the 3rd September to 22nd October 1857, when they withdrew, after inflicting great injury on the population south of Jhansi. All this time they represented themselves as acting on behalf of the British Government. In January 1858, the Rani's troops began to gain the ascendency, and the Tehri troops were beaten on the 1st March and expelled from the territory between the Betwa and Dhasan rivers. The Rani entered into close relations with the Nana, Tantia Topi, and the Banpur Raja. Meanwhile other districts in the vicinity of Jhansi had risen in rebellion, and the native troops at Banda, Hamirpur, Nowgong, and Nagode had mutinied. At Banda was a detachment of three companies of the 1st Bengal Infantry; at Hamirpur a part of the 53rd Bengal Infantry; at Nowgong a wing of the 12th Bengal Infantry and of the 14th Irregular Cavalry (the regiments which had their headquarters at Jhansi), and a detachment of native artillery. At Nagode was stationed the 50th Bengal Infantry.

Banda.

In the Banda District the insurrection began early in June in Mau on the Jumna, where armed men began to assemble, and were soon

* See page 38.

joined by mutineers and released convicts from Cawnpore and Allahabad. The rebellion soon spread over the district, and Mr. F. O. Mayne, the Collector, hoping to hold the detachment of the 1st Bengal Infantry true by an exhibition of confidence, sent some treasure to their lines for safe keeping.

On the 8th June, it being reported that mutineers were crossing the Jumna at Chilla Tara, the European ladies were sent for safety to the palace of the Nawab Ali Bahadur, and on the same day the European refugees from Fatehpur arrived at Banda. The headquarters of the 1st Bengal Infantry were among the troops that mutinied at Cawnpore, and, having heard of this, the sepoys at Banda became beyond control by the 14th June. It was on that date resolved by the European authorities, with the aid of the Nawab and his troops, one hundred and twenty-five in number, to try and ge possession of the two guns at the jail, and then disarm the 1st Bengal Infantry. The Nawab's troops were drawn up in the court-yard, ready to start. But a tumultuous crowd of townspeople assembled; the Nawab's sepoys, who were under Lieutenant Bennett, Commandant of the detachment of the 1st Bengal Infantry, refused to move, and the Europeans would in all probability have been killed then but for the personal interposition of the Nawab. The Banda sepoys marched straight off to the lines to join the regiment, which rose at once, the men seizing their arms and sounding the alarm.

Mutiny of the 1st Bengal Infantry.

The Europeans were now helpless, surrounded by enemies in a hostile country, while it was reported that troops were advancing from Cawnpore to occupy the place. The Nawab, when appealed to, replied that he could do no more, that his sepoys had mutinied, that he himself would stand up and fight for the Europeans, but could not answer for their lives. Accordingly the party, which included seventeen women and children, left Banda that night, and fled to Nagode, seventy-six miles distant, in two marches. They had hardly left, when a blaze that lighted the country for miles round announced the burning of the cantonments. The prisoners were released from the jail, and the Nawab Ali Bahadur proclaimed his rule, giving out that the Collector had deputed his authority to him.

Flight of Europeans.

Destruction of the Cantonment.

On the 15th Mr. Cockerell, Joint-Magistrate, rode into Banda from Kirwi, and was murdered at the palace gate by the Nawab's sepoys.* The same day the sepoys of the 1st Bengal Infantry proclaimed their own *raj*, in opposition to the proclamation of the Nawab, who, however, appeased their wrath by acknowledging their authority and entertaining them with a dinner of sweetmeats. Next day some East Indians, who had remained in hope of the protection of the Nawab, were dragged out and murdered on the parade ground.

On the 19th the sepoys left with their plundered treasure (two lakhs), guns and ammunition, accompanied by some of the sowars and the agent of the Nawab, who assumed the government on their departure.

* It does not appear that the Nawab, who was asleep at the time, was a party to this deed.

On the 30th June a portion of Captain Scott's party from Nowgong were brought prisoners to Banda, and were kindly and hospitably received by the Nawab and his mother, and sent in safety under escort to Nagode, which they reached on the 12th July. The others of the party were hunted from village to village through Sihonda and Badausa, and plundered of all they possessed, while many were killed by the villagers.

The Nowgong fugitives.

On the 2nd September the 7th and 8th Bengal Infantry arrived from Dinapur, bringing with them many wounded comrades, and were well received by the Nawab, who by this time hoped to be able to maintain the independence he had assumed. On the 3rd September emissaries came from Nagode, and on the 12th a large party of mutineer sepoys and of the Nawab's followers and troops marched for Nagode, and returned on the 27th with the 50th Bengal Infantry* and the plunder, guns, and ammunition from that place. On the 29th September Kour Singh with 2,000 men, including the 40th Bengal Infantry, reached Banda and was received with great honour and hospitality by the Nawab. The people of the town were again called upon to supply the Nawab's requirements, and if anyone refused to pay, his house was levelled to the ground and himself tortured and imprisoned. Other mutinous corps and many armed men from Oudh continued to arrive at Banda.

The mutineers flock to Banda.

During this period strife had arisen between the Nawab of Banda and the Chief of Ajaigarh, who claimed prior possession of the country, and in the middle of August the two parties came into conflict at Nimnipar. On the 8th October the mutineers joined with the Nawab in an attack on the Ajaigarh fortress at Nimnipar, and although the garrison fought bravely against a numerically superior and better-armed enemy, they were forced to surrender on the third day owing to lack of provisions, water, and ammunition. The three chiefs were confined in the Nawab's palace, and cruelly murdered in their prison on the 19th April 1858, the day of General Whitlock's victory at the battle of Banda.

Hostilities between the Nawab and the Ajaigarh Chief.

On the 15th October the 5th Irregular Cavalry, 500 strong, reached Banda from Bhaugalpur. On the 18th Kour Singh and his men went away towards Kalpi, and on the 28th the 7th and 8th Bengal Infantry and other mutineers with three guns marched for Chilla Tara. These latter were afterwards met and defeated by British troops at Kadjowa in the Fatehpur District.

Meanwhile Narayan Rao and Madhu Rao had proclaimed their rule at Kirwi, where the Nawab was a minor, nine years of age. The Nawab of Banda opened negotiations with them for a loan, and on the 15th November marched to Kirwi at the head of 2,000 men. He was there joined by two companies of the 32nd mutineers, and succeeded in getting two lakhs from the Raos, with the promise of more. He then entered into

Events at Kirwi.

* Subadar Shiulal Tiwari of this regiment, a well educated man who could read and write English, was most bitter in his animosity.

a compact with them, dividing the district and agreeing to assist each other against all enemies. Collections of revenue were carried on vigorously by both parties, and their armed bands of retainers forced money from the people by every species of torture and oppression.

Banda in 1858.

On the 3rd December the Nawab returned to Banda and found two more companies of the 32nd mutineers, who had arrived with 18 guns during his absence; they left for Kalpi on the 26th. In February 1858, the Church, Christian cemetery, public offices, jail, and records were destroyed. All the fords over the Jumna were carefully guarded; a force was sent to assist Tantia Topi in the attack on Charkhari, and another to attack the fort of Kalinjar, where Lieutenant Remington gallantly held out with a party of matchlockmen and guns furnished by the Raja of Panna.

It was not until the beginning of April that the Nawab and his adherents heard of the advance of the Madras Column under General Whitlock. He recalled his forces from Kalinjar, and sent a force towards Mahoba to meet this attack He had expected enemies only from across the Jumna, having been told that there were few English left in the country.

Nowgong.

The revolt at Jhansi was quickly followed by the rising of the 12th Bengal Infantry at Nowgong, some sixty miles east of the former place. Nowgong was garrisoned by a wing each of the 12th Bengal Infantry and 14th Irregular Cavalry, as well as a detachment of Native Artillery.

On the 30th May it was reported that the native gunners were about to rise, and Major Kirk, who commanded the station, had the guns moved to the quarter-guard of the 12th. On the 9th June news arrived of the murder of the Europeans at Jhansi, and that evening the havildar-major of the 12th was shot dead at guard-mounting and the guns were seized by the mutinous sepoys.

Revolt of the troops.

The officers vainly attempted to reason with the men, but all the native troops in the station were now in open revolt, and the Europeans left, accompanied by a few men who remained faithful. The fugitives fled from place to place in Bundelkhand, generally ill-treated by the inhabitants, but at times sheltered and protected. At Chhatarpur they were kindly treated by the Rani, but left after a halt of two days. Near Kalinjar they were attacked on the 17th June, and Lieutenant Townshend was shot through the heart. Here most of the sepoys who had hitherto accompanied them deserted, and they retreated to Kalrai, with the loss of Major Kirk and Mrs. Smalley, who died of exhaustion. Here some remained in Chhatarpur territory, and others went on to Mahoba, losing Dr. Mawe, Lieutenant Barber, Lieutenant Ewart, and Mrs. Smalley's child, who all died on the way. In the Sihonda district the inhabitants were especially hostile, and at Madhupur the fugitives were attacked, and an unfortunate lady

Adventures of the fugitives.

who was left behind was stripped of her clothes and plundered, whilst the *zemindars* disputed as to who should be her husband. In the midst of this rivalry she was rescued by the Nawab Ali Bahadur of Banda, taken to Banda, and very kindly treated by the Nawab and his mother, and sent under escort to Nagode. A number of people were afterwards rewarded for protecting these and other European fugitives, and others were punished for their hostility.

Hamirpur.

Hamirpur lies almost due north of Banda on the south bank of the Jumna. Mr. T. K. Loyd was the Collector, and the Treasury was guarded by a detachment of the 53rd Bengal Infantry. There were about twenty other Europeans* in the station. Mr. Loyd, on hearing of disturbances elsewhere, sent to the chiefs of Charkhari, Behri, and Baoni for assistance, and received a hundred men and a gun from each; he also entertained five hundred new levies, and brought in a number of *chaprassis* and *barkandazes* from the district.

Early in June the *zemindars* in Dauda and Manjkhore banded together for plunder. On the 12th June there was a meeting at the large house occupied by the Charkhari troops, attended by the headmen of each band of auxiliaries, the Subadar of the 53rd Regiment, and other officials.

On the 13th some troopers arrived from Baoni, and Rahim-ud-Din, a headman of the Nawab, who had come overnight, withdrew the guns posted in Mr. Loyd's compound, and turned them on the house, saying it was by his master's orders, and at the same time news was brought that some sepoys had released the prisoners in the gaol. In the early morning two officers of the 1st Regiment, Lieutenants Raikes and Browne, whose detachment had mutinied on the way to Orai, had arrived as fugitives, and they with Messrs. Loyd and Grant, who up to that time had refused to quit their post, although asked by the Collector at Banda to join him there, called for their horses, which were ready saddled under charge of two troopers, who at once turned traitors, and made off with the horses, calling to the mutineers then approaching that the Europeans were escaping.

The outbreak.

There was now not a moment to be lost, and the fugitives hastened down the bank where an iron boat was ready, in which they embarked. When half way across the Jumna they were fired at from the bank, and the bullets falling thickly among them, they jumped into the water and swam ashore. Here they were badly treated by the men of Rampur, near which place they landed, being plundered of all their possessions. They then separated; the two officers proceeded towards Allahabad, and Browne† reached Fatehpur in time to accompany Havelock on his march to Cawnpore, but Raikes died on the way.

* Mr. Donald Grant, Joint Magistrate; Mr. W. D. Murray, Landholder; Mr. James Crawford, Head Clerk; Mr. W. Bunter, Judicial Clerk, and Mrs. Bunter; Mr. and Mrs. Anderson and four or five children; Jeremiah, Catechist of the Church Missionary Society, with his wife and four children.

† He subsequently died of cholera.

Messrs. Loyd and Grant hid in the fields until evening, and then, swimming with the current, reached the Hamirpur bank near the junction of the Betwa with the Jumna, three miles below the town. There they stayed from the 14th to the 19th June, spending the days standing up to their necks in water among the reeds, and only daring to go ashore at night. Many seem to have been aware of their concealment, and Mr. Loyd's syce and shepherd told Harri Mohan, a Bengal writer in the office, who kept them supplied with food and sent them some clothes; this loyal man performed this kindness at the risk of his life, and was afterwards ill-treated in consequence.

Flight of Europeans.

On the evening of the 18th three Ahirs discovered Mr. Lyod's place of concealment, and he sent his ring by one of them to Ganga Sahai, his *Serishtadar*; but the Ahir instead took it to the Subadar Ali Bakhsh, who had proclaimed the Delhi dynasty, and himself its Agent. On this some of the sepoys went down and escorted them bare-footed to a tree outside the *Cutcherry* compound, where they were bound and made to kneel, and then shot. Mr. Grant fell dead with a bullet in the brain; Mr. Loyd received three bullets in the chest, and called out—"Are not the English troops yet come?"—when another volley completed the tragedy.

Murder of Messrs. Loyd and Grant.

Meanwhile, much blood had been shed in Hamirpur. Messrs Murray and Crawford and the Andersons had made for the house where the Charkhari troops were, hoping to find protection there, but had at once been butchered. The Bunters were cut down at the hospital and Miss Anderson was severely wounded, but was saved and concealed by some cultivators, and eventually escaped to Cawnpore.

Massacre in Hamirpur.

After the murder of the Europeans, the mob and sepoys rushed to the town, plundered every one they could lay hands on, paying off old scores, and slaughtered the Christian preacher Jeremiah and his whole family. The Bengali Babus, as writing and speaking English, were next attacked and robbed of all they possessed. On the 18th June three boat-loads of unarmed sepoys of the 44th and 67th, who were disarmed at Agra, were passing by when the guns were turned on them, many killed and the boats and their contents taken.

On the 20th a body of the Nana's troopers came, and took the contents of the treasury (about a lakh and a half of rupees) to Cawnpore, having had their turn at plundering the place. On the 1st July the Peshwa's rule was proclaimed, native officials were directed to act in his name, and land-holders to pay revenue to the Nana's Agents.

While these events were going on in Hamirpur, Mr. Carne, the Assistant at Mahoba, had fled to Charkhari, after a series of adventures in which he joined the Nowgong fugitives. The Raja of Charkhari remained loyal, and took charge of the neigh-

The Raja of Charkhari.

bouring districts on behalf of Government. Mahoba was, however, taken possession of by the chief of Gursarai. In January and February 1858, the fort at Charkhari* was besieged and the town plundered and burnt by the forces of Tantia Topi, and from that time until the battle of Banda, the Banda Nawab held the country.

* It was to relieve this place that Sir Hugh Rose received orders to turn aside on his march to Kalpi, but he very rightly proceeded with the main object of the campaign. See page 106.

CHAPTER III.

THE SAUGOR AND NARBADA TERRITORIES.

The Saugor and Narbada territories comprised the greater portion of the country now known as the Central Provinces. On the north the districts of Saugor and Damoh form part of the Vindhyan plateau, while to the south, in the valley of the Narbada river, are Jubbulpore, Narsinghpur, Hoshangabad, and Nimar, the latter extending to the Tapti river. Like the rest of the central portion of the Indian Peninsula, the level of this country is broken by frequent hill ranges, and a very large proportion of these territories is covered with forests, through which pour the Narbada and Tapti rivers and their tributaries.

Physical features.

This region formed at one time the great Kingdom of Gondwana, subsequently subject to Delhi, and afterwards overrun by the Mahrattas. The Saugor and Narbada Territories were annexed by the British on the deposition of Apa Sahib, Bhonsla of Nagpur, in 1818. The remainder of the dominions of the Nagpur Rajas lapsed to the British Government in 1853.

When the mutiny broke out at Meerut in May, 1857, the troops stationed in the Saugor and Narbada Districts were as detailed in the margin. These districts had been in rebellion at the time of the hostilities with Gwalior in 1843, which culminated in the battle of Maharajpur. Their proximity to other areas of disturbance in 1857 naturally rendered them liable to infection with the spirit of revolt that was spreading from Northern India. Moreover, signs of organised rebellion were not wanting. In January, 1857, Captain Ternan, Deputy Commissioner of Narsinghpur, noticed the circulation of the *chapathis* which had been a mysterious sign of the coming trouble.

Troops in the Territories.

Saugor—1 Company, European Bengal Artillery.
3rd Irregular Cavalry.
31st Bengal Infantry.
42nd Bengal Infantry.
Damoh—2 Companies, 42nd Bengal Infantry.
Jubbulpore— 52nd Bengal Infantry.
Mandla—A Havildar's Guard, 52nd Bengal Infantry.
Seoni—1 Company, Madras Infantry.
Narsinghpur—4 Companies, 28th Madras Infantry.
Hoshangabad— 4 Companies, 28th Madras Infantry.
Betul—2 Companies, 28th Madras Infantry.

Events at Saugor.

The news of the outbreaks at Meerut and Delhi caused some excitement in Saugor and Jubbulpore, which increased when the facts of the Jhansi massacre were made known. The sepoys at several stations expressed great fears of being disarmed.

On the 13th June Brigadier Sage, who commanded at Saugor, sent the marginally noted troops to the relief of Lalitpur, the Deputy Commissioner of Chanderi having reported that the Gwalior Contingent stationed there were not to be depended on, and that he doubted the loyalty of the Raja of Banpur, who had been called in to assist, but had surrounded the station with his followers. At the same time reports were received by Major Erskine, Commissioner of the District, that the Raja of Shahgarh was raising soldiers and making preparations for war.

Major Gaussen.
One Company, 31st, Bengal Infantry.
One Company, 42nd Bengal Infantry.
One Troop, 3rd Irregular Cavalry.
Two 9-pounders.

On the 14th some men of the 42nd reported that four of their sepoys had endeavoured to prevent the detachment from marching. These men were seized, tried by a Native Court-Martial, and sentenced to six months' imprisonment.

On the 15th Lieutenant Miller, Adjutant of the 52nd, was inspecting guards, when a sepoy made a thrust at him with his musket. The man was seized by the Subadar-Major and confined in the guard-room, there being some show of sympathy towards him by his comrades. The man was pronounced mad by the medical officer of the regiment, and was sent to the lunatic asylum at Benares, where he was found to be sane and was hanged.

The 31st and 42nd Bengal Infantry at Malthone.

Major Gaussen's detachment arrived at Malthone on the 18th June, and finding the passes to the north were held by large bodies of the Raja of Banpur's troops, he halted to protect the northern frontier of the Saugor District where it bordered on Bundelkhand, and keep the Raja in check, being reinforced by 250 men of the 31st, 100 of the 42nd, and 50 sowars of the 2nd Irregular Cavalry from Saugor. He then took the small fort of Bala Bahat, which had been occupied by the insurgents, and sixteen men in it were captured.

On the 25th June some men of the 31st and 42nd Infantry at Malthone broke into open mutiny, insisting that the Bundela prisoners should be brought into their camp from the custody of the police. Major Gaussen was obliged to comply, and on the arrival of the prisoners in camp they were released on the demand of the sepoys.

The Lalitpur prisoners.

Meanwhile the Europeans at Lalitpur had been confined by the Banpur Raja, who sent them to Tehri, where they were kindly treated through the influence of the young Raja of Orchha's tutor, and befriended by Muhammad Ali Khan, Mukhtiar of the Banpur Raja. They were then sent towards Saugor, but seized and imprisoned on the way by the Raja of Shahgarh, who kept them in confinement for three months, only allowing them one anna a day each for food, and then sent them into Saugor.

On the 27th June Brigadier Sage, suspecting the troops in Saugor Cantonment, resolved to take possession of the old fort in the town, which was used as an arsenal and magazine and was garrisoned by sepoys from the cantonment. It was of great consequence that this fort should not fall into the hands of rebels, for, independent of its large stores, it was the only safe place of refuge for the European and Christian residents in the event of mutiny.

Measures of defence at Saugor.

Immediate steps were, therefore, taken to lay in supplies and prepare accommodation for the European families. The bulk of the treasure was lodged in the fort. The same afternoon the sepoy guard was relieved by twenty European artillerymen, and on the 29th the whole of the European artillery, with their guns, were marched into the fort. The Brigadier then sent for the native officers of the 31st and 42nd, and told them that if they wished to prove themselves true, they must give up the bad men of their corps, as there had been mutiny in a portion of each (at Malthone). The native officers expressed regret, and volunteered to send good men to bring in the mutineers from Malthone. This was agreed to, and the men selected marched that evening; but the Brigadier would allow no European officers to remain with the men.

On the morning of the 1st July the 3rd Irregular Cavalry at Saugor, with the exception of some of the native officers and about fifty men, broke into open mutiny, went to the Masjid, and sharpened their swords. At the same time Subadar Shaikh Ramzan of the 42nd raised the Muhammadan flag and called for followers by beat of drum. He was joined by the whole of the 42nd, by a few of the 31st, and by all the mutineers of the 3rd Irregular Cavalry; and the same day the mutineers, in conjunction with the bad characters of the bazaar, plundered the officers' bungalows; the Europeans having already taken refuge in the fort.

Mutiny at Saugor.

On the 2nd July some of the mutineers went towards Damoh, with a view to inciting the two companies of the 42nd there to join them.

Meanwhile the men sent out by the 31st to Malthone relieved the Light Company of that regiment, which had been most mutinous, and it returned to Saugor. Some of the men of this company expressed contrition, but about forty-five at once joined the mutineers. The men sent out by the 42nd on the same errand were overtaken by some of the mutineers, whom they joined, with the exception of six, who were put to death by the latter.

From the 1st July Subadar Shaikh Ramzan, 42nd Bengal Infantry, assumed command in Cantonments, with the rank of General. The mutineers seized the large saluting gun on the artillery hill, which had been left there when the rest of the guns were taken into the fort, and brought it down to the quarter-guard of the 42nd, which they had made their head-quarters. The 31st Bengal Infantry, * with the exception of the forty-five above referred to, kept aloof from the mutineers. The native

Loyalty of the 31st Bengal Infantry.

* Now the 2nd Queen's Own Rajput Light Infantry.

officers of this corps daily went to the fort, and the men protected and conveyed much of their officers' property to them.

The 31st now requested permission to attack the mutineers. This the Brigadier sanctioned, but would not allow their European officers to accompany them. However, a strong party of the Customs *Chaprassis*, who had just been armed with muskets, were sent out by the Deputy Commissioner, Major Western, to make a demonstration in favour of the 31st, and were accompanied by the officers of the Customs Department, and by Captain Pinkney, who had not been able to proceed beyond Saugor in consequence of the mutiny at Malthone, and by Lieutenant Hamilton, the Assistant Commissioner.

The mutineers, seeing they were about to be attacked, fired a round shot into the 31st from the saluting gun, and both regiments kept up a desultory fire with their muskets nearly the whole day, but little damage was done on either side. Next morning, thinking the 31st would be aided by the artillery of the fort, the mutineers left the station for the north in great haste, taking with them some conveyances belonging to the officers, which they soon abandoned on the road.

It is perhaps permissible to conjecture what might have been the effect both on the mutineers and the rebellious people of the surrounding country had a resolute man directed an attack by the loyal regiment, led by their British officers and supported by the guns of the European artillery. The history of the mutiny and its suppression shows that such action, fearless and aggressive, never failed in its effects.

Damoh.

Meanwhile the Saugor mutiny created great alarm at Damoh, where there were two companies of the 42nd Bengal Infantry, and the Deputy Commissioner resolved to place his treasure in the jail fort, as the rebels from Saugor were sending a detachment to seize it, while plundering by the Bundelas from Shahgarh had begun. The detachment at Damoh was accordingly moved into the jail fort on the 3rd July. As the men appeared to be in a mutinous state, the Jemadar and some loyal non-commissioned officers warned the Europeans that they would not be safe in the jail fort, and they accordingly fled that night seventy miles to Narsinghpur. The mutineers arrived next morning, and the infantry proceeded to the jail and demanded the treasure, which was refused by the Subadar-Major and Havildar Ranjit Singh, on which the mutineers left the station. It appears to have been due to the management and gallant conduct of Ranjit Singh that the treasure was saved, and that the whole of the men of this detachment of the 42nd remained faithful to Government.

Jubbulpore.

Meanwhile it was feared at Jubbulpore that the 52nd Bengal Infantry would follow the example of the mutineers, and, as there were many ladies and children, it was decided by Major Erskine in consultation with Colonel Jamieson, commanding the 52nd, that the Christians should assemble in the Agency house, occupied by the former, which could in a short time be made defensible against musketry. Accordingly sixty people, including ten ladies and fifteen children, assembled in the house before 7 P.M. on the 4th July, subordinates being accommodated in tents and out-houses. Picquets were posted, and the place was intrenched and put in a state of defence.

Progress of events in the districts.

A few villages were plundered at this time in the Jubbulpore division, and, to suppress this, detachments were sent out to different places, and to Katangi on the Hiran river towards Damoh. Meanwhile the Rajas of Banpur and Shahgarh had sent emissaries to the petty chiefs in these territories, and had induced some of them to join in the rebellion; while on the 9th July they attacked Kurai and Benaika in the Saugor District, where most of the police joined the rebels.

On the 9th July some of the 3rd Irregular Cavalry and 31st Bengal Infantry were sent to assist Major Gaussen on his return from Malthone to Saugor, where he arrived on the 12th. The greater portion of the men of this detachment of the 7th Irregulars and the 42nd had deserted, and as Major Gaussen retired, the Raja of Banpur took possession of the northern part of the district, and plundering became general.

Harda.

The police at Harda broke out into open mutiny, but the Deputy Magistrate, Mazhir Jamil, maintained a bold front, and they were unable to do much harm there, although they attempted to raise the Muhammadan standard, and, seeing that they could not succeed, nine deserted, leaving their muskets. They were afterwards captured, some hanged, and some imprisoned.

Seoni.

In Seoni there was some alarm, but the Munsif Ali Husain behaved admirably, allayed the fears of the people, and kept the police loyal.

Hoshangabad.

On the 8th July Colonel Durand and his party arrived from Indore at Hoshangabad, and that place was put in a state of defence. Other fugitives from Sehore, Agar, and Sipri arrived during the ensuing week.

The Deccan Road.

In the middle of July 200 Bundelas took possession of the old fort at Bilheri, between Rewah and Sleemanabad, on the great Deccan road. Next day two companies of the 52nd from Jubbulpore marched against them, but they fled on the approach of the sepoys, only to return and take possession of the fort again, while they stole the post horses and robbed the Calcutta mails. Fresh detachments were again sent against them, and the fort was destroyed after the rebels had taken to flight. Thus peace was established and maintained in the districts by the 52nd, a regiment which afterwards mutinied.

Action at Benaika.

On the 18th July a company of the 31st, with two European officers, was sent from Saugor to Benaika. On the 21st the rebels near Benaika, having been reinforced from Shahgarh, advanced with one gun to attack this detachment, but they were repulsed, and their gun was captured. The Raja sent a messenger on the 25th July to say that he would give up the European prisoners from Lalitpur, and the detachment moved out to receive them, but was treacherously fired on. He then sent word that he would exchange them for the gun, but this was evidently false; and as Major Legard, who commanded the detachment, was not strong enough to attack the rebels, he withdrew to Saugor, taking the captured gun.*

About this time the Saugor district was nearly all in the hands of the rebels. The fort of Rahatgarh was taken possession of by the Nawab of Ambapani in Bhopal, the police being driven out or joining the enemy; and the fort of Garhakota was taken and occupied by the Shahgarh troops. At the same time the Raja of Banpur, at the head of some 1,400 men, moved down from the north towards Saugor, and took up a strong position at Nariaoli, 12 miles from Saugor fort, and on the 25th some of his troops advanced to the cantonments, but decamped on the garrison turning out.

Meanwhile the detachment of the 42nd at Damoh had not only held the place but attacked and driven the rebels out of the town. Captain Pinkney marched to Damoh with two companies of the 31st; and took over the fort and treasure. The Subadar-Major of the 42nd, aided by the Munsif, whom Havildar Ranjit Singh had kept in the fort with him, had managed to carry on duty in the town and a few miles round it, keeping the prisoners in jail and the police at their posts.

Events at Damoh.

A detachment from Damoh then attacked Hindoria, 12 miles from that place, the seat of the rebel Kishor Singh, who had been instigated by the Shahgarh Raja to attack Damoh some time before; the rebels were beaten and many of them killed. The European officers who had fled from Damoh returned on the 25th.

The two companies of the 31st, with two guns which they manned, and some eighty of the 3rd Irregular Cavalry, as well as the two companies of the 42nd, remained at Damoh, and had several engagements with the rebels, killing some fifty men in one fight. On the 28th July Damoh was attacked, but the rebels were driven off with loss. The whole of the Damoh District was now swarming with rebels, who plundered in every direction, and the Shahgarh insurgents were joined by nearly every man of the Lodi caste in Damoh, with the exception of the petty Raja of Hatri, who remained faithful throughout.

On the 17th July Colonel Millar left Nagpore with the Nagpore Moveable column, which had been organised at that station, composed of the troops detailed in the margin. The cavalry arrived at Jubbulpore on the 30th July, and was followed by the remainder of the column two days later, the 52nd going out to welcome them in.

The Nagpore Moveable Column—Colonel Millar, 33rd Madras Infantry.

1 Squadron, 4th Madras Cavalry—92 sabres.
D. Company, 3rd Battalion, Madras Artillery—65 rank and file, 6 guns.
33rd Madras Infantry—425 rank and file.
Rifle Company, 1st Nagpore Irregular Infantry—91 rank and file.

Colonel Millar informed Major Erskine, the Commissioner, that his column was placed at the disposal of the latter to march on any place in the Saugor and Narbada Territories, but not to gar-

* See page 24.

tison Jubbulpore; nor was it to be divided. The column was joined at Jubbulpore by two companies, 52nd Bengal Infantry, and two companies, 28th Madras Infantry, from Narsinghpur.

Some of the European residents desired the retention of the column, or a portion of it, at Jubbulpore, but Colonel Millar could not divide his force, and it was deemed necessary to send it to the relief of Damoh. As heavy rain was falling, the guns and carts of the column could not move although urgent calls for help came from Damoh, and on the 7th August the fort of Rehli, south of Saugor and west of Damoh, was taken by the rebels. The two companies of the 52nd attached to the moveable column, being lightly equipped, were ordered off on the 6th, with their four European officers, to Katângi, twenty miles on the Damoh road, to keep the boats safe on the Hiran river. They marched on the 7th, and did their duty well. Shortly after these two companies reached Katangi, Lieutenant Oakes, who was in command, received an urgent requisition from Damoh, and marched there in two days, having several engagements with the rebels near that place.

The districts of Saugor and Damoh were now, with the exception of the larger stations, entirely in the hands of the rebels; all the police had deserted or been driven in, and hundreds of Malguzars, although well inclined, were forced either to join the rebels or to assist them with men and food, or were plundered and often tortured; no posts were received in Saugor or Damoh for many weeks, and several *harkaras* (messengers) were killed or mutilated.

March of the Moveable Column.

The Moveable Column was unable to leave Jubbulpore, owing to rain, until the 17th August, when it marched nine miles. Next day the force marched to Katangi, crossing the Hiran river. The guns and a portion of the infantry did not arrive until three days later, owing to incessant rain. It is noteworthy that the detachment of the 52nd Bengal Infantry at Katangi, who were housed in a comfortable *serai*, brought their tents and pitched them with their own hands for the Madras sepoys.

On the 26th the column marched 17 miles to Jabbera, the guns being dragged through the mud by elephants, preceded by the Rifle Company, which was sent ahead to seize the boats at Nohta on the Birma river, and on the 29th August Damoh was relieved, and the rebels all moved off to a distance.

On the 1st September, 1857, at 3-30 A.M., Colonel Millar marched from Damoh, with the force detailed in the margin, against Balakot, 15 miles off, a large village with an old fort on a neighbouring hill, the residence of Sarup Singh, a Raja of the Lodhi caste, who with his followers had assisted in the attack on Damoh.

Capture of Balakot.
Colonel J. Millar, Commanding.
Captain Harrison, Staff Officer.
Captain Ludlow, Field Engineer.
Squadron, 4th Madras Cavalry, Captain Tottenham.
3rd Battalion, Madras Artillery. 3 guns—Captain James.
2 Companies, 33rd Madras Infantry—Captain Apthorp.
2 Companies, 52nd Bengal Infantry—Captain Oakes.
1 Company, 1st Nagpore Irregular Infantry—Lieutenant Sutherland.

After traversing dense jungle, the last four miles up a steep and rugged path, Colonel Millar arrived at 11 A.M. within a mile of Balakot, and sent the cavalry to surround the village and cut off the enemy's retreat. When the infantry approached within twelve hundred yards of the village, the enemy opened a brisk fire, but were soon driven in by the 33rd and 52nd, which advanced in skirmishing order, and drove the rebels out of the village, which was then set fire to and destroyed. The 33rd lost three men wounded, of whom one died. The detachment returned to Damoh next day.

Disaffection at Jubbulpore.

Early in September Captain Moxon of the 52nd received information from the *pundit* and sepoys of his regiment, in whom he placed great confidence, that mischief was brewing, and that some of the sepoys of the 52nd were conspiring with a pensioned Gond Raja, Shankar Sa,* residing close to Jubbulpore, to attack and murder the Europeans at that station. It was found on enquiry that at least eight or ten of the sepoys were in the habit of visiting the Raja and his son Raghunath Sa, where they met some disaffected Malguzars.

The Raja and his son and some others were arrested, and in his house were found several documents of a treasonable nature.

Captain Tottenham.
D. Company, 3rd Madras Artillery, 2 guns.
4th Light Cavalry, 1 Troop.
33rd Madras Infantry, 2 companies.

On the 7th September, in consequence of this news, a force, as noted in the margin, was detached to Jubbulpore under Captain Tottenham, 4th Light Cavalry, and arrived in time to save the place from destruction.

Attempted relief of Saugor.

Meanwhile, with his reduced force, Colonel Millar did not consider it possible to effect much, but he marched towards Saugor with the intention of relieving that place, and, on the 8th September, had got as far as the right bank of the Sunar river, when his further progress was arrested by the intelligence that the Dinapur mutineers were menacing the Rewah territory, and might come down on Jubbulpore.

The aspect of affairs was at this time very unpromising, the Rewah Raja having intimated to Lieutenant Osborne, the Political Agent at his Court, his inability to protect him. The column, therefore, returned to Damoh, round which the rebels had again gathered, and arrived there on the 13th, finding that Lieutenant Dickins, who had been left there with a portion of the 31st, had exchanged shots with the enemy's picquets.

Destruction of rebels at Narsingarh.

1 Troop, 4th Madras Cavalry, 2 guns.
2 Companies, 33rd Madras Infantry.
2 Companies, 52nd Bengal Infantry.

On the 17th September Major Jenkins marched from Damoh, with the force detailed in the margin, for the purpose of collecting grain from certain rebel villages. On arriving with a reconnoitring party at Narsingarh, he found that the fort, a strong stone-built place with a wet ditch, and well covered by gardens and stone enclosures, was occupied by about 250 matchlockmen, Shahgarh rebels. Behind the fort runs the Sunar river, having a very deep and difficult ford immediately in rear, and a better ford half a mile lower down.

* Raja Shankar Sa was the descendant of the Gond Kings of Garha Mandla. After his death his widow seized Ramgarh, and took part in several skirmishes. At length being closely pursued, she dismounted from her horse and plunged a sword into her own bosom. She was taken into the English camp, where she died.

Finding that the enemy were so strongly posted, Major Jenkins extended some infantry to cut them off from the lower ford, and brought the guns into position for throwing shrapnel. Before a shot could be fired from the guns, the rebels retreated, and the infantry advancing came upon them crossing the upper ford. The river was here about 250 yards wide, running with great force, the stones were slippery, and the water so deep at one place as to oblige the men to swim. The enemy had to make their way across this under a heavy and continuous fire, poured in from the bank above, and the panic was so great that hardly a shot was fired in return. They lost about 50 killed, and 33 prisoners were taken, of whom 13 were hung at Narsingarh, and the rest taken into Damoh where the detachment returned next day.

Affairs at Jubbulpore.

Affairs at Jubbulpore were now coming to a crisis. On the second night after the arrest of Raja Shankar Sa, the Deputy Commissioner heard of a plan on the part of 52nd to rescue the prisoners. The Madras detachment turned out and remained some hours under arms; and during the night a few shots were fired in the 52nd lines, a bungalow close to the lines was burned down, and eight sepoys deserted with their arms.

Execution of Raja Shankar Sa.

Raja Shankar Sa and his son were tried by a commission composed of the Deputy Commissioner and two officers, and, the evidence being conclusive against them, they were lashed to two guns and blown away on the morning of the 18th September.

Mutiny of the 52nd Bengal Infantry.

At 10 that night the whole of the 52nd Bengal Infantry left Jubbulpore, with the exception of one native officer and fifteen rank and file, taking their arms and ammunition and marching by a circuitous route towards Patan on the Hiran river, where there was a detachment of the corps under Lieutenant Macgregor. Directly this became known, the lines, magazines, and property of the 52nd, which they had evidently left behind them in a panic, were secured by the Madras troops. Expresses were sent off to the officers commanding the detachments at Sleemanabad and Patan, warning them of what had occurred and ordering them into Jubbulpore at once. Lieutenants Barton and Cockburn at Sleemanabad told their native officers of what had occurred, and at once mounted their horses. Their men expressed their regret at parting with these officers, and did not molest them, but said they must make the best of their way towards Delhi. Some of them shook their officers by the hand; they then robbed the *tehsili* of the little money that was there, the Pay Havildar handing one of the officers the balance of his pay, and marched off quietly towards Nagode. The two officers reached Jubbulpore in safety, and their baggage was sent in by their men.

Lieutenant Macgregor was less fortunate. When the 52nd reached Patan they confined him, and were joined there by the detachment, the men of which had plenty of ammunition. They then plundered Patan and crossed the river, and, with Thakur Mirhban Singh of Narsinghpur and his followers, marched towards Katangi and were joined by the detachment there with the exception of one loyal Muhammadan Jemadar, who went to Jubbulpore.

On the 18th news was received at Damoh of the mutiny of the 50th at Nagode and the detachment at Narsingarh, which included two companies of the 52nd, was at once called in, and arrived on the evening of the 19th.

Mutiny of the 50th Bengal Infantry.

About midnight on the 19th September an express arrived at Damoh conveying the intelligence of the mutinies of the 50th and 52nd Bengal Infantry at Nagode and Jubbulpore. It now became necessary for the column to return at once to Jubbulpore, but the two companies of the 52nd were first disarmed, on the morning of the 20th, without trouble, although their muskets were loaded, as they had just returned from Narsingarh.

Events at Damoh.

The column was marched out on the Saugor road at daybreak on the 20th ostensibly to attack some rebels, the 52nd forming the advanced guard and the Nagpore Rifles* the rear-guard. On arriving on an open plain three miles from Damoh the column was halted. The guns were unlimbered, double shotted, and drawn up in rear of the 28th Madras Infantry, who were deployed. The 28th moved to the right, and Colonel Millar, riding up to the 52nd, told the officers what was to be done. The men were ordered to pile arms; and were told of what had occurred at Jubbulpore. They were taken by surprise and hesitated, but seeing the guns pointed at them with the port-fires lighted, they with vehement expressions of loyalty and much lamentation piled arms, took off their pouches, and moved to the right.

Owing to the mutiny of the 52nd Bengal Infantry it was decided that the town and district of Damoh should be abandoned by the regular troops, and that the Nagpore Moveable Column under Colonel Millar, taking with it the Damoh Treasure, should retire on Jubbulpore, as it was thought that the small force could not hold both districts. Damoh was accordingly handed over to the Panna troops under Kour Shamleju, who entered the place with a considerable force and two guns on the 20th September. The column left Damoh on the 21st September, 1857, and after having been delayed three days in crossing the river at Nohta, reached Singrampur on the evening of the 26th September, where intelligence was received that the mutineers, 500 rank and file, with 1,000 matchlockmen, had taken up a position at Kani on the west of the Hiran river, about 12 miles below Katangi.

Abandonment of Damoh.

At 2 A.M. on the 27th Colonel Millar sent 12 troopers of the 4th Madras Cavalry and a company, 33rd Madras Infantry, under Lieutenant Watson, accompanied by Major Jenkins, A. Q. M. G., to seize the boats on the Hiran at Katangi. The main body marched at 5 A. M., and at the village of Gobra, three miles from Singrampur, which commands the mouth of the pass, the 52nd mutineers † were seen marching along the road in column of sections with colours flying. On being fired at by the guns,

Fight with the 52nd Bengal Infantry.

* The loyalty of these men, many of whom were from Oudh, was suspected, but they remained faithful throughout.

† For an account of the mutiny of the 52nd, given by a sepoy of that regiment captured at Garhakota in February, 1858, see Appendix III.

the rebels left the road and advanced through the jungle on both sides, but were driven back in about half an hour, and were followed up for some miles, a few being killed and some prisoners taken on the hills near Katangi.

Murder of Lieutenant Macgregor.

At the entrance to the town the body of Lieutenant Macgregor of the 52nd was found, with the throat cut, a shot in the chest, and a bayonet wound in the body. The mutineers had made him a prisoner on the occasion of the outbreak, and had killed him at 3 A.M. that day. The whole force behaved well, the Madras troops proving that they had no sympathy with the Bengal mutineers.

During the first advance, Major Jenkins and Lieutenant Watson had fallen into an ambuscade, but had succeeded in cutting their way through, and concealing themselves in the hills until the arrival of the column. Lieutenant Watson was wounded, Farrier G. Cartright, 24th Cavalry, mortally wounded, 2 sepoys wounded, 1 follower killed and 2 wounded. The two disarmed companies of the 52nd came up shortly after the action and were kept in the *serai* about a mile from camp that night, when ten deserted. The remainder were afterwards sent to Saugor.

Return of the Moveable Column to Jubbulpore.

Next day, while the column was crossing the river in boats and rafts, a detachment went out in search of the enemy, but only came on a few stragglers who were cut up or dispersed.

The river was not passed by the whole force and its baggage until September 29th, and on October 1st the Nagpore Moveable Column marched into Jubbulpore. The two companies of the 28th Madras Infantry were sent back to Narsinghpur, the *thana* of Tendukhera in that district having been driven in by rebels. The force at Jubbulpore was joined by the remainder of the 4th Madras Cavalry and two companies, 33rd Madras Infantry, on the 10th October.

Events at Saugor.

On the 17th September the Banpur rebels from Nariaoli, twelve miles west of Saugor, advanced to the Rahatgarh gate of the city and fired a few shots at the sentries, but, finding the guards alert, they retired. Next day Brigadier Sage, commanding at Saugor, sent out a detachment under Colonel Dalzell of the 42nd to attack the rebels, and the Deputy Commissioner also sent 200 Customs *Chaprassis* under their European officers, but they found the place too strong and the attack failed. Colonel Dalzell was killed, and Lieutenant Prior, Executive Engineer, was wounded. The party returned to Saugor on the following day.

About the end of the month the *thanas* of Kundam and Bargi were attacked and driven in; both these places are in the Jubbulpore District, the latter south of the Narbada, and there was much alarm in Seoni, lest the rebellion should spread south. A company of Madras Infantry was sent from Seoni to Dhuma near Bargi.

The rebels in Nimawar, in the Hoshangabad District, were now very numerous under Thakur Daulat Singh* and were too strong for the police, who were obliged to retire to Harda on the 3rd October. They plundered the town of Nimawar, and confined and tortured several of the most respectable inhabitants who refused to rebel, besides committing other excesses.

Hoshangabad District.

On the 8th October Lieutenant Wood, Deputy Commissioner of Hoshangabad, with a small detachment of the 28th Madras Infantry and two guns, under Lieutenant Lemarchand of the Gwalior Contingent, marched twenty-three miles towards Nimawar, and next day moved on twenty-one miles, the journey taking nineteen hours owing to the heavy and bad state of the roads. On arriving at the old city of Hindia on the south bank of the Narbada on the 12th, they found the rebels in great force on the opposite bank. The enemy at once commenced firing from behind walls and temples at the water's edge, but were dispersed by the fire of the guns. Next day Lieutenant Wood crossed over; the police captured one of the leaders, who was hanged.

Action at Hindia.

After the 52nd were beaten off by the Nagpore Moveable Column they, joined by many rebels, marched to Damoh, where they attacked the Panna troops, whom they soon beat. They then went to the jail, which was most gallantly defended by the guard, but the latter falling short of ammunition and food and attacked by the prisoners at the same time, were obliged to give in, and were nearly all murdered. The mutineers and rebels then plundered the town of Damoh, burned the records and public buildings, blew up the *Kutcherry*, and gutted the Deputy Commissioner's house. After staying some days they joined the Shahgarh rebels at Garhakota, plundering the surrounding country, until they were driven out by Sir Hugh Rose when he took that place. They were subsequently almost entirely destroyed at the battle of Kunch. After a few days the Panna troops returned to Damoh, and held it unopposed until February 1858, when the charge of the district was resumed by the British.

Attack on Damoh.

On the 2nd October the Deputy Commissioner of Saugor resolved to send a body of police to secure Rehli, and asked Brigadier Sage to aid him with troops. A hundred sepoys of the 31st Bengal Infantry were sent under Lieutenant Dickens, 31st, and Ensign Grant, 42nd, but before they arrived the fort had been recovered by a gallant inhabitant of the place, Girdhari Naik, who was made *Killadar* until relieved by Lieutenant Dickens. On the 13th Rehli was attacked by the mutineers and rebels from Garhakota, but Lieutenant Dickens replused them with loss, aided by the police under Girdhari Naik. The 52nd sepoys did their utmost to get the 31st to join them, but without success. Lieutenant Dickens held Rehli

Capture of Rehli.

* Daulat Singh and his following were defeated and mostly killed or captured at piplia on the 28th October, by Major Orr with the Hyderabad Contingent Field Force on his way to Malwa.

throughout, and co-operated with Sir Hugh Rose in his advance against Garhakota.

Invasion of rebels from Bhopal.

About the 20th October Nawab Ali Khan of Bhopal invaded the Narsinghpur District north of the Narbada with 150 Pathans from Rahatgarh, accompanied by some 500 local rebels and some Customs *Chaprassis*. They again plundered and burned Tendukhera and Bilkari and moved down to Hirapur on the right bank of the river, some fifteen miles from Narsinghpur. At the same time the rebels of Bargi in Jubbulpore threatened the south-east of Narsinghpur. Captain Ternan, the Deputy Commissioner, and some police, accompanied by two companies of the 28th Madras Infantry and two six-pounders, worked by the sepoys, marched to Sakal, opposite Hirapur, to oppose Mihrban Singh, a noted rebel leader, who occupied a small fort commanding the village. The guns opened fire, and the rebels fled with loss, while those at Tendukhera, evacuated that place.

Sack of Patan.

On the 21st a large body of rebels crossed the Hiran river to attack Patan. The Deputy Collector and Tehsildar and Police went to meet them, but after exchanging a few shots, the Tehsildar and one of the police being wounded, they gave way and fled before superior numbers. The rebels then entered Patan, destroyed the Government buildings, and burned and plundered many houses in the town. A small force was sent out from Jubbulpore, but the insurgents had left and taken refuge in the heavy jungle on the hills. A hundred infantry and a troop of cavalry were left at Patan.

Mandla.

There were many rebels in Mandla, and it was not until the 22nd that the Deputy Commissioner, having collected a few police and ten men of the 52nd Bengal Infantry who had remained loyal, was able to proceed to his district. On reaching Mandla on the 25th October, he sent out a party of police who attacked a small body of rebels at Ramnagar, and killed a few. Other parties went out, but the enemy took the town of Naraingan j on the road from Mandla to Jubbulpore, and thus cut the communications.

Rebels on the Mirzapur road.

On the 25th the *thana* of Bartalla in Jubbulpore was attacked and burned, and the town plundered; and during the next few days other posts were driven in, and the rebels were formidable in the villages near the Mirzapur road, where the Bijeraghugarh Thakur, Surjupersad, murdered the Tehsildar, placed bodies of men on the road, and closed it for some time. On the 30th Captain Woolley's detachment in Narsinghpur crossed the Sunar river, and taking the enemy by surprise, routed them and cut up a great many.

Rout of the Bijeraghugarh rebels.

On the 4th November Major R. S. Sullivan marched from Jubbulpore with a wing of the 4th Cavalry to support the infantry and artillery on the Mirzapur road, which had moved towards Chaka to check the Bijeraghugarh rebels, and on the morning of the 6th was advancing from Ghosalpur towards Kailwana when he was surprised by a heavy fire from two guns, jingals, and matchlocks. As soon as he could get his guns into position he returned the fire, but one of the guns broke down at the second round owing to a damaged axletree. The enemy now attempted to surround the detachment, and Major Sullivan ordered his squadron of cavalry to attack them by a flank movement from his left, the infantry making a similar movement along the road to the right. The 4th Madras Cavalry under Lieutenant Clerk charged and captured one of the enemy's guns, and cut up some 30 of the rebels, Lieutenant Clerk killing three himself. The 33rd sepoys entered the village, bayonetted several of the rebels, and captured the remaining gun.

The enemy, who numbered some 1,500 or 2,000, left 60 dead on the field. On the British side five men were wounded and one killed.

Death of Captain Tottenham.

On the 7th November Captain Tottenham and Lieutenant C. S. Stewart marched from Jubbulpore along the Mirzapur road with a troop of the 4th Madras Cavalry. On arriving at Pownalgarh, they heard that Ghosalpur was being looted by rebels from Nimkhera and galloped on, but found on arrival that the rebels had left. Following them up, they caught sight of about a thousand people running towards the village of Ramkaria, who, owing to bad ground and having some two miles start, reached the village before their arrival. No one was to be seen in the village, but at length a man pointed out the Raja's house as likely to afford concealment. They burst open the door, and searched the house, but could find no one, until Captain Tottenham went up to another door, when four or five shots were fired through the door and from the balcony above, and Captain Tottenham was mortally wounded. The troop of cavalry was then posted to watch the village until sunset, when they were withdrawn. Seven or eight men were killed, and 18 prisoners taken, of whom one died of wounds and the rest were hung.

Fight at Katangi.

At midday on the 14th November, 1857, information was received at Katangi that a party of Bundelas were looting the village of Rakrita about two miles from camp.

Lieutenant R. Oakes.

½ Troop, 4th Madras Cavalry.
33rd Madras Infantry, 50 rank and file.

Major W. P. Jenkins, A. Q. M. G., Nagpore Field Force, had been sent out from Jubbulpore with a detachment, and ordered a party, detailed in the margin, under Lieutenant R. Oakes, 52nd Bengal Infantry, who was commanding the post at Katangi, to march against the insurgents at once. The cavalry proceeded in advance, accompanied by Major Jenkins and Captain Pinkney, and found that the enemy had retreated to Enota, where they were followed and watched by the cavalry. The infantry on arriving skirmished through a jowari field at the back of the village, but the rebels succeeded in escaping through the jungle to a hill in the vicinity. The infantry followed, and Major Jenkins was mortally wounded by a matchlock ball on the top of the hill. Of the rebels 12 were killed and 9 prisoners taken. Lieutenant Oakes burnt the village before returning to Katangi; he shot with his pistol the man who killed Major Jenkins.

Several other skirmishes took place, and in November Captain Ternan with Captain Woolley's detachment of Infantry and two guns was operating north of the Narbada on the Saugor road, in co-operation with a detachment under Captain Roberts of the 31st and Captain Mayne of the 3rd Irregular Cavalry.

Destruction of Dalganjan Singh's band.

The districts north of the Narbada were cleared of rebels. On the 23rd November an encounter took place with Dalganjan Singh, who had about two hundred followers, in which the troops were completely successful. Captain Ternan, who had his horse shot under him, charged at the head of some of the 3rd Irregular Cavalry, who had remained loyal, and the rebels were surrounded and nearly all killed, Dalganjan Singh and his chief men being taken prisoners and hanged.

The Bargi rebels.

Meanwhile the rebels remained in great force on the Deccan or Mirzapur road and completely cut off direct communication between the north-west and Calcutta and Bombay; all who attempted to pass were searched and plundered, some killed, and others mutilated. On the 30th November the rebel leader Debi Singh Guntia burned the *thana* of Shahpura on the road to Narsinghpur, and when pursued by the cavalry, escaped over the Narbada to Bargi. The Bargi rebels now became very bold, and it was necessary to undertake measures for their destruction. A simultaneous advance of detachments was made from several directions, and on the 7th December Captain Woolley forced the passage of the Sunar river which was held by some 1,500 insurgents under Debi Singh Guntia. On the 10th Captain Ternan with a detachment came upon the insurgents, and captured their guns and tent, and four days later Captain Woolley caught and hanged Debi Singh. The Bargi *pargana* was thus completely settled.

The Saugor District.

On the 15th December Brigadier Sage sent a party to attack the rebels at Bhaplye, but failed, and lost seven men killed and four wounded. On the 26th Rehli was again attacked by the mutineers and rebels from Garhakota, but Lieutenant Dickens drove them off.

Reinforcements.

On the 20th December two companies, 28th Madras Infantry, and two guns under Lieutenant Standon arrived at Jubbulpore, and next day a troop of the 2nd Cavalry, Hyderabad Contingent, came in.

Expedition in the Katangi Hills.

The rebels in the hills near Katangi in Jubbulpore were still causing great trouble, and were plundering the villages near Koni on the right bank of the Hiran river. On the 24th two detachments were sent out from Jubbulpore under Colonel Millar, one direct to Patan to attack the front of the enemy's position, the other to ascend the pass at Katangi.

At 6 A.M. on the 26th December Colonel Millar marched from Patan with the detachment detailed in the margin to attack the rebels reported to be on the Koni Pass. There appeared to be about a thousand rebels on the brow and sides of the hill, with an advanced piquet about a third of the way up the ascent, where they had made a stone breastwork, behind which was a small gun.

Fight at Koni Pass.

Headquarters and one troop, 2nd Cavalry, Hyderabad Contingent.

Two guns, D. Company, Madras Artillery.

Headquarters and 300 rank and file, 33rd Native Infantry.

After crossing the river, Colonel Millar extended the Grenadiers and Light Companies of the 33rd, which covered the advance of the guns. The fire of the artillery soon cleared the way for the skirmishers, who advanced up the hill without a check, followed by the cavalry under Captain Macintire,* who pursued the enemy over rough ground and cut down and captured some of them. There were no casualties.

This expedition had an excellent effect and the rebels gave no further trouble in this part of the country. In January, 1858, the Rahatgarh and Bhopal rebels invaded the Narsinghpur district, 4,000 strong, and attacked and burned Tendukhera. Captain Ternan with two companies, 28th Madras Infantry, two guns, two troops, 2nd Cavalry, Hyderabad Contingent, and some mounted and foot police, marched against the rebels, who fled up the Ghauts towards Rahatgarh. The cavalry under Captain Macintire and Lieutenant Ryall, with Dr. Bradley and Captain Ternan, made a long march, and dashing into the rebel village of Mandanpur, surprised the place, captured some insurgents, among them a son and grandson of Dilan Singh, the rebel leader of 1842, and killed others. Captain Ternan shot three, and Dr. Bradley dragged two armed men from under an earthen jar.

Defeat of the Bhopal invaders.

Troops were now coming up from various directions. Sir Hugh Rose was advancing from Sehore to begin his famous campaign in Central India by the capture of Rahatgarh, while General Whitlock, with a Madras Column, was marching from Nagpore, to undertake operations in the Saugor and Narbada Territories.

Advance of British columns.

* Afterwards General Macintire, C.B.

CHAPTER IV.

THE MUTINIES IN RAJPUTANA.

Rajputana.

Rajputana includes some twenty Native States,* as well as the British District of Ajmer-Merwara. It is of irregular shape, touching on Sind and the Punjab and a number of the States of Central India, the British District of Ajmer being in the centre. The Aravalli Mountains intersect the country from north-east to south-west, the heights of Mount Abu lying at the south-western extremity of the range. The tract which stretches from Sind on the west to the Punjab near Delhi on the north-east is mainly a sandy desert, comparatively fertile, however, towards its eastern extremity, and characterised by sandhills of varying height and length, sparsely clothed with vegetation. But the south and south-eastern division of Rajputana is more fertile, being well watered by the drainage of the Vindhya mountains, the Chambal, the Banas, and the Parbati rivers. This region is characterised by wooded hills and valleys, fertile plains, and rich cities.

The people are mainly Hindu, but there is also a large Muhammadan population. The Rajputs are the ruling race, but there are numbers of Brahmans, Jats, and others, as well as such aboriginal races as Bhils, Minas, and Mers.

Previous history.

On the decline of the Mughal Empire and the rise of the Mahrattas, the States of Rajputana came under the domination of that enterprising people, and were long subject to extortion and desolation. The Mahratta power was severely shaken by the campaigns of Wellesley and Lake in 1803, and Sindhia and Holkar then loosened their hold on some of the Rajput States. But the fatuous policy which followed the departure of Lord Wellesley, Governor-General during a period of warlike and political activity, was sufficient to eliminate a great part of the results which had been obtained by that illustrious statesman at the cost of so much bloodshed. A policy of non-interference and unmasterly inactivity soon reduced the British from the position of dominant power in India, a condition so necessary to the security of peace, to that of the co-equal of the neighbouring States, a situation resulting in many years of anarchy and intrigue which terminated only with the final destruction of the Mahratta Confederacy.

* Alwar, Banswara, Bharatpur, Bikanir, Bundi, Dholpur, Dungarpur, Jaipur, Jaisalmir, Jhalawar, Jodhpur, Karauli, Kishengarh, Kotah, Lawa, Mewar or Udaipur, Partabgarh, Shahpura, Sirohi, Tonk. The British Government was represented by an Agent to the Governor-General, with head-quarters at Mount Abu, while there was a Political Officer at each of the courts of Jaipur, Jodhpur, Bharatpur, Kotah, and Udaipur.

The country was overrun by the Pindari freebooters, encouraged and protected by the Mahratta States, and in 1814 the Pindari Amir Khan had established himself in the heart of Rajputana with an army of some 30,000 horse and foot and a strong artillery. This state of anarchy was put an end to in 1817, when the Marquis of Hastings assembled two great armies, one at either extremity of Central India, and crushed the Pindaris out of existence after turning them out of their fastnesses on the banks of the Chambal and the Narbada. Amir Khan was confined to the State of Tonk, of which he was the first ruler; plundered territories were restored to their Rajput owners; Ajmer was ceded to the British; and Mahratta pressure on Rajputana was terminated.

The Governor-General was able to write on the conclusion of the war—"The Rajput States have been delivered from an oppression more systematic, more unremitting, more brutal, than perhaps before trampled on humanity. Security and comfort established where nothing but terror and misery before existed; nor is it within a narrow sphere. It is a proud phrase to use, but it is a true one that we have bestowed blessings upon millions."

In 1857 the rulers and the people of the Rajput States remembered the deliverance of forty years before. Those millions on whom the British conferred blessings in freeing them from Mahratta domination and Pindari cruelty had not forgotten their benefactors and were mainly loyal to the Government in the day of trouble. But, bordering closely on the disturbed regions of Central India it was not to be supposed that the Rajput States would be entirely untainted by the spread of rebellion.

Garrisons in Rajputana.

Moreover the regular troops quartered in Rajputana belonged principally to the Bengal Army. And there was not a European soldier in the country.

When the mutiny broke out, the garrisons in Rajputana were as follows

Nasirabad.—No. 6 Native Field Battery*; 15th† and 30th Bengal Native Infantry; 1st Bombay Cavalry (Lancers).‡

Neemuch.—4th Troop, 1st Brigade, Bengal Native Horse Artillery; a wing, 1st Bengal Cavalry; 72nd Bengal Native Infantry; 7th Infantry, Gwalior Contingent.

Deoli.—The Kotah Contingent.

Beawar.—The Mhairwarra Battalion.§

Erinpura.—The Jodhpur Legion.

Kherwara.—The Meywar Bhil Corps and a Troop, 1st Bengal Cavalry.

* This battery fought well with Sale at the siege of Jalalabad in the First Afghan War.

† The 15th Bengal Infantry had come from Meerut in March, 1857.

‡ Now the 31st Duke of Connaught's Own Lancers.

§ Now the 44th Merwara Infantry. The Mers are a tribe of low caste people of local habitation.

Ajmer magazine* was garrisoned by a Company of the 15th Bengal Native Infantry, and a company of the Mhairwarra Battalion was posted in the city for duty at the gates. The Jaipur Political Agent had an escort of a company of the 30th Bengal Infantry; the Political Agent of Haraoti—a detachment of the Jodhpur Legion; the Political Agent of Meywar, when absent from Neemuch, took as escort a detachment of the Meywar Bhil Corps.

It was not usual to garrison Rajputana with Bengal troops; but the Bombay regiments had been withdrawn for service in the Persian War, and had been replaced from the Northern Presidency; and at Naśirabad the European troop of Artillery had been relieved by a Bengal battery. The nearest European troops were at Deesa, a hundred and thirty miles from Nasirabad.

Reinforcements from Deesa.

The first intelligence of the outbreak at Meerut and Delhi reached Colonel G. St. P. Lawrence, the Agent to the Governor-General in Rajputana, at Mount Abu† on the 19th May, and a requisition was at once made on the Brigade at Deesa for a Light Field Force, strength as noted in the margin, to proceed with all expedition to Nasirabad. This force marched on the 23rd of May, and reached Nasirabad on the 12th June. On the 23rd May a proclamation was issued to the Chiefs of Rajputana, calling on them to preserve peace within their borders, to intercept rebel fugitives, and to collect their followers on their frontiers. This was promptly replied to, and anticipated by Jodhpur with the most friendly assurances and offers of aid.

3 Horse Artillery guns (European).
1 Squadron, Native Cavalry.
250 European Infantry.
200 Native Infantry.

The Jaipur troops.

On the requisition of the Lieutenant-Governor of the North-Western Provinces, and with the consent of the Maharaja of Jaipur, Captain W. Eden, the Political Agent, marched with 5,000 troops of that State towards the Muttra and Gurgaon districts to maintain order and aid in the re-establishment of the civil government. These duties were not fully discharged, but considering the number of Hindustanis in the force, it is surprising that it ever returned unbroken to Jaipur. It was tampered with in June, when it fell in with Rawal Shiu Singh,‡ the *ex*-Minister of Jaipur, and his escort returning from a pilgrimage to Delhi, but the efforts of the latter to induce their comrades to mutiny were unavailing, and the precautions taken by the loyal Sirdars, and the fearless bearing of the Political Agent, prevented their

* "The careless habits we had got into in this country were never better exemplified than they were in this case. Here was a fort, the walls of which were so old and rotten that it was generally believed a gun being fired from any one of the bastions would have brought them down, close to the large and thickly populated city of Ajmer, and commanded by the heights outside the town, containing an arsenal large enough to supply the troops in the whole of Rajputana, capable of furnishing a siege train of great strength, guns, ammunition, besides an immense quantity of treasure, for the protection of which nothing more than a company of sepoys was allowed." *The Mutinies in Rajputana*, by I. T. Pritchard.

† Brother of Sir John (afterwards Lord) Lawrence, and Sir Henry Lawrence.

‡ This man on his return to the capital did his best to subvert the young Maharaja, who, however, with the advice of such good counsellors, as his Private Secretary Pandit Shiu Din, Nawab Faiz Muhammad Khan, and others, remained loyal throughout, preserved his army from mutiny, and maintained peace in his State.

carrying out their design of murdering that officer. Captain Eden rescued several Europeans in the Gurgaon district, and employed his force in punishing the Mewatis. On the 20th July he returned to Jaipur; a disaffected spirit prevailed among the men; some had deserted, and they were suffering from cholera and the inclemency of the weather.*

The Kotah Contingent.

The Kotah Contingent marched from Deoli for Agra on the 19th May under Captain Dennys, and did good service in the Muttra district until the 14th July, when it mutinied at Agra.

Bharatpur, Alwar, and Jodhpur.

The Bharatpur troops also took the field under Captain Nixon; Alwar sent a force of about 2,500 men to co-operate with Captain Nixon; while 2,000 horse and foot with six guns were despatched from Jodhpur to Beawar and Ajmer.

Relief of Ajmer.

On the first signs of trouble the grenadier company of the 15th Bengal Infantry was sent to act as a check on the light company at Ajmer, as it was supposed to be less tainted. The light company at first refused to admit them, alleging that they were not trustworthy; but their objections were overruled, and for a few days both companies garrisoned the fort. The Commissioner, Colonel Dixon,† however, to prevent the arsenal from falling into the hands of disaffected Bengal sepoys, ordered in another hundred Mers from Beawar to take the place of the 15th at Ajmer. This operation was carried out by Lieutenant Carnell; by a forced march of thirty-seven miles from Beawar he relieved the Bengal sepoys before they could communicate with their comrades at Nasirabad, which was sixteen miles distant.

Nasirabad.

Soon after receipt of the news of the Meerut outbreak, some precautions were taken to prevent the occurrence of a similar catastrophe at Nasirabad. A cavalry piquet under a European Officer was sent to the artillery lines every night to look after the guns, and an artillery officer slept every night at the quarter-guard; the cantonment roads were patrolled by cavalry, and a troop ready accoutred was kept in the cavalry lines. These precautions may have prevented an outbreak at night; but they were relaxed by day.

On the 28th May, 1857, the ordinary duties were gone through in the morning, but after noon it was reported that the sepoys were returning from the bazaar in an excited, state saying that bone-dust had been mixed with the flour for the purpose

* In reply to Captain Eden's report that he had been obliged to return to Jaipur with his force, the Lieutenant-Governor of the North-West Provinces, who had been invested with the supreme authority in Rajputana, wrote—"I greatly regret of course your being unable to retain your position between Muttra and Pulwul. The existence of a force there acting in co-operation with us was always valuable, and you did excellent service in keeping up frequent communication with the Delhi Camp. If you could have kept near the high road, and returned again, it would have been preferable, but you could not foretell the movements of the Neemuch mutineers; and I think that, under all the circumstances, you have done wisely in acquiescing in the strong desire for a return to Jaipur."

† This action of Colonel Dixon, who died at Beawar on the 25th June, saved Ajmer, and secured Rajputana.

of destroying their caste. This was reported to the Brigade-Major, who said it was no use going to Brigadier Macan, who was in command, as he was unwell, and he would see him next day. In the afternoon about four o'clock the report of a cannon was heard, and it was found that the guns had been seized by some sepoys of the 15th, who were joined by the 30th Bengal Infantry. The 1st Bombay Cavalry then assembled in rear of the artillery lines, which were on the left of the cantonment, the cavalry lines being on the right, and those of the two infantry regiments in the centre.

Mutiny at Nasirabad.

The cavalry were ordered to charge by squadrons. They charged, but as soon as they got within a few yards of the guns, the men went threes about, the officers going on.* Major Spottiswoode fell mortally wounded; Cornet Newbury was cut to pieces among the guns; and Captain Hardy and Lieutenant Lock were badly wounded.

The Europeans then assembled in rear of the cavalry lines, where the Lancers were drawn up but would not act. Some of them, † fired at by the mutineers, escaped with difficulty.

That night the Europeans fled to Beawar, thirty-seven miles distant, the party including a number of ladies and children, and a few sepoys who had remained faithful, as well as the 1st Bombay Lancers. On the road Colonel Penny, commanding that regiment, fell dead from excitement and exhaustion. The party reached Beawar next morning Captain Fenwick of the 30th remained in the quarter-guard of his regiment until 8 P.M., when the sepoys made him go. It is noticeable that the 30th offered no violence to their officers, but only told them to go. A party of this regiment, about 120 strong, under a native officer, left the rebels and followed the Europeans to Beawar, but about half the number deserted before the return to Nasirabad, which took place a few days later.

Flight of the Europeans.

After destroying the cantonments, the mutineers next day took the road to Delhi. They were pursued by a thousand of the Jodhpur troops under British officers, but these would not attack them and the mutineers passed unmolested through the country.

March of the mutineers.

On the 1st June Colonel Lawrence received intelligence of the mutiny at Nasirabad and at once left for Beawar, where he received a letter from the Lieutenant-Governor appointing him Brigadier-General in command of the forces in Rajputana, an appointment he held until relieved by Major-General Roberts in March, 1858

Movements of Colonel Lawrence.

* It was afterwards said that there was an understanding between the mutineers and the Cavalry: that the latter agreed to refuse to act provided their families remained unmolested. The 1st Bombay Cavalry afterwards performed good service, notably at the battle of Kotah-ki-Serai and capture of Gwalior in June, 1858.

† Among these was Lieutenant Thackwell, afterwards murdered in the streets of Lucknow, who was in charge of the guard over the magazine. The guard fired at but missed him. He then rode to the parade ground where a hundred muskets were levelled at him, and he was fired at by each company in succession, but escaped to the cavalry parade. The Adjutant of the 15th had his horse shot under him, but it carried him out of danger before falling dead. It was said that he was afterwards refused compensation for the loss of his charger by the Military Auditor-General on the ground that the regiment having mutinied, he had no longer occasion to keep a charger, and therefore it was not necessary to replace it.

About a hundred and fifty miles south of Nasirabad is Neemuch, a cantonment built on an elevated ridge, and having a fortified square which had been constructed as a place of refuge, and was used as a magazine. Here the mutinous spirit first showed itself on the 28th May, when, on a rumour that the bazaar was being plundered, the 72nd Bengal Infantry and the 7th Gwalior Contingent rushed to their arms, but were pacified by their officers. On the night of the 3rd June, at about 9 P.M., four or five troopers of the 1st Bengal Cavalry galloped down the front of the 72nd, calling out—"Get ready," "Get ready." The men rushed to the bells of arms demanding their weapons for self-defence, and were allowed to take them. At about 11 o'clock two signal guns were fired by the artillery, and all the troops rose, the cavalry galloping with torches in the direction of the jail, and the officers' houses were soon fired. The officers of the 72nd assembled in the quarter-guard, and the artillery brought a gun to bear on it. But their own men protected them, and at about 1 A.M. they left for Jawad, and reached Dekan, twenty-five miles distant, next night, where they found Major Burton, Political Agent of Kotah, with a force of native levies.*

Mutiny at Neemuch.

For some time previous to the outbreak, Captain Macdonald, commanding the 7th Gwalior Contingent, remained in the fortified square with the right wing of his regiment, for the purpose of observing the behaviour of the men, and watching over the treasure entrusted to the corps.

The 7th Gwalior Contingent.

On the night of the 3rd June he had about two hundred men accoutred, with their muskets loaded, upon the walls, and intended to pass the night himself on one of the bastions, so as to be on the spot in case of need. A little before midnight some of the men awoke him, and told him that two signal guns had been fired by the artillery. Being ready dressed, he was instantly on the walls. Everything seemed perfectly quiet, but the tranquillity was only temporary, for a few minutes afterwards he plainly saw that attempts were being made to set fire to the officers' houses in Cantonments; this was quickly effected, those bungalows being the first to burst out into flames at which night guards were posted.

The gate of the fort was that night in charge of a company under Subadar Hari Singh, described as being by no means a leading character in the corps,† and on this occasion he kept constantly at Captain Macdonald's side, apparently exerting himself to carry out that officer's orders. When there was no longer any room for doubt that the expected crisis had arrived, Captain Macdonald

* A troop of the 1st Bengal Cavalry under two native officers, on detachment duty at Kherwara, remained at that station throughout the mutiny, the native officers being loyal, although disaffection appeared among the men. The remainder of the regiment mutinied at Mhow on the 1st July.

† In this connection Mr. Pritchard remarks that it is curious how often leading parts were taken in the several regiments by men of whose character their European officers had had no idea; and relates how a subadar of his own regiment, the last man he would have expected to take the leading part in anything, attained the rank of Brigadier-General among the mutineers at Delhi, and frequently had four or five corps of all arms under his command.

ordered a messenger to be sent to his second-in-command, Lieutenant Rose,* who was in the lines with the left wing of the regiment, directing him to bring his men down to the fortified square. He heard the order repeated by Subadar Hari Singh from the gate, but nevertheless it struck him while standing on the wall that no messenger left the fort. Lieutenant Rose subsequently informed him that he received no message.

It had previously been arranged that, in the event of any crisis, Lieutenant Rose was to parade the left wing and join Captain Macdonald; while getting the men under arms he was deliberately fired at by a sepoy, without effect.

Captain Macdonald now heard Lieutenant Rose calling to him that the men would not come with him; but the wing marched into the fort on the orders of their Commandant. Being under the impression that the gate would be first attacked, Captain Macdonald directed Ensign Davenport to join the party at the gate; at the same time another strong party on the walls was told off to support the defence of the gate, if needed. On visiting all the posts Captain Macdonald was met everywhere by assurances of loyalty, the only doubt expressed of their making an effectual defence being in the event of guns being brought to bear on the place. The colours of the regiment were unfurled and placed on the bastion, and the men called on to protect them from dishonour. Nothing was left undone that could add to the security of the place, or induce the men to act properly.

At half past two, men were observed leaving the walls in small parties and in silence, and half an hour later a more combined movement was made, and Lieutenant Gordon and Ensign Davenport informed the Commandant that the gate had been thrown open by the Subadar's orders and that they had been forced to quit the post at the point of the bayonet. Captain Macdonald hastened to the gate, which was wide open; for a short time he succeeded in keeping the men in, and then they went out in a body. The officers followed, and, on coming up to the regiment, seized the colours, and endeavoured to recall the men to duty and rally them round the colours; at that moment two guns were fired by the artillery and the cavalry was heard advancing. The men would listen to no orders. Nothing could be done. The officers left the station accompanied by four men; two left them few miles out, and the remaining two accompanied them thirty-six miles, and then returned to rejoin their comrades. Immediately on rejoining they were seized, accused of having aided the escape of the European officers, and cruelly put to death. A Jemadar took possession of Captain Macdonald's property, donned his epaulettes, mounted his charger, and rode off with the mutineers. Within eleven hours of the mutiny the whole force left the station, carrying away all they could and destroying the remainder, and burning down the whole cantonment with the exception of a few houses. Two

Retreat of the officers.

March of the Neemuch Brigade.

* Lieutenant Rose, 25th Bombay Infantry, distinguished himself in many actions during the campaign in Central India in 1858, and was killed in capturing the Fort of Gwalior with a handful of men of his Corps.

months' pay was first issued all round on the regimental parade ground. A Subadar of the 1st Cavalry was appointed Brigadier. They made their first march of sixteen miles to Nimbahera, where they were entertained by the native authorities of the town, and continued their march next morning after shooting some troopers and sepoys who had rejoined the column after seeing their officers to a place of safety.

Meanwhile the fugitive Europeans fled to Daru and thence to Sadri, in the direction of Udaipur. All reached Daru in safety, with the exception of the wife and children of Sergeant Supple of the Artillery, who were brutally murdered in their quarters.

Re-occupation of the Cantonment.

Next day, hearing that the station was evacuated, Captain Lloyd, Superintendent, with his assistant Lieutenant Ritchie, and Lieutenant Stapleton, 1st Cavalry, accompanied by 17 Sadri troopers, returned to Neemuch, and re-occupied the ruined Cantonment.

Kotah.
500 infantry.
200 cavalry.
2 guns.
Bundi.
100 troopers.
5 camel swivel guns.
Jhalawar.
125 infantry.
75 troopers.
10 camel swivel guns.

On the 7th Major Burton, Political Agent of Kotah, reached Dekan with the force detailed in the margin, and next evening he marched into Neemuch, leaving a hundred Kotah Infantry and ten troopers at Jawad. This force remained in garrison at Neemuch until relieved by British troops on the 18th July, when the Irregular troops returned to their respective capitals. The returned fugitives occupied the fortified square which was placed in a state of defence, and where guns were mounted.

Pursuit of the mutineers.

Meywar.
50 cavalry.
500 infantry.
2 guns.
6 camel swivel guns.
Partabgarh.
25 cavalry.
80 infantry.

Captain Showers, Political Agent in Meywar, who was at Udaipur when the mutiny broke out, pursued the mutineers with the Meywar troops noted in the margin as far as Jehazpur, but without success.

Mutiny of the Malwa Cavalry.

On the 9th June the cavalry of the Malwa Contingent, which had been sent from Mehidpur to the assistance of the Neemuch party by Colonel Durand, mutinied fourteen miles from Neemuch, after murdering their officers, Captain Brodie and Lieutenant Hunt, whose mangled bodies were found on the road, and interred by the native civil authorities. The men then returned to Mehidpur, marching eighty miles in two days, and attempted to seduce the artillery and infantry of the Contingent, but without success. They then left, and joined the Neemuch brigade somewhere beyond Deoli.

Movements of the Neemuch mutineers.

Meanwhile the Neemuch mutineers marched in the direction of Nasirabad, but did not attack that station, where the British detachment from Deesa arrived on the 12th June. They carried on their movements with the greatest precision, making a point of gaining accurate intelligence by means of scouts mounted on swift camels, who scoured the country and accompanied the brigade at some distance on each flank. Their camp regulations were conducted in the most approved style, and they made a point of halting on Sundays. On their way to Agra they sacked Deoli, burning the cantonment, and taking with them the 24-pounder time gun, and some of the guard of the Kotah Contingent.* The Kotah Contingent had gone to Agra, and the ladies and children left in the station had fortunately fled to Ajmer the day before the mutineers arrived.

Sack of Deoli.

Reaching Agra on the 5th July, they were met by a force under Brigadier Polwhele, which they drove back with loss after a severe action. They then marched by way of Muttra to Delhi, and formed part of the force defeated by Nicholson at Najafgarh. On the fall of Delhi the remnant of the Neemuch mutineers joined Khan Bahadur Khan in Rohilkhand.

Arrival at Agra.

On the 1st July Captain Forbes was sent to Deoli to restore confidence and to raise a corps of 800 Minas† to supply the place of the Kotah Contingent. This corps was afterwards commanded by Captain Macdonald, late 7th Gwalior Contingent, and took part in the campaign against the Kotah rebels.

Enlistment of Minas.

In June Lieutenant Mildmay proceeded to lead the Bikaner troops, which were co-operating with General Van Cortlandt's Punjab Levies in the revolted districts of Sirsa, Hissar, and Hansi. Lieutenant Mildmay found the Maharaja, with a zeal rare in a native prince, at his frontier fortress of Bhadra, commanding his own troops. From there Lieutenant Mildmay joined General Van Cortlandt with a reinforcement of 800 Bikaner Horse.‡

The Bikaner Raja.

On the 12th June the first detachment of the troops which had been called for from Deesa arrived at Nasirabad, consisting of the force detailed in the margin. A hundred of the 83rd were sent to Ajmer, which was as important to Rajputana as Delhi was to India, being a holy spot for both Hindus and Musalmans, and only six miles from the sacred city and tank of Pohkar. The city and arsenal were commanded by Taragarh Hill, on the summit of which was a Muhammadan shrine and a

Arrival of European troops at Nasirabad.

Her Majesty's 83rd Foot 400,
Troop, European Horse Artillery.
2nd Bombay Cavalry.
12th Bombay Infantry.

Events at Ajmere.

* Subadar Raghubar Singh, who commanded the guard, concealed the wives and children of the absent sergeants in the neighbouring village of Jehazpur, where they remained until the arrival of Captain Showers with the Meywar troops. The Subadar and 60 out of his 120 men, although forced to accompany the rebels, made their escape a few days afterwards and returned to Deoli.

† The Minas are a predatory tribe, numbering some 500,000. They are most expert thieves, and at one time their depredations extended as far south as Hyderabad. The corps is now the 42nd Deoli Regiment.

‡ Lieutenant Mildmay kept the field with the Bikaner Auxiliaries in the Punjab until October, when he was invalided. He was with them on the 19th August when they repulsed an attack by 3,000 mutinous sepoys and rebellious villagers. Like the troops of Meywar and Marwar, it was found that these levies would not act on the offensive.

fort. The chief priests offered their services for the defence of this post, a duty which they performed regularly until all danger was past.

From June 1857, to January 1858, Brigadier-General Lawrence resided alternately between Ajmer, Beawar, and Nasirabad, carrying on his civil duties uninterruptedly and having a guard of a native officer's party of the faithful Merwara Battalion.

On the 9th August there was an outbreak in the Ajmer jail, when about fifty prisoners escaped after cutting down the policeman on duty at the gate and overpowering the guard. Brigadier-General Lawrence started in pursuit accompanied by some of the leading Muhammadans of the city, and met the civil mounted police on their way back, who had killed and wounded about fifteen and captured twenty-five.

Second outbreak at Nasirabad.

On the 10th August a commotion was caused at Nasirabad by a trooper galloping down the front of the lines occupied by the 1st Bombay Cavalry, calling to the men to rise. The men for the most part, however, remained quietly in their lines. He then rode down to the wing of the 12th Bombay Infantry,* and did the same there. The men passively sympathised with him, did not seize him, and refused to give him up or to proceed to the rendezvous at the guns. Brigadier Macan was by this time on the parade, the guns were called out, and the fanatic fired at the Brigadier. He was shot by an artillery officer, and afterwards died in hospital. The men of the 12th were disarmed, and on the 25th five of the ringleaders were hanged; twenty-five of the disarmed men deserted, and all the Hindustanis were discharged. The regiment afterwards performed good service in the field, taking part in the battle of Kotah-ki-Sarai and the capture of Gwalior.

And at Neemuch.

At Neemuch, on the 12th August, Colonel Jackson, 2nd Bombay Cavalry,† commanding the station, called out the Europeans,‡ having received what he considered reliable information of an intended mutiny of the native troops. Some of the ringleaders were seized and some escaped; the affair was mismanaged, and one of the soldiers of the 83rd was shot by accident, while Lieutenant Blair of the Cavalry was wounded in the melée.

Mount Abu.

Mount Abu, the hill-station of Rajputana (3,930 feet) lies at the south-western extremity of the Aravalli Hills, some forty miles north-east of Deesa and 50 south of Erinpura. It is a sacred place of the Hindus, and particularly of the Jains who have there one of the finest temples in India. It was in August 1857 garrisoned by some sixty men of the Jodhpur Legion. There were also about thirty-five sick and convalescent soldiers of the 83rd, some civil officers, and the families of officers serving in the plains. Four men and a corporal of the 83rd were posted at the school. The remainder were in the barracks.

* Now the 112th Infantry.

† Now the 32nd Lancers.

‡ 100 of the 83rd Foot, 1 squadron, 2nd Bombay Cavalry, 200 of the 12th Bombay Infantry, and two guns from the Ajmer Arsenal had been sent to Neemuch from Nasirabad on the 10th July and arrived there on the 18th; relieving the Kotah and Jhalawar troops.

The Jodhpur Legion was a force of the three arms under Captain Hall, with headquarters at Erinpura. The cavalry consisted of 3 troops, and was noted for the excellence of the horses and equipment. There were two 9-pr. guns drawn by camels. The infantry had 8 companies of Oudh sepoys and three companies of Bhils.* The Legion belonged to the same class of troops as the Gwalior and Kotah Contingents, and other similar forces in Central India. These corps were maintained by the rulers of Native States under the terms of treaties with the British Government,† were officered by three or four British officers, and equipped and drilled according to the English system. They were generally recruited from the same sources as the Bengal Army.

The Jodhpur Legion.

On the 19th August a company of the Jodhpur Legion reached Anadra, two miles from the foot of the mountain pass leading up to Abu. A troop of cavalry of the Legion had arrived a few days before, and was distributed in small parties to protect the road from Deesa to Abu.

On the afternoon of the 20th August, Captain Hall, Commandant of the Jodhpur Legion, was at Anadra giving orders for the distribution of the detachments The party had marched in heavy rain from Erinpura, but the men were in good spirits, and there was no sign of mutiny. After completing all arrangements, Captain Hall returned towards Abu, meeting on the way a havildar from the Abu Guard, named Gozan Singh, who said he was going to see his comrades. It was afterwards discovered that he had been deputed to arrange the attack for the following morning.

The morning of the 21st August was thick and hazy. Under cover of a dense fog the detachment left at Anadra by Captain Hall the morning before crept up the hill. It was almost as dark as night, so they were able to approach the barracks, unperceived by the sentry. Creeping up to the barracks, the mutineers poured in a heavy fire through the windows, which was replied to by the soldiers as soon as they could

Attack on Mount Abu.

* A predatory and nomadic race of aborigines, inhabiting the hilly tracts of Rajputana. They had no sympathy with the Hindustanis.

† Of the corps thus maintained, the Hyderabad Contingent alone remained faithful.

It is interesting to note that the Home Government of India wrote on the 3rd April, 1814, with regard to such corps :—

"We are led to apprehend more danger from the extension of the European system of military discipline amongst the troops of the Native Powers than we can expect to derive from their services. To the superiority of European discipline is to be attributed the establishment of the British Empire in India; and in proportion as that discipline is extended among the natives not in our service, we must consider the power we have acquired exposed to hazard.

The various contingencies which occur in the conduct of the affairs of so large an Empire as we possess in India have at all times made it advisable to avail ourselves of the assistance of native troops not actually in our service, and to place them, upon such occasions, under the command of officers belonging to the Company's Army.

But we look upon the adoption of such temporary expedients in a very different light from the establishment of a system formed for the express purpose of introducing European tactics, in all their regulations and details, into the armies of any of the native governments. . . . . . . The possible consequences of its establishment we deem of a magnitude sufficient to deter us from authorising its further encouragement; particularly with reference to the Artillery—an arm which it ought to be our policy not to extend the knowledge of it to the natives."

get their arms. One of the attacking party fell, and the rest ran away. Their bullets had gone high and done no damage.

While the main body of the Legion were attacking the barracks a party under a subadar marched through the mist to Captain Hall's house, extended in line in front of it, and by word of command fired a volley through the windows and doors. Here also the shots struck high, and as the mutineers did not surround the house, Captain Hall and his family escaped from the rear into the school. The party of the 83rd turned out and loaded as soon as they became aware of Captain Hall's position; they had not heard the firing or alarm at the barracks, which were at a distance, but some men from the barracks soon arrived and gave an account of what had occurred there.

The only casualty among the Europeans was Mr. A. Lawrence* of the Civil Service, who, hearing the firing, ran towards Captain Hall's house, and was fired at and severely wounded in the thigh. Captain Hall and Dr. Young took five men and went in the direction of the sepoys' lines, and after some firing drove the mutineers down the hill. Owing to the small number of men present, pursuit was inadvisable, and the British residents were assembled at the school, which was soon put in a state of defence.

Erinpura.

The headquarters of the Jodhpur Legion were at Erinpura. The lines occupied by the eight companies of Hindustani sepoys faced south, with the main guard, flanked by the bells of arms, in front of the centre. The bazaar was to the right and a little to the front of the lines; to the left were two small houses occupied by the quarter-master-sergeant and the gun-sergeant; to the left of these the magazine and two 9-pounder guns, and beyond them the Sergeant-Major's house. In front of and at right angles to this row of buildings were the cavalry, and to the front of them the Bhil lines. The hospital was behind the Sergeant-Major's house; and to the rear of the whole space of ground thus occupied were the officers' houses, with the rear-guard behind them, and in rear of the whole a dry water-course, intersected by the road to Pali, running due north.

The only European inhabitants were Lieutenant Conolly, Adjutant of the Legion, and the sergeants and their families. As the mutineers descended the hill they gave out that they had massacred all the Europeans in Abu. They did not reach Erinpura until the 23rd August, but the fame of their exploit preceded them, or the intention of carrying it out was previously known to the garrison.

Mutiny of the Legion.

Lieutenant Conolly was informed of the supposed massacre by one of his men who had received a letter from one of the Mount Abu party. As soon as it was daylight next morning he rode towards the parade ground, and found the troops in disorder; the gunners were running to their guns, and shouted to him to keep off; he then rode towards the Bhil lines, and saw the cavalry galloping about in a disorderly manner as he passed their lines. He found the Bhils ready and orderly, but powerless to

* Son of Brigadier-General G. St. P. Lawrence.

act against the cavalry, infantry, and guns arrayed against them. He ordered them to remain where they were, and galloped off to reason with the infantry, but they were mad with excitement and would listen to nothing. With the Wordie-Major and a few troopers of the cavalry, he rode towards the guns, but the gunners shouted to him to keep off, wheeled the guns round, pointing the muzzles at him, and held the port fires ready. He halted, turned his horse's head, and again rode towards the guns, taking them in flank. Several mutinous troopers then galloped down in front of the guns pointing their carbines at Conolly, and telling him to go back or they would fire ; some sepoys also levelled their muskets at him. The sepoys had now begun plundering the houses, and Conolly rode to the cavalry lines with the small party who remained faithful, and sent for the sergeants and their families.

Abbas Ali and Lieutenant Conolly.

Two Risaldars, Abbas Ali and Abdul Ali, came forward and laid their turbans at the feet of the mutineers, and declared that their lives should be sacrified before the Europeans should be harmed, and some of their comrades followed suit. Although these men, some forty-five in number, would not allow Conolly to leave them, they swore to save his life or die in his defence. They offered to let him ride off and save his life, but he would not leave the sergeants and their families. The troopers offered to take the children, but said it would be impossible to save the parents. At length the artillery brought their guns down upon the cavalry lines, and threatened to open fire on the little party* and their defenders if all the horses in the lines were not brought out and picketed by the guns. This was done. At night the captives were confined in a small tent on the parade ground.

In the morning the Abu and Anadra mutineers marched in under Subadar Mihrwan Singh, were received with a salute, and told the story of their exploits. They completed the plunder of the station, and demanded the surrender of the captives, but Abbas Ali and his men refused to give them up.

Next morning all except Conolly were allowed to go, and Mihrwan Singh, who had now the rank of General, ordered a march. Conolly, mounted on his horse, was carefully guarded on the march.

After several narrow escapes from the mutinous sepoys, during which he was protected by the troopers, he was allowed to ride off, accompanied by three sowars, and returned to Erinpura. These were Nasiruddin, Elahi Bakhsh, and Momin Khan, who had stood by him throughout. Abbas Ali, on the advice of Captain Conolly, afterwards communicated with Captain Monck Mason, Commissioner of Ajmer, and offered to desert with a large party of his own men and the guns and bring the party into Jodhpur, provided he and his comrades were pardoned and reinstated in the service of Government. But Captain Monck Mason's hands were tied owing to the stringent orders of Government that no

* Three men two women, and five children.

officer was, on any pretext whatever, to make terms with mutineers as long as they had arms in their hands.*

As soon as the intelligence of the mutiny at Abu reached Brigadier-General Lawrence at Ajmer, he ordered the portion of the Legion at Nasirabad to be disarmed. The men continued doing duty in the station for six months, and behaved well; their arms were restored to them in March, 1858, and they were eventually drafted into other corps.

March of the Jodhpur Legion.

The Jodhpur Legion continued their march from Erinpura up the road towards Pali, and on their way passed through the territories and near the fort of Khushial Singh, the Thakur of Awah, who had for some time been in rebellion against the Raja of Jodhpur. He had been collecting men, arms, and supplies, and strengthening his stronghold, and had adopted a warlike attitude. The mutineers encamped under the walls of the fort, with the object of making common cause with the Chief of Awah. The latter sent an emissary to Captain Monck Mason at Jodhpur, offering to co-operate with the British on certain terms. But, as in the case of Abbas Ali, the British Agent could make no conditions, and Khushial Singh made common cause with the mutineers.

The Thakur of Awah.

As soon as it was known that the latter intended to enter his territory, the Maharaja of Jodhpur sent a force against them under Anar Singh, Commandant of the Jodhpur Fort, a brave and loyal soldier. The force was accompanied by Lieutenant Heathcote, Deputy Assistant Quarter Master General of the Rajputana Field Force. That officer found the two forces encamped close to one another, but no picquets posted, a measure he recommended, but either by treachery or neglect his advice was disregarded. Just before daylight on the 8th September the mutineers and rebels made a sudden attack on the Jodhpur camp. Anar Singh called his men to arms, and took post with the guns, but his troops were routed after a show of resistance, and Lieutenant Heathcote was forced to mount his horse and gallop from the field. The brave commander, surrounded by a small band of gallant soldiers, fought to the last, until all who stood were cut down at the guns, which fell into the hands of the enemy, together with the camp equipage and military stores.

Defeat of the Jodhpur Army.

Fate of the Jodhpur Legion.

The Jodhpur Legion remained at Awah until the 10th October, and then marched through Marwar towards Delhi, and occupied Rewari. A force under Brigadier Gerrard was sent against them from Delhi, and found that on the 16th November they had taken up a very strong position at Narnoul. Here they were completely defeated and dispersed, with the loss of their guns, after a hard-fought action, in which Brigadier Gerrard was killed during the pursuit.

* This was one of many evils of centralization, many such orders being issued by Lord Canning, surrounded by councillors who knew little or nothing of the state of Upper India. More discretionary power in the hands of local authorities would no doubt in many cases have been productive of good in the application of measures suited to local and peculiar circumstances. Abbas Ali left the mutineers soon after they marched from Awah, and remained in concealment in Bikaner until he was pardoned.

CHAPTER V.

THE SITUATION IN CENTRAL INDIA IN AUGUST 1857.

Before proceeding to describe the measures undertaken for the suppression of the revolt in Central India, it will be as well briefly to recapitulate the events that had taken place, and to review the state of the country when the first British column arrived within the disturbed area. The situation, as it presented itself to one of the principal actors in the events narrated, is well described in a very illuminating report, written by Colonel Durand at Mhow on the 13th August 1857, for the information of the Government of India. Colonel Durand had arrived at Mhow with Brigadier Stuart's column only eleven days before.

This report, the substance of which is embodied in this chapter, is most interesting and instructive, as it enables the reader to place himself in the position of those who had to decide on the measures necessary to deal with the situation in which they found themselves. The student of history is frequently too prone to criticise in the light of concurrent and subsequent events, which was not available at the time to those who had to deal with the position.

As the season was now approaching when the rains would cease, and military operations become comparatively easy, Colonel Durand submitted a general view of the state of Central India and of the measures which appeared to be essential for the effectual and rapid establishment of British power and influence throughout the country. At the commencement of the revolt among the native troops in the North-Western Provinces the whole of this region had the several military posts within its circle reduced to a minimum of strength, and with the exception of the European Battery of Artillery at Mhow there was not a single European soldier within the limits of the Agency.

The strongest military posts were those of Gwalior and Mhow; the former composed entirely of Contingent troops; the latter consisting of Regulars of the Bengal Army, *viz.*, the 23rd Native Infantry, Wing of 1st Light Cavalry, and Battery of European Foot Artillery. Neither of these forces was large, but both held important points, and although separated from each other by a distance of 50 miles, the intervening posts of Goona and Sipri on the Agra and Bombay road maintained their military connection with each other, whilst the stations of Mehidpur and Agar were not so far removed from the line of communication between Mhow and Agra as not materially to add to its general security.

The military posts of Nagode and Nowgong, held by regular Native Infantry and Irregular Horse, and that of Sehore held by the Bhopal Contingent, were too far removed from the line of the Agra and Bombay road to influence its security; and the same may be said of the intervening tract of country and of the post of Lalitpur, held by Gwalior Contingent troops. In addition Sehore connected Mhow with Saugor, and Nagode might be held to give security to the general line of communication between Mirzapur and Jubbulpore.

It must be observed that the Central India Agency was crossed transversely by a line of military posts with which the Agent had nothing to do, the territories they occupied being under the control of the Commissioner of the Saugor and Narbada Territory. Jhansi, Lalitpur, Saugor, Damoh, and Jubbulpore separated the Agency into two main blocks; Bundelkhand and Rewah forming one, Malwa and Sindhia's territories forming the other.

Early impressed with the importance of maintaining the integrity of the line of communications of Agra and Bombay, no pains were spared by Colonel Durand to effect this purpose. When Gwalior met the urgent calls of the Lieutenant-Governor of Agra by detaching largely from the Contingent troops to his aid, the breaks caused by immediate attention to those sudden requisitions were filled up by the movement of troops from Mehidpur and Agar, and for some time the security of the Agra and Bombay road, and the postal and telegraphic establishments were perfect.

Entirely distrustful that Contingent troops could be brought to act in opposition to their brethren of the native infantry and cavalry of the Regular Army, the aim was to keep the former in considerable force at particular points where their numbers would hold in check neighbouring cantonments of regulars. With this object in view Colonel Durand was anxious to maintain a good strength of troops under Brigadier Ramsay at Gwalior, for they awed on one hand the troops and petty States of Bundelkhand, and on the other were a support and check to the Agra force. Mehidpur and Agar (only 30 miles apart) held in check Neemuch, whilst Holkar's troops, supposed to be faithful, and the strength of which was little known, curbed the troops at Mhow.

The exigencies of the spreading insurrection soon disturbed this arrangement. Gwalior was weakened by strong reinforcements being sent to Agra and Etawah. Nasirabad and Neemuch rose, and the Mehidpur Cavalry, 800 strong, were swept at one stroke ino the ranks of the mutineers.* Jhansi was the scene of revolt of Regular Troops, and, anxious to crush what he felt to be extremely dangerous for the Bundelkhand States under his supervision, Colonel Durand ordered without a moment's delay a movement from Gwalior, Sipri, and Lalitpur, which, if carried out as rapidly as it was ordered, would have destroyed the mutinous troops. But they dared not move the troops from Sipri, and those from Gwalior, too weak in strength, halted, whilst those from Lalitpur never moved. The Gwalior Contingent was in fact infected, and the examples around it had corrupted the fine feeling which originally animated its ranks.

Jhansi was followed by the Saugor and Nowgong revolt of Regular and Irregular troops; and the Gwalior Contingent caught the mania of revolt and rose

* They mutinied on the way to Neemuch and murdered their officers.

at Gwalior. Then followed the hasty retirement from Sipri and Goona, and the loss of the line of communication between Agra and Biaora, in consequence of these premature withdrawals.

Acting on the principle already noted, Colonel Durand had on the 20th May brought together from Sirdarpur and Sehore detachments of the Bhil and Bhopal Contingents to reinforce the escort of Mehidpur Horse and Foot, which were on duty at Indore; and notwithstanding the defection of the Mehidpur Cavalry, and the loss of the whole of that body, so intimately connected with Holkar's Horse, the appearance of strength which these detachments of three different Contingents yielded, and the belief that Holkar and his troops were true to the British Government, succeeded for a time in keeping in check the most dangerous temper of the Mhow troops.

The circle of insurrection had now closed round Indore; it was well known that all the military stations and treasuries of the North-Western Provinces were lost to Government; Nasirabad, Neemuch, Jhansi, Saugor, Gwalior, Sipri had gone. Delhi was not taken, and the Bombay Column, long promised and anxiously looked for by chiefs and people, was reported to be countermanded; under these circumstances Colonel Durand would have called to Indore the European battery from Mhow, but in a conversation with Colonel Platt, he found that whilst he spoke confidently of his regiment, the 23rd Native Infantry, and Major Harris equally so of the Wing of the 1st Cavalry, every plan for the maintenance of the force, the security of the magazine and its battering ordnance and stores, and the safety of the European officers and families, a large number, hinged on the presence of the European battery and the reliable power it afforded to Colonel Platt. He determined, therefore, to forego its assistance, or even that of a portion of it, and to trust to the check, which had up to that time held good, of the Contingent troops and Holkar's.

How treacherously the latter troops acted has already been shown, and there cannot be a doubt that their attack on the Indore Residency was concerted with the consent of the infantry of the Bhopal and Mehidpur Contingents, and with the conspiracy of the Mhow troops. Colonel Durand had since learnt that the Bhopal Infantry, not content with driving off their sergeants and threatening to shoot their officers, were only deterred from joining in the attack when they found that the two Bhopal guns opened fire in his favour; and that Holkar's troops dared not close upon his guns. The Mhow troops were in that state, that for a month previously the European battery horses were all night harnessed with the wheelers at the pole, and the reason that the battery on the day of the attack on the Residency was not ready to move until a quarter to twelve, though Colonel Durand's note to Colonel Platt must have reached at a quarter to ten A.M., was that during the day the horses were unharnessed, and the drivers scattered over the bazars had to be collected which, as they were in the plot, took time. Such was the feeling with respect to the troops at Mhow that the European battery which started about noon from Mhow to proceed towards Indore, advanced, it was said, at a trot to Rao, a village about half-way, and reached it about two, so that the trot must have been slow, in time to learn that the British had been forced to withdraw. Instead of a trot in returning it retraced its steps at a gallop, and at 3 P.M. was again in cantonments, but rushed straight into the fort, expecting throughout that the native troops would have taken advantage of its temporary absence to rise.

Colonel Durand wrote—"Here it must be permitted me to say one word of that truly chivalrous soldier, Colonel Platt. I saw him but once, when, finding that his every arrangement hinged on the presence of the European battery, I would not ask for any portion of it, but decided to take the chance of the conduct of the Contingent troops at Indore and agreed with Colonel Platt as to the points to which the Contingent Cavalry and guns should move out to support or to rescue the European battery, and European officers and families in case the native troops rose. His last words to me were that if his regiment rose, it must rise over his body; I need not add, that he kept his word, and that he fell riddled with bullets fired by the men to whose welfare a great portion of his li e had been devoted.

He now lies side by side with Major Harris, the equally resolute commander of the wing of the 1st Light Cavalry, and Lieutenant Fagan, the adjutant of the 23rd Native Infantry, who so gallantly responded to the call of his commanding officer when death stared both in the face; all three are laid in the south-east angle of the Mhow fort, and the noble devotedness to duty which worked their end will always be a credit to their memory, for the sense of duty sent them forth to meet certain death."

The insurrection at Indore and the revolt of the Mhow troops was followed by that of the 5th Regiment, Gwalior Contingent at Agar, which had behaved so well under Captain Carter, and the three bodies—the Indore, the Mhow, and the Agar mutineers—poured northwards towards Gwalior, after plundering the Indore treasury.

The effect on Malwa was instantaneous. When asked by Lord Elphinstone* what effect on his position the countermand of the advance of General Woodburn's column would have, Colonel Durand replied that after the fact was known, he would not answer an hour for Malwa, where all, and native Princes especially, agreed that the presence of European troops was indispensable. The result was to the full as rapid as he had anticipated, and though with the view of hastening to the uttermost the advance of that column, the rumour of the countermand of which had produced such terrible consequences, every exertion was made both by the officer upon whom the command devolved, Colonel Stuart, and by those engaged in facilitating the march of the column, yet, on the Agent's arrival with that column at Mhow, a great portion of Malwa and Central India were in a state of anarchy and rebellion.

Nimar, though endangered by the mutiny at Aurangabad and the mutinous conduct of the Gwalior Contingent Infantry at Asirgarh, was perfectly quiet.

* Governor of Bombay.

The suppression and punishment of the mutineers at Aurangabad and the military execution of the mutineer leaders at Asirgarh* had a salutary effect, which was strengthened by the march of the column through Nimar to the Narbada

All north of the Narbada in Malwa was in a different state, Lieutenant Hutchinson† having left Bhopawar in consequence of the proceedings of the Amjhera chief; not only was that chief guilty of hostile acts, but the Bhils had in part resorted to their old habits, and a considerable tract of country was in an unsettled and disturbed state. The Bhil Corps detachments left at Bhopawar and their head-quarters Sirdarpur behaved exceedingly ill; and their conduct wherever they had been, at Indore, Mandlesar, and Bhopawar was certainly not calculated to secure to this body the respect of Western Malwa. The Bhil disturbances spread south of the Narbada and the Magistrate of Khandesh complained of raids by the Bhils of Barwani on the frontier villages of the Sultanpur *Ilaqua*.

In the neighbourhood of Jaora the Mewatis and other turbulent races were up, and the Nawab of Jaora, whose conduct was exemplary, applied for aid from the Malwa Contingent at Mehidpur, having troubles to contend against both to the north of Jaora about Mallagarh, and to the south and east of Jaora.

At Kachrode, in the Ujjain District, a prince of the House of Delhi‡ was reported by Major Timins at Mehidpur to be assembling a Musalman armed rabble with the view of raising the Green Standard.

In the Sundiah country, those plunderers from time immemorial, the Sundhias of Sindhia's Sathmahela, being relieved from the curb of the Agar force, were again active, and insecurity reigned wherever the Sundhias could reach.

The petty States such as Dhar and Dewas were embarrassed rather than strengthened by the Mewatis, *Walayatis*, and others whom they engaged prior to the outbreak at Indore.

The Rajgarh and Narsingarh chiefships had maintained order in Umatwara far better than might have been anticipated, but they made no attempt to check the march of the mutineers, though both chiefships suffered by the plunder of some of their villages which lay on the Agar road.

Sindhia's district of Ujjain, though in a very perturbed condition, was kept in tolerable order by the Sir Subah Baba Apta, and by the officers of the

* *Note.*—The Malwa Field Force turned aside on the way from Ahmadnagar to Mhow to quell an incipient mutiny in the 1st Cavalry, Hyderabad Contingent, at Aurangabad.

Only a portion of the regiment was infected and the only act of violence was that of a trooper who fired a pistol at the Commandant and was afterwards hanged. The regiment afterwards retrieved its honour in the campaign in Central India. Full particulars of the mutiny at Aurangabad will be found in the *History of the Hyderabad Contingent*, by Major R. G. Burton.

In July Lieut.-Colonel LeMesurier disarmed the Gwalior Contingent at Asirgarh and ejected them from the fort, and admitted two companies of Captain Birch's Bhil Corps and two companies, 19th Bombay Infantry. The leaders were executed when the column reached Asirgarh on the way to Mhow.

†In his flight Lieutenant Hutchinson was protected by Holkar, who sent him under escort to Mhow.

‡ Feroz Shah, who headed the insurgents at Mandesar.

Baiza Bai, who prior to the Indore insurrection drew a lakh of rupees from the treasury and levied additional men. The conduct of the Agents of the Baiza Bai was such as everywhere to excite suspicion, and public rumour made no other mention of the Baiza Bai's name than as the active instigator of opposition to the British Government. Throughout Sindhia's districts in Malwa the agricultural population evinced marked and systematic hostility to such officers and families as were forced to traverse the country in making towards places of refuge.

Of the state of Sindhia's districts in the north little had been heard since the outbreak at Gwalior; at that time those bordering the Chambal were in insurrection.

Sindhia's *Vakil* had remained in attendance at Indore throughout, but subsequent to the outbreak at Gwalior no communication from Sindhia was made, until within the last few days. The excuse was the state of the roads and *dâks*, but it was not a valid one, as Sindhia's posts of horse were along the line of road from Gwalior to Indore and the communication between Gwalior and Ujjain had been constant. Sindhia, Colonel Durand wrote, had been observing, either from necessity or choice, a neutral line, seeking neither to compromise himself with the mutineers, nor to give serious umbrage to our Government. His subordinate officers in charge of the districts were less guarded, and whether acting under secret instructions, or from their knowledge of the feelings of the Durbar, they spoke and acted in a manner unfriendly to the British Government, and as if anticipating the moment when a greater degree of weakness on the part of the British would enable them to recover and occupy all Sindhia's ceded Districts.* The *Vakil* of Tonk absented himself from Indore contrary to orders. Tonk Territories were reported as being the focus of a Musalman insurrection and there was some inter-communication with the disaffected of the Bhopal territory No reliable information had of late been received; but the Sironj Districts and all Tonk territory were hostile in spirit.

The Assistant in charge of Bersia with several of his *amlahs* was murdered, the treasury and town plundered, and British authority subverted by a Pindari chief and a gang of ruffian followers who as yet had escaped with impunity.† The detachments of the Bhopal Contingent horse and foot who were at Bersia at the time left the place and the Government officials to their fate, and without striking a blow marched back to Sehore.

* *Note.*—In commenting on Colonel Durand's report, Lord Canning wrote on the 28th January 1858—" Whatever may have been the grounds for suspicion against Sindhia, or at least for withholding from that Chief complete absolution of all complicity against us, at the time when Colonel Durand wrote, there can be no doubt that His Highness, in restraining the Gwalior Contingent from leaving Gwalior until after the Dusserah festival, performed an essential service to the British Government, and perhaps saved Agra from the risks of a siege, and whatever may have been the conduct of Sindhia's Agents in remote parts of his territory, there has proceeded from himself no overt act indicative of anything but friendship and goodwill."

The subsequent loyal conduct of this Chief will be set forth in the ensuing narrative.

† A large number of these met with their deserts when Sir Hugh Rose captured the fort of Rahatgarh on the 20th January 1858.

The Bhopal territory, under the rule of a Regent Begum of great ability, but known to be friendly to the British Government which had given her for years support and countenance, was in a very dangerous state. The chiefs of the family had long borne with ill-disguised impatience the rule of the Sikandar Begum. They took advantage of the present crisis to side with the fanatic and disaffected, and several times nearly succeeded in inducing the *Walayatis* and the Begum's troops to rise and declare for a religious war against the British Government. With her usual dexterity and by much temporising the Sikandar Begum had averted a catastrophe which would certainly have involved her life as well as her rule. Her troops, however, were not sound, and they had been endeavouring to form a coalition with the disaffected and mutinous Bhopal Contingent at Sehore. That body of troops, with the exception of a few, refused to obey orders and to march to the relief of Bersia, and was in fact in a state of open mutiny. It was also reported that Rahatgarh in the Saugor Territory, a post of some renown and strength, was in the hands of the insurgent *Walayatis* that is, of Afghans, and it was said that one of the chiefs of the Bhopal Family was at the head of this movement.* This Regent Begum had a difficult part to play, and some of her propositions betrayed an exaggerated idea both of the weakness of the British power in her neighbourhood and of its necessities, but in no territory were the orders so stringent, or on the whole so well attended to, that all British officers and families passing through were to be well treated and provided with all they required. The contrast with Sindhia's was most remarkable.

The tragedy at Jhansi, the Bundela insurrection in the Chanderi District, and the rise at Nowgong shook and tried the fidelity to the British Government of the Bundelkhand Chiefs under this Agency; but with few exceptions their conduct had been staunch, and Major Ellis had the satisfaction of finding them run true when the examples around them were calculated, whether in our own provinces to the north, or on the Jhansi, Chanderi, and Saugor side to the west and south, to encourage rebellion.

The conduct of Rewah, both under Major Ellis and Lieutenant Osborne's supervision, had been most satisfactory.

At Indore the body of the troops engaged in the attack on the Residency, in the murder of unarmed Europeans, men, women and children, in the plunder

* The report was correct, Rahatgarh being in possession of the Chief of Ambapani.

In a minute on Colonel Durand's report, dated 28th January 1858, Lord Canning wrote: "Personally Holkar has so conducted himself as to give no good reason for distrusting his fidelity; although he has been much too weak to control his troops. As it is, he saved the treasure and sent it to Mhow; and did what he could to save European life. Captain Hungerford, who was in political charge during Colonel Durand's absence, as acknowledged His Highness' aid warmly. His Highness has further been active in the disarming of his troops, and if he acts up to his promises in bringing the guilty, especially the highest and most prominent among them, to punishment, there does not appear to the Governor-General in Council, as at present advised, any reason for withholding a complete and cordial acknowledgment of his good and faithful service."

The views expressed in this minute were embodied in a letter of thanks to Colonel Durand for his clear and interesting report.

of the treasury and destruction of public and private property, remained unpunished in the service of the Maharaja, who had no confidence in them and was unable to control them. The armed rabble of Indore, who took an equally prominent part in the plunder and atrocities of the 1st July, of course also remained unpunished, and generally in the enjoyment of their ill-gotten gains.

According to the report of the Durbar, the numbers whether of troops or rabble who accompanied the Mhow mutineers in their march northwards were comparatively small. Such was the condition of Indore and Holkar's troops, that the first paper put into Colonel Durand's hands after ascending the Simrol Ghat was a requisition for aid on the part of the Durbar in case of a revolt on the occasion of the Eed.

Elsewhere Holkar's territories partook of the general perturbation, and on the side of Rampura there was every prospect of disturbances. Were the Mehidpur Contingent perfectly reliable, the infantry and artillery would be strong enough to maintain order in those parts, but the conduct of a portion of it at Indore on the 1st July was so bad that there could not now be the same reliance on this tainted body as would before have been warrantable.*

The position was summed up as follows by Colonel Durand on the 13th August 1857—"In the north of this Agency Sindhia, after quietly awaiting the turn affairs might take, hearing of Havelock's success to the north of his territories, and that Mhow in the south was occupied by an efficient and reliable force, makes advances to the re-opening of friendly communication. Holkar, compromised by the conduct of his troops, and wholly unable, as he says, to control them, evinces much anxiety for the friendship and support of the British Government, the fact being that whatever his original policy, whether intended, like Sindhia, to be observant and neutral, or, which I should be sorry to believe, intended to be more decided of character, it broke down in consequence of the troops breaking loose from him, and taught him his inherent weakness and dependence. Sindhia keeps under rein the assembled Gwalior Contingent, a force he can use against us should it suit his convenience, or claim merit for restraining its hostile activity if that suit his purpose.† Holkar cannot do one or other. His troops are compromised, his influence over them gone; and his only chance of standing is in the favour and support of the British Government.

"The Chiefs of Western Malwa with the exception of Amjhera are not obnoxious to the charge of disloyalty; they are most of them weak and helplessly in the hands of the troops they raised in a hurry, whatever the motive that led them to entertain the troublesome levies of *Walayatis*, Mewatis, etc., they now feel the dangers which beset them from troops whose conduct and temper may at any moment involve them in ruin.

"Eastern Malwa is, as before observed, endangered by the critical state of Bhopal, the loss of the British District of Bersia, and the disposition to resume

* They mutinied at Mehidpur on the 8th November.

† As already noted Sindhia was adjudged to have been loyal and faithful to the British Government throughout.

ancient habits which this event proves the Pindari Chiefs still to nourish. Umatwara fortunately is only disturbed by the Sundhias of Sindhia's Sathmahala, feeling themselves free of the curb of the Agar force.

"Bundelkhand is in insurrection along the line from Jhansi, by Chanderi to Saugor, and the Shahgarh Raja said to have joined; but in the north the mass of Bundelkhand, though perturbed, has not broken out, and Rewah is staunch and as actively friendly as several of the Bundelkhand Chiefs under Major Ellis."

The means of coercion at Colonel Durand's disposal were extremely inadequate for the restoration of order, and the stay of anarchy. The Gwalior Contingent had wholly gone from our colours and was now, with its well-equipped artillery, in Sindhia's hands and of course at his disposal. It might act against us, it never could act for us. The Malwa Contingent had lost all its cavalry, a body of 800 good horse, and the infantry so misbehaved at Indore that it was impossible not to hold the whole body in suspicion, though the artillery and infantry were still together at Mehidpur under European officers. The Bhopal Contingent, after disgraceful and treacherous behaviour at Indore, was now in open mutiny at Sehore, and not likely to hold together long. The Bhil Corps was in course of reassembly, but with its character and influence deteriorated, and having to be thinned of many native officers and men whom the utmost latitude of consideration could not permit to remain in the ranks. At Nagode up to the latest advices the 50th Bengal Native Infantry still stood and was dutiful;* but with that single exception from north to south of the Central India Agency there was not a gun, there was not a sabre, there was not a musket which could be called in aid of the maintenance of order and British supremacy except Brigadier Stuart's small column at Mhow, consisting of one battery of European Artillery, thoroughly effective, one battery of European Artillery paralyzed by loss of drivers, 230 Dragoons of Her Majesty's 14th, 250 of Her Majesty's 86th, the 25th Bombay Native Infantry, details of Madras and Bombay Sappers and Miners, and 3rd Nizam's Cavalry—the total of this effective force amounting to 700 Europeans of all arms, and 1,200 native troops of all arms.

This force might for the present be considered in observation of Holkar's force at Indore, composed of 30 guns of various calibres, about 1,400 Horse, and 5 battalions of Infantry, besides a city which had shown itself hostile and seditious. The Mhow force was sufficient to dispose of anything likely to oppose it at Indore; but it could scarcely move from Mhow and act elsewhere until the compromised body of guns and troops at Indore was either disarmed or dispersed.† Neither could this force advance northwards, leaving bodies like

* The 50th mutinied on the 27th August. They had been ordered to march against Kunwar Singh, reported to be advancing on Nagode, but two miles out they halted, and told their officers to go. These were escorted to Mirzapur by a few faithful men. The regiment then returned and plundered and burnt the place.

† It did so move and act, however, as will be seen in the ensuing chapter; but this, it must be remembered, was the situation as it presented itself to Colonel Durand at Mhow on the 13th August 1857

the Bhopal and Malwa Contingents in an embarrassing state of mutiny in the one case, and of half mutiny in the other, in the centre of territories abounding with the most inflammable material. A combined revolt of the Bhopal Contingent and of the Begum's own troops might throw all Eastern Malwa into greater temporary confusion than then existed; and should the Malwa Contingent artillery and infantry join the disturbances then arising in Western Malwa, all that great tract of country would be in a blaze of rebellion. There must therefore be a settlement of the question as to the Bhopal and Malwa Contingents as a preliminary to further operations.

To meet the situation thus described, Colonel Durand made the following propositions :—

" I have before recorded my opinion that all the troops between the Narbada and the northernmost limits of this Agency should be under the command of one person, and that the whole of the tract thus placed under one military head should also be under the Agent for Central India. It will be at once seen that any settlement of Bhopal affairs requiring military coercion should not be an isolated movement but form part of a general plan, so that after the combined action of the troops from the Saugor and the Mhow sides, the advance into Bundelkhand and the putting down of insurrection in the Chanderi and other districts might be effectually and vigorously carried out.

The operations might be so executed that the advance upon Bundelkhand should at the same time enable the forces to re-establish the integrity of communications along the Agra road, and thus an object which is one of primary moment that should not be delayed an hour longer than can be avoided would be attained at the same time that the country to the east of that line of road is restored to order and pacified.

If there is to be no union of plan, and if the commands are to remain isolated, and military operations in Central India to be a series of independent movements in two distinct lines by two distinct bodies having little or no connection with each other, double the number of troops will be requisite and the work will not be half so well or rapidly done.

I am averse to the contemplated advance of a heavy column, chiefly composed of European troops, and bringing with it a Battering Train. I consider the idea not borne out by strategical considerations; and it certainly is not by political ones.

The latter demand that Indore, Ujjain, and Bhopal should not be left in an uncertain or an unsatisfactory state; whilst the strategical importance of Mhow, where all the roads from the heads of good passes converge, is beyond calculation. So also the value of the rapid re-establishment of the integrity of the Agra road north of Mhow. I do not advocate, if the force be very large, the advance by a single line of communication; if need be it can advance by a double one; but that should depend on the strength of the column and the state of affairs on the plateau of Malwa.

The forces cannot be assembled for some time to come, and by that time, as the Sendwa jungles are safe after November,* the march of the troops up the Bombay road will be safe and practicable ; whilst the line of road by Asirgarh, Barwai and the Simrol Ghat is known to be practicable throughout the year.

The amount of force requisite to crush anarchy and restore order will depend somewhat on the fall of Delhi, and the success of our arms in the North-Western Provinces ; the unfortunate delay which has taken place in the capture of Delhi has been a blow to our power in Central India difficult to estimate ; and which now will not be wiped away from the feeling of the people even by its recapture.

I hesitate therefore at suggesting the amount of European force which would be sufficient for the work before it in Central India.

It must be borne in mind that a post like Mhow or Saugor cannot be left without some few European troops ; and that between Gwalior and Mhow, whether at Saugor or at Goona, there will be a necessity probably for an intermediate post.

Under these circumstances the force to be effective should be four complete regiments of European infantry, one battery of horse and two batteries of foot artillery, besides spare companies for the siege train. There should be at least one full regiment of European Dragoons ; two would be better. The native troops with the force should on no account exceed the proportion two natives to one European soldier.

This force should be in addition to the strength of the column at Mhow.

I am writing with reference to the aspect of affairs at the present moment, and deem the force specified far from large for the work now before it. I trust the Governor-General in Council will excuse my presuming to enter upon these details ; but it is clear that in future wherever there is a large treasury, a magazine, and sick and families to be left behind a force, they cannot be left wholly at the mercy of native troops and a native population.

Forts like those at Mhow, Saugor and Neemuch should be made capable of effective defence by a few heavy guns and a small detail of European infantry and artillery, so as to set free a maximum of force for operations in the field, without risks to magazines, treasure, sick, and families of the European force. I hold it of some importance that this necessity be foreseen and provided for and that the attention of competent officers be turned to this momentous subject. It is here being carried into execution as well as the nature of the Mhow fort will admit.

Early arrangements will have to be made for facilitating the march of and finding supplies for a large force, for parts of the country it must traverse, whatever the line of country selected, are poor in supplies of every description.

* The Sendwa jungles are very unhealthy until the country begins to dry up after the rainy season.

The Telegraph Department should be prepared to restore telegraphic communication along the Agra and Bombay road as fast as the advance of the army northwards of Mhow and Indore admitted of this being done.

Great latitude of acting without reference should be given for the improvement of the lines of road to be used by the column so as to facilitate its movements; I have to a certain extent taken upon myself the responsibility of ordering a very necessary short piece of road to join on Mhow with the Simrol Ghat.

In conclusion the strength of the column should be that above Ghats; whatever may be requisite for convoys from the rear; for protection of line of communication to foot of Ghats, should be extra force."

The measures undertaken for the suppression of the revolt, and to meet the general situation that has been described, will be detailed in the next part of this narrative.

CHAPTER VI

OPERATIONS OF THE MALWA FIELD FORCE.

The Malwa Field Force.

While the events that have been narrated were taking place a force had been assembled in the Bombay Presidency to open up communications with Central India and the North-West Provinces.

Major-General Woodburn.

5 Troops, 14th Light Drgns.*
Woolcombe's Horse Battery.
4-2 Bombay Artillery.
25th Bombay Infantry.
Pontoon train.

This column, consisting of the troops detailed in the margin, marched from Poona on the 8th June under command of Major-General Woodburn, with orders to proceed to Mhow, to prevent the spread of the insurrection in Malwa, and protect the frontier of the Bombay Presidency.

On arrival at Ahmadnagar, however, the column was diverted to Aurangabad, where disaffection had manifested itself in the 1st Cavalry, Hyderabad Contingent, and it was not until the 12th July that it resumed its march. General† Woodburn having fallen ill, the column proceeded under Brigadier C. S. Stuart† who assumed command at Asirgarh, where Colonel H. M. Durand, Officiating Agent to the Governor-General in Central India, joined the force on the 22nd July.

On the 27th July the 14th Dragoons swam the Narbada, the infantry and guns crossing at Mortakka, a ford near Barwaha. Then ascending the Vindhya mountains, they were joined on the 28th at the Simrol Pass, at the top of the Ghauts, by the 3rd Cavalry, Hyderabad Contingent, under command of Captain S. G. G. Orr.

Relief of Mhow, 2nd August.

On the 2nd August they marched into Mhow, the artillery horses being so exhausted that those of the Bengal battery had to be sent for to drag the guns in. On the 6th August the column was joined by four companies of the 86th Foot. The force remained

* This fine regiment had just returned from service in the Persian Campaign.

† Woodburn was first relieved by Major Follett, commanding 25th Bombay Infantry, who died of cholera at Antoli. In his *History of the Indian Mutiny*, Colonel Malleson, in his anxiety to do justice to Colonel H. M. Durand, has done injustice to Brigadier C. S. Stuart, who commanded the Malwa Field Force throughout this campaign, and who subsequently commanded a brigade under Sir Hugh Rose with gallantry and skill. Colonel Malleson writes as though Colonel Durand commanded the force; but he accompanied it only in his political capacity. The military operations were directed by Brigadier Stuart. Apparently with a similar object, Colonel Malleson says with regard to the question of Holkar's loyalty :—"Durand would be relieved by Sir Robert Hamilton, and Sir Robert Hamilton, an old and much regarded friend (of Holkar) would, he (Holkar) felt confident, accept explanations regarding the events of the 1st July (the rising at Indore) which Durand would utterly contemn." This is scarcely fair to Sir Robert Hamilton; and it is at least open to believe that Holkar, while he showed weakness in the first instance, proved himself to be on the side of the British throughout. His actions subsequent to the outbreak certainly were not those of an enemy of the British.

some time inactive at Mhow, partly because of the impassable state of the country from unusually heavy rains, and also owing to the impossibility of striking a decisive blow at the scattered forces of the enemy. Meanwhile, as already related, a large body of Sindhia's revolted troops, reinforced by Afghan, Makrani, and Mewati levies, had assembled at Mandesar, a large and important town on a tributary of the Chambal river, 120 miles from Indore. This rebel force was in September estimated at 15,000 men with 16 or 18 guns, under the command of Feroz Shah, a prince connected with the Imperial House of Delhi. They plundered Bhopawar and Sirdarpur, and then marched on Dhar, which they occupied on the 31st August.

The rebels at Mandesar.

This, added to other events in progress, showed that the situation in Central India was becoming desperate, and further inaction appeared impossible.

The court of Dhar,* some 20 miles north-west of Mhow, was known to be intriguing, and had, as already related, given shelter to the insurgents and mounted the guns which they had captured at Sirdarpur, in the Raja's palace. It was consequently decided to march on that place as soon as the monsoon had cleared off, and a siege train was organised.

March on Dhar.

An advanced guard under Major Robertson, consisting of a troop of the 14th Dragoons, 3 companies, 25th Bombay Infantry, 2 guns, and some Hyderabad Contingent Cavalry, proceeded to Manpur in the direction of Dhar, and thence to Guzeri, where it awaited the arrival of the main body. The latter marched on the 20th October in two parties by different routes so as to invest the fort simultaneously on two sides, and arrived before Dhar on the 22nd.

A cavalry reconnaissance under Captain Mayne was fired on from the *pettah*.† The column under Major Keane, directed against the north face of the fort, was the first to arrive, and immediately engaged the enemy. The country was dotted with lakes and trees, and to the south between the fort and Brigadier Stuart's column stretched a wide expanse of water; the western side was a series of hills, rocks, and ravines.

On the approach of Brigadier Stuart, the rebels advanced to the attack, covering the movement with the fire of four brass guns posted on a hill south of the fort. The British force formed line to meet them, and the artillery, opening on the fort and guns, soon disabled one of the latter. The guns were then charged and captured by Captain Gall with a troop of the 14th Dragoons, and turned on the enemy by the sepoys of the 25th. The two columns advancing had now driven the enemy from their outworks, but as they continued to threaten the right (east) of Brigadier Stuart's flank, the cavalry under Captain Orr made a determined charge, and routed and dispersed them in all directions. The cavalry then made a complete circuit of the fort, and drove the enemy into it, where they were invested, the troops

Action at Dhar, 22nd October.

* The chief was a minor, and the Durbar was held responsible.

† The native town.

occupying a ridge of hills commanding the fort. In his report on this action, Major Gall drew attention to the gallantry of the cavalry, both British and native, saying with regard to the latter, "all proved themselves true and gallant soldiers, men indeed with whom I am proud to serve under the same flag."

Investment of the fort.

The fort of Dhar, built of red granite, stood on a slight eminence detached from the town. The walls, built of stone, are about thirty feet in height, having towers at intervals. The siege train not having arrived, the bombardment had to be delayed until next day, and the force was assembled in a basin among the hills, leaving strong posts to watch the fort. A small party of the garrison broke out on the 24th, but was pursued by a detachment of cavalry, which came up with them at the village of Chiklia. The village was burnt, some of the enemy were killed, and a number of elephants captured. On the 25th a sand bag battery was constructed 2,000 yards south of the fort, and fire was opened. On the night of the 29th the breaching guns were in position, and 24-pound shot were fired at the curtain close to the entrance, firing continuing at night, as there was bright moonlight. On the 30th the enemy displayed a white flag, and asked for terms, but were informed that nothing less than unconditional surrender would be accepted.

The breach was found to be practicable on the night of the 31st, but two Madras Sapper Sergeants, who were reconnoitring it prior to the assault, found that the enemy had evacuated the fort. The cavalry pursued them in the direction of Mandesar, but only a few stragglers were captured.

The British loss during these operations amounted only to a few killed and wounded.

The Hyderabad Contingent Field Force.

After the conclusion of the siege of Dhar, the Malwa Column was joined by the Hyderabad Contingent Field Force, which had been assembled at Edlabad in July for the protection of North Berar and to prevent disaffected parties from crossing into the Nizam's territory. This force, under command of Major W. A. Orr, was composed of the 1st and 4th Cavalry; 1st, 2nd, and 4th companies Artillery, and two howitzers; and a wing each of the 3rd and 5th Infantry—all of the Hyderabad Contingent.

The force remained in observation at Edlabad for some time, and its advance was further delayed by heavy rains and by a severe outbreak of cholera among the troops in camp. At length in October Major Orr moved forward to Hoshangabad, where several rebel Thakurs had broken out, and took the fort of Piplia on the 28th, capturing a number of insurgents. He then marched to join Brigadier Stuart's force before Dhar.

Amjhera.

Before leaving Dhar, Colonel Durand directed Major Orr to march with his force upon Amjhera, and dislodge all *Walayatis*, Makranis, and other rebels, and thus to protect the rear and left flank of Brigadier Stuart's column as it advanced northwards. Lieutenant Hutchinson, Bhil Agent and Political Assistant, was at the same time directed to proceed to Rutlam, and, with a detachment of troops, to take charge of Dhar and Amjhera, while Major Orr afterwards rejoined Brigadier Stuart at Barnagar. Lieutenant Hutchinson, with a detachment of the Hyderabad Contingent, took the hill fastness of Lalgarh on the 8th November, and after dismantling it and hurling its guns down the hill, followed in the track of the rebel chief and captured him on the 11th. The chief was subsequently hanged. Captain Keatinge, Political Assistant, was at the same time directed to proceed to Rutlam, and to bring into active co-operation the troops of Rutlam, Silana, and Jaora. He was to march parallel with the British force at a distance of ten or twelve miles, and to act against the right flank and right rear of the enemy according to circumstances. Boha Aptiah was also warned to advance with Sindhia's troops from Ujjain.

Advance from Dhar.

Having dismantled the fort, the British column marched from Dhar on the 6th November, its advance being hailed with joy by the people of the country through which it passed. Captain H. O. Mayne of the Intelligence Department who marched with a detachment ahead of the column, reported that at the large town of Barnagar, which had just been evacuated by the insurgents, the demonstration made by the inhabitants was remarkable. "On our coming into the main street every shop was shut, and only a few loiterers with gloomy faces were visible. But on our reaching the *Kotwali* and announcing our errand, the populace swarmed up as bees from a hive, and in one minute the whole place was densely crowded, as if by magic, and it was difficult to pass through the concourse." In Sindhia's districts the column was dependent for its supplies wholly upon the exertions of the Nawab of Jaora, whose loyal conduct was the more remarkable as many of his kinsmen had joined the rebels.

Mutiny at Mehidpur, 8th November.

On arrival at Noyla, two fugitive British officers came into camp from Mehidpur,* the headquarters of the Malwa Contingent, which was attacked by a body of the Mandesar rebels on the 8th November. The Cavalry had already mutinied on the way to Neemuch in June and murdered their two officers. Major Timins, Commandant of the Contingent, had six guns, but the infantry did not defend them well. They expressed a great dread of the *Walayatis* and did not wait to receive their charge. Major Timins having in vain endeavoured to rally his men, left the station accompanied by Lieutenant Dysart and thirty-five faithful men of the 2nd Cavalry, Gwalior Contingent. The infantry dispersed in various directions, and some of them went over to the enemy. The rebels set fire to the hospital, which was full of sick and wounded men; and forty crushed and burnt bodies were afterwards taken from the ruins. Captain G. L. Mills, who commanded the infantry, was deliberately shot by one of Holkar's sepoys as he was lying wounded in a litter; Dr. H. T. Cary, in medical charge of the contingent, was also murdered. Mrs. Timins, whose horse was shot under her as she was

* Mehidpur is notable as the scene of the battle gained over Holkar by the British Army under Sir Thomas Hislop on 23rd December, 1817, during the great war with the Mahratta Confederacy.

attempting to escape with her husband, was concealed in the town by a faithful tailor, and so escaped. The rebels left the station with the guns of the contingent, and with a large quantity of ordnance stores which they took from the magazine. They had also in their possession two guns of native manufacture which they had taken from Barnagar to Mehidpur, and which they were anxious to convey to Mandesar for the siege of Neemuch, where they had only one piece of heavy calibre, and little ammunition for it.

Pursuit of the Mehidpur rebels.

On receipt of this news Major Orr was despatched to Mehidpur with 337 sabres of the 1st, 3rd, and 4th Cavalry, Hyderabad Contingent. Major Orr found Mehidpur evacuated by the rebels, who had taken the road to Kasari, with the guns and plunder of the cantonment. Proceeding at once in pursuit, he found a 12-pounder gun on the road about two miles from the cantonment, and in the bed of the Sipra river were discovered two 12-pounder howitzers complete with wagons, and two native guns of considerable calibre, as well as a number of carts containing stores. Had these guns and stores reached Mandesar they would have added greatly to the resources of the insurgents at that place.

Combat of Rawal, 12th November.

After a pursuit of twelve miles, at 4 o'clock in the afternoon of the 12th November Major Orr came up with the enemy at Rawal, where some 500 men with two guns had taken up a position near the village. On nearing Rawal Major Orr divided his force into two portions, one under Captain Abbott to attack from the right, while the other under Captain Murray advanced from the left.

The troops formed line and advanced at the gallop, and, charging the guns, each party received the fire of one, and cut down the gunners. The rebels broke up at once, but continued to fight to the last with much obstinacy and determination, losing about 100 killed and 74 prisoners.

The men had been in their saddles since 4 A.M., and this gallant fight did not end until sunset. In this action Lieutenant Samwell* was dangerously wounded, and two other officers had horses killed under them.

March on Mandesar.

Continuing his march, Brigadier Stuart reached Harnia on the Chambal river on the 18th November, † crossed it next day unopposed, and arrived in the vicinity of Mandesar at 9 A.M. on the 21st, where he encamped in a position covered to the front by some rising ground, flanked on the left by a little village and gardens, beyond which were several groups of trees and another village surrounded by gardens.

Mandesar is a large straggling town full of trees on the river Sohna, having a fort which was occupied by a strong force of insurgents. The British force was here on historic ground, where the army of the Deccan had encamped during the Mahratta War in 1817. In rear was the Chambal river, deep and rapid with rugged and almost perpendicular banks, formerly the haunt of Pindari bands, and in

* Afterwards Colonel Samwell, C.B., 42nd Highlanders.

† The Mehidpur prisoner were tried by Court-Martial at 5 P.M. this day, and 74 were shot.

crossing which Monson's ill-fated column had met with disaster during its retreat before Holkar in 1804.

The passage of the river was difficult, particularly as the transport consisted mainly of bullock-carts, with a few camels, and it is fortunate that it was not defended. Lowe describes the crossing in his *Campaign in Central India*. "I never saw a more animated and beautiful picture in my life than when our brigade crossed this river. The steep, verdant, shrubby banks, covered with our varied forces, elephants, camels, horses, bullocks; the deep flowing clear river, reaching on and on to the far east, to the soft blue-tinted horizon; the babble and yelling of men, the lowing of the cattle, the grunting screams of the camels, and the trumpeting of the wary, heavily-laden elephant; the rattle of our artillery down the bank, through the river, and up the opposite side; the splashing and plunging of our cavalry through the stream—neighing and eager for the green encamping ground before them; and everybody so busy and jovial, streaming up from the deep water to their respective grounds; and all this in the face, almost, of an enemy formed a *tableau vivant* never to be forgotten."

At about 3 o'clock in the afternoon the enemy moved forward in force, threatening the British flanks and centre, and advancing steadily with banners flying. The troops at once fell in, the guns opened fire on a village * occupied by the enemy, and on approaching the right front the insurgents were charged most gallantly by a picquet of the 14th Light Dragoons under Lieutenant Dew, supported by the 3rd Cavalry, Hyderabad Contingent, and were driven back with heavy loss, including 100 killed.

Lowe relates that in this action "Lieutenant Strutt's shooting was very true. All the while this firing was going on at the village a fine fellow, dressed in white with a green flag, coolly walked out of the cover, and sauntered leisurely along the whole line of our guns, while round shot and shell were whizzing about him in awful proximity. He occasionally stooped down, but never attempted to run; he then quietly retraced his steps when a shot from Lieutenant Strutt struck him just before he regained the village."

In this action Lieutenant Dew with only some 20 men dashed into a mass of 300 of the enemy, for which act of valour he was recommended for but not awarded the Victoria Cross.

Next morning, in order to cut the communications with Neemuch, which the rebels were besieging, and from whence an attempt to break the investment of Mandesar might be expected, Brigadier Stuart moved forward in order of battle, crossed the Bahri ford about 1,400 yards to the south-west of the town, and skirted the town until he gained the Neemuch road, and encamped facing the west of the town, with the flanks well protected by two branches of the river Sohn.

Flight at Piplia.

While making a reconnaissance Major Orr obtained intelligence that some of the enemy's baggage had just left the village of Goraria on the Neemuch road. The rebels were at once pursued by the Cavalry, and after a gallop of five or six miles, were over-

* This village was probably Kalatepuram.

taken about two miles south of Piplia and some 200 were cut up. Finding the village strongly held by the enemy's infantry, and many standards displayed, the cavalry returned to camp.

Concluding that the infantry seen at Piplia was the advanced guard of the rebel force from Neemuch, Brigadier Stuart moved forward at 8 A.M. on the 23rd, crossed the northern branch of the river Sohn, and found the enemy in great force some four miles to the north, where they occupied a strong position with their right on the village of Goraria, their centre with guns on a hill where the gunners had cover from a large mud hut, and their left covered by a nullah and lines of date trees in the *jowari* fields, where the crops were uncut, and stretching along a ridge to the east of the village. Behind their guns were some ruined houses, which sheltered the infantry and some Mehidpur Contingent Cavalry; on the left of their battery of six guns was a deep cart-road in a cutting.

Battle of Mandesar, 23rd November.

Covered by a cloud of skirmishers, the British line advanced, the hostile infantry, with green banners flying, moving forward through the intervening millet fields to meet them, whilst their guns at the same time opened fire, and the dense masses of their main body appeared like dark clouds on the near horizon, lit up by the flash of arms, and accompanied by the rumbling thunder of distant drums.

Brigadier Stuart halted his line, and Hungerford's guns opened at 900 yards, and then, moving to the right front, enfiladed the enemy's line. A gallant charge was then made by Lieutenant Martin* with 30 of the 14th Dragoons, who took the enemy's guns, but were forced to retire by the musketry fire from the huts with the loss of their leader, who was severely wounded.

The infantry having by now opened a well-directed fire on the enemy's guns, they were charged and taken by Gall's reserve squadron of Dragoons and the gunners sabred. The rebels then fled in great numbers towards the village of Goraria, when the 3rd Cavalry under Captain Orr swooped down upon them and killed many. A further advance having been made, the village was shelled, and strong infantry picquets were posted round it.

While this action was in progress, the rear-guard and baggage were attacked by a strong body of some 2,000 of the enemy from Mandesar. Major Orr accordingly received orders to reinforce that portion of the column with two guns, and, conceiving that it would conduce to the success of the day's operations, he at the same time moved to the rear with the whole of his mounted troops, the 1st and 4th Cavalry, Hyderabad Contingent, and a squadron of the 14th Dragoons. This operation having been rapidly effected, Major Orr found that the enemy had advanced to within 800 yards of the rear-guard. The guns at once opened fire, and the cavalry then charged the retreating masses of the insurgents, killing many and pursuing them until they took refuge in some gravel pits which adjoined a small pond. Here they again opened fire, and Lieutenant Redmayne, 14th Dragoons, who

Attack on the rear-guard.

* Colonel Martin, C.B., Commandant, Central India Horse, 1878-87.

was leading, wheeled round the pond, closely followed by a few of his men, when he was killed by a volley, and cut to pieces by the rebels, who carried off his charger and accoutrements.* Most of the men were wounded by the same fire.

Defeat of the rebels.

The infantry now coming up, and Captain Abbott's cavalry, which had arrived by a different route, threatening their rear, the rebels retreated to Mandesar.

Storming of Goraria, 24th November.

Next morning, the 24th November, the whole force proceeded to storm the village of Goraria, which was shelled for three hours and then assaulted. The following account is by an officer who was present :—

"After a shower of shot and shell to clear the walls and houses of their sharp-shooters, the Royal County Downs (86th), the 25th Regiment, Nizam's Infantry, and Madras Sappers and Miners, led by Majors Keene, Robertson, and officers commanding the two remaining corps, rushed across the range under fire, over the mud walls, and amid the burning houses began to shoot and bayonet the mutineers, who had themselves fired some of the houses, and poured a deadly matchlock fire from the eaves into our red coats, as they dashed along the streets.

From midday until evening the bloody work went on, the County Downs despising all means but the bayonet. Occasionally a son of the sister isle, all covered with sweat and dust, his face blackened by powder and smoke, would be seen leading tenderly outside the walls a woman or child, and a cavalry Assistant Surgeon humanely carried to a place of safety a Rajput girl whose leg had been smashed by a carbine shot. She was of good family and had lost a father and brother in the fray. All the rebels who ventured to rush from the burning village were sabred by the cavalry. Hand-to-hand fights were going on in the patches of sugar-cane near the village, and about two hundred *Walayatis* came out *en masse* under a flag of truce, surrendering as prisoners. At evening some few only remained, in strongly-built houses at the upper end of the village. Captain Robertson was taking a nine-pounder in to blow open the doors as the infantry bugles rang out the assembly, and a more thirsty and powder-besmeared body of soldiers could not exist than came forth after the day's work. Cavalry picquets were again thrown out around the ruins in which this handful of desperate men remained, and the Brigade encamped. The next day not a living soul remained in Goraria."

Flight of the rebels.

This holocaust was a fitting conclusion to the campaign in Western Malwa. The rebels evacuated Mandesar, and dispersed in all directions. One party appeared before Partabgarh, but the loyal chief of the State attacked and killed eighty of them, and the remainder fled across the Chambal. The main body of the insurgents retreated to Nangarh, where they broke up their standards, saying their gods had forsaken them.

* These were subsequently recovered at the capture of Rahatgarh.

The insurgents defeated at Mandesar* had been besieging Neemuch, which was thus relieved, and Captain Mayne, with a few sowars as escort, rode there and returned, accompanied by some of the officers of the garrison.

Relief of Neemuch.

Colonel Durand now directed the force to march on Indore. The Hyderabad Contingent Field Force under Major Orr remained at Mandesar, and the remainder of the Brigade, marching by Mehidpur† on 9th December and Ujjain 11th December, reached the vicinity of Indore on the 14th December, 1857. Here Holkar's troops were disarmed without opposition, and on the 15th the troops marched in and encamped in the Residency grounds. The Residency was unroofed by fire, and the walls bore the marks of shot. The windows of the Church had gone, the bell was torn down, and the furniture had been removed. Over the altar rail a European had written—"They have thrown down thine altars, and slain thy Prophets with the sword; and they seek my life, to take it away." The blood of the murdered Europeans was still fresh about the jail, and a woman's scalp, with long fair hair, was found in the fields. But vengeance had been taken. Some of the mutineers were hanged, and some blown from guns.

March to Indore.

* Over the gateway at Mandesar was found the head of Captain Tucker, who had been killed at Neemuch. The heads of two rebel chiefs replaced it before the column marched for Indore.

Note.—In his Despatch, Brigadier Stuart acknowledged the assistance he had received from Colonel Durand, and mentioned the officers of his staff (see Appendix), Major Orr, Hyderabad Contingent; Captain Gall and Lieutenant Leith, 14th Light Dragoons, Captain S. G. G. Orr, 3rd Cavalry, H.C., of whom he said "his daring courage is admired by all, and in every affair in which he is engaged his personal combats are most prominent features;" Captains Hungerford, Woolcombe, Brown, and Major Keane; Major Robertson and Captain Little, 25th Bombay Infantry, Assistant Surgeon Butler, Artillery and Gunners Maitland and Thomson, Artillery.

In his Despatch to the Governor-General Colonel Durand wrote:—"Much of the success in quelling this insurrection is due to the judicious daring, the thorough gallantry with which, whenever opportunity offered, Major Gall, his officers and men, sought close conflict with the enemy—a bold one, who often fought most desperately." He also noted the splendid services of Major Orr and the Hyderabad Contingent, and of the 25th Bombay Infantry, and the Bombay artillery.

† At Mehidpur the parade ground, on which Dysart fought to the last for his guns, was found strewn with accoutrements and ammunition, and one gun, too large for the rebels to move, remained. The walls of the houses were blackened ruins, and the trees were torn to pieces by grape and canister.

CHAPTER VII.

SIR HUGH ROSE'S CAMPAIGN IN CENTRAL INDIA.*

On the 16th December 1857, Sir Robert Hamilton, Bart., assumed office at Indore as Agent to the Governor-General in Central India. Next day Sir Hugh Rose took over command of the forces in Central India.

Sir Hugh Rose.

Major-General Sir Hugh Rose, K.C.B., was an officer with a distinguished record both as a soldier and statesman. Entering the army in 1820, he had fought in Syria twenty years later, when he was severely wounded, and captured with his own hand the enemy's leader, the Pasha of Egypt. At Constantinople he had succeeded Lord Stratford de Redcliffe prior to the outbreak of the Crimean War, had ordered the British fleet to Turkish waters, and borne a distinguished part in the subsequent campaign. Brave, resourceful, and possessed of experience in war, he was well-fitted to lead an army during the present crisis.

Plan of Campaign.

The general plan of operations for the coming campaign provided for the advance of three columns, one of which, operating from Mhow under Sir Hugh Rose, would sweep the country from that place to Kalpi on the Jumna, relieving Saugor and recapturing Jhansi; at the same time a Madras Force, under General Whitlock, was to cross Bundelkhand from Jubbulpore to Banda, while a Bombay Column under Major-General Roberts operated in Rajputana.

The Central India Field Force.

The Central India Field Force, of which the Malwa Field Force formed the nucleus, consisted of two Brigades, which were assembled, the first at Mhow, the second at Sehore.†

1st Brigade.

Brigadier‡ C. S. Stuart, Bombay Infantry.
One Squadron, 14th Light Dragoons.
One Troop, 3rd Bombay Light Cavalry.
86th Regiment, 2 companies.§
25th Bombay Infantry.
Two Batteries, European Artillery
Sappers.

A portion of the Hyderabad Contingent Field Force, under Major W. A. Orr, detailed in the preceding chapter, formed an advanced guard to this Brigade.

*Afterwards Field Marshal Lord Strathnairn, G.C.B., G.C.S.I.

† For route of 2nd Brigade from Aurangabad to Sehore, see Appendix VIII.

‡ Afterwards Sir Charles Stuart, K.C.B.

§ The remainder of the 86th joined on the 16th March, during the siege of Chanderi, together with the 21st Company, R.E., and a battery, Royal Artillery.

2nd Brigade.

Brigadier C. Steuart, C.B., 14th Light Dr goons.
Headquarters, 14th Light Dragoons.*
Headquarters, 3rd Bombay Cavalry.
3rd Bombay European Regiment.
24th Bombay Infantry.
Battery, Horse Artillery.
One Field Battery.
Madras Sappers and Miners.
Siege train (joined on 15th January 1858).
A detachment of all arms from the Hyderabad Contingent Field Force.

Intelligence received at Indore made it desirable that the relief of Saugor should be undertaken as soon as possible, and Sir Robert Hamilton and Sir Hugh Rose joined the 2nd Brigade at Sehore, two days' march from Indore, on the 8th January 1858.

At Sehore the mutineers of the late Bhopal Contingent were tried by Court-Martial, and 195 executed, 274 dismissed, and 228 re-entertained. Some faithful Sikhs of the Contingent were placed under Captain H. O. Mayne, and formed the nucleus of the 1st Regiment, Central India Horse.†

Rahatgarh.

A hundred miles from Sehore, and twenty-five miles south-west of Saugor the fortress of Rahatgarh, venerated by the natives as a place of traditional strength, forms the key of the Western Frontier of Saugor and Bundelkhand, the former of which was partially and the latter completely in the hands of the rebels. It is situated on the extremity of a long, high hill, in the midst of hills, nullahs, and dense jungle. The rocky sides of this eminence are scarped and precipitous, falling at one point sheer to the deep and rapid waters of the Bina river. The fort was as strong as Mahratta art could make it, and commanded all the country, and the road from Bhopal and Western India to Saugor. The only means of access to the fort was by a steep and narrow road. The north face was covered by a strong wall and a ditch twenty feet wide. On the west it overlooks the town and the road to Saugor, having bastions at intervals along the walls, in the angles, and flanking the gateways. Before this formidable stronghold Sir Hugh Rose arrived with his 2nd Brigade on the 24th January.

Importance of Rahatgarh.

The fort was garrisoned by warlike *Walayatis* and Pathans under command of Nawab Muhammad Fazal Khan, a man of energy and courage, and a relative of the Regent of Bhopal, who, having failed in an attempt to usurp the power of the latter, had become a chief leader of the rebels. The Shahzada of Mandesar and other rebels of note had also assembled at Rahatgarh. If the garrison could have made a successful resistance, the moral effect would have been most

* The remainder of this regiment had arrived from Poona with other reinforcements.

† Now the 38th Prince of Wales' Own Central India Horse.

unfavourable; Saugor could not have been relieved and the rebellion would have spread in every direction. The Raja of Banpur, one of the most dangerous enemies of Government, who had already sent troops from Kurai across the river Bina to cut off supplies which were coming from Udepur, and other parts of Sindhia's territory, would have intercepted communications with the west, the only base of the British force, which would have been left, destitute of supplies, in a country swarming with rebels. These, if Rahatgarh held out, could have attacked the rear from their fortified camps of Nariaoli and Kurai, the former of which had already beaten off an attempt made from Saugor to take it.

Deeds of the rebels.

The insurgents made war cheaply, paying their followers with the plunder of thriving villages. The Government had many friends in Saugor and Bundelkhand, but the Raja of Banpur, Muhammad Fazal Khan, and others, by acts of the most barbarous cruelty, had intimidated and crushed the well-disposed, and rendered the rebel sway paramount. All persons, on the mere suspicion of being friendly to the Government, were mutilated by having their noses and hands cut off.

Advance on Rahatgarh, 24th January.

As he approached Rahatgarh, Sir Hugh Rose received information of the assemblage of rebels at Udepur in Sindhia's country and in his front; and in order to ensure the safety of his siege train, which was a day's march in rear, and to save time, he brought it up by a night march to his force, and adopted precautions against surprise.

In going through a pass over a range of hills five miles from Rahatgarh on the 24th January the officer commanding the leading flankers, embarrassed by thick jungle, took by mistake the right instead of the left road, and crossing in consequence the river Bina by the upper, the wrong ford, got into a skirmish with the rebels posted in the suburbs of Rahatgarh. The General had just arrived with the advanced guard at the encamping ground; to extricate the flankers from a position so unfavourable to cavalry, he advanced and covered, with the infantry, guns, and supports, their return to their proper position. In rectifying this mistake he had gained a good deal of ground to the right front, and a company of the 24th Bombay Infantry had taken one or two houses and gardens. In reconnoitring he found that they were the commencement of the suburbs, and that to keep all this would compromise his right, and his plan of attacking the fort from the left flank. He therefore ordered the troops back to their camp.

Reconnaissance.

Next day Sir Hugh Rose made, with Major Boileau, C.R.E., and a small party of the 3rd Europeans and 3rd Bombay Cavalry under Captain Forbes, a complete reconnaissance of eighteen miles of the whole country round the rock of Rahatgarh. He ascertained that the rock, a mile and a half in length, covered and surrounded with thick jungle, sloped from the west, where it is precipitous, to the east, where it is accessible. The north front of the fort was alone inhabited; the other parts were merely fortifications. The river Bina runs under the west face.

The reconnaissance confirmed in all essentials the information on which he had based his plan of attack. He carried it out by investing the same evening the rock of Rahatgarh as closely as the great extent, hills, thick jungle, and a difficult river would allow. But it was impossible with the small force at his disposal to invest completely such ground, because a great part of it was covered with dense jungle, which, hiding all view of the enemy's movements, enabled him, by a feint, to concentrate videttes and picquets on one point, and then pass through the interval. The south-west of the fort was invested by 600 or 700 Bhopal Infantry which took the village of Pattan after firing a few shots.

Investment of the rock.

Next day, as soon as the Artillery and Engineer Officers reported that they were ready for the siege, the fort was attacked from the left, the south-west end of the rock, under cover of a feint from the right against the town, from which all possible advantage was to be derived. Both succeeded.

The first attack, 26th January.

Leaving a troop of the 3rd Bombay Cavalry at the foot of the slope to cover the rear, Sir Hugh Rose mounted the slope, with the troops named in the margin, two companies of the 3rd Europeans skirmishing and covering the breadth of the rock, two companies supporting, and the rest in reserve. They made their way through thick jungle, and reached, without being discovered, the edge of the open ground in front of the east curtain of the fort, which Major Boileau had selected for the breaching batteries. The General directed a road to be cut immediately by the Sappers and Miners from the foot of the slope to the battery; the left to open a communication down the south of the rock with the troop of the 3rd Bombay Cavalry investing the south of the rock; the right to open a communication down the north side of the rock with the camp, and rifle pits to be made at night in front of the attack, enfilading as much as possible the enemy's line of defences.

3rd European Regiment.
Detachment, Siege Train, two 8-pounders, 15 men, Bombay Artillery.
Two 5½-inch mortars, 10 men, Bombay Artillery.
90 Madras Sappers and Miners.
Two 6-pounder guns, Hyderabad Contingent.
One Troop, 3rd Bombay Cavalry.

The enemy having perceived the position, commenced a sharp fire on it from their jingals and small guns in the curtain and bastions, which were kept down by the fire of the 6-prs. of the Hyderabad Contingent and the 5½-inch mortars, the former firing at the loopholes and embrasures, the latter with half charges dropping their shells on the banquette.

The bombardment.

Quarter Master Thompson, commanding the half battery of the Hyderabad Contingent, was twice hit, but continued working his guns successfully until the close of the day. The General thanked his battery on the ground. The two 18-pounders with elephant draught were brought up the hill at 4 P.M., the 3rd Europeans dragging them up the steep where the elephants could not go.

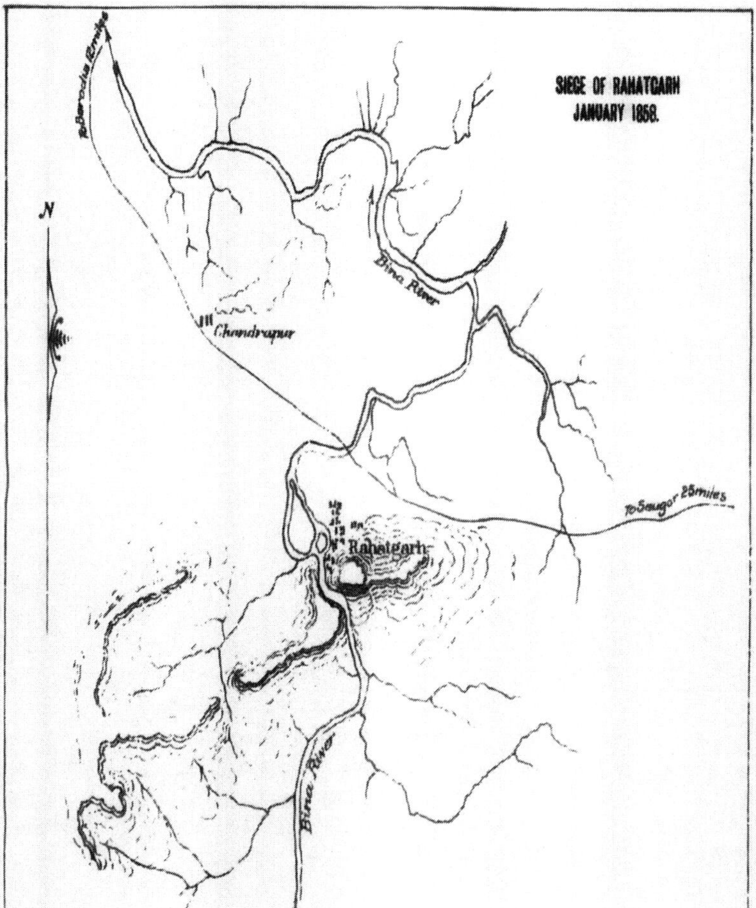

I. B. Topo. Dy. No. 7,076,
Exd. C. d. A.. January 1908.

No. 4,247-I., 1908.

The feint against the town drove the enemy out of it into the fort, and enabled Brigadier Steuart, with the force detailed in the margin, to take possession of the Eedgah, a Musalman place of prayer opposite the north face, commanding the town and within range of the main gate of the fort; on this height, and another to the left, he skilfully placed Captain Lightfoot's 9-pounder battery, one 8-inch howitzer, and two 8-inch mortars. These batteries, forming the right or town attack, kept up night and day an effective fire on the line of defences and buildings of the fort.

Four 6-pounder guns, Bombay Horse Artillery.
Six 9-pounder guns, Bombay Light Field Battery.
50 Bombay Sappers and Miners
Detachment of Siege Train.
Two 8-inch mortars, one 8-inch howitzer, and 26 men, Bombay Artillery.
Two Troops, 14 Light Dragoons, 24th Bombay Infantry.

On the 27th January Sir Hugh Rose changed the 8-inch howitzer from the right to the left attack, in order to enfilade with its fire the defences of the north face. He was constantly between the two attacks, which were two and a half miles apart.

From the town attack the General directed a detachment of the 3rd Europeans, supported by another of the 24th Bombay Infantry, with two companies of the 24th in reserve and under cover of houses and trees and of a heavy fire from the Eedgah battery, to take a low massive tower close to the main gate, Captain Lightfoot being of opinion that a howitzer might be placed in it which would batter the gate and strengthen and shorten the cordon of investment. A couple of 8-inch shells were thrown into the tower to drive out the enemy should they be there, and the storming party, gallantly led by Captain Lightfoot, who volunteered to accompany it, entered the tower, under a heavy fire from the walls, by the postern opposite the walls, from which it was only fifty yards distant.*

Captain Lightfoot and Lieutenant Bonus of the Engineers, after a thorough examination of the tower, reported that the massive construction and nature of its defences prevented their being used for the offensive, and the troops were withdrawn from it before daylight. At 8 o'clock on the 28th, the sandbag batteries having been completed, the two 18-pounders and the 8-inch howitzer having been brought up to them, commenced their fire against the outer wall of the east curtain of the fort with such good effect that it was evident that a practicable breach would soon be made.

Advance of the Raja of Banpur, 28th January.

Sir Hugh Rose had just returned to the camp from the battery when the rebels, coming in force out of the thick jungle crossed the river Bina and attacked the vedettes of the right rear of the camp; another large body† appeared at the same time on the opposite bank, the two bodies amounting to 1,500 or 2,000 men, many of them sepoys and *Walayatis*. The General moved rapidly with the outlying picquet of the 14th Light Dragoons, who in less than a minute were in their saddles,

* Private Davies, 3rd Europeans, was recommended for his gallantry and intelligence on this occasion.

† This was a body of insurgents under the Raja of Banpur, who advanced rapidly with great boldness, drums beating, colours flying, and the shout of warlike songs; but, as related, their courage vanished with no less rapidity on the approach of the Dragoons.

against the rebels, ordering two guns and the rest of the picquets to follow in support. The enemy, who were skirmishing with a picquet of the 3rd Bombay Cavalry, on seeing this, fired a discharge of muskets and rockets at the Dragoons, and ran into a gorge of the Bina and up its rocky banks. Captain Hare, who was following in rear with his detachment of the Hyderabad Contingent, was directed to move by a short line and cut off their retreat.

Defeat of the enemy.

Brigadier Steuart, who had been called up, advancing from the Eedgah, with a few rounds from the guns, sent the enemy on the other side of the river into the jungle, and the whole retreated rapidly to a precipitous ridge above the village of Chandrapur, four miles to the north-west of Rahatgarh, from whence they had started in the morning. Captain Hare came up with their rear before they reached the ridge, and cut up some of them.*

After nightfall the rebels made a feeble and unsuccessful attack on the left of the camp from the Saugor road. The rebels, who had come from their fortified camp of Nariaoli and from the fort of Kurai, failed completely in their attempt to surprise the camp and relieve Rahatgarh; and during the whole time of their attack the breaching batteries continued their fire. Colonel Turnbull reported that the breach would be practicable for an assault next day at sunset.

Attack on a convoy by the rebels.

Information was now received that the rebels from the Chandrapur ridge had early in the morning attacked, in the difficult pass already mentioned, a convoy of supplies coming for the force from the west, and had killed Sindhia's *vakil* who was in charge of it. The safety of the supplies rendered it necessary that the rebels should be driven from Chandrapur during the night, and Sir Hugh Rose was on the point of marching against that place when two spies reported that they had left for Barodia.

Flight of the garrison, 29th January.

On the General visiting the Eedgah, Brigadier Steuart reported that at about 4 A.M. the enemy had attempted to make a sortie from the main gate, which he had driven back with Captain Lightfoot's 9-pounders. A Bhopal officer came up and reported that he had cut up 25 out of 50 of the garrison who had attempted to force their way by his patrol. Colonel Liddell reported also at the same time that, judging from the stillness in the fort that its garrison were escaping, he had entered it by the incompleted breach with part of the 3rd Europeans who, after receiving some shots from the few rebels still there, had killed them and taken possession of the fort. The main body fled by an ancient sally port and a hole dug under the parapet to the south-west, from which the ropes were hanging by which they had let themselves down.

"The most amazing thing was to see the place from whence they had escaped. To look down the precipitous path made one giddy, and yet down this place, where no possible footing could be seen, they had all gone—men and women—in the dead of night! One or two mangled bodies lay at the bottom, attesting the

*Captain Hare and Lieutenant Westmacott were mentioned for their services on this occasion, and Lieutenant Moore, 3rd Bombay Cavalry, who served a gun with effect, owing to the paucity of gunners.

difficulty of the descent. Nothing but despair could have tempted them to have chosen such a way." (*Central India during the Rebellion of* 1857-58.—*Lowe.*)

The reports of all the officers on duty stated that these rebels, crossing a ford over the Bina to the south-west, under the Bhopal camp, passed through the Bhopal lines into the jungle. The Bhopal troops fired a few shots at the fugitives, and two or three of their dead baggage animals in the ford showed the track they had taken.

The garrison, despite their determination that they would hold Rahatgarh or die, had not been able to stand the shelling or meet the approaching assault. The investment of the rock prevented the escape of most of the chief rebels. Muhammad Fazal Khan, a relation of the Regent of Bhopal, and the military chief of the rebels in these districts, and all his staff attempted to cross the Bina, but seeing the vedettes of the 14th Light Dragoons on the other bank, turned back and hid themselves in a cave under the rock, where they were captured. The vedettes and piquets round the rock cut down and took many of the fugitives during the day, and eighty prisoners were made over to Sir Robert Hamilton, of whom 24 were executed, and 48 more to the civil authorities.

The Hyderabad Contingent Cavalry sent in pursuit of the fugitives came up with and killed forty of them.

Execution of rebels.

At sunset Muhammad Fazal Khan and the Nawab Kamdar Khan, a pensioner of the British Government and a son of the great Pindari Chief taken by Sir John Malcolm in 1818, were hanged over the gate of the fort, and next day 17 more, most of them rebels of note and all part of the garrison of Rahatgarh, were executed. Two of them, brothers of the Pindari Chief, had taken part in the murder of the British Assistant at Bersia; Kishen Ram, Secretary of Muhammad Fazal Khan, was stated to have been instrumental in atrocities committed on forty Christians.

Contents of the fort.

The fort was provided with a fine tank fifty feet deep, cut out of the rock; in it were found great stores of salt and grain, sufficient for a year's consumption, a few camels, cattle, and several horses, two of them belonging to Muhammad Fazal Khan, one with a silver bridle; a mould for casting cannon and shot, and an immense mass of native correspondence and English accounts. There was also found the effigy of the head of a decapitated European female, which these supporters of a change of rule in India carried before their troops as a fitting emblem of their deeds. Other standards taken here as at Mandesar were marked with the crescent and the bloody hand. In the fort were found many women and children who, it is needless to say, were not harmed by the troops, whose passions might well have been excited by the atrocities whch had been committed on their fellow countrymen and women throughout India.

The rebels assemble at Barodia.

After the capture of Rahatgarh, the rebels who had retired fom Chandrapur to Barodia concentrated in the latter place, having been reinforced by such of the garrison of Rahatgarh as had escaped and by rebels from Kurai and other places in Bundelkhand.

Barodia, on the left bank of the river Bina, was a strong village with a small fort, with dense jungle on each side, about twelve miles from Rahatgarh on the road to Kurai, a strong fort twenty-nine miles to the north of Saugor. The object of the rebels in concentrating at this place was to prevent or endanger the British advance to Saugor, by retaking Rahatgarh, or by placing themselves in their rear, on the road from Bhopal to Saugor, to cut off, as they had already attempted to do, the supplies coming from the friendly States of Sindhia and Bhopal. It was consequently necessary to drive the enemy out of Barodia.

4 Guns, Horse Artillery.
4 Guns, Captain Lightfoot's Battery.
Two $5\frac{1}{2}$-inch Mortars, with 15 men of Captain Woolcombe's Battery under Lieutenant Strutt.
3 Troops, 14th Light Dragoons.
2 Troops, 3rd Bombay Light Cavalry.
25 men, Madras Sappers and Miners.
3rd European Regiment.
Detachment, Hyderabad Contingent, under Captain Hare.
British order of march.

Sir Hugh Rose marched from Rahatgarh at midday on the 31st January, with the force detailed in the margin, leaving Brigadier Steuart with the remaining troops to protect Rahatgarh and the camp. He moved forward in the order of march which he always adopted when near rebels, as a precaution against their system of surprises; that is, a line of flankers of the 14th Light Dragoons on each side of the road, fifty yards in front of the leading file of the advanced guard, which, with a file of Irregulars, had charge of the guides; another line of Irregular Cavalry 150 yards in echelon in front of the outward flanks of the 14th, and should thick jungle border the road, a company of infantry in extended order on each side of it to support the flankers of the 14th and the advanced guard. By this means all dangerous ground was searched, surprises were almost impossible, and spies lying concealed at a great distance from the road were frequently seized.

The rebel ambush.

As the column approached Barodia and the river Bina they had very thick jungle, long grass, and ravines on the left. The flankers of the Irregulars, suddenly halting, reported that they perceived the enemy in force in ambuscade on the left. Being with the advanced guard, which was under Lieutenant-Colonel Turnbull, Sir Hugh Rose ordered the two guns of his troop* to open fire on the enemy; before they could do so, the enemy poured in a musketry fire, killing Lieutenant-Colonel Turnbull's horse, although the division of Horse Artillery was reinforced with four of Captain Lightfoot's 9-pounders, firing grape and round shot; it was too close for shrapnel.

Action at Barodia, 31st January.

Lieutenant-Colonel Turnbull with the Horse Artillery took ground to the right with a view to enfilade the enemy, but he could not get a slant at them. However, this movement enabled him to obtain good views of a body of rebel horsemen with a red standard, endeavouring to gain a wood and outflank the British right. A charge

* The "Eagle" Troop—1st Troop, Bombay Horse Artillery.

of cavalry was directed against them, but could not be carried out in consequence of the Staff Officer being unable to find a passage down the high banks of the Bina; two rounds of spherical case burst among this body, and they disappeared.

The 3rd Europeans had been placed in skirmishing order in front of the flanks of the guns; their fire diminished but did not silence that of the rebels. The skirmishers of the 3rd Europeans under Lieutenant-Colonel Liddell then charged their advanced position, and gallantly drove the rebels out of the thick jungle and twisting nullahs, and took possession of the bank of the river, commanding the ford to Barodia which now first became visible. The rebels had displayed so much obstinacy in defending this position in order to prevent the advance across the Bina to Barodia. In this advance Lieutenant-Colonel Liddell, Captain Neville, R.E., Captain Campbell, 3rd Europeans, Captain Rose, A.D.C., and Lieutenant Macdonald, A.Q.M.G., were conspicuous.

The cavalry attack.

The advantage gained by the 3rd Europeans was immediately turned to account, and the Hyderabad Contingent Cavalry, supported by the 3rd Bombay Cavalry, under Captain Forbes, was sent to cross the ford, covered by the skirmishers, to pass through the jungle to the front and fall on the enemy in the open plain between the jungle and Barodia. The General followed with the four guns of the Horse Artillery, and a troop of the 14th Light Dragoons in support under Lieutenant-Colonel Turnbull, ordering the rest of the force to follow, with the exception of Captain Hare's Infantry and guns, which remained at the ford to prevent the rear being cut off.

Captain Forbes found the enemy's flanks, particularly their left, posted in thick jungle, their centre in comparatively open ground; he charged and broke their centre, cutting up thirty or forty of them. The third and a very strong position, the village of Barodia, now came within sight. Captain Forbes, having observed a body of cavalry retreating leisurely on the village, endeavoured to cut them off, but their flight on seeing his intention became so rapid that he only succeeded in killing eight or ten of them before they got well under the protection of their guns in position at the village, and of the matchlockmen posted in the dense jungle which surrounded three sides of it, and lining a wet *nala* which ran along the front. In this action Subadar Sujat Singh killed three of the rebels, and Jemadar Ahmad Hussain Khan, 3rd Cavalry, Hyderabad Contingent, was mortally wounded in courageously attacking singly a knot of the enemy.

Advance of the guns.

Although the ford was a bad one, Colonel Turnbull took his guns across it rapidly in support of the cavalry, and when by the strength of the enemy's position they were compelled to give up the pursuit, he unlimbered in front of the village and of the enemy's guns, and opened an effective fire on their position. Captain Lightfoot with the battery arrived shortly afterwards.

The enemy answered with guns and rockets, killing at the General's side Captain Neville, R.E.,* who was acting as his A.D.C. Driven from their position by the fire of the guns, the enemy retreated across a wall and open space into the village and jungle. Captain Lightfoot, being directed to conform to this movement, took ground to the left with the guns, and gave them before they reached cover an enfilading and destructive fire; the 5½-inch mortars threw shells into the small fort of the village and jungle into which the rebels had retired.

Retreat of the enemy.

It was now getting dark, and taking two companies of the 3rd Europeans which had just come up, Sir Hugh Rose crossed the wet *nala*, and bringing their right shoulders forward, occupied the wall round the village and surrounded it with the skirmishers and a troop of the 3rd Bombay Cavalry. Lieutenant-Colonel Liddell afterwards occupied it and the little fort, but the enemy, except for a few *Walayati* skirmishers who were killed, had fled to Kurai through the jungle, leaving baggage unpacked and other signs of a precipitate retreat.

Not being sure that his camp with the Siege Artillery and numerous stores, left under a small guard at Rahatgarh, would not be attacked, the General halted only for a short time to rest his troops, and marched back to Rahatgarh the same night, the men having been marching or engaged for fifteen hours.

Casualties.

The enemy's loss amounted to four or five hundred, and included Anant Singh, their ablest military leader and a nephew of Muhammad Fazal Khan,† killed, and the Raja of Banpur wounded. The *Walayatis* and Pathans fought with their usual courage, even when dying springing from the ground and inflicting mortal wounds with their broad swords. On the British side two were killed and 21 wounded (two mortally).

Results of the victory.

The results of this defeat exceeded expectations. Not only were the communications with the west and Saugor completely opened, but the rebels, flying from Barodia to Kurai, left in their panic that place, a strong position, and Krulassa, which is between thirty and forty miles to the north-west of Saugor. Nariaoli, their fortified camp, was also abandoned. All these places and the country about them had been in their hands for the last eight months. The rebels also left at Kurai the guns they had at Barodia.

Behaviour of the troops.

The troops behaved at Barodia with discipline and courage, keeping their formation in very bad ground and obeying with eager alacrity any orders which brought them closer

* This officer, who had served throughout the Crimean War with distinction, only joined the previous day. Sir Hugh Rose, knowing what excellent service he had done as an Engineer Officer before Sevastopol, had brought him up by forced marches to assist in the reduction of the forts in this country. During the action he exhibited to the last the courage and intelligence which had obtained for him so honourable a reputation.

† Killed by Lieutenant H. H. Lyster, 72nd Bengal Infantry, Interpreter.

to the enemy. The 3rd Europeans, although very young and now for the first time in the field, qualified themselves for a career of honour.*

There was now nothing to prevent the march to Saugor, which Sir Hugh Rose entered on the morning of the 3rd February. As the troops approached the town, not only the Europeans, who had been beleaguered for seven months, but the whole native population came out to welcome them, and there appeared to be the greatest joy among all classes.

Relief of Saugor, 3rd February.

The Europeans, 173 men, 67 women, and 130 children had been confined in the fort since the 29th June 1857, without much more than bare necessaries, and deprived of all ordinary conveniences and comforts. The mortality had amounted to twenty-two. The men, during this trying period, cut off from all communication, and with the knowledge that succour could not be sent them for many weeks, performed their duty well, and nobly maintained the character of their country, adding another to the many instances of devotion and firmness which the sepoy mutinies elicited.

Before the arrival of Sir Hugh Rose's force, the rebels of the Bundelkhand, Shahgarh, Saugor, and Narbada Districts had not only invested Saugor but occupied the forts of Sanoda and Garhakota to the east and Nariaoli and Kurai to the north-east. The fort of Rehli to the south-east was gallantly held by Lieutenant Dickens with a detachment of the faithful 31st Bengal Infantry. The relief of Saugor had opened the roads to the west and north, permitting of communication being entered into by Sir Hugh Rose with Major Orr, commanding the advanced guard of the 1st Brigade at Goona on the Mhow and Agra Grand Trunk Road. It remained for the 2nd Brigade to open communications from Saugor towards the east, and cut the rebel line from Jhansi to the Narbada. As the best means of doing this, Sir Hugh Rose determined to capture the fort of Garhakota, which was garrisoned by sepoys of the 52nd and other regiments that had mutinied.

On the 8th February Captain Hare, with his detachment of all arms of the Hyderabad Contingent, was sent to take the little fort of Sanoda where the rebels had stored their supplies, with orders at the same time to make practicable for siege artillery for use against Garhakota, the ford of the river Bias.

Capture of Sanoda.

Next day, knowing the good effect which rapid movements have on the enemy, and the value of cool weather for the extensive operations before him, Sir Hugh Rose marched ten miles to Sanoda, and on Tuesday, the 11th, made a double march of 21 miles to Bassari, close to Garhakota, arriving there in the afternoon.

March to Garhakota.

After turning off the high road between Saugor and Damoh at Saorpur, the jungle became more and more dense, until the force had cleared a low range of

* Mentioned in the Despatch—Lieutenant-Colonel Liddell, Captain Campbell, 3rd Europeans; Captain Forbes, 3rd Bombay Cavalry; Captains Wood, Macdonald, and Rose, Staff. Subadar Sujat Singh, Naiks Hanmanth Singh and Babadin Khan, Trooper Vas, 3rd Bombay Cavalry.

hills, when it grew more open. In passing under the hillside the skirmishers came upon a party escaping, who fled over the hill, leaving their baggage. Shortly afterwards a *chaprassi*, whom Sir Robert Hamilton had sent out, returned from Garhakota with information that the mutinous sepoys were all in their lines near the ford under the fort, and that the Bundelas, amounting to a thousand or more, were in the fort, apparently unaware of the approach of the force, but that a post was occupied on a spur near the fort.

On receiving this intelligence Sir Hugh Rose pushed forward a party of cavalry which took the post and shot the sixteen men occupying it except two horsemen who escaped.

The fort of Garhakota.

The fort of Garhakota is situated at the confluence of the Sunar and Gidhari rivers which wash the outer wall on two sides. It is surrounded on all sides except the east by forest and the towns of Garhakota and Hardanagar. In the general form of a semi-circle its greatest length is 900 yards and breadth 300 yards. The Sunar is easily fordable except during the rainy season. The interior wall, built of stone, is 29 feet high and from 15 to 24 feet in thickness. About 1,600 yards from the ditch, a wall extends between the two rivers, and is continued for the space of a few hundred yards along the Sunar.*

Investment of the fort, 11th February.

On the evening of his arrival the General drove in, with some guns of the Horse Artillery and Captain Lightfoot's Battery, and skirmishers of the 3rd Europeans, the enemy who wished to prevent the occupation of the village of Bassari; the 3rd Europeans, covered by the artillery, storming some houses still more in advance, and taking a ridge close to the walls. During the night and next morning the sepoys attempted to retake the position, but were immediately repulsed by the advanced posts and two 9-prs.

On the following morning a hamlet was shelled and occupied; the mutineers came in numbers out of the fort and an entrenched camp to the south, to oppose the advance of the 3rd, their buglers repeating the English skirmishing calls; but with the difference that the 3rd went as rapidly to the front as the mutineers went to the rear when the advance was sounded.

* Colonel Malleson, in the History of the Indian Mutiny, states that this fort was attacked in 1818 by Brigadier Watson with 11,000 men, and he was unable in three weeks to effect a breach in the walls, and was glad to allow the garrison to evacuate the place with all the honours of war. This is not quite correct. Watson had under his command on this occasion a force from Saugor, which could not have amounted to 11,000 men, for the whole garrison of Saugor and its dependencies comprised only a detail of Horse Artillery, 4 squadrons, Native Cavalry, 2 Companies, Foot Artillery, 5 Battalions, Native Infantry, and one Risala of Irregular Horse.

Brigadier Watson laid siege to Garhakota on the 18th October 1818, and on the 29th the breach was reported practicable, and the storming party was ordered for the assault proposed to take place the following morning. But the garrison were not prepared to stand a storm, and asked to be permitted to retain their arms and private property, and return to their homes. They were certainly in no condition to insist on these stipulations; but as their opposition had been to Sindhia and not to the British Government Brigadier Watson preferred not to risk the lives of his troops in an assault. At 7 o'clock on the morning of the 30th October, the garrison, which originally amounted to five hundred men, marched out and dispersed to their homes. They had lost about a hundred killed and wounded during the siege.

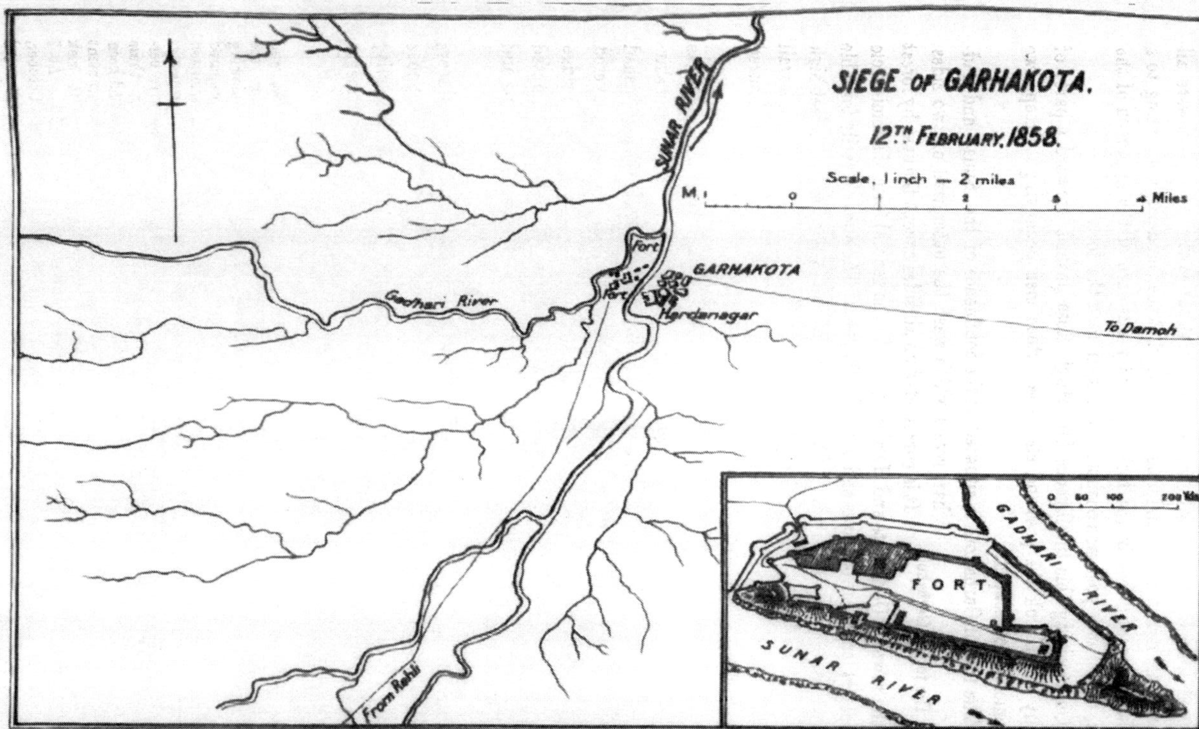

I. B. Topo. Dy. No. 7,074.
Exd. C. J. A., January 1908.

No. 4,248-I., 1908.

A reconnaissance was pushed through Hardanagar to the Panch Ghat to co-operate with Lieutenant Dickens who had intended to advance and hold that ford, but did not do so, as he heard that it could not be held, being too close to the enemy's defences at Hardanagar and Garhakota. Skirmishers attempted to oppose the passage across the ford, but were driven back, and their intrenchments taken. The reconnaissance returned to camp after thirteen hours' marching, having seized a noted rebel, the Lambardar of the village of Majiowa.

The reconnaissance having made a circuit of the fort, detachments of all arms were left in position, investing the north-east, east, and south-east, the troops in camp guarding the north and north-west. Having reckoned on the Rehli detachment for the southern investment, Sir Hugh Rose left that part unoccupied. On his return to camp he sent Captain Hare to guard the south, but before the latter

Flight and pursuit of the rebels.

arrived at about 10 P.M. the whole garrison fled by the gate on the south side, and then turned northwards in the direction of Shahgarh, leaving all their cattle and stores, and their 13 guns loaded. No doubt they were intimidated by the energy of the investment, the lesson of Rahatgarh, and fear for their line of retreat. In any case, with the numbers at his disposal, it would have been impossible for the General to have made a complete investment. His troops were, strictly speaking, only sufficient to guard the camp and artillery. His force was unusually weak, as he had left a troop of the 14th Dragoons and two companies of the 24th Bombay Infantry at Saugor. He had also sent the 31st and detachment of the 42nd Bengal Infantry to Kurai to guard Saugor against a possible attack from the north. During the reconnaissance Lieutenant-Colonel Turnbull fired the first shot with the 8-inch howitzer which blew in an embrasure, dismounted a gun, and took off the head of a sepoy in a red jacket with an English medal and two clasps, who served it. The defences of the fort were demolished by a party of Sappers left for the purpose. The casualties during the operations amounted to only four wounded. The insurgents were pursued by Captain Hare, with half a troop of Horse Artillery, a troop of the 14th Dragoons, and a troop of Hyderabad Cavalry. He came up with their rear just as they had crossed the river Bias at the village of Bear, but the guns could not get over. However, the cavalry under Captain Need went across the river, and, pursuing until dark, cut up about a hundred of the enemy, mostly sepoys of the 52nd and other regiments, of whom Captain Need killed five with his own hand.

In his report to Government, Sir Robert Hamilton wrote :—" I cannot but consider it most fortunate that the fort at Garhakota has been so easily obtained, for it is beyond exception the strongest and most difficult I have seen in Bundelkhand, indeed as formidable as any I have met with in India. We have not only saved a great deal of time, but we have not lost a life ; whilst the impression which the fall of this celebrated fort will make throughout this country will be far greater than can well be conceived, it being deemed impregnable."*

* Captains Hare and Need were mentioned in the General's Despatch.

After the capture of Garhakota, the British force marched back to Saugor to prepare for a further advance. The Rajahs of Shahgarh and Banpur met on the 11th February to plan future operations, and information was received that nearly all the rebels from Garhakota had gone to Maraura, having skirted Shahgarh, which was abandoned. Maraura was one of the strongest forts in Bundelkhand. The road to it led through dense jungle and dangerous ground. In its rear the ground was open. Bundelkhand is a rugged country full of passes through rocky hills, thick jungle, deep *nalas*, and winding streams.

Return to Saugor.

Bundelkhand.

The country was, therefore, suited to the guerilla tactics of the enemy, and not to the British force, which was weak in infantry, and proportionately strong in guns, a great part of which was heavy artillery.

Moreover, Sir Hugh Rose would be encumbered by the transport of several days' supplies, which he had to carry as the country had been stripped by the enemy, and he had no organised military train. Under these circumstances, the General decided to take the road to Jhansi, through the more open country skirting the dangerous part of Bundelkhand, and falling when feasible on the flank or rear of any strong position of the enemy, assisting Tehri, and getting into communication with the first Brigade, which was to arrive at Goona about the 28th February. He would then make a combined attack on Jhansi with both brigades.

Plans of the British General.

The unavoidable delay at Saugor for the repair of the siege guns did away with much of the good effect of the speedy fall of Garhakota. The rebels, not seeing any further movements to the front against them, re-gained courage, and again occupied in force the strong positions in the Shahgarh and adjoining districts, such as the forts of Surahi and Maraura, and the difficult passes in the mountainous ridges which separate the Shahgarh and Saugor Districts.

These passes are three in number, the pass of Narhat and the fort of Karnalgarh near Malthone, and the passes of Madanpur and Dhamoni. Resistance was anticipated at the forts of Surahi, Maraura, and Talbahat, at which latter place it was said the Raja of Banpur intended to make his last stand.

The General determined to force these obstacles, and accordingly gave orders to Brigadier Stuart, commanding the 1st Brigade, to move from Goona westwards and take Chanderi, while he forced his way northwards, and crossing the Betwa, he would then march with both Brigades against Jhansi.

An operation against the passes was more than usually difficult on account of the great length of the line of march. For knowing the danger of a want of ammunition, Sir Hugh Rose took abundant reserves, as well as a convoy of fifteen days' supplies. The pass of Narhat was by far the most difficult, and the enemy, having concluded that the British force must cross it, had increased its natural difficulties by barricading the road with abatis and parapets 15 feet thick, made of large boulders. Passage by the sides of the road was rendered impracticable by the almost precipitous hills, covered with jungle, which descended to it. The Raja of Banpur, who was said to be both enterprising and courageous, defended this pass with 10,000 men.

In the meantime the General directed Major Orr to reconnoitre the passes, while he was detained at Saugor for supplies.

Major Orr's operations.

Major Orr had advanced to Barole with some Hyderabad Cavalry, and on the 18th February received information that a strong party of insurgent Bundelas in the service of the Banpur Raja had advanced from Dhamoni towards Barole and had taken possession of and fortified a post about five miles off. As the country was impracticable for cavalry, and Major Orr had nothing else, he obtained 150 *Barkandazes* from the Customs Police detachment at Bandri, under Mr. Bartie and Mr. Verrier of the Customs Department, and came upon the rebels four miles along the road. They had fortified a ridge, covered with thick jungle, with stone breastworks, beyond a stream which crossed the road. From this they opened a heavy fire on the head of the column, but the infantry, gallantly led by the two Customs officers, carried the position, and killed eight or ten of the enemy, taking two prisoners, who were shot.

Advance of Sir Hugh Rose, 27th February.

Supplies having come into Saugor, Sir Hugh Rose marched on the 27th February, reaching Ranipur the same day, and Rajwas, 4 miles short of Barodia, on the 1st March. Here he was joined by the force under Major Orr, who had collected information which decided the General to select the pass of Madanpur for his point of attack.

The fort of Barodia was taken that afternoon, the village being carried at the point of the bayonet by the 3rd Europeans, who killed fifty of the enemy and took fifty-two prisoners; and the place was then garrisoned by the Gond Levy. A heavy fall of rain prevented a further advance on the 2nd.

Major Scudamore.

2 Troops, 14th Dragoons.
1 Troop, 3rd Light Cavalry.
100 Irregular Cavalry.
1 24-pounder howitzer.
3 Bhopal 9-pounder .
24th Bombay Infantry.

Sir Hugh Rose's Force.
Advanced Guard.
500 Hyderabad Cavalry.
200 Hyderabad Infantry.
4 guns, Artillery.
1 Company, 3rd Bombay Europeans.

In order to deceive the enemy as to his intention, and prevent the Raja of Banpur from coming from the pass of Narhat to the assistance of the Raja of Shahgarh who defended Madanpur, a feint was made against Narhat by the force under Major Scudamore, detailed in the margin, who was sent to the town of Malthone while the real attack was carried out against Madanpur. The remainder of the force under Sir Hugh Rose marched on the 3rd March by a country road, and proceeded without obstacle to Lunia, a mile in advance of which the pass commenced. Up to the verge of the descent the ground was open for some space, but flanked by

N 2

Central.

1 Troop, 14th Dragoons.

Sappers and Miners.

4 guns, Horse Artillery.

Right Wing, 3rd Bombay Europeans.

39-pr. guns, Captain Lightfoot's Battery.

2 5¼-inch Mortars.

1 8-inch Mortar.

1 8-inch Howitzer.

Left wing, 3rd Bombay Europeans.

Siege Train.

3rd Bombay Light Cavalry.

Baggage and Convoy.

Rearguard.

125 Hyderabad Infantry.

1 Howitzer and 1 gun, Horse Artillery.

1 Troop, Her Majesty's 14th Light Dragoons.

50 Hyderabad Cavalry.

hills and thick jungle. The descent is steep through a deep glen, through which the road was rugged, being in the dry bed of the water-course, completely shut in by dense jungle. For close upon a mile after this it becomes more open, entering on the ordinary level of the country, with the village of Madanpur two miles in front on the bank of a tank in which the water flowing down the pass during the monsoon is collected. The road ran round the side of the tank, the left being lined by rocky and precipitous hills. Here opposition was expected.

The hills on the right of the advance to Lunia draw in and circle round so as to form the gorge of the pass, against which Sir Hugh Rose marched on the 3rd March.

Battle of Madanpur Pass, 3rd March.

As the column approached the pass, skirmishers fired on the advanced guard, keeping to the jungle and hill sides, but they were driven back by a party of the Salt Customs under Mr. Bartie. On clearing the village of Lunia, the rebels were seen in great numbers on the hills on the left of the pass. Major Orr's guns opened on them with effect, with round shot and spherical case, and very soon a sharp fire from matchlocks and muskets proved that the enemy were in force in the glen.

At this time the ardour of an excellent officer induced him to make an incautious movement with his guns to his right front, with the view of pouring an enfilading fire into the enemy. But he had not taken into consideration that this movement brought him to within fifty or sixty yards of the edge of the glen, in which lay concealed some hundred sepoys who, before he could unlimber, opened a heavy fire on his guns, which he was unable to depress on them. The sepoys fortunately fired too rapidly, and the officer retired his guns out of range with only a few casualties. The rebels hailed this event with exultant shouts, but their joy was short lived. A hundred of the 3rd Infantry, Hyderabad Contingent, under Captain Sinclair, charged into the glen at the double and drove the insurgents rapidly up the hill on the left. At the same time a movement of the 3rd Europeans was made against their front, and of the Salt Customs, from the extreme right, against their rear. Still further to discomfit them, the General sent a troop of the 14th Dragoons to a knoll quite in rear of the glen, and commanding a view of the lake and the other end of the pass. The rebels were driven with loss from the glen, and, crossing the road, ascended the hill on its left, for the purpose of joining a large body of their comrades who had occupied the hills divided by ravines on the left of the road. The troop of the Horse Artillery would have swept them away with grape had not the officer commanding it mistaken the rebels, on account of similarity of dress, for men of

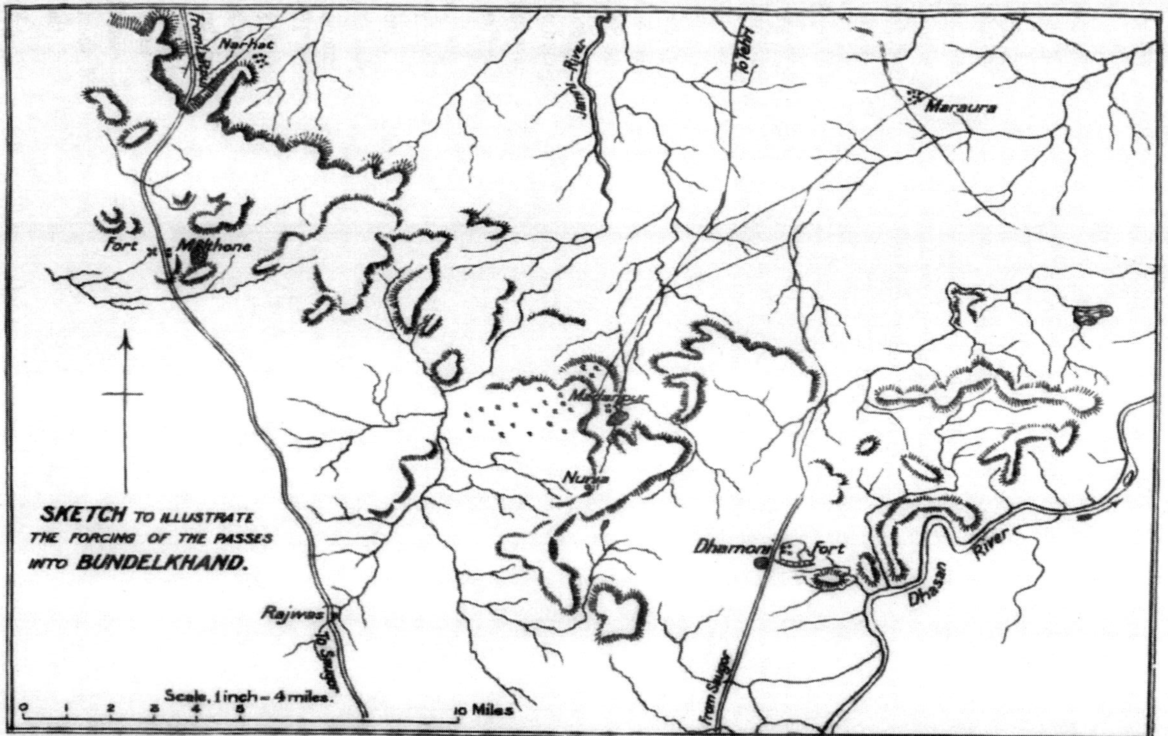

I. B. Topo. Dy. No. 7,075.
Exd. C. J. A., January 1908.

No. 4,244-I., 1908.

the Salt Customs. Not giving the rebels time to breathe, Sir Hugh Rose directed Captain Macdonald, A.Q.M.G., to storm the hill to the left of the road with two companies of the 3rd Europeans. Captain Macdonald conducted them ably up the almost precipitous height, and extending the Grenadier Company from the right, and supporting them with the other company drove the rebels from the first to the second line of hills. As soon as Lieut.-Colonel Liddell came up, with the rest of the 3rd Europeans, he moved up in support of the other two companies, and drove the enemy successively from all the hills commanding the pass.

Captain Abbott, with the 3rd Cavalry, Hyderabad Contingent, then cleared the pass and drove in the enemy's front. The insurgents, repulsed in flank and front, retired to the village of Madanpur, in rear of the end of the lake. The village was fortified by a formidable work, a *bund* of great thickness of solid masonry and earth, which dammed up the lake. The enemy had placed their six guns in rear of the *bund*, and had been firing with them on the 3rd Europeans on the hill.

The pass having been gained, the General sent directions to Brigadier Steuart, who had halted in rear with the reserve and siege train, to advance through it and occupy the head of the lake. As soon as they arrived, fire was opened on the enemy's guns with the 8-inch howitzer and the 9-pounders.

At this time a message was received from the officer commanding the rear-guard that the enemy had fired on the long line of baggage from the range of hills running to the pass of Narhat, and some cavalry were sent to cover the rear-guard. A few rounds drove the rebels from their position in rear of the *bund*, and they retired from Madanpur, through the jungle, towards the fort of Surahi.

Major Orr and Captain Abbott, pursuing along the road through the jungle came up with the rear of the insurgents, consisting principally of the 52nd Bengal Infantry, and killed a number of them, including Lal Tribedi, the Havildar Major, who was the instigator of the mutiny in the regiment, and whom they had made their commanding officer. The enemy's total loss was estimated at three hundred.*

Sir Hugh Rose marched several miles into the open country, and encamped at Piprai, but did not arrive until long after sunset, the troops having commenced moving at 3 A.M. The baggage did not come up until next day. The success at Madanpur had important results. The pass had been occupied by the sepoys of the 52nd and other regiments and by 7,000 picked Bundelas. The sepoys and Bundelas quarrelled, the former declaring that the latter had run away, and left them to fight at the pass, and general mistrust and panic ensued in the rebel camp.

Capture of Surahi and Maraura, 4th March.

The pass of Narhat was turned, although considered impregnable by the rebels, and the British force was placed in rear of the passes. Next day the fort of Surahi, a fortified palace of the Raja of Shahgarh, perfect in architecture, and used as an arsenal for the manufacture of powder and shot, fell

* In his Despatch reporting this action, the General mentioned Lieut.-Colonel Liddell, Major Scudamore, Major Orr, Captains Abbott, Sinclair, and Macdonald, A.Q.M.G., and Mr. Bartie. Dr. Vaughan, Staff Surgeon, was mentioned for having on account of the paucity of officers gallantly led a party of Hyderabad Contingent Infantry, who cleared a difficult position of the enemy.

into the hands of the troops. The following day Sir Hugh Rose took possession of Maraura, an ancient fort with a double line of defences, in an important position on the road from Saugor to Jhansi and from Shahgarh to Malthone. The passes of Narhat and Dhamoni were abandoned, the Shahgarh territory was annexed to the British possessions, and the flag hoisted on the fort of Maraura. The whole country between Saugor and Jhansi, to the east of the river Betwa, which, since the outbreak of the rebellion, had been in the hands of the insurgents, was now with the exception of Tal Bahat restored to Government.

March of the 1st Brigade.

The 1st Brigade was detained at Mhow pending the arrival of the 21st Company, Royal Engineers, a British Battery, and six hundred of the 86th Regiment, and did not march until the 6th February. Meanwhile Major Orr's Force had marched up the Agra road, restored the telegraph wires, and taken part in the operations already described. Brigadier C. S. Stuart now moved against Chanderi, reaching Tonk on the 11th February and Rijwas, 1st March, where Major Orr was detached to co-operate with Sir Hugh Rose in forcing the passes. The siege train joined at Dewas.

As far as Goona the Brigade kept to the Grand Trunk Road, and then marched into Bundelkhand in the direction of Isagarh. Here it was reported that the rebels had mustered strong at Chanderi, and were manufacturing guns and powder in the fort, and that they had determined to oppose the passage of the river near the town. Accordingly the force was directed on Chanderi, an important town lying some 50 miles to the east of Goona.

Chanderi.

Chanderi had been a great city in the time of Akbar, and its fort, manned by the rebels who had sworn to defend it or die in the attempt, was of great strength. The fort was of historic interest. Babar had taken it from Ibrahim of Delhi in 1526, and conferred it on one of his followers. But in 1528, Babar, coveting the place, vowed to wage feudal war against it, and entered it by escalade; the Rajputs, after performing their fearful rite of *juhar* by the massacre of their women and children, rushed naked and desperate on the Musalmans until they were slain to a man.

At a more recent date it had been taken by Sindhia's General, Jean Baptiste Filose, the remains of whose old road for guns up the ridge were still visible.

Advance on Chanderi.

On the 5th March Brigadier Stuart reached Khukwasas, and next day marched on this formidable stronghold, to which the rebels dispersed by Sir Hugh Rose had flocked in large numbers, and encamped at Kursara, a small village six miles short of Chanderi. From this place a reconnoitring party of cavalry was sent on through the dense jungle, warning of its approach being given by fires lighted in the forest by rebels, so that columns of smoke towered in the air every half mile as far as Chanderi itself. The party reached a gorge in sandstone hills, covered with trees and underwood, and were about to emerge from it, having caught a glimpse of the distant fort, and a temple which stood still nearer, when they were received with a volley of musketry; and, having no infantry to clear the jungle, they returned to camp.

Next day, covered by a strong advanced guard under Major Robertson, the Brigade moved forward, and a brisk fire was opened on them when they reached the gorge. But the hill sides were cleared by the infantry, the 86th on the right, and the 25th Bombay Infantry on the left, while barricades which had been placed across the road were removed by the Engineers.

When the troops arrived at the level ground beyond, large numbers of the enemy were seen in the ruined temple and summer houses in front. The Artillery opened with round shot and shell, driving the mutineers into another tract of jungle beyond, from which they were driven still nearer the fort, and took shelter behind a temple, called Fatiabad, and wall of recent construction which extended from one ridge of hills to another opposite, the valley intervening. The wall was loopholed and furnished with bastions twelve or fourteen feet in height and several feet in thickness. The field pieces made no impression on it, and if well held it prevented any advance on the fort and town in that direction. But the infantry rushed on, and the 86th, led by Lieutenant Lewis and Major Keatinge, rushed the wall, jumped into the enclosure and drove out the enemy, who fled to the fort and town, about half a mile distant. The wall was destroyed, and a force, subsequently relieved by some of Sindhia's troops, left in the position, while the remainder of the brigade skirted round a range of hills commanding the fort, and encamped.

Investment of the fort, 7th March.

On the 7th March the troops proceeded to clear the ridge, which was of sandstone, thickly wooded, about a hundred feet in height, with a passage cut through the solid rock, called the Kati Gati. The fort was visible through this tunnel, over which was an inscription stating that Ghaziuddin, King of Delhi, had caused to be made the lofty gate of Gumti and Karauli, near one of the many tanks near the town.

A few of the enemy were killed here and at the small village of Ramnagar at the foot of the hill. From the heights Brigadier Stuart obtained a panoramic view of the country beneath. The fort was of about the same altitude as the ridge, built on an isolated hill, and only separated from the heights by a wide jungle-clad ravine about as broad as the range of a nine-pounder. At first sight it looked almost impregnable, but at one spot a ridge of rock ran across the valley, forming a sort of road. Across this was evidently the vulnerable part, but the fortifications had been strengthened at the spot where the ridge joined the fort hill, by means of two towers and a bastion of solid masonry. This curtain was chosen for breaching.

With great difficulty some siege guns and mortars were got up the ridge, and fire was opened on the palace, which was a prominent feature. But the enemy's guns made good practice, and could not be silenced. It was now necessary to make a road along the crest of the ridge, in order to get the heavy guns into position. The men were much exposed, the trees being the only protection, and much work had to be done at night.

On the 10th March the Artillery and Engineers, with the aid of elephants, dragged up the 24-pounders. The cavalry reconnoitred daily but could not do much as the ground was unsuitable for their action.

On the night of the 10th the enemy made a sally, and captured the wall at Fatiabad from Sindhia's troops, but the place was retaken and occupied by the 25th Bombay Infantry.

An officer who was present wrote :—" The breaching commenced, the range being a very short one and point blank. As the battery was slightly over the eminence, anyone, to approach it, had to run the gauntlet of the enemy's fire. It was evident Chanderi had not been so disturbed for many a year. Most of the trees were of a flowering description, and covered with gorgeous blossoms, while flights of parrots screamed among them, monkeys chattered at the soldiery, an occasional panther was turned out of his lair, and wild duck wheeled overhead. But the sun was fierce and hot, and it was a very thirsty tour of duty in all the batteries, which were five in number. The breaching battery being nearest the fort was the object of the enemy's especial attention, and they kept up an incessant fire on it both from their cannon and small arms. One individual, who possessed a European rifle and had learnt to use it, caused much annoyance and many wounds, and the bullocks bringing up ammunition afforded them excellent marks. They appeared to have an unlimited number of guns and wall-pieces, extending completely round the fortifications. Our shells fell thick and fast into the fort, and did them much damage ; but as it was so large they had plenty of space and shelter to escape from them, and an underground passage down the rock, into the town close beneath, whereby they got both provisions and water, and occasionally stole the baggage animals which had left camp to graze ; on one occasion killed some camp followers when foraging ; and on the night of the 13th they ascended a hill overlooking our camp and fired a regular volley into it, but did us no damage."

In the Royal Battery Lieutenant Moresby* was killed by a round shot which struck his head.

On the night of the 15th Lieutenant Dowker and thirty of the 1st Cavalry, Hyderabad Contingent, arrived with despatches from Sir Hugh Rose, after a long march, losing one man on the way. Next morning the remainder of the 86th Regiment marched into camp, and the same day the breach was reported practicable. Two storming parties were told off, one for the breach under the Brigadier, and the other under Captain Little. The latter was directed to make a false attack in order to lessen the resistance at the breach, but also to enter the fort if possible. This party was to attack opposite the Kati Gati where the rock could be climbed and the wall was not very high. The cavalry was left in charge of the camp, which was struck, as it would have been useless to attempt a pursuit with mounted men in this country.

Under cover of darkness, Captain Keatinge† inspected the breach, passing along the scarp of rock which connected the ridge of hills with the fort. He found the breach practicable, but in the rock a deep trench, some 14 feet in width and depth, had been cut.

* The name of this officer does not appear in Brigadier Stuart's list of casualties.

† Afterwards General Keatinge, V. C.

At 3 A.M. on the 17th the attacking parties formed up, and after a salvo, fired at dawn, the stormers rushed the fort, both parties arriving simultaneously. The enemy's guns were loaded, and they returned the fire, but most of their shot passed over the heads of the assailants. Scaling ladders were thrown across the trench at the base of the breach, and the soldiers dashed into the fort, taking gun after gun, shooting or bayoneting the rebels, or dashing them down the precipice into the ravine below. A magazine exploded and blew up seven of the 86th, but the fort was soon cleared, and then the palace and buildings beyond it. Most of the enemy fled through the town beneath and into the jungle beyond. A number were intercepted and cut up by a force of cavalry under Major Orr on the 18th. This force had gone to Tal Bahat for the purpose on the 12th, and the enemy abandoned the fort there next morning.

Attack on the fort, 17th March.

Flight of the rebels.

The fort was dismantled, and a great number of guns were taken, whilst about a hundred dead were found. On the British side 1 officer and 2 men were killed, 4 officers and 19 men wounded.

A garrison of Sindhia's men was left in the fort. On the 19th the 14th Dragoons marched to join the 2nd Brigade.

Marching in the direction of Jhansi, Sir Hugh Rose with his 2nd Brigade reached Banpur on the 10th. The palace, a very strong and extensive fortified residence, was abandoned by the Raja, and was destroyed. In it was found a complete manufactory for casting guns and mortars, as well as a quantity of clothing belonging to corps that had mutinied. The town was quite empty. The British force marched on to Tal Bahat, which was reached on the 14th, and from there opened communication with the 1st Brigade.

Advance on Jhansi.

Here news was received that the rebels had taken the fort of Barwa Sagar, and were besieging the fort of Orchha, about 30 miles to the north-east. On the 17th Sir Hugh Rose encamped on the left bank of the Betwa river, and on the 19th he reached Chachanpur, 14 miles from Jhansi. The following interesting Abstract of Intelligence is recorded as having been received here by Sir R. Hamilton from one Ganeshi Lal, dated Jhansi, 14th March :—" Bala Bhao Pundit, Dulaju, and Guneshju (Thakurs of Kerwa) in the service of the Rani, who since last month were at Mhow, have returned to Jhansi with two guns and two thousand horse and foot. Jowahir Singh, Killadar of Tal Bahat, with sixty followers, coming back to Jhansi, reported that Tal Bahat was occupied by the British Force. One Harkara came in from the village of Khajurahu in the Pachor District, and reported that the son of the Raja of Narwar with 1,500 men had come to the village of Madeyra and intends going to Tantia Topi, the Nana's Agent. The Kamdars of the Rani sent word that he should proceed to his destination without passing through Jhansi. All the inhabitants of the town wish to get out of it, but the Rani does not allow them to do so, acting upon the Hindi proverb—" A dying leper wishes to have companions." A camelman from Datia came into camp this morning and stated

Intelligence regarding enemy.

that yesterday morning he saw about 200 horse and foot of the Rani of Jhansi at the village of Lohar; asking them what was going on at Jhansi, he was informed that Mardan Singh of Banpur reached Jhansi on the 15th instant. He stated to have seen about 400 horse and foot at the village of Babina. No one on the part of the Rani of Jhansi was seen by the camelman on this side of Babina."

Information reached Government that the rebels had defeated the troops of the Charkhari Raja, taken the town of Charkhari, and burnt half of it, and were besieging the Raja in the fort. Sir Hugh Rose was accordingly directed to operate in that direction if possible; but in consultation with Sir R. Hamilton he decided that it would be inexpedient to turn aside from Jhansi, the direct objective of the campaign.

On the 30th the cavalry, horse artillery, and light field guns of the 2nd Brigade were sent on from Chachanpur to reconnoitre and invest Jhansi, the great stronghold of the rebel power in Central India, held by one of the bitterest enemies of Government, and the scene of one of the most atrocious massacres of the mutiny.

Jhansi.

Next day the General encamped at Simra, and arrived before Jhansi on the 21st. His cavalry had the day before sabred about 100 armed Bundelas who had been summoned by the Rani and were endeavouring to enter the place.

Having no plan, or even correct description of the fortress and city, the General had to make long and repeated reconnaissances, which delayed siege operations for some days. The great strength of the fort, natural as well as artificial, entitles it to a place among fortresses. Its aspect was imposing, standing as it did in bold relief on a hot and inhospitable looking granite plain, from which sprang a few huge hills and bold, woodless crags. The fort stands on an elevated rock, rising out of the plain. It is built of excellent and most massive masonry and commands the city and surrounding country. It is difficult to breach, because composed of granite, its wall varying in thickness from sixteen to twenty feet.

The fort has extensive and elaborate outworks of the same solid construction, with front and flanking embrasures for artillery fire, and loopholes, of which in some places there were five tiers for musketry. Guns placed on the high towers of the fort commanded the surrounding country. One tower, called the "white turret," had lately been raised in height by the rebels, and armed with heavy ordnance. The fortress is surrounded by the city of Jhansi on all sides except the west and part of the south face. The steepness of the rock protects the west, the fortified city wall, with bastions springing from the centre of its south face, running south and ending in a high mound or mamelon, protects by a flanking fire its south face. The mound was fortified by a strong circular bastion for 5 guns, round part of which was drawn a ditch of solid masonry 12 feet deep and 15 feet broad. Numbers of men were always at work in the mound.

The city of Jhansi is about 4½ miles in circumference, and was surrounded by a fortified and massive wall, from 6 to 12 feet thick, and varying in height from

18 to 30 feet, with numerous flanking bastions armed as batteries with ordnance and loopholes with a banquette for infantry.

Outside the walls the city was girt with wood, except some parts of the east and south fronts. On the former was a picturesque lake and water palace; to the south, between the British camp and the city, were the remains of the cantonments. Temples with their gardens, one the Jokan Bagh, the scene of the massacre of the English inhabitants; and two rocky ridges, the eastmost called Kapu Tekri, both important positions, faced and threatened the south face of the city wall and fort. The enemy was visible in great numbers near the ruined bungalows intervening between the camp and city. After the interchange of a few shots, and a show of cavalry and artillery, they retreated into the gardens near their defences and Sir Hugh Rose and his staff proceeded to reconnoitre the position, and drew the fire of most of their batteries.

On the 23rd March the place was thoroughly invested by the cavalry. Seven flying camps of cavalry were established; one large outpost, on the most distant side of the town, was under Major Gall, who had also two nine-pounders; another, opposite the water palace, was commanded by Captain Thompson; Captain Forbes commanded one of the 3rd Bombay Cavalry; and Captains Abbott, Murray, and Clerk those of the Hyderabad Contingent. These camps detached to the front outposts and vedettes, which watched and prevented all issue from the city, day and night, each camp, on any attempt being made to force its line, was to call on the others for help. The road from the city was obstructed by trenches and abatis. Prisoners were taken every night, and one party from Kalpi was captured bringing a convoy of rockets.

Investment and siege of Jhansi, 23rd March.

The 1st Brigade joined on the 25th and encamped about two miles from the other one, and a mile from the fort.

The attack of Jhansi offered serious difficulties. There were no means of breaching the fort except from the south, but the south was flanked by the fortified city wall and mound above described. The rocky ridge was excellent for a breaching battery, except that it was too far off, 640 yards, and the fire from it would have been oblique. The mound enfiladed two walls of the city, and commanded the whole of the south quarter of it, including the palace.

It was evident that the capture of the mound was the first most important operation, because its occupation ensured, in all probability, that of the south of the city, and of the palace, affording also the means of constructing, by approaches, an advanced breaching battery.

It was, therefore, desirable to concentrate a heavy fire on the mound and on the south of the city in order to drive the enemy out of them, and facilitate their capture; to breach the wall close to the mound, and to dismantle the enemy's defences which protected the mound and opposed an attack. This was effected, first, by occupying and placing batteries on a rocky knoll, the right attack, which the General had found during his reconnaissance to the south of the lake opposite the Orchha gate, and south-east wall of the town, which took in reverse the mound and two walls running from it. Secondly, on the rocky ridge the left attack.

"The right attack was always a busy spot, for there were gabions to be made, sand-bags to be filled, furnaces for heating shot requiring constant attention. Advantage was taken of a height hard by to erect a telegraph, which was worked by signal flags, and in case of necessity indicated to the flying outposts, "enemy escaping," "enemy advancing," and, like a weather vane, the direction in which they might be coming or going, and was the signal for officers commanding outposts to "let loose the dogs of war." At night also a shell was despatched into the city every few minutes, which occasionally fired their stacks of hay and forage, causing vast conflagrations, illuminating the city, and there were minor fires and flames resulting from the burning of the dead."

The batteries could not be completed until the arrival of the 1st Brigade and their siege guns on the 25th. In the meantime the right attack opened fire from an 8-inch howitzer and two 8-inch mortars on the rear of the mound and the south of the city. Sir R. Hamilton estimated the numbers of the garrison at 10,000 Bundelas and *Walayatis*, and 1,500 sepoys, of whom 400 were cavalry, and the number of guns in the city and fort at 30 or 40.

The chief of the rebel artillery was a first rate gunner, who had under him two companies of *golandaz*. The manner in which the rebels served their guns, repaired their defences, and reopened fire from batteries and guns repeatedly silenced was remarkable. From some batteries they returned shot for shot. The women were seen working in the batteries and carrying ammunition. The garden battery was fought under the black flag of the Fakirs.

Everything indicated a general and determined resistance, which was not surprising; as the inhabitants from the Rani downwards were more or less concerned in the murder and plunder of the English. There was hardly a house in Jhansi which did not contain some article of English plunder, and politically speaking the rebel confederacy knew well, that if Jhansi, the richest Hindu city and most important fortress in Central India, fell, the cause of the insurgents in this part of India would fall also.

The fire of the right attack opened on the 28th, and on the first day cleared the mound of workmen and the enemy.

The bombardment.

On the 24th the rocky ridge was occupied by Captain G. Hare with a detachment of the Hyderabad Contingent, and two 5½-inch mortars which played on the mound and the houses adjacent to it. On the 25th, the siege train of the 1st Brigade having arrived, batteries were constructed and opened fire from the 26th to the 29th on the rocky ridge as follows, forming the left attack:—Two 18-prs. to dismantle the defences of the fort, two 10-inch mortars to destroy the fort, two 8-inch mortars and one 8-inch howitzer to act on the mound and adjacent wall and city. One 18-pounder to breach the wall near the bastion of the mound, which was thus exposed to a vertical and horizontal fire on its right face and left rear. The 18-pounders were changed from travelling to garrison carriages.

The enemy had thirteen batteries, all of which were named by the general to avoid confusion.

The fire of the two 18-pounders was so effective that towards sunset the parapets of the white turret, the black tower, and the tree tower, which faced the attack, were nearly destroyed. The two 10-inch mortars created great havoc in the fort, and a powder magazine was blown up on the third shot.

The breaching gun, so solid was the wall and so hard the masonry, did not make a practicable breach until the 30th. The enemy retrenched the breach with a double row of palisades filled with earth, on which fire was directed with red hot shot, and part of the stockade was destroyed. Riflemen to fire at the parapets, embrasures, and loopholes were placed in all the batteries, with sand-bag loopholes, and posts of riflemen were distributed in the temples and garden of the east and south side of the city, while the Jokan Bagh was occupied by a picquet of rifles. All these caused numerous casualties among the rebels in the town as well as in the parapets.

Two of the enemy's defences, which annoyed the left attack the most, were the wheel tower on the south and the garden battery on a rock in rear of the west wall of the city. To silence the former a new battery called the Kapu Tekri or East Battery was established on a ridge to the east of the rocky ridge, with two 5½-inch mortars, which, not proving sufficient, had two 8-inch mortars and a 9-pounder substituted for them. A 24-pounder howitzer was afterwards added to enfilade the wall running eastwards from the mound.

Before the sand-bag battery could be made for the 9-pounder, acting Bombardier Brenna, quite a lad, commanded and pointed the 9-pounder in the open, silenced the enemy's gun in battery in the bastion, besides destroying its defences. The General praised him for his good service on the ground and promoted him.

The two 8-inch mortars, and occasionally the two 10-inch mortars of the left attack, answered the garden battery, shelling also the Naya Basti, and five wells where the sepoys had taken up their quarters on account of the good water. After the capture of Jhansi the havoc caused by the shelling and cannonade was seen in the city, and the rebels acknowledged to have had from sixty to seventy men a day killed.

By the 30th the defences of the fort and city were dismantled or their guns disabled. The rebels had made on the white turret an excellent parapet of large sand-bags, which they kept always wet, and still ran up fresh in lieu of disabled guns; but their best guns had been disabled and their best artillerymen killed; their fire was therefore no longer serious. However, the obstinate defence of the enemy, the breach, and the extent fired on, had caused a great consumption of ammunition, so much so that it was evident there would not be sufficient to multiply breaches in the town wall, or to establish a main breach in the south double wall of the fort.

It was accordingly determined to assault the place by escalade, at the same time making use of the breach, upon which and the adjoining houses a heavy fire was directed day and night, in order to prevent the enemy from working. Lieutenant Strutt, Bombay Artillery, meanwhile made excellent practice, throwing shells on to the spots occupied by the guards of the city walls.

Advance of Tantia Topi, 30th March.

Arrangements had been made for the assault, when the besiegers were threatened with a fresh danger. Tantia Topi,* a relation and Agent of the Nana, had collected and organised a large body of troops in the neighbourhood of Mau and Nowgong in Bundelkhand, which was called "The Army of the Peshwa," and displayed the standard of that obsolete authority. After the fall of Charkhari, where he had captured 24 guns and 3 lakhs of rupees, Tantia, at the urgent request of the Rani, marched against the British camp before Jhansi at the head of 22,000 men, including five or six regiments of the Gwalior Contingent and 28 guns. On March 30th Sir Hugh Rose received information that the main body of this army had arrived at Barwa Sagar, about three miles from the Betwa, with the object of crossing the river during the night and attacking him next morning.

In the hope of forcing the enemy to engage with the river in his rear, the British General left the park and heavy baggage of the 2nd Brigade, with which he was, with the 1st Brigade, and marched at 9 P.M., from Jhansi to the village of Bapoba, six miles off, which commands the two fords of Rajpur and Kolwa by which the enemy coming from Barwa Sagar must cross the Betwa.

At Bapoba he received reports from the two outposts which he had sent to watch the ford, that they had seen and heard nothing of the enemy. A similar report being made next morning, he came to the conclusion that the insurgents would not cross the river while the British were so close to it, and that nothing would be more likely to encourage them to do so than a retrograde movement, which they would construe into a retreat. He, therefore, returned to camp, leaving the outposts to watch the fords. The ruse was successful, and the same day the enemy crossed the Rajpur (upper) ford in great numbers, preceded by an advanced guard of *Walayatis*, and after sunset took up a position in order of battle opposite the rear of the camp of the 2nd Brigade. At sunset they lit an immense bonfire on a rising ground on the hither side of the Betwa, as a signal to Jhansi; it was answered by salvos from all the batteries of the fort and city and shouts of joy from their defenders.

It was evident that the enemy sought a battle. This confidence was explained afterwards by prisoners, who stated that Tantia Topi had been informed by his spies that nearly the whole British force was scattered and engaged in the siege and investment, and that he could easily destroy the few who guarded the camp.

Disposition of the British army.

Jhansi had proved so strong and the ground to be watched by cavalry was so extensive that the force had enough to do in investing the place. But the General relied on

* In November 1857 General Windham had suffered a reverse near Cawnpore in action with the Gwalior Contingent under Tantia Topi, who was afterwards driven across the Jumna by Sir Colin Campbell.

the spirit of British soldiers, which rises with difficulties and which no dangers can appal, and resolved, whilst he fought a general action, to relax neither the siege nor the investment. It was a resolution worthy of a great commander and of the soldiers whom he led.

The detail of troops at his disposal showed how weak he was compared with the enemy. On the first news of their approach he had sent Major Orr with a party of his cavalry along the road to the Betwa to watch their movements. Sir Hugh Rose drew up his force across the road from the Betwa, half a mile from camp. On the right flank of his first line, the 2nd Brigade, he placed the Hyderabad Contingent Cavalry under Lieutenant Clerk, a troop of the 14th Light Dragoons and 4 guns, Horse Artillery; in the centre, detachments of the 24th Bombay Infantry and 3rd Europeans, 3 heavy guns and detachment, Hyderabad Contingent Infantry; and the left flank, Captain Lightfoot's Battery and two troops, 14th Light Dragoons.

16th Light Field guns.		
14th Dragoons	.. 243	rank and file.
Hyderabad Cavalry	207	"
86th Regiment	.. 208	"
3rd Europeans	.. 226	"
24th Regiment, N.I.,	298	"
Siege guns	.. 3	"

The second line was in contiguous columns at quarter distance, a weak troop, 14th Light Dragoons, on the right, and Hyderabad Cavalry on the left flank; in the centre the 86th Regiment, Captain Woolcombe's Battery of 6-pounders, and Captain Ommaney's Battery of 9-pounders, and detachment of the 25th Bombay Infantry.

He threw out strong picquets and lines of vedettes of the 14th Light Dragoons and Hyderabad Contingent Cavalry well to the front and flanks. During the night the rebel outposts called out that they were very numerous and the British very few, and that in the morning they would finish them off. In consequence of the lateness of the enemy's advance, and the distance of the 1st Brigade, the British force was not in position until long after dark. The silent regularity with which the assembly was carried out did credit to the discipline of the troops. The opposing forces slept opposite each other upon their arms.

A little after midnight a sowar galloped in from the Kolwar ford, and reported that the enemy were crossing in great numbers. The General had expected this move, the object of which was to turn his left flank and force a way along the Bangaon road, through Major Scudamore's flying camp, into Jhansi.

Brigadier Stuart was at once detached with the 1st Brigade, along the road to Bangaon, 8 miles from Jhansi, close to the Betwa river, from whence he could oppose and outflank the enemy who had crossed by the ford above Bangaon.

The departure of this Brigade left Sir Hugh Rose without a second line, so he was constrained to form this from detachments of the 24th Bombay Infantry, drawn from the first line. Knowing well that the best way of making up for numerical inferiority is by a determined attack on the enemy's weak point, the British General had intended to commence the attack at daylight, advance in line, pour in the fire

1st Brigade.
Brigadier Stuart.
14th Dragoons, 40 rank and file.
H. C. Cavalry, 107 sabres.
2 guns, Col. Ommaney's Baty.
Captain Woolcombe's Battery.
86th Regiment, 208 rank and file.
5th Bombay Infantry.

of all his guns, and then turn and double up the hostile left. But before daybreak the enemy advanced, covered by a cloud of skirmishers. The picquets and vedettes retired steadily, closing to each flank in order to unmask the guns. Before the British line was uncovered, the enemy took ground to his right. Sir Hugh Rose conformed to prevent his left being outflanked, but very cautiously, lest the enemy should draw him away too much to the left, and then fall on his right flank. This was probably his intention, for a body of horse was seen towards his right. He halted and fronted; the enemy did the same, and immediately opened a very heavy artillery, musketry, and matchlock fire from the whole of his front, to which the British batteries steadily replied.

Battle of Betwa River, 31st March.

The rebels had taken up an excellent position, a little in rear of a rising ground, which made it difficult to bring an effective fire on him. The General ordered the front line of his infantry to lie down, the Troop of Horse Artillery (the Eagle Troop) to take ground diagonally to the right, and enfilade the enemy's left flank. In this movement a round shot broke the wheel of a Horse Artillery gun, a mishap which gave the enemy courage, and which they greeted with cheers. Captain Lightfoot took up an advanced position to his left front, which made the fire of his battery much more effective.

While the rebels were suffering from the fire of the troop and battery, the General directed Captain Prettijohn, 14th Dragoons, to charge the enemy's right with his troop, supported by Captain MacMahon of the same regiment, while he himself headed a charge against their left with Captain Need's troop of the 14th Dragoons, and a strong troop of the Hyderabad Cavalry. To the charge headed by the General were opposed the enemy's best troops, sepoys and *Walayatis*, who, throwing themselves back on the right and resting the flanks of their new line, four or five deep, on two rocky knolls, received the charge with a heavy fire of musketry. Breaking through this dense line, which flung itself among the rocks and bringing their right shoulders forward, the cavalry took the first line in reverse and routed it. The rebels were hurled back on the Betwa in confusion by this irresistible attack, which was followed up by a general advance of the whole line, when the retreat became a rout.

The whole of the artillery and cavalry moved forward in pursuit, the Horse Artillery following the road to the Betwa, from which it had enfiladed the enemy's position, the Field Battery going across country. Occasionally the bravest of the rebels rallied and fought in groups to the last, taking the best advantage of the ground. One body wedged themsleves so dexterously into the banks of a nullah that neither musketry nor artillery fire could destroy them. Lieutenant Armstrong, 3rd Europeans, coming up with a few skirmishers, dashed at them and bayonetted them all. The further the enemy were pursued, the thinner and fewer they became, until at last only little groups and fugitives dotted the plain. Six guns with their wagons were abandoned in the flight.

Pursuit of the rebels.

The pursuit had now penetrated and cleared away the first line. A cloud of dust about a mile and a half to the right pointed out the line of re treat of another large body, the second line of the rebels, which was under Tantia Topi, and must have been three miles in rear of the first line. The whole force pursued, and came up with the skirmishers in rocky and difficult ground, covering the retreat of the second line. Driven in, they closed to the right, and uncovered the main body which commanded the troops in pursuit with an 18-pounder, an 8-inch mortar, and other guns. Colonel Turnbull answered with a few rounds. Captain Lightfoot who had come up, thinking that he could bring his guns to ground from which he could enfilade the enemy's left, was directed to join the cavalry which had been sent to turn the enemy's left and take their guns. But the insurgents did not await this attack, and retired precipitately by the high road to the Rajpur ford, firing the jungle to try and check their pursuers. But the mounted troops galloped through the burning forest. Once on the road, guns and cavalry galloped without a check until they came within gunshot of the village of Rajpur, where the enemy made their last stand.

The Troop of Horse Artillery and the Field Battery, advantageously placed on two eminences, crossed their fire on the enemy, who rapidly left this, but kept up a heavy fire of musketry, and with a 12-pounder from the opposite bank; the 12-pounder, hit by a round shot, retired disabled. Two troops of the 14th Dragoons and the Hyderabad Contingent Cavalry now crossed the river, which was crowded with the enemy's artillery, ordnance park, and quantities of stores, the 18-pounder and the 8-inch mortar, drawn by two elephants, ammunition wagons, and carts full of ammunition, of the Gwalior Contingent. The rebels kept up a heavy fire on the cavalry as it was crossing the ford, but the men pressed on, ascended the steep bank on the other side, and, surmounting all opposition, sabred such of the insurgents as still held their ground. Parties were sent in pursuit, aud all the guns, eighteen in number, and two standards were captured.

In crossing the river Captain Need was surrounded by the enemy, and received nine sword-cuts on his horse and trappings, but no wounds. He was rescued from his perilous situation by Lieutenant Leith, 14th Dragoons, who received the Victoria Cross for his gallant action.

Meanwhile the 1st Brigade under Brigadier Stuart, having found no enemy at or near Bangaon, was marched back towards the sound of the battle, the cavalry being sent on ahead. After about an hour's march, some fugitives were observed on the left front and were pursued and cut up by a detachment of the 14th Dragoons. The Brigade now approached the village of Kushabir, and found that a large body of all arms of the enemy, upwards of two thousand in number, were prepared to oppose their progress, having placed guns in position in and about the village.

Movements of the 1st Brigade.

Brigadier Stuart advanced with his infantry in skirmishing order, his cavalry on either flank, and his guns on the main road until within about 600 yards of the enemy's position; effective fire was then opened by the artillery, and the moment the guns ceased firing the skirmishers of the 86th and 25th dashed forward, carried the village at the point of the bayonet, capturing all the enemy's six guns and their ammunition. The line then steadily advanced, driving the rebels over some difficult ground in rear of the village, until a second village was reached, on the outskirts of which they made another stand, but were immediately dislodged by the 86th. They then retired in a compact body covered by a strong rear-guard. Two elephants and some camels were captured, and about 250 of the enemy killed by the 1st Brigade, which had been under arms 36 hours.

Horses and men being completely exhausted by the incessant marching and fighting of the last 48 hours, and being nine miles from Jhansi, Sir Hugh Rose marched the troops back to camp. In his report of the action he brought "to the favourable notice of the Commander-in-Chief, the conduct of the force under his command, which, without relaxing in the very least the arduous siege and investment of a very strong and fortified city, garrisoned by 10,000 desperate men, fought, with the few numbers left in camp, a grand action with a relieving army; beat and pursued them nine miles, killing 1,500 of them, and taking from them all their artillery, stores, and ammunition." Many officers were mentioned in the despatch.* The casualties in the battle of Betwa river numbered 15 killed and 66 wounded (4 mortally).

Assault on the city, 3rd April.

The arrangements made for the assault on the 30th March were interrupted by the advance of Tantia Topi, the scattered remnants of whose army now fled to Kalpi; but the enterprise was only delayed for 48 hours. During the battle the besieged had redoubled their fire, and poured forth volleys of musketry which appeared to menace a sortie. But the defeat of Tantia's army, while it inspired the besiegers with fresh ardour, diminished to a corresponding extent the spirits of the besieged.

On the 2nd April all necessary preparations had been made for the attack. A 24-pounder howitzer had been placed in front of the Jokan Bagh for the purpose of enfilading and clearing during the night the wall from the mound to the fort and the rocket bastion which was on it. A division order was issued for the assault of the defences of the city wall, of which a copy, with a plan of attack, was furnished to the officers in command.

The attack of the 1st Brigade.

The assaulting columns were formed up at daybreak on the 3rd April, that of the 1st Brigade ready to move on two points which had been indicated, the breach at the mound and the rocket tower and low curtain immediately to the right of it. Led by Lieutenant Colonel Lowth, 86th Regiment, and Major Stuart of the same corps, both parties moved on the given signal, under a heavy fire from the enemy.

*Lieutenant Fox, Madras Sappers and Miners, killed eight men with his own hand, Lieutenant Hastings Fraser killed three of the enemy, and were mentioned in despatches. The following were also mentioned:—Brigadier Stuart, Lieutenant-Colonel Turnbull, Captain Lightfoot, Captain Need, Lieutenant Leith (recommended for V. C.); Lieutenant Armstrong, 86th; Lieutenant Prendergast, Madras Sappers and Miners; Major Orr, Captain Prettijohn, Captain Hare, Lieutenant Haggard, Lieutenant-Colonel Lowth, Lieutenant Cochrane, 86th, who had three horses shot under him; Lieutenant Mills, 25th Bombay Infantry; Sergeant Gardener, 14th Dragoons, who killed a cavalry soldier and two armed men on foot; Ressaidars Sikander Ali Beg, 3rd Cavalry, H. C., and Allauddin Khan, 1st Cavalry, H. C. Sir Hugh Rose also mentioned his staff officers.

The stormers forced the breach and drove the enemy before them at all points, while at the same time Major Stuart's party escaladed the rocket tower. The stormers were led by Lieutenant Jerome,* and the first man up the ladders was Lieutenant Dartnell,† who jumped down among the defenders and received several severe sword cuts before Lieutenant Fowler and others of his comrades could come to his assistance. On gaining the town, Lieutenant-Colonel Lowth moved part of his force to the right, and thus took the enemy in flank and rear when they were meeting the right attack of the 2nd Brigade with great vigour. In the streets and at the palace, to which the column was led, the insurgents offered a desperate resistance, each room in the palace being contested to the last. During these operations several officers were wounded, and Surgeon Stock was shot dead while nobly and courageously attending the wounded under a hot fire. After an entrance into the city had been effected a number of rebels were found to have taken refuge in the recesses of a large well, the only approach to which was by steep and narrow stairs, having a sharp turning at which one resolute man could have kept off any number. While measures were being arranged for seizing these rebels, Havildar Shaikh Daoud, 25th Bombay Infantry, volunteered to capture them, and fixing his bayonet he boldly descended the well, and, followed by others, brought up thirteen of the enemy.

The 2nd Brigade, right attack.

The 2nd Brigade at the same signal (which was given by a small detachment under Major Gall, who made a false attack on the west wall) moved to the assault in two columns. The left column led by Captain Robinson, 3rd Europeans, the right by Lieutenant-Colonel Liddell, advanced with great steadiness through a very heavy fire of musketry and wall pieces, described by Lowe as a "sheet of fire out of which burst a storm of bullets, round shot, and rockets destined for our annihilation." The advance of this column is best described by an officer who accompanied it—"All being ready, the signal was waited for in breathless anxiety. We fancied there was some little delay in it, for it began to get light. The columns had some way to go from the right attack, and the enemy must have been aware of their approach, for they had manned the ramparts, and opened a murderous fire, but nothing could exceed the ardour of the stormers, cheering as they rushed forward across a field and then down a road; but here the Sappers began to fall thick and fast, while the roaring of the enemy's fort guns became something terrific and for a moment, to gain breath, the party take advantage of the shelter of some ruins. Another dash and the walls are reached, and up go the ladders amid a hail of bullets, rockets, and huge stones, and every possible description of missile. Up go three ladders; Lieutenants Dick, Meiklejohn, and Fox are on the rampart, but alas! the crush of men to follow breaks the ladders." Left on the wall, Meiklejohn jumped into the mass of insurgents below, and, fighting to the last, was cut to pieces. Dick, pierced by shot and bayonets, fell dying from the wall; and Fox was shot through the neck.

* Afterwards Colonel Jerome, V.C.

† Afterwards Major-General Sir John Dartnell, K.C.B., C.M.G., who served with distinction in the War in South Africa, 1900-1901.

Repulsed at this point, owing to the ladders breaking or being too short, the party was doubled round to the breach to the left, where an entry was effected and the ramparts were sufficiently cleared to enable the remainder to mount by the ladders unopposed. Meanwhile, Lieutenant-Colonel Liddell, finding his ladders of no use, ordered Lieutenant Goodfellow,* Bombay Engineers, to try a bag of powder at a postern, but from being built up inside, no entry could be effected. However, by this time Captain Robinson had made good his lodgment, and was followed by the right column, when all proceeded in the direction of the palace and there joined the remainder of the force.

Fall of Jhansi.

The right and left attacks being now concentrated in the palace, Sir Hugh Rose gained possession of a large portion of the city by advancing the 3rd Europeans to the north-east, and occupying the Bargaon gate, on which he rested their right flank, forming an oblique line from the gate to the palace with the 3rd Europeans and the 86th in the palace, the two regiments occupying with picquets the commanding houses to their front. This line was a prolongation of the second line leading from the mound under the front to the palace. This done, it was necessary to clear the large portion of the city in rear of this oblique line of the numerous armed rebels who remained in the houses and who were firing on the troops. This was not effected without bloody, often hand-to-hand combats. One of the most remarkable encounters was between detachments of the 86th Regiment and the 3rd Europeans and thirty or forty *Walayati* sowars, the Body-Guard of the Rani, in the palace stables under fire of the fort. The sowars, full of *bhang*, defended their stables, firing with matchlocks and pistols from the windows and loopholes, and cutting with their swords from behind the doors. When driven in they retreated behind their houses, still firing or fighting with their swords in both hands until they were shot or bayoneted, struggling to strike again even when dying on the ground. A party of them remained in a room off the stables which was on fire until they were half burnt; their clothes in flames they rushed out hacking at their assailants, and guarding their heads with their shields.

All the sowars were killed. The gallant soldiers captured in the quarters of the sowars the Rani's standards, three standards of the body-guard, three kettle drums and an English Union Jack of silk which Lord William Bentinck had given to the grandfather of the Rani's husband, with permission to have it carried before him as a reward for his fidelity. The soldiers hoisted on the palace the flag of their country which they had so bravely won. Captain Sandwith, who was wounded, commanded the 3rd Europeans on this occasion, and Sergeant Brown of the Commissariat Department was the first to dash boldly into the stables.

Numerous incidents marked the desperate feeling which animated the defenders. A retainer of the Rani attempted to blow up himself and his wife; failing in the attempt, he cut her to pieces and then killed himself. Two *Walayatis*

*Afterwards General Goodfellow, V.C.

attacked by the vedettes threw a woman who was with them into a well and then jumped down it themselves.

Retribution Hill.

While engaged in the town Sir Hugh Rose received a report from the Officer Commanding one of the Hyderabad Cavalry Camps that a large body of the enemy flying from the town had tried to force his picquet at about 3 P.M., but that the main body, some 400 strong, had been driven back, and had occupied a high and rocky hill about 600 yards to the west of the fort; and that he had surrounded the hill with cavalry and awaited reinforcements. He immediately ordered out from the camps all available troops of all arms, consisting of Woolcombe's battery, some companies of the 24th Bombay Infantry and Hyderabad Contingent, and a few dragoons. The rebels were surrounded and shelled, while many lay down on their powder-flasks and blew themselves up. Finally the infantry went up and cleared the hill with the bayonet, killing practically the whole of the insurgents on this place, which was henceforth known as Retribution Hill. In this attack Lieutenant Park, 24th Bombay Infantry, was killed whilst gallantly leading a party of his men along the ridge of the hill, and about a dozen men were killed and wounded. The Rani's father, Mamu Sahib, was among the rebels; he was wounded on the hill, and captured some days afterwards and hanged in the Jokan Bagh.

Next day Sir Hugh Rose and Brigadier Stuart occupied the rest of the city by a combined movement, assisted by Major Gall, who scaled the bastion at the Unao gate from his flying camp, captured a gun there, and threw it down the rampart.

Flight and pursuit of the Rani.

The following morning a wounded Mahratta retainer of the Rani stated that she had fled that night from the fort, accompanied by 300 *Walayatis* and 25 sowars; and that after leaving the fort they had been headed back by one of the picquets, where the Rani and her party separated, she herself taking to the right with a few sowars in the direction of her intended flight to Bhander. The observatory also telegraphed "enemy escaping to the north-east." Strong parties of cavalry were at once sent in pursuit, with guns to support them, as it was said that Tantia Topi had sent a force to meet her. Brigadier Steuart, with cavalry, was sent to watch the fords of the Betwa.

In sight of Bhander, 21 miles from Jhansi, the cavalry came in sight of the Irregular Horse sent to meet the Rani, which separated, probably with a view to mislead her pursuers as to her real course. Lieutenant Dowker, Hyderabad Contingent Cavalry, was sent by Captain Forbes through the town of Bhander, whilst he with the 3rd Bombay Cavalry and 14th Dragoons passed it by the left. In the town Lieutenant Dowker saw traces of the Rani's hasty flight and her tent in

* General H. C. Dowker, C.B, informed the present writer that he received a severe wound and would have been almost cut in half, but that the blow was turned by the revolver on his hip.

which was an unfinished breakfast. On the other side of the town he came up with and cut up forty of the enemy, consisting of Rohillas and Bengal Irregular Cavalry. Lieutenant Dowker was gaining fast on the Rani, who with four attendants was seen escaping on a grey horse, when he was dismounted by a severe wound and forced to give up the pursuit.

Final resistance of the rebels and capture of the Fort.*

From the time the troops took the palace, the rebels lost heart and began to leave the town and fort. Nothing could prove more the efficiency of the investment than the number of them cut up by the picquets of the flying camps; the woods, gardens, and roads round the town were strewn with the corpses of fugitive rebels. The Rani's flight was the signal for a general retreat. Early in the morning the General caused the outskirts of the city to be scoured by cavalry and infantry; and a party of the 14th Dragoons alone killed 200 in one patrol. The rebels, who were chiefly *Walayatis* and Pathans, sold their lives as dearly as they could, fighting to the last with their usual dexterity and firmness. A band of forty of these desperadoes barricaded themselves in a spacious house with a courtyard and vaults in a suburb called the Naya Basti, which was attacked by a party of Hyderabad Contingent Infantry under Captain Hare. Captain Sinclair was here killed, and the house was battered to pieces with siege artillery, but the rebels still fought in the vaults until all were destroyed.

In his despatch Sir Hugh Rose brought to notice the conduct of the troops under his command. "They had to contend against an enemy more than double their numbers behind formidable fortifications, who defended themselves afterwards from house to house in a spacious city, often under the fire of the fort, afterwards in suburbs and in very difficult ground outside the walls. The investing cavalry force were day and night for 17 days on arduous duty, the men not taking off their clothes, the horses saddled and bridled up at night. The nature of the defence and strictness of the investment gave rise to continued and fierce combats, for the rebels having no hope sought to sell their lives as dearly as they could. But the discipline and gallant spirit of the troops enabled them to overcome difficulties and opposition of every sort, to take the fortified city of Jhansi by storm, subduing the strongest fortress in Central India, and killing 5,000 of its rebel garrison . . . . ."

"The Commander-in-Chief will learn with pleasure that the troops under my command treated with great humanity the women and children of Jhansi; neither the desperate resistance of the rebels nor the recollections of Jhansi of last year could make them forget that in an English soldier's eyes women and children are spared; so far from hurting, the troops were seen sharing their

* In the fort was found a great deal of property of the murdered Europeans, including books, writing desks, ladies' work-boxes, apparel of both sexes, and the toys of the innocent children who had not been spared by the assassins.

rations with them. I gave orders also that the destitute women and children of Jhansi should be fed out of the prize grain."*

The casualties during the siege amounted to 38 killed and 181 wounded, of whom 22 subsequently died.

Twenty-six guns were taken in the town and nine in the fort.

* In his despatch the General mentioned many officers:—Brigadiers Stuart, and Steuart, C.B.; Lieutenant-Colonel Lowth, 86th; Lieutenant-Colonel Liddell, 3rd Europeans; Major Scudamore, 14th Dragoons; Major Orr; Major Forbes, C.B., Commanding 3rd Bombay Cavalry; Major Robertson, 25th Bombay Infantry; Captains Lightfoot and Woolcombe, Artillery; Captain Fenwick, R.E.; Captain Hare, 5th Infantry, Hyderabad Contingent; Captain Brown, Madras Sappers and Miners; Lieutenant Goodfellow, Bombay Sappers and Miners; Lieutenant Lowry, R.A.

Captain Wood, A.A.G.; Captain Macdonald, A.Q.M.G.; Major Boileau, C.R.E.; Captain Ommaney, C.R.A.; Lieutenant Haggard, Commissary of Ordnance; Doctors Arnott and Vaughan; Captain Rose, A.D.C.; Lieutenant Lyster, Interpreter; Major Stuart, Lieutenants Dartnell, Fowler, and Jerome, Ensign Sewell, 86th Regiment; Lieutenant Webber, R.E.: Captains Todd and Coley, Brigade-Majors; Captains Bacon and Lecky, D.A.Q.M.G.'s; Captains Sandwith and Robinson; Lieutenant Parks, Ensign Newport, 3rd Europeans; Lieutenant Fox, Madras Sappers and Miners; Lieutenant Bonus, Bombay Engineers.

Of these officers Lieutenant Jerome assisted by Private Burns, 86th, carried Ensign Sewell, who was wounded, to a place of safety, under a murderous fire. They were awarded the Victoria Cross.

Many lower ranks were also mentioned for gallant conduct, including Corporal Hard and Privates Rogers and Archibald, Drummond and Doran, 3rd Europeans, who fought gallantly at the head of the ladders until they gave way; Ensign Newport, Corporal Hard, and Private Gillman, 3rd Europeans, carried off the body of Lieutenant Fox through the hottest fire.

CHAPTER VIII.

SIR HUGH ROSE'S CAMPAIGN IN CENTRAL INDIA—(contd..)

Movements of Majors Orr and Gall.

While Sir Hugh Rose was detained at Jhansi by the necessity of protecting it against the Kotah rebels and the late Chanderi garrison, who made an incursion on the road from Jhansi to Goona, he sent Major Orr across the Betwa to clear the village of Mau, on the road from Jhansi to Charkhari, where rebels were said to have re-assembled, with orders to proceed northwards to Gursarai, the chief of which district was an ally. From him Major Orr was to gain all possible information, and move against Kotra, an important ford said to be occupied by the rebels.

Major Gall.
1 Squadron, 14th Dragoons.
3rd Cavalry, Hyderabad Contingent.
3 Guns, Bombay Artillery.

He was to co-operate with Major Gall, who had been sent along the road from Jhansi to Kalpi, with the force detailed in the margin, to gain information respecting the enemy, as to whose numbers and movements the most conflicting reports were current. The General's intention was to pick up these two forces when he moved from Jhansi. He wished to clear Kotra and the line of the Betwa because he apprehended that the Rajas of Banpur and Shahgarh would either hurry on and annoy his right flank or rear as he advanced on Kalpi, or double back across the Betwa and again create trouble and disorder in the north of Bundelkhand.

Major Orr found no enemy in Mau, but between Gursarai and the Betwa he came upon a fort occupied by the rebels, some of whom escaped, while 40 surrendered, with 3 guns. He found that Kotra was garrisoned by friendly Gursarai troops. Major Orr marched to the fort of Erich, across the Betwa to the west of Kotra, and entered into communication with Major Gall, who advanced as far as Punch, 14 miles from Kunch, and ascertained that the enemy in force in that town intended to oppose the advance to Kalpi.

Major Gall, in order better to observe the enemy, had a Jemadar's party of Hyderabad Contingent Cavalry at Lohari, a village and mud fort about 8 miles north-west of Punch, garrisoned by some 70 or 80 men of the Raja of Samthar, who was said to be an ally. These men betrayed the cavalry to the rebel cavalry in Kunch in the basest manner, but the Contingent sowars cut their way through their assailants with the loss of one man killed, all their baggage, and three or four camp-followers.

March of Sir Hugh Rose, 25th April.
Garrison left at Jhansi.
Lieutenant-Colonel Liddell.
Wing, 3rd Europeans.
Wing, 24th Bombay Infantry.
Wing, 3rd Bombay Cavalry.
100 Hybad. Congent. Caly.
½ C. B. S. and M.
3 Guns, Bhopal Contingent.

Leaving a small garrison at Jhansi, Sir Hugh Rose marched at midnight on the 25th April with the 1st Brigade, directing the 2nd Brigade to follow two days later. Jhansi was now protected from attack by the Kotah rebels by the advance of Major-General Roberts with the Rajputana Field Force.*

The hot weather had now set in, and the troops suffered severely in consequence. The country they marched through was flat and without vegetation. The dust was several inches thick on the roads, and the heat during the day obliged the troops to march at night. Many of the soldiers who slept during the time the sun shone never woke again and were found dead. The further the column marched the scarcer became the water, which was now only found in small round wells at a very great depth, while it was lukewarm and often had a brackish flavour.

Capture of Lohari, 2nd May.
4 Guns, Royal Artillery.
1 Squadron, 14th Dragoons.
100 Sabres, Hyderabad Contingent.
Left wing, 3rd Europeans.
Left wing, 25th B. I.
20th Bombay Sappers.

On the 1st May the 1st Brigade reached Punch, and was joined by Major Gall's force, and on the 5th the 2nd Brigade, which had been reinforced two days earlier by the 71st Highlanders,† also arrived. On his arrival at Punch Sir Hugh Rose sent Major Gall, with the troops detailed in the margin, to punish the garrison of Lohari, who, it turned out, were in great part sepoys of the 12th Bengal Infantry.

Major Gall marched at 2 A.M. on the 2nd May. The cavalry rapidly pushed forward and completed an investment of the place soon after day-break, the main body halting on the plain to the east of the fort and within cannon shot, at half-past-six. In passing Sirsa, Major Gall sent a party of the Hyderabad Cavalry under a Duffadar towards Kulliah, on his right, reported to be occupied by the enemy, with orders to watch any hostile movement that might be made from that quarter. On arrival, Major Gall rode through the village up to the wall of the fort, and summoned Manowar Singh, the *killadar*, to surrender; the latter eventually came out with a small retinue, and gave up his sword. He appeared to have no command over the garrison.

The skirmishers now advanced through the village, until on the right and left they had reached some low mud enclosures beyond which was an open space between it and the fort, about 150 yards in extent. Two guns were placed on the Khullia road, and a howitzer and one gun opposite a guard house that stood outside and on the east side of the fort. The fort and village are situated on an extensive level plain, the village being separated from the fort by the open space above referred to. The little fort was square, built of mud and sunburnt bricks, flanked by round towers at the corners, with a ditch and a second line of works outside the ditch; the length of the interior side was about a hundred

* See page 200.

† It is interesting to note that the 71st wore a loose holland blouse and overalls of khaki colour, and a light shako-shaped hat with cover and curtain of the same colour.

yards. A company of the 3rd Europeans crossed the open space between the village and the fort and established themselves in the guard house, close to the ditch. Two of the fort gates were opened by Lieutenant Armstrong, 3rd Europeans; they were undefended, the garrison having retired and taken post behind a third gate, which was closed.

The enemy still refusing to surrender, Major Gall directed Captain Field, R. A., to open fire with two 9-pounders and a 24-pounder howitzer, on a building at the summit, and fire was continued on various parts of the wall when the enemy appeared in any numbers. To this they replied with matchlocks, and a 9-pounder brass gun that fired grape and round shot alternately upon the dragoons in the plain and all who came near a well, commanded by the bastion on which it stood.

The walls were difficult to escalade, so it was decided to blow in the gate, and Lieutenant Bonus of the Bombay Engineers found a pair of forge below, in a gunsmith's shop in the village, which were charged with 50 lb of gunpowder obtained from the Artillery.

Twenty-five files of the 3rd Europeans under Lieutenants Armstrong and Donne and Ensign Newport were told off as a storming party; and an equal number of the 25th Bombay Infantry under Lieutenant Rose formed a support. The gate was blown in, and the stormers rushed through the smoke and met the enemy hand-to-hand at a fourth gateway, at right angles to the third, and from which a very narrow curved passage, with a seven foot wall on either side, led to the place where the garrison was assembled and from which they rushed yelling sword in hand and firing matchlocks. A desperate combat commenced, and as the stormers advanced, they were assailed by a shower of stones and brickbats from above as well as by men who cut and stabbed and shot at them from the walls on either side as they passed. The enemy were giving way when a burning cloth full of loose powder was dropped from above into the midst of the crowded stormers, who, thrown into some confusion, fell back to avoid the explosion. The enemy, following up their advantage, came close up to the bayonets of the Europeans and dealt sword-cuts at them, but were repulsed. Again advance and retreat were made under precisely similar circumstances.

A third time Lieutenant Donne and Ensign Newport led their men into the midst of the enemy with daring valour, and were severely wounded, but beat off their assailants.

Lieutenant Rose now arrived, and the fight was continued in the narrow lane until with a shout and charge the Europeans and some of the 25th broke and drove the enemy before them along an uncovered way passing round the walls of the fort; but at less than fifty yards behind the first corner, the fugitives rallied behind two trees, and, firing their matchlocks, again advanced. A bloody *mêlée* took place beneath the trees, and on this spot ten of the garrison were killed. The remnant, now reduced to some 25, fled; some vainly sought refuge in a mud guard-house below the south wall, some in the interior of the place itself, but were followed up and killed. A last stand was made by a few desperate men to the immediate left of the gateway near which the conflict had commenced, and here the last man fell. Fifty-seven bodies were counted within the gateways of the fort; and all who endeavoured to get away were cut down by the dragoons outside or shot down by the infantry. Not a man escaped. There were several indications of the presence of sepoys among the garrison; a European drum and bugle were found in the fort and many brass cap plates of the 12th Bengal Infantry, which had mutinied at Jhansi; also some red coatees with yellow facings. Lieutenants Armstrong, Donne, and Rose, and Ensign Newport were wounded; one man of the 3rd Europeans was killed and 15 were wounded, and the 25th Bombay Infantry had four men wounded.

Movements of the insurgents.

After the fall of Jhansi the Rani and Tantia Topi fled to Kalpi, arriving there the same day. The rebel force there was commanded by Rao Sahib, a nephew of the Nana, to whom the Rani appealed for "an army, that she might go and fight." The garrison, consisting of some regiments of the Bengal Army, and of the Gwalior Contingent Cavalry from Kotah, the levies of rebel Rajas, and the remains of the Jhansi garrison, was accordingly assembled, and marched to Kunch under Tantia Topi and the Rani. Here they threw up intrenchments, which they armed to defend the road from Jhansi, and to make a vigorous opposition to the advance against Kalpi. Kunch is an open town difficult to attack, as it is surrounded by woods, gardens, and temples with high walls round them.

Action at Kotra.

Major Orr had been directed to do his utmost to prevent the Rajas of Banpur and Shahgarh from crossing the Betwa and doubling back southwards. For the purpose of carrying out this very manœuvre the Rajas separated from the rebels at Kunch, and drove the troops of the Raja of Gursarai, who held Kotra, commanding a ford across the Betwa, to the south bank of the river.

Major Orr crossed the Betwa, engaged the Rajas, drove them from their position at Kotra, and took one of their guns. But it was impossible to cut off the retreat of the Rajas who, while Major Orr was attacking one part of their force, retired precipitately with the remainder some distance down the river, where they crossed at a ford and took the road southwards, carriage and supplies being furnished them by the treacherous Raja of Jigni. Major Orr, who was in camp at Ait, was then directed to march on Kunch.

Battle of Kunch, 7th May.

In order to turn the flank and defences of the rebels, and as the excessive heat rendered it* advisable that he should not undertake a long operation or a siege, Sir Hugh Rose made a flank march with his whole force to the north-west. The force marched

* There were on this day 46 cases of sunstroke, 14 of them fatal. An officer who was present wrote:—"The heat at daybreak was intense, and the mirage most remarkable. The whole of the surrounding country was dried up and covered with light brown soil, and perfectly flat, yet it appeared one beautiful lake of water, and the few trees assumed the appearance of gigantic height; and when Major Orr's force approached, so distorted was it that we could not tell whether it was friend or foe The horses appeared twenty feet high, and riders in proportion, and the heated air ascending made them tremulous and crooked."

Sir Hugh Rose suffered much from the sun, and was obliged to dismount for a time and seek shade, when he was attended by Dr. Vaughan, and subsequently resumed his duties.

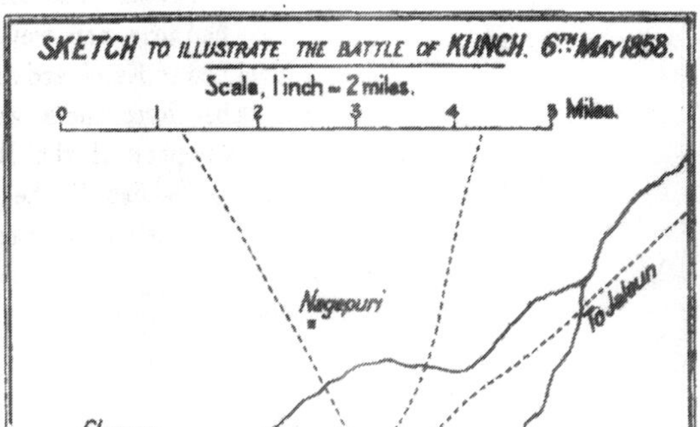

I. B. Topo. Dy. No. 7,078.
Exd. C. J. A., January 1908.

No. 4,242-I., 1908.

at 10 P.M. on the 6th May, the left, the 1st Brigade, resting its left flank on the village of Nagepura; the centre, the 2nd Brigade, under Brigadier Steuart, in the village of Chamer; the right, Major Orr's force, in front of the village of Umri.

This position threatened seriously the enemy's line of retreat to Kalpi; and the north-west of the town, which was not protected by intrenchments, was exposed to attack. The three columns were directed to effect a lodgment in the town as soon as they had taken up their positions. When the force arrived within sight of Kunch, vedettes and strong picquets of the enemy's cavalry were perceived outside the wood. They conformed to the flank movement and posted themselves nearly opposite Nagepura. A few rounds of shrapnel from Captain Lightfoot's guns emptied some of their saddles and they disappeared in the wood. The rebel infantry now showed in force behind a long wall to the front, and in the wood to the left of it.

The 1st Brigade had marched a distance of 14 miles from Lohari that morning for the purpose of surprising the enemy by the flank movement, and not giving them time to alter their plan of defence. So, to rest and refresh the men, the General ordered their dinners to be cooked for them, and in the meantime battered the wall with the two 18-pounders and the 8-inch howitzer. The half troop of Horse Artillery, advancing diagonally to their left, shelled the infantry to the left of the wall; and the enemy in return shelled the troop and the siege guns from a battery to the right; but this was soon silenced by two guns which were turned on it

Lieutenant-Colonel Gall now bravely galloped into the wood to reconnoitre, accompanied by Lieutenant Arbuthnot, Royal Artillery. The enemy, although he was in easy musket range of them, did not fire at him, because the shelling from the Horse Artillery had caused confusion in their ranks; he ascertained that the infantry to the left had retreated further into the wood, having in their rear a large body of cavalry; that the siege guns had driven the enemy from the cover of the wall, but that some way in rear of it was posted a large body of infantry with elephants.

Sir Hugh Rose determined to drive the enemy out of the wood, gardens, and temples, which surround Kunch, and then to storm the town, including a dilapidated mud fort, on which the rebels' red flag was flying, on a rising ground, a strong position which was opposite to the right of the 1st Brigade. Once in possession of this position in the town, the enemy in front and to the left would be cut off from their comrades in the intrenchments on the right, who would be forced to retreat to the plain on the other side of the town, pressed by the 2nd Brigade and Major Orr's Force, the 1st Brigade passing through the town and pressing the enemy with whom they had been engaged.

This operation was effected by throwing the left wing of the 86th Regiment, under Major Stuart, and the whole of the 25th Bombay Infantry, under Lieutenant-Colonel Robertson, into skirmishing order, the 86th on the left, the 25th on the right, their flanks, supported by the half Troop, Horse Artillery, and a troop of the 14th Dragoons; and Captain Ommaney's Battery and two troops, 14th

Dragoons. Captain Woolcombe's Battery, a troop of Dragoons, and the right wing of the 86th were left in a second line in reserve under command of Lieutenant-Colonel Lowth.

The rapidity and precision with which this formation was made must have surprised the sepoys. The 25th skirmishers charged into the wood, temples, and walled gardens, and occupied them under a fire of musketry and artillery from the Battery on the British right, which re-opened its fire; but the sepoys took the guns, and thus an important position was gallantly gained.

Capture of the town and fort.

The 86th, covered by the three Horse Artillery guns, under Captain Lightfoot and the troop, 14th Dragoons, made a circuit to their left, took all the obstacles to their front, and then bringing their left shoulders forward, advanced, despite the artillery and musketry fire, through the whole north part of the town, and took the fort.

Just as the General, with the 86th and 25th, was about to enter the town, a large number of rebel infantry, strongly posted in cultivated ground, was observed threatening the line of the right attack of the 1st Brigade. Captain Field's Battery with Captains Thompson's and Gordon's troops of the 14th Dragoons and a troop of the 3rd Cavalry, Hyderabad Contingent, were ordered up to dislodge them. But the enemy held their position obstinately and they did not retreat until a portion of the infantry of the 2nd Brigade moved down upon them from another direction; the Cavalry then charged and broke the mass, cutting up several of them, while clumps of trees favoured the escape of the remainder. The 2nd Brigade, owing, to some misconception, did not enter the town, but moving round to the south of it, their artillery and cavalry joined in the pursuit.

Meanwhile Major Orr had moved from the village of Umri direct upon Kunch. In his immediate front were some gardens and walled enclosures held in force by the enemy, from which a heavy fire was directed upon his line. The Artillery under captain Douglas advanced, and his fire having silenced that of the enemy, the 5th Infantry quickly drove them from the gardens and enclosures. At the same time the whole of the Hyderabad Contingent Cavalry moved to the right, charged the enemy's horsemen, who had the whole time been threatening that flank, and drove them from the field on to the line of their infantry supports, which occupied several deep ravines and broken ground from which they opened a heavy fire. The cavalry were subsequently joined by a squadron, 14th Dragoons, and two Horse Artillery guns under Major Scudamore, and retained possession of their ground until the general advance, when they joined in the pursuit.

Major Orr's movements.

The Artillery of the Hyderabad Contingent had meanwhile advanced so far as to arrive within range of the enemy's guns, which opened on it from two Batteries with round shot, shell, and shrapnel, causing several casualties. The rebel infantry was also strongly reinforced and suddenly came forward with a rush in great numbers and forced back the infantry holding the garden. Major Orr was about to advance once more at this point, when he learnt that the 1st

Brigade had forced the town and fort. The whole of his force now advance, the enemy was driven from the enclosures, and joining in the retreat of the main body, proceeded in the direction of the Orai Road.

The pursuit.

The whole of the cavalry of the Force, a Troop of Horse Artillery, Captain Field's guns, and No. 18 Light Field Battery now took up the pursuit, the infantry being too exhausted to co-operate.

The enemy commenced their retreat across the plain with resolution and intelligence. The line of skirmishers fought well to protect the retreat of the main body, observing the rules of Light Infantry drill. When charged they threw aside their muskets and fought desperately with their swords.* The pursuit was commenced by Captain McManus with a squadron and a troop (Blyth's) 14th Dragoons charging, the first the right and the latter the left of the enemy's skirmishers. A piece of very heavy plough caused a check in the pace, of Captain McManus' squadron, which was exposed to a heavy fire. But the squadron got through and the enemy, fighting fiercely to the last, was cut to pieces. Captain McManus received three sabre wounds, but continued the pursuit. In the centre the Horse Artillery opened a hot fire on the skirmishers. The enemy now threw back the extreme right of their skirmishers so as to enfilade the line of pursuit. But Captain Prettijohn formed to the left, and charged and cut off this enfilading line. Captain Blyth, 14th Dragoons, and Captain Abbott, 3rd Cavalry, Hyderabad Contingent, each gallantly charged and captured a gun under heavy fire, and other guns were taken in the course of the pursuit. Lieutenant Lyster, Interpreter on the Staff, sent with an order to the cavalry, came across a group of some thirty sepoys, but cut his way through them, single-handed.

Dispersal of the insurgents.

The greater part of the enemy's line of skirmishers being killed, the remainder driven in, and the rebel artillery captured, the main body lost their nerve and crowded into the road to Kalpi, a helpless column of runaways. The Horse Artillery and Cavalry were now

* An officer who was present wrote:—"Each of the rebels was provided with a Government musket, belt, and cartouch box, in capital order, and well provided with cartridges. After firing, down went the musket and out came the sharp-cutting native sword. They cut and slashed our horses and men so long as one of their band remained alive. I counted thirty-six regular sepoys lying dead at that spot. To show the force with which they cut with their native swords, it is only necessary to instance Line Sergeant Wilson, who had his bridle arm completely severed above the elbow, and on another occasion the thigh of a Gond was cut through at one blow. On the other hand, I have seen the blunt sword of a dragoon bound off the skull instead of cleaving it; while on the same day a native cut off part of a dragoon's foot, shoe, sole, and all! I have seen a dragoon cut a man across the face with sufficient force to slice the top of his head off, yet he scarcely cut through the cheek bones. But in spite of all this inferiority of arms, exhausted and almost dying as half the force was, we drove them before us on the Orai road, killed five hundred, and took nine guns and a quantity of ammunition. Captain Abbott led his men on with his usual praiseworthy valour, and showed that in a pursuit no weapon equals the spear. In this action nothing could have been more praiseworthy than the valour displayed by the sepoys of the late Bengal Army, and nothing more disgraceful than the behaviour of the cavalry, who, in every fight I saw, distinguished themselves signally by cowardice! Tantia Topi's order book was found subsequently at Kalpi, and the last order in it expressed his thanks to the spirit of bravery which animated his men at Kunch.

so beaten by sun and fatigue that they were reduced to a walk; the guns were only able to rake the column in its depth with round shot and shell, but could not approach sufficiently close to give it grape. The cavalry on their part had only strength to reach the numerous stragglers who could not keep up with the enemy's main body. On reaching some wood and broken ground about a village seven or eight miles from Kunch, profiting by this cover, they sought safety from attack by breaking into scattered flight across country.

The scorching rays of the sun and the pace at which they retreated told even on the sepoys; several fell dead on the road, struck by apoplexy; many, exhausted, threw away their arms, whilst others, to quench their thirst, rushed to the wells, regardless of the cavalry. But the sun, fatigue, and scarcity of water told still more on the British cavalry and artillery, who had been marching or engaged for sixteen hours. At the village where the enemy dispersed a halt was called; and the horses having been watered, the force was marched back to Kunch at sunset.

The enemy must have lost five or six hundred men in the action and pursuit, and the 52nd Bengal Infantry, which covered the retreat, was almost destroyed. Nine guns and quantities of good English ammunition and stores, furnished to the late Gwalior Contingent, were taken.

The British loss amounted to 1 officer and 7 men killed; 2 officers and 43 men wounded; the cases of sunstroke amounted to 2 officers and 43 men; 12 of the 71st alone died from this cause.*

The defeat at Kunch gave rise to animosities and distrust in the rebel army.

Effects of the British victory.

The infantry sepoys accused their brother mutineers of the cavalry of having pusillanimously abandoned them; and all three arms brought the same charge against their General, Tantia Topi, who had disappeared at Kunch as rapidly as he had done at the Betwa, leaving to its fate, at the most critical moment, the force which he had called into existence under the pompous title of the "Army of the Peshwa."

The *Walayatis* also were charged with not having exhibited at Kunch the stern courage on which they prided themselves. They were accused of having left the field too soon; and their excuse that they had felt it their duty to escort the Rani of Jhansi to a place of safety was not accepted. It was said that the destruction of the *Walayatis* at Jhansi had made their countrymen less anxious than usual to try the fate of war.

These various causes created confusion in the councils of the Kalpi mutineers, and the immediate British advance caused a panic among the sepoys at that place, as well as those retreating towards it, and it was said that at one time there

* Mentioned in Despatches:—Captain Macdonald, A. Q. M. G.; Captain H. H. A. Wood, A.A.G.; Captain Cockburn; Lieutenant Baigrie, A. Q. M. G., who was severely wounded, but continued to perform his duties Lieutenant Lyster, Interpreter; Doctors Arnott and Vaughan; Captains Fenwick, Coley, Bacon; Lieutenant Henry, Staff Surgeon Mackenzie; Major Gall; Captains Abbott, Light-foot, Field, R. A.; Lieutenants Strutt, Bombay Artillery, Edwards, Engineers, Gossett, R. E.; Lieutenant-Colonel Lowth; Major Robertson; Captains Todd and Locky; Captains Douglas, H. C. Artillery; Hare, Murray; Lieutenants Dowker, Macquoid, Dun, Fraser, Westmacott, Hyderabad Contingent.

were only eleven sepoys in the town and fort. But the unexpected arrival of the Nawab of Banda* with a large force of good cavalry mutineers, some guns, and infantry, and his energetic exertions, backed up by those of the Rani of Jhansi, produced one of those sudden changes from despair to confidence which mark the Indian character.

The rebels at Kalpi.

Their leaders again exhorted the sepoys, as the General learnt from an intercepted letter, "to hold to the last Kalpi, their only arsenal, and to win their right to paradise by exterminating the infidel English." The rebels returned to Kalpi, re-occupying the strong positions in the labyrinth of ravines which surround it, and the intrenchments which they had thrown up and armed to arrest the British advance a few miles in front of the Chaurasi (84) temples, which are two or three miles from Kalpi. They had already cut deep trenches across the road near the intrenchments, and in several other places, which were serious obstacles, because the ravines on each side of the road made it very difficult to turn them. When driven out of the intrenchments, the rebels could fall back on the eighty-four temples, built, as well as the walls round them, of most solid masonry, the net work of ravines afforded them a third; the town of Kalpi a fourth; another chain of ravines between the town and the fort a fifth; and finally the fort, a sixth and last line of defence.

The fort of Kalpi is wretched as a fortification, but as a position it is unusually strong, being protected on all sides by ravines; to its front by five lines of defence and to its rear by the Jumna, from which rises the precipitous rock on which it stands.

In a Despatch, dated Gwalior, the 22nd June 1858, Sir Hugh Rose details the difficulties with which he had to contend in the advance on Kalpi, as follows:—"It is my duty, in justice to the unvarying devotion and discipline of the troops under my command, to state the new and very serious difficulties which beset them after leaving Jhansi. They had to contend not only against the rebel army, fighting as usual with all the advantages on their side of very superior numbers and knowledge of the ground, but they had to encounter a new antagonist, a Bengal sun at its maximum of heat. This formidable ally of the rebel cause was more dangerous than the rebels themselves; its summer blaze made havoc amongst troops, especially Europeans, who, already exhausted by months of over-fatigue and want of sleep by continuous night-watching and night-marches, were often exposed to its rays, manœuvring or fighting as at Kunch, from sunrise to sunset. At Kunch the thermometer was 115°; before Kalpi 118° in the shade, and on the march to Gwalior it burst in an officer's tent at 130°.

Difficulties with which the General and army had to contend.

Her Majesty's 71st Highland Light Infantry, less inured than any other corps to the sun, because it had just arrived in India, suffered the most from it. Besides

* The Nawab retreated to Kalpi after his defeat at Banda by General Whitlock on the 19th April.

Kalpi was besieged and taken by a British force in 1803.

the twelve men of a weak wing of this regiment killed in the ranks by the sun at Kunch, a great many more had to go into the Field Hospital sick from sunstroke and the whole wing was more or less affected by it.

The number of officers and men on the sick list, all of whom had to be carried on the march in doolies, increased with each day's operations, and in proportion as I was deprived of fighting men, the difficulties of taking care of the sick and transporting them in continued marches increased. Whilst my force suffered so much from sunstroke, they were deprived in a great measure of its antidote —water. Between Jhansi and Kalpi we found no streams ; all was well water ; the wells, which are neither numerous nor abundant, being of extraordinary depth as we approached the Jumna, which increased the difficulties of obtaining water. Forage was as scant as water.

The scarcity of these two essentials hurt the efficiency of the cavalry and the transport at the very time that they were both urgently required—the first against the rebel cavalry, whose numbers and organisation made them unusually enterprising ; and the latter for the numerous and daily increasing sick.

The scarcity of water had another disadvantage ; it prevented concentration of my force, when the strength of the enemy and my difficulties rendered it necessary, for a rapid advance against Kalpi. The Enfield rifles had made up a good deal for my inferiority in numbers ; that advantage, however, no longer existed. The heat and other causes had had such an effect on the ammunition of the rifles that, their loading becoming difficult, and their fire uncertain, the men lost confidence in their arms.*

The above were some of the military disadvantages of my position. They were increased by political causes. The inhabitants of the valley of the Jumna were the most disaffected my force had yet met with. They had been under rebel rule and had never felt the influence of British power since the commencement of the insurrection. Every village had its one or two Mahratta *Pundits*, who had made a most successful propaganda in favour of Nana Sahib as Peshwa. The villagers did good service to the rebels, betraying to them our *dâks* and movements as well as some carts, when their drivers, on account of the exhausted state of their cattle, could not keep their place in the column, or sought water at a distance from the road.

The rebels had another great source of strength. They fought their best because they were defending Kalpi, their best fortified stronghold in Central and Western India, and only arsenal full of warlike stores and ammunition. Kalpi, on the right bank of the Jumna in the hands of the rebels, prevented the concentration of the British armies in the west with those in the east of India ; exposed to attack, from the line of the Jumna, the army engaged in operations against the insurgents in the Doab, the line of the Ganges, Oudh, and Rohilkhand ; and so long as Kalpi was rebel, so long had it in their power to say that

* An officer present at the Battle of Kunch wrote :—"The 3rd Europeans seemed much more annoyed by their useless Enfield rifles than by the sun. No amount of force exerted by the men would drive the bullets down to the breech of their weapons."

the east and west of India might be British, but that the pivot of its centre was theirs.

Whilst so many drawbacks weakened me the enemy, physically speaking, was unusually strong. They were under three leaders of considerable influence, Rao Sahib, a nephew of Nana Sahib, the Nawab of Banda, and the Rani of Jhansi. The high descent of the Rani, her unbounded liberality to her troops and retainers, and her fortitude, which no reverses could shake, rendered her an influential and dangerous adversary. The rebel army was composed of the Gwalior Contingent, the finest men, best drilled and organised native troops of all arms in India; other mutinous Bengal Infantry regiments, such as the 52nd; rebel cavalry from Kotah, and a chosen band of *Walayatis*; the whole reinforced by the force of all arms of the Nawab of Banda, comprising a great deal of mutinous Bengal Cavalry, of which the 5th Irregulars, dressed in their red uniforms, formed a part. All the sepoy regiments kept up carefully their English equipments and organisation; the words of command for drill, grand rounds, etc., were given, as we could hear at night, in English."

March on Kalpi.

At 2 A.M. on the 9th May Sir Hugh Rose marched with his first Brigade, intending to follow up the enemy and attack him as rapidly as possible, while still suffering from the defeat at Kunch. The enemy abandoned the fort of Hardoi, one march from Kunch, and its chief, an influential adherent of Nana Sahib, surrendered. But a further advance was prevented by the detention of the 2nd Brigade, which was unable to march from Kunch until the 11th owing to a storm of rain having made the tents too heavy for transport.

The General's instructions were to take Kalpi. He was subsequently directed to make his appearance at some point on the right bank of the Jumna, to enter into communication with Lieutenant-Colonel Maxwell, commanding a column of the Bengal Army, who was to co-operate with him for the purpose of supplying ammunition for the siege of Kalpi, to make good the large amount expended at Chanderi and Jhansi. He had written to Colonel Maxwell that he would be on the Jumna, a few miles below Kalpi, on the 14th May; this letter never reached its destination. Communications were hazardous and only effected by spies in disguise, who conveyed letters in the soles of their sandals or in quills in their mouths.*

On account of the want of water, Sir Hugh Rose was unable to concentrate his force against the defences before Kalpi. He determined, therefore, to turn them, to break off to the right from the high road from Orai to Kalpi, march to the Jumna to the village of Golauli, about five miles below Kalpi, effect a communication from thence with Lieutenant-Colonel Maxwell, and then, his right resting on the Jumna, and covered by the flank fire of Colonel Maxwell's batteries, and riflemen from the other side of the river, advance up the right

* The enemy also had their spies, and one of these, disguised as one of the cavalry, was detected in camp and hanged on the 13th May.

bank against Kalpi. The fort of Kalpi and the part of the town facing his advance was to be well shelled before his attack.

The Jumna is fordable at Golauli; which stands in the nullah running down to the Jumna, just outside the dangerous labyrinth of ravines surrounding Kalpi.

The march to Golauli was, with the exception of a few bad and unbridged *nalas*, over a table-land, from which, during the monsoon, the waters run into the ravines.

To mislead the enemy and mask this movement the 2nd Brigade was ordered to close up to Orai* from Kunch, and following the high road to Kalpi, take up a position at the village of Bandha. This plan was foiled by the Brigade losing its way, and instead of going on from Orai to Bandha, making a double march and following the General to Sakhali. Their long exposure to the sun in this protracted march caused a great many casualties, and the general prostration of the Brigade; Brigadier Steuart and the whole of his staff forming part of the sick list.

It was important to keep the appointment with Colonel Maxwell to be on the Jumna on the 14th, but the 2nd Brigade was not in a condition to co-operate, and, weak as it was, it would have been hazardous to go too far away from it; for the enemy, aware of these difficulties, had concentrated their forces in the villages round Kalpi for the purpose of harassing the British, part of their tactics being to force the troops to exposure to the sun, which they knew was fatal to Europeans, at the hottest time of day

Sir Hugh Rose consequently delayed one day at Itaura to give the 2nd Brigade a rest at Sakhali, detaching all his carriage for the sick to their assistance, and calling off the attention of the enemy from them by a diversion in another direction.

The two Brigades were concentrated without molestation on the night of the 14th. A few hours later Sir Hugh marched with the 1st Brigade and Major Orr's force for Golauli, which was reached with no other opposition than an attack on the baggage by the rebel cavalry concealed in a ravine. They were put to flight by a troop of the 14th Dragoons which had reinforced the rear-guard in anticipation of an ambuscade. In this march the high road from Jalalpur to Kalpi was crossed. Major Orr was directed to drive in a strong picquet of the enemy posted on this road in the direction of Kalpi; to halt afterwards on the road; cover the march of the rear-guard to Golauli; and then encamp at the village of Tehri near the road, for the purpose of watching it and keeping up communication with the 2nd Brigade, and assisting it in its march during the night of the 15th to Deopura, a village near Tehri. On his arrival at Golauli Sir Hugh despatched two sowars to Colonel Maxwell, who was about thirty miles off on the other side of the Jumna, requesting him to move up the river immediately. He also ordered two pontoon rafts, which he had brought with great

*At Orai a luxury was found in the shape of a tank of muddy water. Previous to the mutiny two companies of Bengal Infantry were stationed here, and three European bungalows were found in ruins.

trouble from Poona, to be floated on the Jumna by sunset, for communication with Colonel Maxwell and transport of the ammunition. The rebels had destroyed or taken to Kalpi all the boats on the river.

One of the most important objects of Sir Hugh Rose's instructions had now been attained. His force had marched from Bombay to the Jumna and had effected a union with the Bengal Army; the immediate result of which was a combined operation of Bengal and Bombay troops towards Kalpi.

The advanced-guard and centre of the 2nd Brigade reached Deopura without opposition on the morning of the 15th; but its rear-guard under Major Forbes,

Rear-guard action, 15th May.

which had been strongly reinforced, had hardly left Itaura when it was vigorously attacked by about 1,000 or 1,200 cavalry, besides three or four thousand infantry and guns.* About a mile from Itaura a broad and deep ravine, only passable for carts by one narrow road, intersects the route. While halted here on account of the baggage, Major Forbes first saw the rebels approaching from the Kalpi direction towards his left flank. They took up a position on his left rear and rear, occupying the village of Itaura, and from their strength, particularly in cavalry, it was apparent that the bold front shown by the rear-guard, assisted by the Hyderabad Contingent Field Force under Major Orr, alone saved them from being driven in. During the two hours or more that the rear-guard was halted, the enemy's cavalry made several advances, one or two at a rapid pace, but, deceived by the steadiness of the troops into supposing that a larger force was concealed in the broken ground, they did not charge. As soon as the road was clear, Major Forbes withdrew first the guns and infantry to the further side of the ravine, and lastly the cavalry retired first at a walk, and then at a gallop when concealed by the ground.

The enemy at once occupied the position that had been vacated, but their advance was for some time checked by the rifles of the 3rd Europeans, and the excellent practice of two guns of the Royal Artillery, until the baggage had got to a considerable distance. For the first three miles of the remainder of the march the rear-guard was almost surrounded by the rebel cavalry, and was fired into by their artillery, but alternately halting and retiring, they succeeded in preserving the baggage, which was brought in safety to Deopura.

Having received at Golauli a report that Major Forbes was hard pressed, and hearing a heavy cannonade in his direction, Sir Hugh Rose marched to his

½ Troop, B. H. A.
1 Troop, 14th Dragoons.
1 Troop, H. C. Cavalry.
3 Guns, No. 4 L. F. B.
38th and 25th Regiments, N. I.

assistance with the troops detailed in the margin. The urgency of the case alone induced him to undertake this operation as he foresaw that a large portion of the force must be struck down by the heat of the sun. He galloped on and found that Major Forbes had reached Deopura, but that the enemy, baffled in their attempt to

* These were heavy guns, drawn by elephants. The cavalry were dressed in the uniform of regiments that had mutinied. More conspicuous than all were those dressed in red and others in light grey; some were in green *alkhaliks* and a few in yellow.

cut off the rear-guard, had taken ground to the left, and reinforced by three or four battalions from Kalpi, who were now swarming out of the ravines, were preparing, firing heavily, to storm the village of Matra, which Lieutenant-Colonel Campbell had judiciously occupied from Deopura. If the enemy possessed Matra the camp at Deopura would no longer have been tenable. A large body of cavalry, deployed across the road from Itaura to Matra, was approaching to support the infantry. The officer commanding in Matra was so hard pressed that he had given orders to evacuate the village, and the enemy were pressing forward.

The General at once gave orders to the troops that were retiring to reoccupy the village, and hold it at any price, ordering up in their support at a trot the artillery and cavalry, with two companies of Hyderabad Contingent Infantry and the 25th Bombay Infantry.

Captain Lightfoot placed the artillery skilfully on the left of Matra; the accurate fire of their shrapnel and round shot broke the rebel cavalry and drove them from their position in support of the infantry, which still held the deep and tortuous ravines in front of Matra. Captain Douglas, commanding the Hyderabad Contingent Artillery, was then directed to post four 6-pounders on the right of Matra, and burst shrapnel just over the heads of the rebels in the ravines; this he did with his usual skill and devotion under a heavy fire of the enemy's riflemen so effectually that the rebels, who were suffering from the admirable fire of the 71st who still had some of the better sort of ammunition, retired from their ambuscades, the main body down the ravines, and a few across country to Kalpi, the 71st making killing practice at the latter at 700 or 800 yards.

The General did not pursue, because fresh exertion in the sun and in most difficult ground would have been fatal to men, the greater part of whom had been marching all night, and engaged all day in fearful heat. His game was a waiting one, and he abstained carefully from playing that of his adversary, which was to disorganise and prostrate his force by continued exposure to the sun. He never yielded an inch to the enemy's attacks, but on the other hand husbanded the health and strength of his men for one great battle for Kalpi.

As it was, upwards of 200 out of 400 men of the 25th Bombay Infantry fell out of the ranks on the line of march, struck by the sun. This gallant regiment suffered as much as Europeans from sun, the constitutions of the men having been weakened by scurvy. Having provided for the protection of Matra, the General returned with the detachments of the 1st Brigade to Golauli.

The enemy on the same day, hoping to prevent support being given to the 2nd Brigade, or to beat the 1st Brigade, weakened by the reinforcement taken from it, strengthened their lines of outposts in the ravines, and supporting them with guns and masses at a distance, menaced and kept up a heavy fire on the position at Golauli from the Jumna to the village of Tehri, advancing against the latter place with a thick chain of skirmishers.

Brigadier Stuart, commanding the 1st Brigade at Golauli, and Captain Hare, commanding at Tehri, met the attack with vigour; the former answered the enemy's cannonade so effectually with mortars and guns that they retired

Captain Hare, repulsed the enemy's advance, and following them up, took a grove of trees in advance of his position, in which they had concentrated in force. The enemy having shown signs of fortifying a high ridge opposite the right front of the position, about half way between Golauli and Kalpi, Sir Hugh Rose had a battery of two 8-inch mortars constructed in front of his right, which shelled with good effect the ridge and the ravines near it.

Next day, the 17th May, at 2 P.M., upwards of 200 of the enemy's cavalry with 3 guns moved suddenly out from the rear of a large village about two or three miles on the left flank of the 2nd Brigade at Deopura, and advanced with the evident intention of attacking the camp.

The small village of Matra, forming the left point of appui, was then occupied by two companies of the 71st and two guns, No. 18 Bombay Light Battery, with a support from the 24th Bombay Infantry. Colonel Campbell* immediately reinforced the post with the whole of the 71st and the remaining two guns of No. 18 Battery, and giving orders for the 14th Light Dragoons and two guns of the Royal Artillery to follow, proceeded at once to meet the enemy, taking with him the 3rd Bombay Cavalry and the half battery which he met on their way to Matra.

He found the insurgents advancing rapidly in line, about a mile and a half off, and so widely extended as to threaten the left rear. The enemy was soon brought to a halt, and a heavy fire commenced on both sides, but the guns quickly stopped their further advance.

An attack on Matra now drew attention, but here the rebels were beaten off by the 71st under Majors Rich and Loftus. Another column of infantry and guns came down from Kalpi on the right of the camp, but were kept at a distance by the artillery and infantry. The whole of the enemy withdrew at sunset.

On this day a mortar battery was thrown up in front of the 86th lines of the 1st Brigade to shell the ravines towards Kalpi.

Sir Hugh Rose's plan of attack on Kalpi.

The details of Sir Hugh Rose's plan of attack on Kalpi were as follows :—

Colonel Maxwell was to construct, on the opposite bank of the Jumna, several mortar batteries ; one to shell vigorously the fort of Kalpi, and blow up if possible the powder magazines in it, destroying also the defences of the fort facing the British position at Golauli. Another was to shell the part of the town fronting the same way, so as to prevent the enemy from holding these localities in force when they were attacked ; another mortar battery to be placed lower down the Jumna, opposite the village of Rayar. Rayar stands on the small sandy plain, bordered by the Jumna, which is situated between the ravines and Kalpi. The enemy had a force and a battery in Rayar for the purpose of sweeping off the right column of attack, when it debouched from the ravines against Kalpi and preventing the occupation of the sandy plain, which was an important point for the British, because, once in possession of it, his right flank resting on the Jumna, the General could bring up all his artillery through the pass through the ravines

* Lieutenant-Colonel Campbell succeeded to the command of the 2nd Brigade when Brigadier-General Steuart was taken ill on the march from Kunch.

and concentrate from the sandy plain a vertical and horizontal fire on the part of Kalpi he wished to attack. Rayar was, therefore, to be destroyed and the ground and ravines about it made untenable by fire from the opposite bank. Maxwell's batteries were to shell their objectives for 16 or 20 hours before and during the advance on Kalpi. Riflemen and field guns were to be stationed opposite the sandy plain on the left bank of the Jumna to clear its right bank and the sandy plain of the enemy.

Sir Hugh Rose hoped to beat the rebel army in one decisive action. He felt certain that if he routed them they would not, with the fate of Jhansi before their eyes, have the heart to shut themselves up in the fort and become the victims of an investment. At the same time it was evident that to take by storm such difficult ground, if well defended, as the ravines surrounding Kalpi, every yard of which was a dangerous obstacle and an ambush, was no ordinary operation, particularly under the difficulties with which the British forces had to contend.

While with his right, the 1st Brigade, the General attacked Kalpi by its left, he intended to make a strong feint against the right of the enemy, to be converted into a real attack, if feasible, with his left, the 2nd Brigade, along the Jalalpur and Kalpi road, Major Orr's force in Tehri keeping up communication between the two Brigades and assisting both as required.

Fresh difficulties compelled a modification of this plan. Some few days must elapse before the mortar batteries on the opposite bank of the Jumna could be ready. The wells of the village where the Hyderabad Field Force and the 2nd Brigade were stationed began to fail, and the sick from sunstroke could not have the water necessary for their treatment; troop horses and baggage animals died from drought. The 2nd Brigade was exposed to constant attack. Concentration and abundance of water were the only remedies for these fresh embarrassments. On the morning of the 19th May the 2nd Brigade and Hyderabad Field Force were brought from Deopura and Tehri to the camp on the Jumna.

Hardships of the troops.

The enemy continued unceasingly their tactics of harassing the British, and forcing them into the sun; large bodies of cavalry hanging round the position, retiring when attacked, but ready to fall on escorts which had to be sent to a distance for forage. Out of 36 of the 14th Dragoons forming part of one forage escort, 17 were brought back to camp in *dhoolies* after only two hours' exposure to sun.

This prostration of more than half a body of men by sun, after two hours' mere marching, and a similar amount of sun-sickness in the 25th Bombay Infantry on the march, showed the dangerous condition of the force before Kalpi.

The prostration of the whole force had become a matter of arithmetical calculation. So many hours' sun laid low so many men. Weakened by every sort of difficulty, the troops had to contend against the greatest odds. The General and his force were suffering from sickness and climate, two evils which have overcome the greatest armies under the most successful commanders.

In a quiet garrison to be on guard every other day is held to be too much for the soldier's health, but the men of the Central India Field Force had been for months making the greatest physical exertions with broken sleep or no sleep at all, watching the camp in unknown and hostile districts against surprise half the night, and marching the other half to avoid the sun; then often all day without a rest, fighting or on the rear-guard, or reconnaissances, or escorts, under a burning sun. The small numbers of the force did not allow of the reliefs which, according to the rules of the Service, are considered indispensable even in peace. In the long march from the west to the centre of India these hardships were augmented by bad roads. The communications consisted generally of country tracks and unbridged nullahs; with the consequence that the guns, baggage, and rearguard were often detained by one deep nullah and for hours exposed to the sun. Rations were also often in arrears owing to bad roads and other difficulties of supply and transport.

Sir Hugh Rose, in consequence of the diminishing strength of his force, had to reinforce himself with some of Colonel Maxwell's troops. In detailing these difficulties and hardships to the Commander-in-Chief, he reported that "these noble soldiers, whose successes were never chequered by a reverse, with a discipline which was as enduring as their courage, never proffered one complaint. They fell in their ranks struck down by sun, and exhausted by fatigue; but they would not increase the anxieties of their General, or belie their devotion by a complaint. No matter how great their exhaustion, or how deep their short sleep, they always sprung to my call to arms with the heartiest good will. To think of yielding or retreating would have been ignominy. All felt that physical strength might fail, but that the spirit and discipline of British soldiers never could. They were often too ill to march, but their devotion made them fight. It is almost superfluous to add that troops animated by so high a sense of duty were sober, orderly, and most respectful to their officers. There was less crime in camp than in garrison."

It was most necessary to take Kalpi. A check there in the advanced state of the hot season, with the rains close at hand, would have resuscitated rebellion throughout India, compromised the safety of Cawnpore,* exposed to a flank or rear attack the extensive line of operations of the Commander-in-Chief in India, and lit the torch of rebellion in the Deccan and Southern Mahrattas, full of ill disposed Arabs and Rohillas and partizans of Nana Sahib.

Colonel Maxwell arrived in camp before Kalpi, on the left bank of the Jumna, on the 18th May, and commenced the construction of batteries the same night. On the following day three 10-inch mortars were in position opposite the fort, and the fourth was ready on the 20th.

Colonel Maxwell's movements.

Colonel Maxwell.
4 Guns, Major Blunt's Battery.
266 Tiwana Horse.
578 His Majesty's 88th Regiment (Connaught Rangers).
682 Camel Corps.
458 Sikh Police Corps.
Four 10-inch Mortars.
Four 8-inch Mortars.

On the night of the 20th he sent a reinforcement to Sir Hugh Rose, consisting of two companies, 88th Regiment, the Camel Corps, and 124 of the Sikh Infantry. On the morning of the 21st he sent also two 8-inch mortars, two field guns, with a company of the 88th, to the village of Rasulpur, about three

* Cawnpore was only 47 miles to the north-east of Kalpi.

miles below Kalpi on the left bank of the Jumna, and opposite the village of Rayar where the enemy had a battery commanding the road by which Sir Hugh Rose purposed advancing on Kalpi. During the night of the 21st two 8-inch mortars were put in position in the village of Dilauli opposite the *kutcherry* and town of Kalpi.

Movements of the enemy.

On the 20th Sir Hugh Rose had scarcely returned to camp from a reconnaissance on the left bank of the Jumna, when the enemy advanced through the ravines, covered by a thick chain of skirmishers, and attacked the British right flank. The picquets were immediately reinforced by four companies of the 86th, two companies, 25th Bombay Infantry, and three 9-pounders. But the General did not allow himself to be drawn into action, and contented himself with directing the picquets to maintain their ground, which they did steadily and gallantly under command of Major Stuart, 86th Regiment, and drove the enemy back, losing in casualties four officers and forty rank and file.

On the 21st May Sir Hugh Rose received information that the rebels intended to make a general attack on his position at Golauli at 8 A.M. next day; that they had sworn an oath on the sacred waters of the Jumna that they would drive his force into the river or die in the attempt; and that afterwards they would march southwards against General Whitlock; * and that large quantities of opium had been issued to the insurgents to make them fight desperately.

Disposition of the British forces.

The British force was disposed of as follows:—The right flank, facing the left of Kalpi, rested on the ravines running down to the Jumna; in these ravines stood the villages of Sarauli and Golauli, both connected and held by strong picquets, preventing the right being turned.

Half the 1st Brigade, the right flank, was encamped perpendicularly to the Jumna, facing the belt of ravines and the left front of Kalpi, on the table-land immediately outside the belt. The remainder of the 1st Brigade facing the continuation of the belt of ravines, which took a sweep outward, and the 2nd Brigade and Hyderabad Field Force facing the table-land or plain stretching from Golauli across the road from Kalpi to Jalalpur, were thrown back *en potence*. This ground was adapted to the movements of cavalry and artillery. The whole front was guarded by strong outposts, with picquets and advanced sentries in the ravines.

On the morning of the 22nd Sir Hugh Rose made the following dispositions to resist the expected attack.

The picquets on the right front of the 86th Regiment and 3rd Europeans were reinforced by the remainder of the 86th in skirmishing order; their right resting on the Jumna. In support were three guns of No. 4 Light Field Battery, the remainder of the 25th Bombay† Infantry, with the 21st Company, R. E., the whole under Lieutenant-Colonel Robertson. The left centre, facing the plain and the

* General Whitlock was at Banda.

† Four companies were left as camp guard.

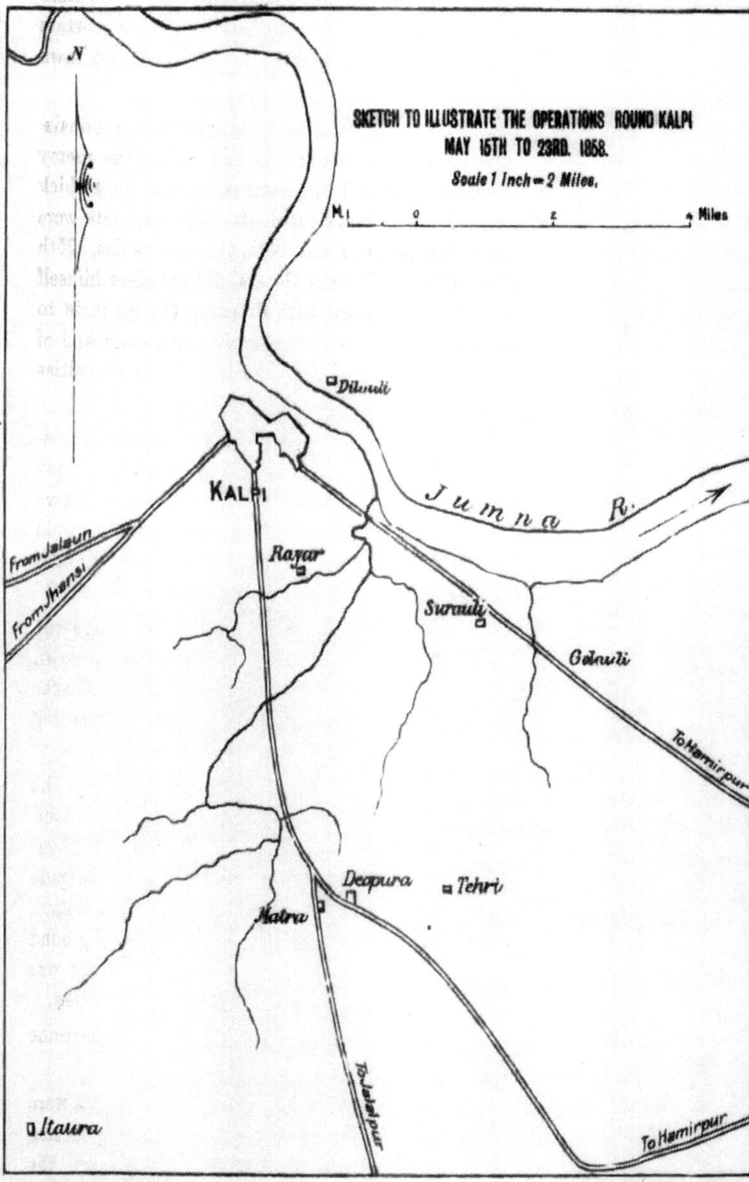

I. B. Topo. Dy. No. 7,878.
Exd. C. J. A., January 1908.

No. 4,248-L., 1908.

village of Tehri, was guarded by No. 1 Troop, Bombay Horse Artillery, supported by two troops, 14th Dragoons.

The siege guns, two 18-pounders, one 24-pounder, and two 8-inch howitzers, their flanks guarded by detachments of the 3rd Europeans, formed the centre, supported by the wing of the 71st Regiment, one squadron, 14th Dragoons, a troop, 3rd Light Cavalry, and Captain Field's Royal Artillery 9-pounders.

The left was formed by the Camel Corps and No. 18 Light Field Battery, supported by a detachment of the Sikh Corps, the Hyderabad Field Force covering the extreme left.

Two companies, 88th Regiment, whose strength was already much weakened by sun casualties, and four companies, 25th Bombay Infantry, were left for protection of the camp.

Battle of Kalpi, 22nd May.

Shortly after 8 A.M. on the 22nd May the enemy were reported to be advancing in great force from Kalpi and its environs towards the belt of ravines on the British right, and along the Jalalpur-Kalpi road against the left. Their left manœuvred so skilfully that they got under cover of broken ground into the ravines without being perceived on the right; and Brigadier Stuart reported to the General, as he was posting the siege guns, that the right was no longer threatened.

Advance against the British left.

The enemy's right, consisting of some 1,400 cavalry, supported by several battalions of infantry and horse artillery 9-pounders, continuing their advance along the Jalalpur road, brought their left shoulders up when opposite the village of Tehri, in front of the British centre, from whence they reinforced strongly their picquets in the ravines opposite the right centre, and deploying their guns and cavalry to the right, threatened to outflank and turn the British left. Sir Hugh Rose still felt convinced that the enemy's real object of attack was his right; and that this ostentatious display of force against his left and the perfect stillness in the deep ravines on his right were ruses to mislead him and induce him to weaken his right, by sending reinforcements from it to his left, when the rebels would have attacked the right with all their energy, endeavoured to take the mortar battery and the camp, their right falling at the same time on his left, and cutting him off, in combination with their left, from the Jumna.

Whilst, therefore, he protected his left against a feint which might become a serious attack, he did not take a man away from his right, and endeavoured to catch the enemy in their own trap. He reinforced the picquets on the left, in the first instance, with a squadron of the 14th Dragoons under Major Gall, and the 3rd Cavalry, Hyderabad Contingent, under Captain Abbott, and afterwards directed these troops to retire slowly before the enemy, obliquely across his front, in order to conceal his heavy guns, and draw the rebel cavalry into their fire. Captain Abbott was directed, after completing this movement, to place his regiment perpendicularly to the front, in order to be able to charge with all his Horse the right flank of the advancing cavalry. The manœuvre succeeded partially; the rebel Horse were enticed into the fire of the siege guns, which caused confusion and numerous casualties, killing among others the Commanding Officer of the 5th Bengal Irregulars. But the mutinous cavalry adhered to their system of never allowing the British Cavalry to close with them, and kept carefully out of reach of the Hyderabad Horse.

To discover the enemy who, Sir Hugh Rose felt assured, were concealed in the ravines in front of his right, he ordered a company of the 3rd Europeans to be pushed some hundred yards forward in front of the outposts into this network of ambushes. The 3rd Europeans, after advancing some distance, found the rebel host crouched in their lair, and started them from it. In an instant a general engagement began along the whole line from the Jumna to the village of Tehri; the belt of ravines in front of the British position becoming enveloped in smoke and fire; the sepoys rose out of their hiding places in thick chains of skirmishers, advancing and firing heavily, followed by large supports and columns in mass at a distance. All the British guns opened fire, and the supports closed up to their threatened fronts.

The rebels attack the right.

The General was watching the determined attack on the centre of his position from the left of the village of Tehri, and at the same time their movements towards his right and left, when he heard a slackening of fire on his right, and at once sent an enquiry to Brigadier Stuart whether he would like to be reinforced by half the Camel Corps, and received a reply in the affirmative. Immediately afterwards, Brigadier Stuart's fire becoming fainter and fainter, and that of the enemy heavier, Sir Hugh Rose understood that his right, the key of the whole position, was in danger, and instantly proceeded to its assistance with the whole of the Camel Corps at a good pace. On the way he met an orderly from Brigadier Stuart asking for reinforcements, which were evidently urgently needed as the enemy's fire was now heard within the position. The Camel Corps under Major Ross, with Sir Hugh Rose at their head, reached the foot of the rising ground on which were the mortar battery and three 9-pounders, and, dismounting, doubled up the rise in line in perfect order.

The moment was critical. Volleys of musketry, which killed or wounded every horse but one of the General's Staff, were coming over the crest of the rising ground from the rebel troops, which had debouched and were debouching in great numbers from the gullies leading into the ravines, and were advancing rapidly, firing heavily, with yells of triumph, their faces distorted by opium and fury, across a small piece of level ground against the mortar battery and guns, and were close upon them. The guns had ceased firing. Brigadier Stuart was on foot at the guns, ordering the few artillerymen who served them to draw swords and defend their pieces; his lines of defence had been driven in, many men having been struck to the ground by sunstroke where they lay, while the fire of the rest was ineffective owing to bad ammunition. Without halting on the crest Sir Hugh Rose charged down it with the Camel Corps, into the dense lines of the mutineers, who were ten times superior in number, the gallant soldiers of the Rifle Brigade and 80th Regiment (forming the Camel Corps) giving one of those cheers which all over the world have been

Critical situation.

Repulse of the enemy.

the heralds of British successes. The rebels wavered, turned, and fled, pursued by the Camel Corps, with all their energy, through the ravines, where numbers were bayonetted or killed by musketry fire.

The General ordered up rapidly the half of No. 4 Light Field Battery from the Mortar Battery to the front to a knoll in the ravines, from whence they fired grape at the nearest rebels and round shot at the more distant masses, which had also made a precipitate retreat.

The men of the Camel Corps fell so fast and thick, struck by the sun, in their violent pursuit of the enemy up and down the steep sides of the rocky ravines, that the whole of them would have been prostrated had they not been called off after they had driven the enemy over and taken the commanding ridge between the position and Kalpi. In these operations, as at Kunch, sunstroke caused death, delirium, and hysterical fits of crying and laughing.

Lieutenant-Colonel Lowth, commanding on the extreme right on the Jumna, relieved from pressure by the success of the Camel Corps, and reinforced by one of its companies, moved forward through the ravines, and by a skilful manœuvre cut off and surrounded a considerable body of rebel sepoys who had advanced too far. Part were killed on the bank of the Jumna, and the rest driven into the river, where they were shot or drowned.

The enemy, simultaneously with their attack on the right, had advanced with equal vigour against the right centre guarded by part of the 25th Bombay Infantry, who, despite a gallant resistance, were driven back by overpowering numbers. But the 21st Company, Royal Engineers, which fought as well in the field as they worked in the trenches, charged under Lieutenant Edwards, and routed the insurgents, pursuing them until out of reach and inflicting considerable loss.

The remainder of the 25th guarding the left centre under Lieutenant-Colonel Robertson, held their ground; the rebels advanced close up to them, firing, and halted and addressed them bitter reproaches, couched in the most revolting language, for their unshaken fidelity to the English. The 25th answered the maledictions of the mutineers in a manner worthy of their reputation and English discipline, with a volley, a cheer, and a charge with the bayonet.

General advance, and defeat of the rebels.

The whole British line was now advancing and driving the enemy from their positions. The left centre under Lieutenant-Colonel Robertson, following up his spirited charge, dashed through the ravines after the rebels, came up with their rear near the village of Tehri, bayonetted numbers, and continued the pursuit beyond the village until his men fell exhausted.

The whole of the infantry on the left now brought their left shoulders forward, and covered by Captain Lightfoot's Troop of Horse Artillery, three guns, No. 4 Light Field Battery, and the whole of the cavalry, made a converging movement on the enemy's right and the village of Tehri. The enemy broke and fled, pursued for some miles by the Horse Artillery and cavalry. Exhaustion and broken ground stopped the pursuit, in which numbers were killed. The rebels were so completely beaten and disheartened that broken parties were seen flying across the ravines in a westerly direction towards Jalaun.

During the fight the mortar batteries on the other side of the Jumna cleared the village of Rayar, and subsequently kept up a fire on the fort and town of Kalpi.*

Capture of Kalpi, 23rd May.

Brigadier Stuart.
14th Light Dragoons, 40 sabres.
Hyderabad Contingent, 50 sabres.
No. 4 Light Field Battery.
No. 18 Light Field Battery.
21st Company, R.E., 84 rank and file.
Wing, 71st Regiment, 210 rank and file.
86th Regiment, 520 rank and file.
88th Regiment, 85 rank and file.
Wing, 3rd Europeans, 190 rank and file.
Sikh Infantry, 200 rank and file.

The complete defeat and serious loss which the enemy had sustained this day, despite their having displayed unprecedented energy and skilful tactics, convinced the General that an immediate advance on Kalpi would be successful. Accordingly, giving the troops only time for rest, he divided his force into two columns of attack, and marched next morning long before daybreak, according to his original plan, the right under Brigadier Stuart, through the ravines,† their right resting on the Jumna; the left, under his personal command, along the Jalalpur and Kalpi road.

When Sir Hugh Rose's column had marched from camp across the plain and reached the Jalalpur-Kalpi road, he brought their left shoulders forward, and, taking the road for the direction of his centre, covered his advance with the Camel Corps, supported by the Hyderabad Contingent Cavalry. From the road he despatched a Staff Officer with a party of Cavalry to communicate with Brigadier Stuart. After marching some distance along the road, the enemy opened fire from a battery in a ravine at a great distance and elevation, but their guns were silenced by a few rounds.

Brigadier Stuart's column met with no opposition until the village of Rayar was reached, when the 86th Regiment received a volley, but at once charged and drove the enemy out. Kalpi town and fort were both found deserted.‡

The Pursuit.

4 Troops, 14th Dragoons, 153 sabres.
6 guns, Horse Artillery.
3rd Hyderabad Contingent Cavalry.
1st Hyderabad Contingent Cavalry, 50 sabres.

A force, as detailed in the margin, under Major Gall was sent in pursuit of the enemy who were observed moving off from Kalpi north-west in large bodies, with elephants. Major Gall pursued along the Kalpi-Jhansi high road, which diverges to Jalaun at about three miles from Kalpi.

About half a mile up the Jhansi road a large tomb was reported to be occupied by the enemy, but on the cavalry approaching it was found to have been evacuated, and the rebels were seen retreating in great numbers across the plain beyond it. The rebels were charged and cut up in all directions, two guns being captured

* A shell from one of the mortar batteries burst in the Rani's room, killing two of her attendants, and hastened her flight. She left Kalpi before midnight on the 22nd.

† The soldiers advancing through the ravines put up a panther and two hares which were killed by the Highlanders.

‡ The Rao Sahib and the Nawab of Banda fled on the morning of the 23rd, their flight being greatly favoured by the nature of the country.

by the 1st Cavalry under Lieutenant Dowker,* who was on the right. In the centre the Dragoons sabred numbers of the fugitives who, firing wildly and completely panic-stricken by the suddenness and rapidity of the advance, fell an easy pray to the pursuers, in some instances casting away their arms.† On the left Captain Abbott charged along the road to Jalaun, and captured a 9-pounder gun. All the enemy's five guns, artillery wagons, ammunition and bullock carts were captured, as well as six caparisoned elephants and some camels and bullocks.

Contents of the fort.

All the artillery in the fort, including a fine English 18-pounder, was taken and 27 silk-embroidered standards of the Gwalior Contingent, bearing Sindhia's device, a cross and a serpent round it, and one of the Kotah Contingent. Also three cannon and mortar foundries, which had been constructed in the town and fort, a very complete and extensive subterranean arsenal, containing 60,000 pounds of English powder; every description of warlike stores and ammunition; numerous boxes of new and old English muskets; quantities of English shot and shell of which there were also piles outside the arsenal in the fort; engineering tools of every description; boxes of brass shells of native manufacture; the whole estimated at a value of £20,000 to £30,000.‡

The casualties § amounted to 24 killed and 43 wounded, besides losses from sunstroke; among the victims of which was Sir Hugh Rose who suffered from this cause on five occasions, and was thus prevented from composing his despatch on these operations until a month later at Gwalior.

Despatch of a pursuing column, 25th May.

It was clear that the main body of the rebels had retreated by the Jalaun road, and Sir Robert Hamilton was of opinion that they would make to the north for the Sher Ghat, a ford across the Jumna, or another ford higher up the river. Colonel Riddell with a moveable column was guarding the former ford. It was of vital importance to make a fresh pursuit of the enemy, in order either to catch him between Colonel Riddell's and the main force, to meet him if he turned, or to ascertain the line of his flight.

Lieut.-Colonel Robertson.
1 Troop, 14th Light Drgns.
1 Squadron, 3rd Bombay Cavalry.
No. 18, Light Field Battery.
Hyderabad Contingent Cavalry, 160.
25th Bombay Infantry.

Notwithstanding the exhausted state of the troops, a force under Lieutenant-Colonel Robertson, detailed in the margin, was sent along the Jalaun road on the 25th May to follow the enemy.

Combat of Bilayan, 31st May.

1st Cavalry, Hyderabad Contingent, 165 sabres.
4th Cavalry Hyderabad Contingent, 162 sabres.

After the occupation of Kalpi Major Orr was sent with the force detailed in the margin down the road to Jhansi to clear it of a band of rebels, under the insurgent chief of Bilayan, Barjur Singh, who were endeavouring to reorganise and cut off the communications with Jhansi.

* Lieutenant Dowker reported that he saw Duffadar Sadhu Singh kill 5 or 6 of the enemy with his own hand.

† From buttons found it appeared that not less than eleven Gwalior and Bengal Infantry regiments were among the enemy.

‡ A box containing important correspondence belonging to the Rani was found in the fort.

§ The European sick and wounded were sent to Cawnpore.

1st Company Artillery, Hyderabad Contingent, two 6-pounders.
4th Company Artillery, Hyderabad Contingent, two 12-pounder howitzers, two 5½-inch mortars.
3rd Infantry, Hyderabad Contingent, 344 bayonets.
Siege Train, one 18-pounder gun, two 8-inch mortars.
Sappers and Miners, 22.

Major Orr marched to Orai, and on the evening of May 30th received information that Barjur Singh was in his stronghold at Bilayan, 19 miles from Orai on the Jhansi road. Marching at 10 P.M. with his whole force, he pushed on with his cavalry at a rapid pace from the village of Girthan, half way to Bilayan. Arriving before the latter place at day-break, he at once surrounded it with his cavalry, and awaited the arrival of the guns and infantry. The alarm was given, and an ineffective fire was opened from the fort. The rebels in a short time appeared outside the town in a large mass, numbering from 200 to 250, and, having formed up under cover of a garden, moved forward in a compact body and in regular formation. Collecting some of his picquets, and leaving some to watch the fort, Major Orr advanced with 81 sabres against this mass. The guns of the Light Field Battery, having got within range, opened with shell and shrapnel with good effect. The cavalry then charged and cut up a number of both horse and foot; but the rebels took refuge in some deep ravines running towards the Betwa, to attack or dislodge them from which was very difficult. Here they fought desperately, but were destroyed or dispersed with the loss of all their property. About 130 were killed and 35 taken prisoners. Barjur Singh's horse and standard were captured, and he himself only got away by threading the ravines on foot, having stripped himself of almost all his clothing. The Hyderabad Contingent lost seven men of the 3rd Infantry killed, and Lieutenant Westmacott, a Subadar and six men were wounded. As Sir Hugh Rose wrote in his despatch*—"Major Orr, in crushing rapidly and effectually this rebel did essential service to the Government and the British Force."

Services of the Hyderabad Contingent.

The services of the Hyderabad Contingent had been very distinguished throughout the campaign, and in his report of the operations before Kalpi the British General wrote:—"So much of the success of the operations is due to the portion of the Hyderabad Contingent which formed part of my force, that I ought not to fail to express my best thanks to Colonel Davidson, Resident at Hyderabad, for the proof of confidence which he placed in me by putting at my disposal troops whose organisation in the three arms, light equipment, knowledge of the Indian language and

* Mentioned in the Despatch—Major Orr, Lieutenants Dowker, Fraser, Dun, Westmacott, Surgeon Orr, Assistant-Surgeon Sanderson; Duffadar Sadhu Singh, Troopers Shah Nur Khan, Jiwan Singh, 1st Cavalry. Subadar Muhammad Ali, Havildar Sivdin, Lakshman Pande, Privates Shaikh Sarwar, Shaikh Kammu, 3rd Infantry.

country, combined with their high military qualities, enabled them to act as the wings of my operations." *

He also wrote, with regard to the Begum of Bhopal:—"Her Highness displayed the very best feeling towards the English interests; she did so courageously in the worst times, when the natives in her part of the world thought that rebellion must triumph. Her Highness gave me two 9-pounder guns and a 24-pounder howitzer, with the gunners belonging to them, very good artillerymen, when I marched through Bhopal, which enabled me to complete No. 18 Light Field Battery. Her Highness was indefatigable in obtaining supplies for my force when it was very much in want of them."

The Begam of Bhopal.

It was thought that with the crushing defeat of the rebels on the 22nd May, and the fall of Kalpi, the campaign in Central India had come to a close. The enemy had been defeated wherever met with and his forces scattered in every direction. The British General even issued a farewell order to the troops, and the Hyderabad Contingent turned towards the Deccan to seek a well-earned repose in their cantonments. Sir Hugh Rose's stirring order to the troops may well be quoted here before we proceed to a description of the final phase of the campaign against the rebel hosts which gathered fresh strength at Gwalior under the able leadership of Tantia Topi.

"Soldiers! You have marched more than a thousand miles and taken more than a hundred guns. You have forced your way through mountain passes, and intricate jungles, and over rivers. You have captured the strongest forts and beat the enemy, no matter what the odds, wherever you have met him. You have restored extensive districts to the Government, and peace and order now where before for a twelvemonth were tyranny and rebellion. You have done all this, and you have never had a check. I thank you with all my sincerity for your bravery, your devotion, and your discipline.

Sir Hugh Rose's order to the troops.

When you first marched I told you that you, as British soldiers, had more than enough of courage for the work that was before you, but that courage without discipline was of no avail, and I expected you to let discipline be your watchword. You have attended to my orders. In hardships, in temptation and danger you

* In 1853 Lord Gough, lately Commander-in-Chief in India, stated before the House of Commons Committee that the Hyderabad Contingent were "the finest Irregular Cavalry in the world," an estimate borne out by their services.

For their services in this campaign Major W. A. Orr was promoted Brevet-Lieutenant-Colonel, and made C. B., Captains H. D. Abbott and G. Hare were promoted Brevet-Majors, and made C. B., Surgeons J. Orr and W. Mackenzie were made C. B. On attaining the rank of Captain, Lieutenant H. C. Dowker was promoted Brevet-Major, and was subsequently made a C. B. Nine Native officers of the Hyderabad Contingent were made Companions of the Order of British India, 71 Orders of Merit were given in the Force and about a hundred special promotions of native ranks were made. Among the most distinguished native officers was Risaldar-Major Nawab Ahmad Bakhsh Khan, Sirdar Bahadur, 3rd Cavalry, Hyderabad Contingent, whose brave conduct in many actions was remarkable. He died at Mominabad in 1906 at the age of 95 years. Jemadar Vilayat Ali Beg, father of Lieutenant-Colonel Muhammad Ali Beg, Afsur-ul-Mulk, C. I. E., and Commander-in-Chief of H. H. The Nizam's Army, was throughout the campaign orderly to Sir Hugh Rose, who presented him with a sword of honour.

have never left your ranks. You have fought against the strong, and you have protected the rights of the weak and defenceless, of foes as wells as of friends.

I have seen you in the ardour of the combat preserve and place children out of harm's way. This is the discipline of Christian soldiers, and it is what has brought you triumphant from the shores of Western India to the waters of the Jumna, and establishes without doubt that you will find no place before which the glory of your arms can be dimmed."

CHAPTER IX.

THE GWALIOR CAMPAIGN.

Movements of the rebels.

After the capture of Kalpi the first reports made to Sir Hugh Rose by Lieutenant-Colonel Robertson, commanding the column of pursuit, were to the effect that the scattered parties of the rebel army, without guns or tents, were making *viâ* Jalaun, in the utmost disorder, for the Sher Ghat, a ford across the Jumna, 35 or 40 miles to the north-east of Kalpi. Subsequent accounts from the same officer stated that a great part of the fugitives had, after leaving Jalaun, made a turn in a more westerly direction, which was contrary to the one Sir Robert Hamilton felt persuaded the rebels would follow; he was certain that they would make for Oudh and cross the Jumna at the Sher Ghat or the ford to the west of it, near Jagamanpur.

Tantia Topi.

After the battle of Kunch, Tantia Topi had taken refuge with his parents at Chirki, four miles from Jalaun, where he remained until after the capture of Kalpi, when he joined the Rani of Jhansi and Rao Sahib at Gopalpur, 46 miles south-west of Gwalior. The Rani, desperate and daring, then conceived the plan of marching on Sindhia's capital, and taking possession of that stronghold.

The Rani's plan.

Movements of the pursuing column.

In his uncertainty as to the movements of the rebels, Lieutenant-Colonel Robertson, with good judgment, took up a position with the pursuing column, which enabled him not to be deceived by a feigned move to draw him off from the real chase, but to follow the rebels by the shortest line, should they move westwards or northwards.

After a short rest to refresh his European troops Sir Hugh reinforced Lieutenant-Colonel Robertson with a wing of the 86th Regiment and two squadrons of the 14th Dragoons.

Subsequent reports from that officer stated that he had reason to think that all the rebels had decidedly taken a westerly direction, and that they had been reinforced by 800 Oudh Cavalry under Rahim Ali, Nawab of Bareilly. Following the line to the west taken by the rebels from Jalaun towards the Pahuj and Sind rivers, Colonel Robertson got into communication with the Raja of Rampura, to the west of the Pahuj, a faithful friend of the English; and his intelligence and knowledge of the natives and their language enabled him to obtain very valuable information from this person to the effect that the Kalpi rebels had certainly taken the road to Gwalior.

So little was any design on Sindhia's power suspected, that the best authority for intelligence could not bring himself to believe the truth of this report.

No. 4 Light Field Battery.
Troops, 14th Light Dragoons.
1 wing, 71st Regiment.
4 Companies, 25th Bombay Infantry.
½ Company, Bombay Sappers and Miners.
Two 18-pounders.
One 8-inch howitzer.

But Sir Robert Hamilton received similar information a few hours after the arrival of Colonel Robertson's express, and the General at once ordered off Brigadier Stuart, with the troops detailed in the margin, to reinforce the pursuing column and then march on Gwalior after the rebels.

The news received the next few days was very uncertain and contradictory. An express letter from Sindhia's Agent at Gwalior removed apprehensions for his safety, and that of his Government; it stated that the rebels, who were in a destitute condition, had, when still several miles from Gwalior, implored Sindhia's favour and protection in language and with a demeanour the reverse of hostile.

The rebels reach Morar.

Subsequent accounts from Lieutenant-Colonel Robertson, which were confirmed by Sir Robert Hamilton, conveyed the news which created a sensation throughout India only equalled by that caused by the first mutinies. On the 30th May Tantia Topi, the Rani of Jhansi, and other leaders at the head of a force of 7,000 infantry, 4,000 cavalry and 12 guns, entered Morar. At daybreak next morning Sindhia marched out with some 8,000 men and 8 guns, and took up a position at Bahadurpur, two miles east of Morar, and awaited the rebel attack, having disposed his troops in three divisions, with his guns in the centre.

Sindhia offers battle to the rebels, 31st May.

The rebels advanced at 7 A.M., and carried the guns by a charge of 2,000 horse. Simultaneously the whole of Sindhia's army, with the exception of his body-guard, went over to the enemy. The body-guard was attacked, and put to flight after a gallant defence, and Sindhia fled to Agra with a few faithful retainers.

Defection of Sindhia's army.

His flight to Agra.

Rebels enter Gwalior.

The rebels then entered Gwalior and took the Treasury and Sindhia's jewels, the latter said to be of fabulous value. The garrison of the fortress, considered to be one of the strongest in India, had, after a mock resistance, opened its gates, and 50 or 60 guns as well as a fine arsenal stocked with warlike stores fell into the hands of the insurgents. In short, the rebels who had fled in the most disorderly and helpless state from Kalpi were now completely set up with abundance of money, a capital park of artillery, plenty of material, and Sindhia's army as their allies.

Effects of the rebel success.

Gwalior itself, without the fort, was a prize of no ordinary value, comprising the old city and the Lashkar, the ancient Mahratta camp, converted into a handsome and flourishing city, both containing a population of 170,000. But other circumstances combined to render the loss of Gwalior the most serious event which had occurred since the revolt.

Sindhia was the faithful ally of the British, and with one exception the most powerful of the independent princes of India. The extent and geographical position of the Gwalior States gave their rulers great political and military power over the whole of India. The main artery of communication and the telegraph line from Bombay to Central India, Agra, and the North-West Provinces traversed Sindia's dominions for hundreds of miles. The troops which went over to the rebels were the best drilled and organized of all the native levies. To render this state of affairs more embarrassing, Gwalior fell into rebel hands at the most unfavourable time of the year for military operations, on the eve of the rainy season and when the heat of summer was at its maximum. No one could therefore foresee the extent of evil if Gwalior were not promptly wrested from the rebels; if Tantia Topi, with the immense acquisition of political influence and military strength which the possession of that place gave the rebel cause, had time to reorganise the Kalpi army, which he could easily do, with the resources of Gwalior at his disposal. The worst forebodings would have come to pass if Tantia Topi, leaving either the Kalpi or Gwalior Army at Gwalior for its defence, marched with the other southwards, and unfurled the standard of the Peshwa in the Deccan and Southern Mahrattas. These districts, and the west of India generally, were very much denuded of troops, and the attachment of the inhabitants to their former Government was too well known to admit of a doubt as to the course they would have pursued if Tantia Topi had appeared amongst them with a large army.

The inhabitants of Indore had given so many proofs of unfavourable feeling that there was reason to fear that they would, if opportunity offered, follow the example of Gwalior. It was of vital importance that the troops should reach Gwalior before the rains set in; there were no pontoons for siege artillery, and it would have been difficult, if not impossible, to transport siege guns across the Pahuj and Sind rivers, swollen by rains; while a siege protracted by the difficulties of monsoon weather would have had disastrous effect on military prestige and the political state of affairs.

Sir Hugh Rose marches on Gwalior.

Sir Hugh Rose received information of the fall of Gwalior on the 3rd June. He had suffered severely in health, and had given up his command, and prepared to go southwards on sick certificate; but he at once resumed his command, and in view of the considerations that have been detailed, decided to march on Gwalior immediately.

1st Troop, Bombay Horse Artillery.
1 Squadron, 14th Light Dragoons.
1 Squadron, 3rd Bombay Light Cavalry.
Madras Sappers and Miners.

Accordingly, leaving at Kalpi a part of the permanent garrison, Captain Ommaney's, R. A., battery of 9-pounders, and a troop, 3rd Bombay Cavalry, 21st Company, R. E., a wing, 3rd Europeans, and 400, 24th Bombay Infantry, to garrison the place until relieved by Bengal troops, he marched on the 6th June with the troops detailed in the margin and followed Brigadier Stuart's column by forced marches, on the road to Gwalior by Jalaun, marching by night to avoid the sun.

One day the temperature in the shade rose to 130°, and on the night of the third day the men of the outlying piquet of the 14th Dragoons fell from their saddles from exhaustion, and were relieved by the Hyderabad Contingent. Owing to the difficulties of bad transport carts in crossing one very deep nullah, and the rapid advance of the column, a detachment of the 25th Bombay Infantry, guarding the baggage, were three days without a meal; but after a bath in the Pahuj and a short rest to enable them to cook their food, these good soldiers were ready to march on.

Difficulties of the march.

Sir Hugh Rose came up with Brigadier Stuart's column at the fort of Indurkhi on the Sind River on the 11th June. Here he received instructions from the Commander-in-Chief that he was reinforced by a Bengal Column under Colonel Riddell. This column was to escort a large supply of siege guns from Agra to Gwalior for the siege of that place. Brigadier Smith, with a brigade of the Rajputana Field Force, was to march from the neighbourhood of Chanderi to Gwalior.

Colonel Riddell.

No. 21 Light Field Battery.
3rd Bengal Europeans.
200 Sikh Horse.
300 Sikh Infantry.
Siege Artillery.

Brigadier Smith.

8th Hussars.
1st Bombay Light Cavalry.
95th Regiment.
10th Bombay Infantry.

The Hyderabad Contingent after their hard service had received permission and orders to return home, and had almost all commenced their march towards the Deccan, and were some of them far advanced on the road. But with a good feeling which cannot be sufficiently praised, all of the Contingent which had formed part of the Central India Field Force instantly countermarched and moved against Gwalior on the wish being intimated to the Commanding Officers that they should perform this fresh act of good service for Government. Major Orr was at Moth, and marched on Gwalior by way of Jhansi on the 7th June.

Movements of the Hyderabad Contingent.

Agra was selected as the base of operations, its communication with Gwalior being the shortest and best, although rendered imperfect by the passage of a very difficult ford across the Chambal. Sir Hugh Rose decided to invest Gwalior as much as its great extent would allow, and then attack its weakest side, the investing troops cutting off the escape of the rebels. He hoped that a successful attack outside or inside the city would be followed by the capture of the fort, as at Kalpi. In order to invest the place from the south, he directed Major Orr with the Hyderabad Contingent to move from Jhansi to Punniar, on the road from Gwalior to Sipri. His force was too weak to attack Gwalior from that direction, but he was perfectly placed for cutting off the retreat of the rebels to the south, assisted, as he would be, by other investing corps.

Sir Hugh Rose's plan of operations.

Information as to the enemy's position is the surest guarantee of success, but Sir Hugh Rose had no plan of Gwalior or its environs.

With great trouble he had ascertained that the weakest side, and consequently the best for attack, was the east, as it was there girt by high hills. The summits of these hills were difficult of access; but slopes which descended gradually from these summits towards and close to the Lashkar would enable him, after taking the heights to drive the enemy down from slope to slope, from the lowest of which he could cannonade the Lashkar, and, covered by the fire of artillery, storm the new town, that is the Lashkar; thus cutting in two the enemy's whole line, consisting of the old city, above which is the fort, and the new city or Lashkar. This point of attack had the additional advantage that it was almost protected from the fire of the fort.

The General directed Brigadier Smith to move from Siprí to Kotah-Ki-Serai, about seven miles to the south-east of Gwalior. He himself with Brigadier Stuart's column, marched against the Morar Cantonments, which were said to be occupied in force by the enemy. These Cantonments for the troops stationed at Gwalior were about five miles from that city, on the river Morar. They had only been partially burnt by the rebels; and Sindhia's Government had been at much trouble and expense to repair the old buildings and construct others for the force which was to be the garrison of Gwalior. Once in possession of the Morar Cantonments, the General could establish there his hospital, parks, etc.

Divested of these incumbrances, and leaving a force to protect the Morar Cantonments, and at the same time form part of the investment of Gwalior and pursue when required, the General was free to join Brigadier Smith at Kotah-Ki-Serai and attack Gwalior with both forces. To complete the investment which, roughly speaking, was to enclose Gwalior from the south-east and north Sir Hugh Rose sent instructions to Colonel Riddell to move with his column by the Agra and Gwalior road to the Residency, about seven miles to the north of Gwalior. Colonel Riddell, by extending his force from the Residency down the west side of Gwalior, invested it from that side. According to the arrangements made, all the columns would be at their posts to carry out this plan by the 19th June.

Movements of the British General.

On the 14th June Sir Hugh Rose arrived at Sopaoli, and on the same date Brigadier Smith was at Mahona, Major Orr near Antri, Brigadier Showers at Dholpur, and the Sipri Force at Punniar.* On the 15th Brigadier-General R. Napier, C.B., joined † and took command of the 2nd Brigade.

On the 16th June Sir Hugh Rose arrived at Bahadurpur, four or five miles from the Morar Cantonments. It was reported that there were much alarm and symptoms of disunion at Gwalior. Sindhia's troops were deserting in great numbers from the Lashkar to rejoin the Maharaja, and were collecting at Hingoera. They had been ordered to move to Jaora on the old Bombay road and intercept fugitives. On the same day the Sipri Force occupied the fort of Kimulgarh, 20 miles south of Gwalior, after a skirmish in which the enemy was defeated and fled to the Lashkar. And on the evening of the 16th the Maharaja Sindhia left Dholpur for Gwalior with Meade's Cavalry.

* Here a portion of the Gwalior Forces was defeated in 1843, and the remainder were beaten at Maharajpur on the same day.

† Afterwards Lord Napier of Magdala.

On arriving at Bahadurpur Sir Hugh Rose directed Captain Abbott with his cavalry to reconnoitre Morar; he reported that the rebels were in force in front of it. The General reconnoitred their position closely; and found that the side of the Cantonments fronting him was occupied by strong bodies of cavalry and that on their right were guns and a good deal of infantry.

His force had had a long and fatiguing march, and the sun had been up for some time. Four or five miles more march in the sun, and a combat afterwards, would be a great trial for the men's strength. On the other hand, Morar looked inviting, with several good buildings not yet burnt; they would be good quarters for a portion of the force; if the attack were delayed until next day, the enemy were sure to turn them. A prompt attack had always the greatest effect on the rebels. The General, therefore, countermanded the order for encamping, and made the following arrangements to attack the enemy.

British dispositions.

He formed his force in two lines, the first line consisting of the 1st Brigade, under Brigadier Stuart, the second line, under Brigadier Napier, in support of the first, consisting of only a small part of the 2nd Brigade, as the rest was at Kalpi. Captain Abbott covered the advance with the 3rd Cavalry, Hyderabad Contingent.

Brigadier Napier was requested to watch well the hills to the left and rear, in which the enemy were supposed to be; and to advance in echelon from the right, which enabled him, his left flank refused, to guard the left rear, on the outer flank of which were placed the baggage and encumbrances. Cavalry patrols were sent far away into the hills to the left and rear to search them. The ground on the right and in front of Morar was full of ravines.

Both lines advanced; No. 18 Light Field Battery and the siege guns in the centre of the first; the 86th Regiment on their right; the 25th Bombay Infantry on their left; the 14th Light Dragoons on each flank. To march to the position in order of battle, the troops passed over the ground on which Sindhia had been attacked and routed by his faithless troops and the Kalpi rebels. It was strewed with dead horses.

The General's plan was to mask the dangerous ground to his left, towards which the enemy evidently wished to draw him; to outflank the enemy's left, double it up, and cut off their retreat from the road over the bridge in rear of the cantonments leading to Gwalior. The first line advanced in line across the plain between Morar and Bahadurpur, dressing by their centre with the regularity of a parade movement. The enemy retired from their position in front of Morar into the cantonments.

The second line, under Brigadier-General Napier, was disposed as follows:—In the centre the Madras Sappers and Miners and wing of the 71st Highlanders; on the right 100 horse of the Hyderabad Contingent; on the left the right wing of the 14th Light Dragoons.

Battle of Morar, 16th June.

Under the guidance of Sindhia's Agent, Sir Hugh Rose took ground diagonally to the right in order to get on the road which led to the Cantonments, which would enable him to turn the enemy's left; but he missed the road; in the meantime the force

THE COUNTRY ROUND GWALIOR.

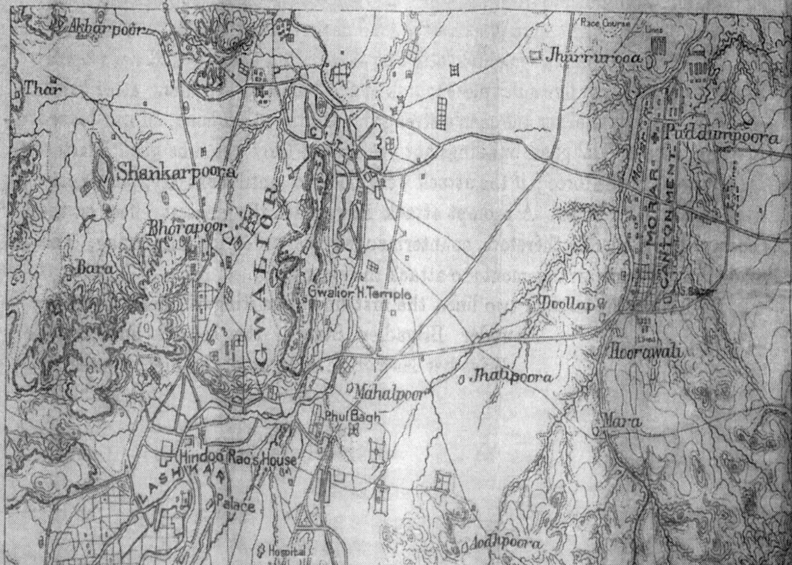

I. G. Topo. Dy. No. 7,060.
Exd. C. J. A., January 1908.

Scale 1 inch = 1 mile.

Furlongs 8 4 0 1 2 3 Miles

No. 4,249-I., 1908.

had got on the edge of broken ground; a masked battery in the enemy's centre concealed by trees, and the guns on their right, opened a cross fire on the British line, causing some casualties among Captain Abbott's Cavalry, which showed admirable steadiness.

The General directed the siege guns under Lieutenant Strutt, and No. 18 Light Field Battery under Lieutenant Harcourt, to be placed in position obliquely to his front, which enabled them to open a telling fire diagonally to their left on the enemy's batteries. The rebel artillery caused some casualties among the horses of these guns.

The lay of the ground favouring the rebels' right battery, the General brought up to his left Captain Lightfoot's 1st Troop, Bombay Horse Artillery, against it.

Ravines and broken ground prevented the advance of Captain Abbott's Cavalry, which were placed under cover; and of the 14th Light Dragoons under Captain Thompson on the right, who reinforced the left.

The enemy's cavalry, of which the 5th Irregulars formed part, showed in force to the front along the road through the cantonments.

The left, now near the dangerous ground on the enemy's right, was reinforced by the 25th Bombay Infantry, and advanced across broken ground. The 86th in skirmishing order, and firing as they advanced, took by storm, under the cannonade of the enemy's right battery, all the Morar Cantonments in front of the advancing line, the rebels retiring at a gallop.

The 86th line of skirmishers now brought forward their right shoulders, and, resting their right on the right bank of the Morar river, swept the whole Cantonments and occupied them.

Captain Abbott, whose horse was killed under him by a round shot, in the meantime had contrived to get round the nullahs further to the right, and wheeling to his left, galloped through the cantonments and joined in the pursuit of the enemy, who retired from their right. But the delay in his advance, caused by the very difficult ground, prevented his arriving in time to cut off the retreat of the enemy across the bridge. The rebels withdrew their batteries, crippled by the fire of the British guns, as soon as they saw their left compromised by the successful advances of the 86th. The British left, which had been refused, conformed to the right, and changed position to the left, fronting the *nalas* on the British right, which it had now approached.

The advanced ravine and others in rear of it were lined with rebel sepoys who gave no sign until the left approached them, when they opened a very heavy fire; and Major Rich moved his skirmishers of the 71st rapidly forward to dislodge them. Lieutenant Neave courageously led the charge, and fell mortally wounded when close to the ravine. The 71st gallantly took this *nala* and others in rear by storm; Lieutenant Rose, 25th Bombay Infantry, co-operating by skilfully placing a party of his regiment so as to enfilade these dangerous intrenchments. The whole of the rebels in them were killed, after a desperate resistance, in which the 71st lost heavily, Sergeant McGill, Corporal Leslie, and two men being killed, and Sergeant Wilson and six men wounded.

In the advanced *nala* alone seventy rebels lay dead, belonging to Sindhia's faithless Guards, and wearing English accoutrements and breastplates on which was engraved "1st Brigade Infantry."

The 71st Highlanders proved on this as well as on every other occasion that they could maintain by their courage and discipline the historic renown of which they bear so many honoured records on their colours.*

Defeat of the rebels.

The success of the day was completed by the destruction of the rebels in the *nala*, and a most successful pursuit by Captain Thompson with a wing of the 14th Dragoons. These rebels had been turned by Captain Abbott's advance from the ford of the river, across which and the bridge the main body had retreated. Captain Thompson caught them in the plains before they could reach the hills to which they were hurrying, and slaughtered great numbers.

The "Eagle" Troop.

In his Despatch the General made special mention of the "Eagle" Troop, Bombay Horse Artillery, under Captain Lightfoot, for their excellent and gallant conduct throughout the campaign. In his actions he made very liberal use of the troop, in pouring an unexpected or flank fire into the enemy. On all these occasions the 1st Troop was worthy of its former fame, and proved that no arm of the service is more dangerous to its foes than fleet artillery.

Sir Hugh Rose brought to notice the good spirit and gallantry which the troops displayed in the rapid and successful operation against the Morar Cantonments. Their march from Kalpi was very trying. In consequence of the great heat in the tents by day, the men could not get the rest which they lost by marching at night to avoid the sun.

Effect of the victory.

Notwithstanding a long march to Bahadurpur, the troops ceased their preparations for encamping, and marched, fasting, with the utmost alacrity and steadiness against Morar, going five miles and taking it in two hours under a heavy and well-directed cannonade and a resolute resistance on the left. The capture of Morar had good results. It was the first defeat which the combined forces of the Kalpi and Gwalior rebels had sustained. Morar, the military station and an outwork of Gwalior, was an important strategical point. It gave to the British the command of the line of the Morar river, of the road to Agra, and enabled the General to communicate with Brigadier Smith to the left and the Residency to the right.

The rebels were surprised by the rapid march from Kalpi. They intended to make a determined stand at Morar, and had commenced storing it with supplies. They had not time to burn the houses, nor the temporary sheds prepared for the troops by Sindhia, which were turned to good account.

* When a wing of this Regiment was prostrated by sun sickness after the action at Kunch, the only complaint heard in the field-hospitals from these gallant young soldiers was that they could not rise and fight.

Sir Hugh Rose immediately got into communication with Brigadier Smith at Kotah-ki-Serai, and reconnoitred Gwalior. His reconnaissance satisfied him that the information* on which he had decided to attack it was good. If he attacked it from Morar, he would have to cross the plain between Morar and Gwalior under fire of the fort and of masked and formidable batteries, established in strong houses and gardens on the banks of the old canal, and a dry river in front of the Phul Bagh Palace.

Action at Kotah-ki-Serai, 17th June.

On the morning of the 17th June Brigadier Smith, with his Brigade of the Rajputana Field Force, marched by Sir Hugh Rose's order from Antri through the pass to Kotah-ki-Serai, which lies about three or four miles south-east of Gwalior. He had reconnoitred the pass the preceding evening, and occupied the difficult points by strong picquets and posts. He, however, met with no opposition, and reached Kotah-ki-Serai at 7 A.M. Upon his arrival he saw the enemy occupy the heights in front, and between him and Gwalior. He had orders from Sir Hugh Rose to halt at Kotah-ki-Serai, and communicate with him, but as the enemy appeared determined to attack, and being also hampered with a large quantity of baggage, and Kotah-ki-Serai not being a secure position, Brigadier Smith thought it best to take the initiative. He therefore collected his baggage under a strong guard in and near the fort, and reconnoitred the ground in front, which was most difficult, intersected with ravines and impracticable for cavalry. About 1,500 yards from Kotah-ki-Serai the rebel guns were in position, and their line ran all under the hills across the road to Gwalior.

Brigadier Smith advanced his Horse Artillery and soon silenced the hostile guns, which began to retire after three or four rounds. He then sent his infantry (95th Regiment and 10th Bombay Infantry)† under Colonel Raines‡ across the broken ground, the 95th in skirmishing order, and the 10th in echelon as a reserve. On nearing their breastwork a heavy fire was met with from both infantry and guns, and when within 50 yards the 95th charged and put the enemy to flight.

On gaining the heights in rear of the encampment, during which a company of the 95th had swept round the base of the hill to the left, Colonel Raines observed that the enemy had guns about 800 or 1,000 yards in front on another hill about the same height, as well as infantry and cavalry. He sounded the halt and assembly, whereupon the enemy opened fire with shrapnel. He then noticed on his immediate right, about 500 yards off on the road to Gwalior, about a hundred of the Gwalior Contingent Cavalry, protected from his fire by a high embankment. And as he anticipated that they would endeavour to turn his right flank by a charge and thus cut him off from his reserve, he retired on the entrenchments. Here he found that Major Vialls, who commanded the reserve, was attacking the Gwalior Contingent Cavalry, with two companies of the 95th, keeping them in check.

* See page 150.

† Now the 110th Mahratta Light Infantry.

‡ Lieutenant-Colonel Raines received special mention in the Despatch; Major Vialls, Major Massey, Captain Forster, Lieutenants Sexton and Maurice of the 95th were also mentioned, as well as Colonel Pelloy, Commanding 10th Bombay Infantry.

Colonel Raines then advanced up the Gwalior road, the cavalry and guns retiring before him.

Meanwhile Brigadier Smith had advanced his cavalry to the head of the pass, and, leaving some infantry to protect the defile in rear, he directed a squadron of cavalry to charge two or three hundred of the enemy's horse who were being formed in front of Gwalior.

Charge of the 8th Hussars.

The squadron of the 8th Hussars under Captain Heneage debouched from the pass in file, formed at a gallop after advancing about 300 yards, and then charged and were upon the enemy in a moment. Many of the rebels were cut down and the rest fled towards the town. The ground being very rough and intersected with small *nalas*, about one-third of the squadron was obliged to diverge to the right under Lieutenant Harding; the remainder with Captain Heneage, Captain Poore,* and Lieutenant Reilly, going a little to the left and continuing the attack, came shortly into the midst of the enemy's camp. Here they took three guns, cutting down the gunners and completely clearing the camp of the enemy's troops, under a heavy fire from the guns in the fort, and field guns on the right and left. After passing through the camp and crossing the road from Gwalior to Morar, the squadron came upon a large force of hostile cavalry and infantry trying to escape in a disorganised mass from the camp to the fort. Many of them made a stand, but the Hussars never slackened their pace and dashing into the midst of them, cut them down by scores, and took two guns, continuing the charge right through the Phul Bagh Cantonment.

Death of the Rani of Jhansi.

Here the Rani of Jhansi, dressed as a cavalry soldier, was cut down by a Hussar, and in her death the rebels lost their bravest and best military leader.

The whole of the ground over which this fine charge had been made, being now completely cleared of the enemy, Captain Heneage withdrew his squadron at an easy pace, and was shortly joined by the detachment under Lieutenant Harding which had charged through the right of the camp, cutting down many of the enemy's gunners and infantry, and taking four guns. Lieutenant Harding was shot at by a dismounted sowar, who missed him, but the bullet struck his charger in the eye. He was attacked at the same time by two sepoys, but killed them both.

After the charge Captain Heneage† was overcome by the heat of the sun and Lieutenant Reilly died almost immediately from exhaustion. Colonel Hicks of the Bombay Artillery and Assistant Surgeon Sherlock charged with the cavalry, the latter being wounded.

* Captain Poore was specially mentioned in the Despatch for his very gallant conduct and "unyielding resolution in remaining in the saddle under a burning sun several hours, and although so ill as to be fit for the sick report, bringing himself, the other officers being disabled by sickness, the brave squadrons in good order to his camp, under a heavy and cross fire from the enemy's guns."

† Colonel Hicks and Captain Heneage were specially mentioned in the Despatch; and Assistant Surgeon Sherlock for rendering great assistance in bringing in the wounded under fire. Lieutenant and Adjutant Harding also received special mention.

The squadron was so completely exhausted from their charge that the men could scarcely sit in their saddles. The moment was critical, as the enemy were collecting both on the front and flanks, but the 95th had arrived near the guns, and the 8th Hussars, in spite of their fatigue, formed to their front in line, in single rank so as to show a more extended front. In the meantime the remaining troop of the 1st Bombay Lancers* had arrived to support, as a second line. The cavalry was then retired by alternate troops, protected by the artillery, during which movement both arms showed the greatest steadiness, and entered the ravines under the protection of the infantry posted there. Brigadier Smith then took up a position on the heights for the night, sending for his baggage, and placing it in a sort of amphitheatre formed by a portion of the hills he had occupied. Both ends of the defile were guarded by strong infantry picquets, and strong cavalry and infantry picquets were thrown out towards the heights on the right; the left was defended against any sudden assault by a steep bank and a canal.

Brigadier Smith's dispositions.

In his despatch Brigadier Smith† wrote that he could not speak too highly of the steady and soldier-like conduct of both officers and men of the 10th Native Infantry and of the 95th Regiment, who, though exhausted by fatigue and want of food, stormed the heights under a burning sun and a heavy fire.

3 Troops, 14th Light Dragoons.
4 Guns, No. 4 Light Field Battery.
25th Bombay Infantry.

Brigadier Smith having asked for reinforcements, he was joined by Lieutenant-Colonel Robertson with the force detailed in the margin.

The General's reconnaissance of Gwalior satisfied him that the information on which he had decided to attack it was good. If he attacked from Morar, he would have to cross the plain between Morar and Gwalior under the fire of the fort, and of masked and formidable batteries, established in strong houses and gardens on the banks of the old canal, and a dry river in front of the Phul Bagh Palace.

Sir Hugh Rose marches to Kotah-ki-Serai, 18th June.

He could not leave Morar, so close to Gwalior, without adequate protection. The arrival of the troops which had been left to garrison Kalpi, on the morning of the 18th June, enabled him, leaving his encumbrances, to march on the same afternoon for Kotah-ki-Serai, with the force detailed in the margin, leaving in Morar a force under Brigadier-General Napier for its protection, the investment of Gwalior, and the pursuit of the enemy when they retreated.

Major-General Sir Hugh Rose, K.C.B.

2 Troops, 14th Light Dragoons.
No. 18, Light-Field Battery.
Madras Sappers and Miners.
Wing, 71st Highland Light Infantry.
Her Majesty's 86th Regiment.
Wing, 5th Hyderabad Contingent Infantry.
Two 18-pounders and one 8-inch howitzer.

* Now 31st Duke of Connaught's Lancers. Captain Anderson, 1st Bombay Lancers, who was mentioned in the despatch, was wounded in the arm by a musket ball.

† Brigadier Smith received special mention in Sir Hugh Rose's despatch, as well as his Brigade-Major, Captain Sir John Hill; Captain MacMullen, late 23rd Bengal Infantry; Cornet Goldsworthy, 8th Hussars and Lieutenant Williams, Sub-Assistant Commissary General.

Brigadier-General R. Napier, C.B.

1st Troop, Bombay Horse Artillery.
3 Troops, 14th Light Dragoons.
3 Troops, 3rd Bombay Light Cavalry.
50, 1st Cavalry Hyderabad Contingent.
3rd Cavalry, Hyderabad Contingent.
2 squadrons, Meade's Horse.
21st Company, Royal Engineers.
Wing, 3rd Bombay Europeans.
4 Compnies, 24th Bombay Infantry.
3 Guns, Hyderabad Contingent Artillery.

The march to Kotah-ki-Serai, about twenty miles, was very harassing; 100 men of the 86th alone were compelled by sun-sickness to fall out and go into *dhoolies*. These same men next day, unmindful of their illness, fell in with their companies, and took part in the assault of Gwalior, thus showing again that the spirit of the soldiers often made them fight when they were too weak to march.*

Sir Hugh Rose's column bivouacked on the left bank of the river Morar. Here the General received Brigadier Smith's report of how he had advanced along the road to Gwalior, by the ford across the river, attacked and driven the enemy from the hills on his right front, occupied the road, which led through a pass about two miles in length through the hills, and to the left or south side of a very deep and dry old canal cut out of the rock, which ran from the ford close by the left of the road through the pass, to the foot of the rock of Gwalior.

The enemy retained possession of the hills to the left of the pass and canal.

The enemy's position.

To the left of the road and canal in the pass rose from a narrow plain a succession of slopes intersected by ravines; a ridge ran along the top of the slopes, on which the enemy had placed a battery of 9-pounders. To protect the battery and position, the rebels had concentrated a numerous force of all arms on the ridge, as well as a large body of cavalry in rear of it. About a mile and a half further back, and about the same distance from the left of the road, was stationed in a gorge of the hills a large body of the hostile infantry with guns. They guarded a road which branched off from the ford southwards through the hills to Gwalior.

Brigadier Smith's position in the hills was weak and cramped. His left and rear were threatened by the two bodies just described. The camp baggage and guns were in the pass, into which came shots from the enemy's battery on the ridge.

It was clear that the enemy must be driven from both positions, the one on the ridge and the other in the gorge, before the advance on Gwalior.

The General's plans.

The enemy by occupying positions of the ridge so far from and unsupported by Gwalior had exposed himself to be cut off. The impediment to such an operation was the canal, impracticable for cavalry and infantry; on this obstacle the enemy probably relied for protection. Sir Hugh directed the Madras Sappers and Miners to make a bridge across the canal, some way to the left rear of his position. The bridge or dam was to be ready by sunset. The General's plan

* A hundred years before the British soldier inspired Haidar Ali of Mysore with so much respect that he said he could conquer India with a corps of them, whom he would have carried in *dhoolies* on the march, so that they might be fresh on the day of battle.

was to cross over this bridge during the night, with a force of all arms, get on the south road to Gwalior through the hills above mentioned, place himself between Gwalior and the enemy's two positions, fall on them a little before daybreak, when the 86th and 95th Regiments, supported by the rest of Brigadier Smith's brigade, were concealed by the ravines to attack their front and turn their left Lieutenant Haggard, Commissary of Ordnance, during the night, moved the two 18-pounders and the 8-inch howitzer from the bivouac up to the top of a steep height to the right of the road and canal and opposite the ridge. The General selected a point at the extremity of a spur of this height towards Gwalior as a position for these guns, from whence they commanded the plain below the entrance to the pass, and could fire on the enemy's battery on the ridge.

Artillery duel.

The enemy's battery opened fire on these siege pieces as they were being taken into position, wounding two draught elephants and subsequently causing some casualties in the battery after it had opened fire under Lieutenant Haggard's orders.

The enemy set on fire with their guns some monster hay-ricks which were close to the canal in the narrow plain, in order that the outposts might not be covered by them.

The carriage of the 8-inch howitzer had been shaken by hundreds of miles' marching that its charge was reduced a pound below the regulation in order to save the carriage; this irregular charge rendered its fire uncertain, and the want of sights on the 18-pounders affected their accuracy.

Colonel Hicks suggested the withdrawal of the siege guns as they did not appear to damage the enemy, who had their range. The General thought it better that the battery should cease firing gradually, when the enemy would probably do the same, than that it should be withdrawn. This was done, and the enemy's battery ceased to fire.

Advance of the rebels.

Before the batteries had begun to diminish their firing, the General had gone to his battery to inspect it and to watch an advance of the hostile infantry, in skirmishing order from the ridge and a spur of it to the left, against the British chain of outposts and left, which rested on the canal. Soon afterwards a large body of troops was seen debouching from Gwalior; and the vedettes reported that fresh guns were ascending the heights to reinforce the battery on the ridge, which was good news, as the more guns the rebels brought up to the heights the more were likely to be taken next morning.

Sir Hugh Rose reinforced the sentries and picquets on his left, on the line of the canal, and ordered the troops in camp to be ready to turn out.

The enemy's skirmishers now became engaged with the British line guarding the canal. At this time the General received an express from Sir Robert Hamilton, telling him that he had received information that the sepoys and *Walayatis* intended to attack that day.

The rebels seemed inclined not to confine their advance to an affair of outposts, but to be determined to attack the left flank, which they knew was weak

The Central India Field Force was the worse for the last night's harassing march, and a bad bivouac on rock. The Madras Sappers and Miners, whose zeal and intelligence no hardships could abate, would have completed the bridge across the canal by sunset; and from it, as a means of cutting off the rebel forces on the hills at night, the General anticipated the best results. He would, therefore, have preferred not engaging the enemy before the time determined on.

Disposition of the British force.

On the other hand, the position in the narrow pass was so false that it became necessary to free it from the risk of a serious attack, and to change the defensive for the offensive. He, therefore, directed Brigadier Stuart with the 86th Regiment which was encamped between the pass and the river Morar, to move from the left rear, supported by the 25th Bombay Infantry, across the canal, crown the heights on the other side of it, and attack the enemy in their left flank, by which means they would mask the fire of the battery.

As a diversion in favour of Brigadier Stuart's attack, he directed Brigadier Smith to move Lieutenant-Colonel Raines with the 95th Regiment, from the left of his right front, across the canal in skirmishing order, over the shoulder of the hill; on which was the rebel's battery, against their left flank.

This oblique movement, and the lie of the ground, prevented the 95th suffering seriously from the guns of the battery. Brigadier Smith was further directed to move up the 10th Bombay Infantry under Colonel Pelly from the right of his right front across the canal, to support the advance of the 95th and cover the right.

Sir Hugh Rose also ordered up the 3rd Troop, Bombay Horse Artillery, to the entrance of the pass towards Gwalior, supported by a squadron of the 8th Hussars.

The rest of the force was disposed in support of the attacking columns and for the defence of the camp from the rear.

Brigadier Smith, crossing the canal steadily, ascended the heights with the 86th Regiment under Lieutenant-Colonel Louth The enemy, taken in flank, retired rapidly from the attack of the British left towards the battery. The skirmishers of the 86th, with their usual ardour, pressed the rebel infantry so hard that they did not make a stand even under their guns, but retreated across the intrenchment in the rear of which they were in position. The gallant skirmishers gave them no time to rally in the battery, but dashing with a cheer at the parapet, crossed it, and took the guns which defended the ridge, three excellent English 9-pounders.

Battle of Gwalior, 19th June.

The 86th, leaving a party with the captured guns, passed on after the enemy's cavalry and infantry, who fled, part towards Gwalior, part to the hills to the south.

Lieutenant-Colonel Raines coming up with a wing of the 95th to the intrenchments, with good judgment, turned the captured guns on the hostile cavalry and infantry which he saw in detached bodies in the plain below at a distance of a thousand yards, as well as on the body which had retired to the British left.

The guns were manned by men of the 86th and 95th who had been instructed in gunnery, and made excellent practice.* Four rebel batteries now opened a hot fire of shot and shell on the advanced lines.

The 10th Bombay Infantry under Lieutenant Roome crossed the pass and the canal, and passing by the haystacks, which were now one burning mass, and moving up in support of the 95th and in protection of the right, found himself exposed to a fire of artillery and musketry from the heights on the enemy's extreme left. Advancing with half his regiment in skirmishing order and half in support, he cleared the two nearest heights of the rebel infantry, and gallantly took two brass field guns and three mortars which were in a plain at the foot of the second height.

Capture of the heights.

The British troops were now in possession of the highest range of heights to the east of Gwalior, and the city could be seen lying below. To the right was the handsome palace of the Phul Bagh with its gardens, and the old city, surmounted by the fort, remarkable for its ancient architecture, with lines of extensive fortifications round the high and precipitous rock of Gwalior. To the left lay the Lashkar or new city, with its spacious houses half hidden by trees. The slopes descended gradually towards Gwalior; the lowest one commanding the grand parade of the Lashkar, which was almost out of fire of the fort and afforded an entrance into the city.

The General felt convinced that he could take Gwalior before sunset. He determined to make a general advance against all the positions which the enemy occupied for the defence of Gwalior, extending from beyond the palace of the Phul Bagh on their right, to the extensive barracks on the left of the grand parade of the Lashkar, and then take the Lashkar by assault.

Advance on the grand parade.

For this purpose he ordered the 3rd Troop, Bombay Horse Artillery, with a squadron of the 8th Hussars, to follow the road which led out of the pass, and advance, covering his extreme right, parallel with the troops attacking Gwalior.

Lieutenant-Colonel Owen, with the 1st Bombay Lancers, had been moved to the heights to cover the captured guns; the rapidity and dexterity with which they got over difficult ground was a credit to the regiment. The General now ordered them to ascend the heights to the rear, get into the road which led through the hills to the south, and occupy the entrance to it, which led to the grand parade, for the purpose of assisting in the attack of that important point and the Lashkar.

He left a sufficient force of all arms for the protection of the camp, which was exposed.

He had some time before ordered up No. 4 Light Field Battery with two troops, 14th Dragoons, to the heights to cover his advanced line, and to answer

*Lieutenant Read, 10th Bombay Infantry, rendered great assistance in pointing and firing the guns.

Privates P. Murphy, Loix, Dempsey, and Colville, 95th Regiment, were mentioned in the Despatch for ably serving the captured guns.

the enemy's batteries in position in front of Gwalior. The hilly and difficult nature of the ground, particularly the deep canal which the guns had to traverse prevented their arrival.

The advanced line was irregular, as it followed the formation of the hills. The 86th formed the left, which was in advance, the 95th the right, which was refused.

The left of the 86th who pursued, across a deep ravine to the range of hills to the south, the body of the enemy who retreated to the left, had returned and rested their left on a hamlet situated on the crest of the range which commanded Gwalior. The rebels immediately brought a battery of two 18-pounders in front of the grand parade to bear on the hamlet, and firing from a great elevation sent round shot into it in rapid succession and with accurate aim.

Skirmishers of the 86th had descended the hill towards the barracks, and were advancing against the enemy who had made a stand in houses amongst trees at the foot of the hill. Lieutenant-Colonel Raines with good judgment detached Captain Smith's Company of the 95th in support of them.

The General now moved the 86th from the hamlet lower down the hill, extending them at wide intervals from the left to the right. This new position of the 86th rendered the fire of the 18-pounders harmless, and gave more support to the skirmishers. who soon gave a good account of the enemy in the houses.

In front of and between the two hills, occupied by the 86th and 95th, was the last slope, a spur of the hill on which were the 86th, commanding the rows of barracks and the grand parade of the Lashkar, to which the enemy, pressed by the British advance, had now withdrawn the two 18-pounders.

Sir Hugh Rose occupied this slope with a wing of the 25th Bombay Infantry which was brought up from the second line, leaving the other wing in support. He moved a party of the 95th down to the right of the slope under Major Vialls who took possession of a strong powder magazine, surrounded by a wall, at the further end of it.

Lieutenant Roome, with the 10th Bombay Infantry on the right, after he had captured the guns and field pieces, took a strong building on his right, used as an arsenal, from which the enemy had poured a galling fire on his regiment and occupied a trench at the bottom of the hill on which was the arsenal. From here the 10th kept up a heavy fire on the enemy, who had retreated to a position in front of Gwalior.

Lieutenant-Colonel Raines, leaving a company of the 95th to guard the captured gun, which kept up an effective fire on the enemy, joined with the rest of his regiment and reinforced Major Vialls on the west slope. He perceived a large body of the enemy's cavalry in the vicinity of the two 18-pounders now placed in battery, who, he believed, were posted there for the purpose of making a dash at the British troops, should they attempt to take the guns. He therefore halted and waited for orders and reinforcements, placing two companies of the 95th in skirmishing order, lying down along the crest of the hill, a part of the 10th Bombay Infantry being in rear as supports. The enemy now came out and fired the 18-pounders with grape and canister at the British position, on which Colonel Raines detached some skirmishers of the 95th to cover ground to his front, who kept up with their Enfields such an effective fire on the 18-pounders and the cavalry, that, after firing eight rounds, the enemy was obliged to cease fire and retire behind the buildings of the grand parade.

Lieutenant Knatchbull and seven or eight men of the 95th dragged a small howitzer and its tumbril, captured by the 10th Bombay Infantry, up the slope and opened fire with it on the enemy behind the buildings.

The Officer Commanding No. 4 Light Field Battery, by following the road through the pass beyond its entrance, had found a passage, a very difficult one, across the canal; but on taking them up a bridle road which led to the heights, a gun upset and delayed very inopportunely the arrival of this artillery on the heights; but one 9-pounder was at last taken up.

The enemy were firing with much vivacity but little effect from the batteries on the right, and the captured guns were answering them. Large bodies of infantry and cavalry were marching out of Gwalior by all its issues, and moving towards the British, but not in order or with resolution as if to attack, or take up a position of defence.

General attack on Gwalior.

Besides storming the grand parade, from which the attacking force could enter the Lashkar and pass by the main street to Sindhia's palace, Sir Hugh Rose directed Brigadier Smith, with No. 3 Troop, Bombay Horse Artillery, and a squadron of the 14th Light Dragoons, to be ready to attack the enemy's positions at the Phul Bagh and beyond it. This attack protected the right of the troops attacking the grand parade, and at the same time turned the enemy's left.

The 1st Bombay Lancers were to debouch from the entrance of the road on which they had been placed, charge the enemy on the grand parade, and assist the 95th in taking it.

The 10th Bombay Infantry were to support these regiments. One 9-pounder, the only artillery which had been able to reach the heights, was to cover from the lowest slope the advance of the 1st Bombay Lancers and of the 95th and to clear the grand parade.

The 86th were to remain in their position on the left of the heights, cover the left, and if necessary assist the camp.

One wing of the 25th Bombay Infantry was to attack the barracks and cover the left of the 95th attacking the grand parade. The other was to be in support on the slopes.

Two troops of the 14th Light Dragoons were in support on the lower slopes.

All being ready, Sir Hugh Rose gave the word for the general attack of Gwalior.

He had placed the 9-pounder in position, opposite the two 18-pounders, and directed it to fire with shrapnel at the enemy who were attempting to load their pieces. The shrapnel burst just over the 18-pounders into about twenty pieces, killed and disabled some of the gunners, and put the rest to flight; at the same time part of the hostile cavalry and infantry on the grand parade began to retire.

An animated scene ensued. The 1st Lancers under Lieutenant-Colonel Owen, the first squadron led by Lieutenant Heath and that in support by Captain Lock, issuing from the road, charged most gallantly in sight of the British troops descending the slopes of the heights into the grand parade, and clearing all the right of it pursued, carried away by their ardour, the rebel infantry into the Lashkar, where Lieutenant Mills was shot through the heart, Captain Lock cutting down the man who killed him.

Colonel Raines with two companies of the 95th charged down the slope and took the two 18-pounders and two small mortars on the grand parade.

After descending the slope and pointing out to Brigadier Smith the position he was to attack, Sir Hugh Rose joined Colonel Raines on the grand parade, and went with him against the town, with the intention of forcing the way, if necessary, to the palace, the possession of which would give them the Lashkar. As he did not know whether the enemy might not, as at Jhansi, defend the streets and houses, he directed Colonel Raines to form four companies of his regiment for street-fighting, and to leave the remainder in reserve on the grand parade

Lieutenant Roome, with the 10th Bombay Infantry, on the general advance being ordered, moved to the front, skirmishing through the buildings of the grand parade, and killed many of the enemy who stood there; those who escaped were afterwards cut up by the 1st Bombay Lancers.

The fort kept up a constant fire during the advance, but, as the General foresaw, his position masked him from it. Shortly after entering the Lashkar he met the 1st Lancers returning with Liutenant Mills just killed, Colonel Owen not thinking it advisable for cavalry to be involved in street fighting with the large numbers of the enemy in the town.

The rebel cavalry and infantry retreated so rapidly through the town that they were not even sighted, although the troops advanced by several streets to cut them off. Their cavalry, instead of covering the retreat, headed it as usua. After marching more than a mile through the streets, Sindhia's palace was reached Patrols were detached in every direction to clear the streets; and before sunset the whole of the Lashkar was in the hands of the British.

Capture of the Lashkar.

Lieutenant-Colonel Robertson,* 25th Bombay Infantry, was appointed Commandant of Gwalior, and directed to occupy it with his regiment, including the fort, which Sindhia's Agent said had been evacuated.

Meanwhile Brigadier Smith engaged the enemy at Phul Bagh which he took, killing numbers of the rebels. He then pursued a large body retiring round the rock of Gwalior towards the Residency, covering their retreat with Horse Artillery guns. After a stout resistance, which did credit to the enemy's

* This brave officer, whose fine regiment had performed such good service throughout the campaign in Central India, received his 5th special mention in despatches for his services at the battle of Gwalior.

artillery, Brigadier Smith captured the guns and killed numbers of the retreating rebels. He pursued them far into the night, capturing more guns, until his men and horses were unable to move on.

The Officer Commanding Old Gwalior reported that the enemy still held the fort, and had fired upon him from it, and as it was now night, the General gave directions for its close investment. The fortress of Gwalior stands upon a vast rock about four miles in length, but narrow and of unequal breadth and nearly flat on the top. The sides are so steep as to appear almost perpendicular in every part; for where not so, the rock has been scarped away and the height above the plain below is from 200 to 300 feet. The rampart conforms to the edge of the precipice all round, and the only entrance to it is by steps running up the side of the rock, defended on the side next the city by a wall and bastion, and further guarded by seven stone gateways, at certain distances from each other. The area within is full of noble buildings, reservoirs of water, wells, and cultivated land; so that it is really a little district in itself.

The fortress of Gwalior.

The morning after the battle the enemy again fired from the fort on the troops. Lieutenant Rose, 25th Bombay Infantry, Lieutenant Waller, and a party of the 25th under his orders, with some of Sindhia's police, burst open the main gateway of the fort, and surprising the other gates before the garrison, a party of fanatical Musalman artillerymen, could shut them, reached an archway on which the rebels brought a gun to bear. Lieutenant Rose and his party got through the archway unscathed by the fire of the gun and then engaged in a desperate hand-to-hand conflict with the rebels, who defended the narrow street leading into the fort. But the determined gallantry of Lieutenant Rose and of the soldiers of the 25th, aided by Lieutenant Waller, who climbed with a few of his men on to the roof of a house and shot the gunners, carried all before it, and they took the fort and killed every man in it. But their brave leader, who had been specially mentioned twice by Sir Hugh Rose for good and gallant conduct, was mortally wounded. Thus Lieutenant Rose closed his brave and early career in capturing the fort of Gwalior; he had, as an officer of the 7th Gwalior Contingent, escaped from Neemuch on the outbreak of the mutiny.*

Capture of the fort, 20th June.

* The men of the 25th with Lieutenant Rose, mentioned in Despatches, were Colour Havildar Gannu Powar, Havildar Ramzan Khan, Privates Bhao Sirka, Gonaji Goura, Matadin, Sen Ami Ahir, Chota Singh; the four last named were wounded.

This gallant capture of the fort of Gwalior may be compared with the first capture of the fortress by the British in 1780. In that year a small force under Major W. Popham, despatched by Warren Hastings in aid of the Rana of Gohad, the former owner of Gwalior, crossed the Jumna in February. After some minor operations Major Popham arrived before Gwalior with four battalions of sepoys and a few guns early in August. On the 3rd August two companies of picked sepoys under Captain W. Bruce were told off as a storming party, Major Popham following with a reserve of two companies. The sepoys, who wore woollen shoes, placed wooden ladders against the scarped rock, and thus ascended the first part of it. The second wall, 30 feet in height, was then climbed by Captain Bruce and twenty sepoys by means of a rope ladder, who, when the garrison was alarmed, held their own until the arrival of the main body. Of the twelve hundred men forming the garrison many were killed including Bapoji, the Governor, and the rest fled, the assailants losing only twenty wounded, and at sunrise the British flag floated from the rock of Gwalior.

Abandoning the defence of Gwalior whilst his troops were still fighting, Tantia Topi, with a considerable body of cavalry and infantry, attempted to retreat southwards by the road to Punniar and Goona; but learning that Punniar was occupied by Major Orr's force, he went to the Residency, where the rest of the rebel army joined him in their retreat from Gwalior.*

Flight of Tantia Topi.

The Residency was to have been occupied by Colonel Riddell, but the difficulty of crossing the ford over the Chambal at Dholpur, where he had arrived on his road from Agra, made it impossible for him to reach to it in time to complete the investment.

Sir Hugh Rose sent an express to Brigadier-General Napier at the Morar Cantonments, requesting him to pursue the enemy as far and as closely as he could.

Next morning, at Sir Hugh Rose's suggestion, Sindhia † arrived with his retinue at Gwalior where he was received by the General and escorted to his palace in the Lashkar by a squadron of the 8th Hussars and a squadron of the 14th Light Dragoons. The road lay through the long and handsome street which leads from the grand parade to the palace, which was lined by crowds of inhabitants who greeted their prince with enthusiastic acclamations. Sindhia was unceasing in his endeavours to prove his deep gratitude to the Government of India and to the gallant soldiers who had restored him to his throne, and asked permission to present a medal to the troops engaged

Restoration of Sindhia, 20th June.

The British loss in the Gwalior operations amounted to 21 killed and 44 wounded, of whom 5 subsequently died.

Brigadier-General Napier received his orders to pursue the enemy at 5-15 A.M. on the 20th June, and marched, with the troops detailed in the margin, within an hour and a half of their receipt. The fort opened fire on him as he passed, and obliged him to make a detour to reach the Residency; and late in the evening he arrived at Samaoli, having marched about 25 miles.

Brigadier-General Napier's pursuit, 20th June.

1st Troop, Horse Arty., 99.
14th Light Dragoons, 62.
3rd Bo. Light Cavalry, 104.
3rd Hyderabad Contingent Cavalry, 245.
Meade's Horse, 180.

The enemy was reported to have 12,000 men and 22 guns, and to have marched from Samaoli to Jaora-Alipur in the forenoon. The pursuing force was too exhausted to go beyond Samaoli, the heat of the sun having been terrific, so they rested until 4 A.M. on the 21st, and then advanced on Jaora-Alipur, where they found the enemy strongly posted with their right resting on Alipur, guns and infantry in the centre, and cavalry on both flanks.

A rising ground hid the approach, and enabled Brigadier-General Napier to reconnoitre their position in security from a distance of 1,200 yards. They opened

* Tantia Topi was prevented from fleeing northwards by a force sent out from Agra by Brigadier Showers.

† Sindhia, escorted by two squadrons of Meade's Horse, left Agra for Dholpur on the 14th, and reached Morar on the 17th after a march of 65 miles within 24 hours.

several guns on the reconnoitring party, disclosing the position of their artillery, which had not previously been discovered. The ground was open to the enemy's left, and a careful examination convinced the General that there was nothing to check the advance of his artillery. He directed Captain Lightfoot to take up a position about 600 yards from the enemy's left flank, and enfilade their line, and to act afterwards as circumstances might dictate.

The column of march was the most convenient formation for attack; Abbott's Hyderabad Contingent Cavalry in advance, Lightfoot's Troop of Horse Artillery, supported by Captain Prettijohn's Troop of 14th Light Dragoons and two Troops, 3rd Light Cavalry, under Lieutenant Dick, with a detachment of Meade's Horse * under Lieutenant Burlton in reserve. When the troops came into view of the enemy after turning the shoulder of the rising ground, the whole were advanced at a gallop, and as soon as the artillery had reached the flank of the position, the line was formed to the left, and the guns opened on the insurgents at a distance of 600 yards.

Action at Jaora Alipur, 21st June.

After a few rounds the enemy's guns were silenced and a rapid thinning and wavering of their ranks took place. Captain Lightfoot limbered up and advanced at a gallop; and Captain Abbott with his cavalry charged at the same moment. The movement was instantaneously followed by the rest of the cavalry, and the whole of the little force swept through the enemy's batteries and camp, and past the villages into the open plain, driving before them and cutting down the rebels for several miles. Detachments of cavalry charged a body of fugitives to the right and cut up many of them.

Wherever there was a body of the enemy collected in front, Lightfoot's guns opened and dispersed them. A party of their cavalry made a move to the left rear of the British as if to cut off the baggage, but on perceiving a body of the Hyderabad Contingent Cavalry, left to cover the road to the rear, and being themselves threatened by the 3rd Light Cavalry, they retreated rapidly out of sight.

Defeat of the rebels.

The pursuers had now advanced about six miles from their first point of attack; the enemy were dispersed in every direction, throwing away their arms; 25 guns had been captured and were lying broadcast over the plain; men and horse were exhausted, and it was necessary to retire. The villages in rear were still full of the enemy, who were cutting up camp followers, and firing on all who passed within range. Two guns and a party of Abbott's Cavalry were sent to clear them out, which was effected by the fire of the guns, and by parties of dismounted cavalry with their swords and carbines. Besides the guns, a considerable quantity of ammunition, an elephant, tents, carts, and baggage fell into the hands of the victors.

* Meade's Horse was raised at Agra in December 1857, and January 1858, by Captain (afterwards General Sir Richard) Meade, who had been for some years Brigade-Major of the Gwalior Contingent. The nucleus of the regiment was formed of a hundred Sikhs and Punjabi Muhammadans. To them were added some 85 Eurasians and native Christians, formed into a Christian troop. In January, 1858, 45 Jats from Rohtak joined, and later 70 horsemen raised by the Thakur of Jhara. Meade was ably assisted by, among others, Sergeant Hartigan, V.C., 9th Lancers, who subsequently received a commission in the 16th. The regiment was afterwards incorporated in the Central India Horse.

Never was the rout of an army more complete, and between 300 and 400 rebels were killed. Of the pursuers four men were killed and eight wounded.

The good discipline of the troops was only equalled by the courage with which they charged such a superior force. Many occasions arose when it was necessary for detached parties to act against the hostile infantry, and they were invariably met with the promptest gallantry. Captain Barrett's Troop of the 14th Dragoons arrived after the close of the action, and a party dismounted turned twenty rebels out of a garden and killed them all. Private Novell, 14th Dragoons, charged alone into the village, and killed one of the enemy under a heavy fire. He was recommended for the Victoria Cross. Subadar Sujab Khan, 3rd Bombay Cavalry, dislodged a party from behind a wall and killed them. Trumpeter Charles Sappery, Meade's Horse, killed a standard bearer and captured a standard. Brigadier-General Napier especially noticed the superb manner in which Captain Lightfoot took up his position on the flank of the enemy, and the dash with which he followed them when broken. Captain Abbott distinguished himself by his activity and intelligence and the gallantry of his charge on the batteries.

In his report* on the Gwalior operations, Sir Hugh Rose wrote :—" I venture to recommend most earnestly all the troops engaged in the Gwalior operations, the Central India Field Force, as well as Brigadier Smith's Brigade of the Rajputana Field Force, to His Lordship's most favourable consideration. It is not for me to describe the importance of the service which they performed. I am convinced that it is fully and generously appreciated by the exalted authorities whose high attributions and experience constitute them the judges of what would have been the state of India if Gwalior had remained for any length of time in the hands of the rebels.

Fine conduct of the troops.

But as the commander of the troops engaged, it is my duty to say, that although a most arduous campaign had impaired the health and strength of every man of my force, their discipline, devotion, and courage remained unvarying and unshaken, enabling them to make a very rapid march in summer heat to Gwalior, fight and gain two actions on the road, one at Morar Cantonments, the other at Kotah-ki-Serai; arrive at their posts from great distances and by bad roads, before Gwalior before the day appointed, the 19th June; and on that same day carry by assault all the enemy's positions on strong heights, and in most difficult ground, taking one battery after another, 27 pieces of artillery in the action, 25 in the pursuit, besides the guns in the fort; the old city; the new city; and finally the rock of Gwalior held to be one of the most important and strongest fortresses in India.

I marched on the 6th June from Kalpi for Gwalior, and on the 19th of the same month the Gwalior States were restored to their Prince."

* Sir Hugh Rose mentioned his Staff Officers in his despatches, including Captain R. Meade, of Meade's Horse, whose zeal and knowledge of the country rendered him of great use during the operations.

The capture of Gwalior and the dispersal of the rebels at Jaora-Alipur brought the regular campaign to an end, although there was a long pursuit of Tantia Topi, lasting many months, before that miscreant was brought to the gallows.

Sir Hugh Rose handed over his command to Brigadier-General R. Napier, C.B., and left for Poona by way of Mhow on the morning of the 29th June 1858.

CHAPTER

GENERAL WHITLOCK'S OPERATIONS AND THE PACIFICATION OF BUNDELKHAND.

It has already been stated that the plan of campaign in Central India provided for the advance of a Madras Column from Jubbulpore to co-operate with Sir Hugh Rose in the relief of Jhansi, and to move through the eastern part of Bundelkhand and suppress the revolt in that area. In November, 1857, Major-General Whitlock was appointed to the command of this column which was to be concentrated at Jubbulpore for the advance on Banda.

The Saugor Field Division.

Major-General G. Whitlock.

A. Troop, European Horse Artillery.
E. Troop, Native Horse Artillery.
Her Majesty's 12th Lancers.
4th Madras Light Cavalry.
6th Madras Light Cavalry.
7th Madras Light Cavalry.
One Squadron, 2nd Cavalry, Hyderabad Contingent.
Detachment, Royal Artillery.
Detachment, Madras Foot Artillery.
Detachment, Madras Sappers and Miners.
3rd Madras European Regiment.
1st Madras Infantry.

Nagpore Moveable Column.

1 Squadron, 4th Madras Light Cavalry.
One Squadron, 2nd Cavalry, Hyderabad Contingent.
D. Company, 3rd Battalion, Madras Artillery.
33rd Madras Infantry.
Rifle Company, 1st Nagpore Irregular Infantry

The Saugor Field Division was composed of the troops detailed in the margin. General Whitlock reached Kamptee on the 10th January, 1858, but with the dilatoriness which, it will be seen, characterised all his operations, he did not march until the 23rd. On the 3rd February he reached Jubbulpore, a distance of a hundred and forty-eight miles, his force arriving a few days later, and there found the Nagpore Moveable Column which had been operating in the southern Narbada territory under Colonel Millar, and had been directed to await his arrival.

On the 11th February the 4th and 6th Madras Light Cavalry, which had been ordered to Allahabad, marched from Jubbulpore, but had not gone far when news was received that the Nana had crossed into Bundelkhand with a large force, and General Whitlock, therefore, ordered them to halt until his force could overtake them.

General Whitlock's advance.

On the 17th February General Whitlock's force marched from Jubbulpore. accompanied by Major Erskine,* Commissioner of the Division, and reached Jukehi on the 24th, finding that place completely destroyed by the Rewah troops. Here he was met by the loyal Raja of Nagode, and, information having been received that the report of the Nana's entry into Bundelkhand was erroneous, the 4th and 6th Madras Cavalry resumed their march to Allahabad. During the march to Jukehi the General was several times requested by Major

* Afterwards Earl of Mar and Kellie.

Erskine to destroy strongholds held by rebels, such as Ramnagar, Mardangarh, and Ramgarh, but refused either to divide his force or turn aside for the purpose. The consequence was that his column passed through the country without any attempt at pacification.

Relief of Damoh, 26th February.

Leaving the Deccan road on the 26th, General Whitlock marched to Damoh in seven stages, the rebels clearing off to the flanks as the column passed, but again closing in behind it. Near Damoh there was a noted rebel, Kishor Singh, at Hindoria, but he was allowed to continue his plundering unmolested.

On the 5th March General Whitlock entered Saugor, which had been relieved by Sir Hugh Rose on the 3rd February, with some artillery and lancers, and was followed by two hundred of the 3rd Madras Europeans and seventy native infantry, who came in by forced marches. He also ordered a hundred of the Madras Europeans and seventy native infantry to escort treasure in the direction of Jubbulpore. The remainder of his force meanwhile remained at Damoh under Brigadier Carpenter. On the 12th General Whitlock returned to Damoh from Saugor, taking with him some lancers and horse artillery. Here Major Erskine left him, having requested him in vain to operate against the rebels who were plundering the country between Damoh and Jubbulpore.

Slow movements of Whitlock.

Having received orders from Government to march on Nagode and Panna by way of Hatta, General Whitlock reached Panna on the 29th March, meeting with no opposition. Here he halted until the 2nd April. It is interesting, at this stage, to compare the hesitating movements of this commander with those of Sir Hugh Rose, who had by this date taken many forts, relieved Saugor, fought several battles, defeated Tantia Topi at Betwa river, keeping his hold on Jhansi, which he was about to assault on the morrow. It is an excellent example of the difference between an active, energetic, and great General, and one lacking in character and decision.

On the 3rd April, the day on which Jhansi was stormed and taken, Whitlock received a despatch from Sir Hugh Rose, with whom he had been directed to co-operate, requesting him to move with all expedition on Jhansi. He had meanwhile marched by a difficult road over Marwa Ghat to Mandala, where he had to halt some days to repair his damaged guns and vehicles, and on the 6th he moved on to Chhatarpur, which he reached on the 9th.

Here Major Ellis, Political Assistant in Bundelkhand, having informed General Whitlock that 2,000 rebels had collected at Jhigan, one of their strongholds and the depôt for their plunder, about seventeen miles from Chhatarpur, the General decided on making a night march to surprise them.

Action at Jhigan, 11th April.

The force marched at 8 P.M., on 10th April, 1858, but, owing to the difficulties of the road and ignorance of the guides, was still four miles from Jhigan at 5 A.M. the following day. General Whitlock then advanced rapidly with A Troop, Horse Artillery, two squadrons of Lancers, and a detachment, 2nd Cavalry, Hyderabad Contingent, when the insurgents evacuated their position. The artillery opened fire, and the cavalry charging killed many of the rebels. The cavalry and guns then moved to intercept their flight through jungle which had been set on fire to impede pursuit, and under a heavy matchlock fire, and again came up with them.

Ninety-seven rebels were killed and 39 prisoners taken, of whom 9 were hanged that evening. The village and stronghold were destroyed. The casualties were only two men of the Hyderabad Contingent Cavalry wounded.

Advance on Banda.

The Saugor Field Division now marched to Mahoba, and thence moved on Banda, where, as has already been related, the Nawab had made preparations to meet this advance.

On the 17th April, when marching through Kabrai, twenty-four miles west of Banda, General Whitlock was surprised by a heavy fire opened on the troops before daybreak. The Cavalry and Horse Artillery immediately went to the front, but the rebels retreated under cover of darkness with very little loss, and on arrival at Banda represented that they had gained a victory over the British, who were few in number and unable to fight.

The Nawab's position.

On the 18th April the Nawab Ali Bahadur took up a position at Goera Mughali,* about 8 miles west of Banda and five miles from the left bank of the river Ken, to oppose General Whitlock's advance on his capital. The position was strong and well-selected. The artillery commanded the main road on which the British force was moving, enabling the Nawab to withdraw his guns if hard pressed. Ground intersected by numerous ravines and nullahs covered his whole front, affording excellent cover to a horde of skirmishers, who skilfully availed themselves of it, whilst movements against their flanks were impeded by ground most difficult for the combined operations of cavalry and artillery. The enemy, some six thousand in number, with three thousand in reserve, comprising many sepoys of the mutinied 50th and other regiments, were under the personal command of the Nawab and the infantry had percussion muskets.

Battle of Banda, 18th April.

A. Troop, E. H. Artillery.
E. Troop, N. H. Artillery.
Her Majesty's 12th Lancers.
1 Squadron, 2nd Cavalry, Hyderabad Contingent.
Detachment, Royal Arty.
Detachment, M. F. Artillery.
No. 1 Horse Battery.
Detachment, S. and M.
3rd Madras E. Regiment.
1st Madras Infantry.
Detachment, 5th M. I.
Total 1,899 of all arms.
Also 414 of the Raja of Charkhari's troops.

General Whitlock had with him the force detailed in the margin; when he approached to reconnoitre, the enemy opened a sharp artillery fire. The advanced guard under Colonel Apthorp, 3rd Madras Europeans, first encountered the hostile infantry, and met with a heavy fire.

The advanced guard was formed in line some six hundred yards from the enemy's position, with Captain Macintire's† squadron of the 2nd Cavalry, Hyderabad Contingent, on the right. Afer advancing a short distance, it was found that two of the

* The villagers of Goera Mughali had captured the Nowgong fugitives and delivered them up to the Nawab on the 30th June 1857 (see page 28) for which they were afterwards punished. The site of the battle of Banda is erroneously placed south instead of west of that town, in Malleson's History.

† Afterwards General Macintire, C.B.

Advanced Guard.
Colonel Apthorp.
1 Troop, 12th Lancers.
1 squadron, 2nd Cavalry, Hyderabad Contingent.
3rd Madras Europeans.

enemy's guns were posted so as to enfilade the infantry as they advanced, so Colonel Apthorp directed Captain Macintire to charge the guns, which was done in gallant style, and one of the guns was captured. This charge overground intersected with deep nullahs full of the enemy's infantry, enabled the infantry to reach the rebels with comparatively trifling loss.

The main body of the force had now come up, and was directed to the left, to co-operate with the advanced guard, which was hard pressed. A flanking fire soon relieved them, and the desperate resistance of the enemy resulted in many hand-to-hand conflicts, where the bayonet did great execution.

The Cavalry and Artillery then turned the enemy's left flank, and the Hyderabad Contingent Cavalry getting into difficulties in bad ground suffered severely. But the 12th Lancers, formed in line by Major T. Oakes, who commanded the Cavalry Brigade, having crossed the deep nullahs in single file, charged the rebels, who did not await their onslaught, but dispersed all over the country. The Lancers followed them up about four miles to the river Ken, cutting up about three hundred of them. Here Brigadier W. H. Miller was cut down, and saved by Private T. Ellis, 12th Lancers, who speared his assailant.

Defeat of the rebels.

Although the enemy was now retreating, it was four hours before the firing ceased; the rebels fell back slowly, occupying all avourable ground fo r opposition, and the guns were continually in action to dislodge them. When they occupied a second position Major Oakes detached a troop of Lancers to protect the art ery on the left flank and a troop of the Hyderabad Contingent on the right The heights having been gained, the 12th Lancers advanced and took a large brass gun, and pursued the enemy, who were in full retreat, covered by the fire of some heavy guns on the left of the fort.

Flight of the Nawab.

The Nawab at length fled, leaving on the field more than a thousand of his men, eight hundred of whom were killed; among them several men of note, while many notorious scoundrels were hanged within a few hours. The British loss amounted to five killed and twenty-nine wounded, the Hyderabad Contingent Cavalry alone losing three killed and fifteen wounded, three mortally.

Services of the British Force.

The General brought to the special notice of the Commander-in-Chief, "Captain Macintire, of the Madras Artillery, commanding a squadron of the 2nd Hyderabad Contingent Cavalry, always distinguished for his zeal, a soldier's spirit, and a judgment well fitting him for his command; his charge on the enemy's guns was the admiration of all who witnessed the affair; and his men followed their leader with an order with which his high bearing had inspired them, and I cannot express myself in too high terms of their spirit and their gallantry." Captain Macintire and the Adjutant of the regiment Lieutenant Ryall cut down several of the enemy in hand-to-hand combat.

The artillery, both British and native, did excellent service, and engaged the enemy at close quarters, and Brigadier Miller in his despatch said with regard to his arm of the service:—"Major Davie cut down one gunner and disarmed another flying from one of the enemy's guns taken; Major Barrow and Lieutenant Henegan, gallantly supported by Lieutenant Blunt, 12th Lancers, with a few of his men, captured another gun; Sergeant Major Dinwiddie, F. Troop, and Sergeant Alford, D. Troop, Horse Artillery, cut down several of the enemy during the action, and the Major-General himself witnessed the daring manner in which Gunner Michael Carroll, A. Troop, Horse Artillery, went in on a mutineer who was fighting with the resolution of despair, and had for some time kept several men, both Europeans and natives, at bay."*

Occupation of Banda.

When the column approached the city a flag of truce was brought out by the principal inhabitants, who informed the General that the Nawab had fled and the rebels had evacuated the place, the mutineers having set fire to their lines. So great was the panic and so sudden the flight that food was being prepared for the Nawab when the British occupied the palace. Thirteen large brass guns were found in Banda, besides several of smaller calibre, as well as much valuable property, specie, grain, elephants, and camels, and for weeks afterwards abandoned horses and property were brought in by the surrounding villagers.

The station was found a heap of ruins, even the trees on the road sides had been destroyed. The church roof had been blown off and the tower made a target of by the rebel artillerymen, and the walls had been undermined. The monuments in the cemetery had been defaced, and the stone and marble tablets taken for use as curry stones.

Retreat of the insurgents.

The main portion of the rebel-column retreated towards Hamirpur by a more northerly road. The Nawab,† as he passed through the town, was said to be weeping bitterly. With a few followers he and the female portion of his establishment crossed the

* In addition to all those mentioned above the following were noted in despatches:—Brigadier Carpenter, commanding Infantry Brigade; Major R. Hamilton, A. A. G.; Captain Lawder, A. Q. M. G.; Captain Mayne, A. J. A. G.; Lieutenant Homan, 50th M.I., A. D.C.; Major Brett, 3rd Europeans; Major Ludlow, Field Engineer; Major Abbott, who was with the troops of the Charkhari Raja; Surgeon Davidson; Field Surgeon Macfarlane; Majors Brice and Mein, Captains Palmer, Holmes, and Harrison, Artillery; Captain Prior and Lieutenant Roe, 12th Lancers.

†The Nawab, who appears to have been of weak character, was undoubtedly duped by his adherents. Mr. Mayne, the Collector, wrote of him as follows:—"At this time (June, 1857) I gave Nawab Ali Bahadur credit for good intentions at heart. He had from his youth upwards courted English society, and was also devoted to field sports and manly exercises. He is a good shot with both rifle and pistol, a first rate whip, and a good plucky rider, and can undergo immense personal fatigue. He possesses, therefore, many of the attributes which would make a good leader of the rebel cause; but he is utterly wanting in brains and judgment. We can indeed have no better proof of his being a fool than that, notwithstanding the above propensities and the possession of a good and extensive stud and other establishments, and his enjoying an annual pension of £40,000 sterling he should have turned rebel. He thought of nothing but his women, his horses, and his English fowling-pieces and rifles, and was ever a mere tool in the hands of others. Essentially a man of pleasure and incapable of transacting the most trifling public business, he was entirely in the hands of those about him, and he acted by their advice. There were naturally great doubts to all at the time whether the British Government would ever again be restored, and the Nawab did the best

river Ken by a ford some miles lower down and rejoined the main body of his troops at Jalalpur. He then marched to Kalpi and joined the rebels under the Rao and Rani of Jhansi at that stronghold, against which Sir Hugh Rose was then advancing.*

General Whitlock's inaction.

Meanwhile the rebel chiefs with their larger armies still stood defiant in the neighbouring districts of Kalpi, Hamirpur, and Jalalpur, while at Kirwi Narayan Rao and Madhu Rao, a minor,† had an army of 15,000 men and 40 guns, calling themselves "Peshwa," retaining possession of the eastern half of the district, and refusing to surrender.

2nd Brigade, Saugor Field Division.
Brigadier J. MacDuff.
No. 6 Field Battery, Royal Artillery.
8th Irregular Cavalry.
Metge's Sikh Horse.
Jhansi Mounted Police.
Detachment, Her Majesty's 43rd Regiment.
Jhansi Military Foot Police.

But General Whitlock was awaiting the arrival of his second Brigade, under Brigadier J. MacDuff. This Brigade, about a thousand strong with four guns, consisting of the troops detailed in the margin, left Jubbulpore on the 18th March, and moving by way of Saugor and Nagode, to prevent the mutineers from heading back into the Mirzapur District, reached Banda on the 27th May. Here he found General Whitlock still halted, and making no attempt to co-operate with Sir Hugh Rose in the advance on Kalpi. The General had not, however, been idle. A strong detachment of all arms had been sent out to march through the district under Major Dallas, 1st Madras Infantry. This column marched by Baberu, Tindwari, and Chilla Tara back to Banda. The inhabitants were reassured and every precaution was taken against plunder and molestation. The villagers flocked to the British camp, bringing supplies and manifesting pleasure in the re-establishment of authority. At Hardaoli, a large Muhammadan village, where rebels were said to be concealed, Major Dallas captured the Nawab's private Munshi, who was riding a horse stolen from an officer, and hanged him on the spot. The villages of Banda and Joharpur on the banks of the Jumna were next pointed out as the terror of the surrounding country, and still occupied in force by the rebels. Joharpur was surrounded at night, and the insurgents took to their boats and made for the opposite bank being well punished with grape from the Horse Artillery guns before they reached it. A few rebels were caught in the village, one of whom had set himself up as a Raja in the surrounding country, and was forthwith hanged, while the others were released after receiving corporal punishment.

Operations of a flying column.

he could to secure his own interests and the sovereignty of the country, which his ancestors had usurped. But I do not believe he was himself at that time actuated by actively hostile feelings to the British Government. He possessed no resources and had no power in the country. He was threatened by the Rajas of Bundelkhand and by the surrounding villagers. He had to make a power for himself and to re-establish order, and with that view he re-entertained all the old establishments, sent for the Government treasure (Rs. 18,000) and appropriated it to his own use, and commenced raising troops and to cast guns. I believe he would have been glad at that time to have seen us return."

* See page 129.

† Madhu or Madhava Rao of Kirwi was a minor, 9 years of age.

General Whitlock marched on the 1st June, the Kirwi Raos still refusing to come in or to allow the British establishments to occupy that portion of the district. On the approach of the British force, Narayan Rao's army made a precipitate retreat to the hilly tracts south of Tirohan, and Narayan Rao and Madhu Rao surrendered unconditionally with 42 guns, and treasure and jewels to a fabulous amount, which were afterwards awarded as prize money to the troops, while the State was annexed by the Government.* General Whitlock then marched back to Banda with the guns and treasure, leaving a force at Kirwi under Brigadier Carpenter. Another column under Major Dallas was sent to patrol the district, and these measures, combined with the defeat of the rebels at Kalpi, tended to pacify the country.

March to Kirwi, 1st June.

During the ensuing months the Saugor Field Division was distributed in the district at various stations, a portion going to Kalpi to relieve the detachment left by Sir Hugh Rose at that place when he marched on Gwalior. Some military operations were carried out in Bundelkhand during the remainder of the year 1858.

When Sir Hugh Rose advanced through Bundelkhand to Kalpi he had no spare troops to occupy any of the country and positions he had passed through, except Jhansi itself; and the rebels, seeing no troops, recovered confidence. The Rajas of Banpur and Shahgarh, who had doubled round Sir Hugh Rose's right flank, reached their own territories, and the fort of Chanderi was again captured by the insurgents.

State of the Jhansi District.

Barjur Singh, a rebel Thakur of the Jalaun district, was plundering the country round Kunch, and the very day of the fall of Kalpi, Moth, 35 miles on the road from Jhansi, was plundered by Thakurs Gambhir Singh and Debi Singh, while places within sixteen miles of Jhansi were attacked. Barjur Singh's band was attacked and dispersed by Major Orr at Bilayan, on the 31st May, as already related, but the Hyderabad Contingent had to march on Gwalior shortly afterwards.

The revolution at Gwalior had a disastrous effect in the Jhansi district, where the rebels soon rose again. At this time, the middle of June 1858, there were in the whole Jhansi Division, including Chanderi, Jhansi, Jalaun, and Hamirpur, only two military posts, one at Jhansi under Colonel Liddell, consisting of the troops detailed in the margin; among these were all the sick and wounded, and, as the fort and town of Jhansi had to be guarded, there remained only 391 of all arms for duty.

3rd Bombay Europeans,	557
24th Bombay Infantry,	538
Bhopal Artillery, 3 guns and 34 men,	34
Hyderabad Cavalry,	113
Sappers,	83
Total	1,325

* Colonel Malleson in his *History of the Indian Mutiny* ascribes the annexation of Banda solely to the desire of General Whitlock to claim the treasure as booty. But the Government had more solid grounds than this for the measure.

At Kalpi—

Royal Artillery	..	124
5th Fusiliers	..	417
19th Madras Infantry		353
Total	..	894

The other post was at Kalpi, but as the place was important, not more than half the 664 available for duty were disposable. There were no troops in the Chanderi and Hamirpur districts.

The rebels in Chanderi.

On the 6th June Captain Maclean, who had been sent from Jhansi to take charge of the Chanderi district, and who had only 150 Gond Police and some Tehri troops, finding that his position at Lalitpur was not tenable, retired to Banpur and from thence to Tehri, and the district shortly after fell into the hands of the rebels.

14th Light Dragoons, 1 Squadron.
3rd Bombay Cavalry, 3 Troops.
Sappers and Miners, 1 Company.
3rd Bombay Europeans, Wing.
24th Bombay Infantry, 4 Companies.
Bombay Horse Artillery, Battery.

The country between the Betwa and Dhasan was overrun by about 2,000 rebels and 500 mutineers, part of whom had come from the Hamirpur district. The Rais of Gursarai, Keshu Rao, alone held out for the Government at Gursarai in the north, while the Tehsildar and Thanadar of Mau held out at the fort of that place in the south, where they were besieged on the 21st June. On the 24th they were treacherously given up to the insurgents by their own men, and cruelly murdered. The reinforcement detailed in the margin was soon after sent to Jhansi by Sir Hugh Rose, and reached that place on the 10th July.

Affairs round Kunch.

On the 2nd July a detachment under Captain Montriou proceeded to occupy Moth, which was rendered necessary by the rebels of Jalaun, and mutineers from beyond the Jumna having again collected in great force and taken Kunch, which until then had been held by the son of the Rais of Gursarai with 500 matchlockmen. On the arrival of Captain Montriou at Moth the Gursarai troops again occupied Kunch, and Barjur Singh, the rebel, took up a strong position at Mau Mahoni.

Surrender of the Banpur Raja.

On the 5th July 1858 the Banpur Raja gave himself up to Mr. Thornton, the Assistant Superintendent at Maraura, but was shortly after allowed to return to the Chanderi district, where he continued intriguing and collecting revenue until early in August, when he finally came in, and with the Shahgarh Raja proceeded under escort to Gwalior.

Jalaun.

Owing to inactivity on the part of the military authorities at Kalpi, Kachwagarh and the west of the Jalaun district fell almost entirely into the hands of the rebels, headed by Barjur Singh and Daulat Singh.

On the 19th July Colonel Liddell sent 150 of the 24th Bombay Infantry, 50 of the 3rd Bombay Europeans, and one gun across the Betwa to garrison Barwa Sagar for the purpose of holding in check the rebels about Mau Ranipur, amounting to some 6,000 men, to whom the Deshpat of Jaitpur had brought a considerable reinforcement from the Hamirpur district. Hamirpur was held by a small detachment, but there were no other troops in the district; most of the taluqdars in Mahoba were banded against British authority, and the Deshpat made an irruption from Mau Ranipur and placed a garrison in Kashipura.

Hamirpur.

On the 26th July information was received from Pachor, 34 miles south-west of Jhansi, that the rebels under Mansaram, an adherent of the late Rani, after taking the fort of Mayapur and hanging some of the police there, were advancing on the fort of Pachor.

Relief of Pachor.

The detachment named in the margin at once proceeded to Pachor and saved that place. This detachment was subsequently reinforced, and drove the rebels out of the west of the Jhansi district, which was then settled.

50, Bombay Light Cavalry.
100, 24th Bombay Infantry.
100, Gond Police.

On the 25th July Captain Ternan reported that the rebels were closing round Jalaun, and that no troops would be sent from Kalpi, and asked for help from Jhansi. But as Jhansi was 76 miles distant, and Jalaun outside the range of operations of its garrison, which had quite enough to do, no aid could be sent. Before assistance came from Kalpi, Barjur Singh again attacked Kunch, and drove out the Gursarai troops, killing thirty and taking two guns. This had a bad effect in Jalaun and the northern part of Jhansi, where the malcontents collected in small parties preparatory to rising.

Jalaun.

On the 2nd August Jalaun was taken by the rebels, who abandoned it on hearing of the approach of a detachment from Jhansi, but first put the Thanadar to death. The Kalpi detachment, consisting of 180 of the 43rd Foot and 130 of the 19th Madras Infantry, under Major Synge, remained in garrison at Jalaun.

On the 11th August Colonel Liddell, having organised a Field Force of 700 men of all arms, moved across the Betwa river towards Mau Ranipur, and advanced to Barwa Sagar. Within a week of his crossing the Betwa there was not an armed band of rebels left between that river and the Dhasan. That part of the country, where the first amnesty proclamation was made known, was then settled and remained peaceful.

Pacification of Mau Ranipur.

On the rebels breaking up, Colonel Liddell divided his force into two parties, one under Captain Thompson, 14th Dragoons, took post at Garotha, which it reached on the 26th August; and the other under Colonel Liddell encamped at Mau Ranipur, where it arrived on the 24th, with a view to intercept the rebels who, it was expected, would retire before General Whitlock's advance on Banda.

About the 13th August Chhatar Singh with a large party of rebels advanced against and attacked Rath in the Hamirpur district, which was given up by treachery, and the Tehsildar and other officials were put to death.

In the middle of August a strong detach ent of the three arms was set under Captain Ashburner, 3rd Bombay Cavalry, towards Mau Mahoni and Kunch to act against Barjur Singh and co-operate with the Kalpi force. Having effectually cleared the rebels out of the Bhander and Moth districts, Captain Ashburner marched from Daboh on the 4th September with the force detailed in the margin, to attack the rebels under Thakurs Barjur Singh, Jowahir Singh, Debi Singh, and Medmi Mall who to the number of three or four thousand had occupied Mau and Mahoni, on either side of the river Pahuj. Continuous and heavy rain since the 31st August had prevented an earlier attack on the position, which the insurgents had chosen on account of its great natural strength, being intersected by ravines.

Captain Ashburner's operations.

3rd Bombay Cavalry	..140
Royal Artillery	.. 11
Bhopal Artillery	.. 41
3rd Europeans	.. 90
24th Bombay Infantry	181
Sappers and Miners	36

On arrival at Mahoni the rebels were found in possession of the *nalas*, from which they opened fire on the advanced guard. Skirmishers were thrown out with the usual supports, and the guns, opening with shrapnel, soon drove the enemy from their position, and allowed the force to advance close up to Mahoni, which was cleared by a few shells. The troops then advanced to the opposite side of the town, facing the fort of Mau, where the enemy had assembled and brought a gun to bear on the approach by the road; this gun was soon silenced by the artillery, and seeing that the enemy had withdrawn it Captain Ashburner advanced his whole line. No European cavalry officer being available at the moment, Veterinary Surgeon Lamb led 50 of the 3rd Bombay Cavalry in the pursuit of the guns. This party soon overtook the enemy, captured their two guns, which were at once turned on their former owners, and cut up about thirty of them, Surgeon Lamb being wounded in the pursuit. Owing to the difficult nature of the ground, which gave secure cover to the enemy, their loss was not heavy, but from 80 to 100 were killed and they were completely dispersed.

Dispersal of rebels.

On the 5th September Brigadier MacDuff defeated the rebels at Sarawan ten miles north of Jalaun. Captain Ashburner subsequently entered Kachwagarh and the combined operations of the two forces broke up the bands of insurgent in the Jalaun district.

General Whitlock, having advanced from Banda, was at Mahoba on the 4th September, from which place he advanced to and destroyed the abandoned fort of Srinagar. In the meantime the rebels in the Hamirpur district plundered and committed outrages unchecked, and extended along the east bank of the Dhasan from its junction with the Betwa to about Kashipura. On the 22nd September Captain Thompson, 14th Dragoons, having moved nearer to Colonel Liddell, was encamped at Simerda, when Chhatar Singh with about 1,200 matchlockmen, some sowars, and two guns, suddenly forded the Dhasan, which was very deep, moved rapidly round Captain Thompson's left flank, and took possession of the town and fort of Garotha, seven miles from Simerda. On the 23rd September Captain

Action at Garotha, 22nd September.

Thompson, finding the roads so flooded and muddy that he could not move his guns, left them in camp with a guard, and taking fifty each of the 14th Dragoons, 3rd Bombay Europeans, and 24th Bombay Infantry, forded the Lakhara river, and attacked and drove Chhatar Singh out of Garotha, killing about sixty men, and taking his two guns, all his ammunition, and much baggage. Chhatar Singh immediately fled over the Dhasan into the Hamirpur district, towards Jigni; but as Brigadier Munsey was at Rath, his band totally dispersed, and he himself went into concealment. General Whitlock had in the meantime advanced in the direction of Panwari, and all the rebels of the Hamirpur district made towards Jaitpur in the south.

The Chanderi District.

At the end of August Lieutenant Fenton, Deputy Commissioner of Chanderi, left Jhansi to take charge of his district. He had with him only a few police, under Captain Sneyd, but was to meet 100 Bhopal sowars and 130 Bhopal Infantry near Banpur, at which place it was at his discretion to remain for further reinforcements, or to proceed to Lalitpur. On reaching Banpur Lieutenant Fenton procured from the Tehri State 700 matchlockmen and two guns, and pushed on to Lalitpur, which he reached on the 28th August. The rebels under the Thakurs of Jakhlaun, Pali, and Nanakpur were assembled south of Lalitpur, but offered no opposition. The district was then settled with the exception of the country round Jakhlaun. About the 22nd September, being probably incited by the emissaries of Tantia Topi, who was approaching Chanderi, the rebels north of Chanderi attacked, drove out, and cut up several of the police at Talbahat and Bansi, and put to death the *thanadar* of the former place. On the 25th September Captain Fenton received intelligence that they intended moving on Banpur *viâ* Baar, and knowing that in case the rebels got possession of Banpur his retreat would be completely cut off should Tantia Topi enter the district, he determined to leave the Bhopal Infantry to hold Lalitpur and march against the rebels with the rest of his force. The Bhopal Infantry, however, who were new levies, refused to remain at Lalitpur which, under the circumstances, was a very dangerous position, and Captain Fenton marched on Banpur with his whole force. Towards evening heavy rain fell, and on arriving at Kalianpur at 8 P.M., the whole country was a sheet of water, and the rivers between that place and Banpur became impassable. In these circumstances Captain Fenton determined to march back to Lalitpur, but a fresh difficulty arose, the Tehri force refusing to move. Next day the rearguard arrived and reported that the rebels had occupied Lalitpur. The Bhopal Infantry became disorderly, and a Jemadar and twenty men deserted. Captain Fenton was detained three days at Kallianpur by the river; it became fordable on the morning of the 29th September, and he and his party under Captain Sneyd crossed it, but shortly after they had reached the other side they were attacked by the rebels, who were beaten off with a loss of 25 killed, who were cut up by the Bhopal sowars under Captain Fenton. The same day the party reached Banpur, and were there joined by Lieutenant Turner with 100 sowars and 150 military Police.

After this Tantia Topi entered the Jhansi district, but his movements and the operations undertaken against him will be described in the chapter relating to the pursuit of that rebel.

Action near Kirwi, 13th August.

Shortly before noon on the 13th August information reached Brigadier T. D. Carpenter, commanding the 1st Infantry Brigade, Saugor Field Division, that a large body of mutineers and rebels, variously estimated at from 2,000 to 4,000 men, were descending the ghats about two or three miles in front of the villages of Nayagaon, Sitapur, Chitrakot, and Kampta, all of which were in imminent danger of attack.

2 brass guns on elephants.
Royal Artillery, 53 men.
Her Majesty's 43rd Regiment 128
1st Madras Infantry.. 154
Sikh Mounted Police.. 21

Brigadier Carpenter marched at 2 A.M., with the force detailed in the margin, guided by Sayyid Akbar Ali, Tahsildar, and Ghulam Awah Khan, Thanadar of Kirwi, both of whom had been most zealous in furnishing him with correct information.

The rebels, according to subsequent information given by a prisoner, came from Dudri, and were said to muster 2,500 men, including some 200 mutinous sepoys.

In less than three hours the advanced guard, preceded by nine mounted men of the Royal Artillery, came in sight of the enemy in force, about a mile distant and apparently in confusion as if taken by surprise; but they immediately formed up with their right resting on one of the passes through the hills, and their left protected by a body of cavalry and infantry *en potence*, with another pass close at hand, and on the left of the cavalry a labyrinth of deep and almost impenetrable ravines, wooded to the summit. The rear of the main position was a precipitous hill, covered with large boulders of rock and thick jungle. The temple of Hanuman, a very strong building on the face of the hill, afforded good cover to the enemy. Brigadier Carpenter halted within three or four hundred yards to allow the guns to come into action, when the enemy commenced a desultory fire along the whole line, accompanied by shouts of defiance. The guns then opened and the infantry advanced in skirmishing order, and the rebels retired by the passes with a loss of about a hundred men, before the British troops could climb the precipitous heights. Only one man of the Sikh Mounted Police was killed and three of the 43rd died of sunstroke.

Fight at Panghati Pass, 27th August.

Horse Artillery 6-pounders, drawn by bullocks.
2 Mortars carried on an elephant.
1 brass gun on an elephant.
Royal Artillery, 46 men.
Her Majesty's 43rd Light Infantry, 160 men.
1st Madras Infantry, 196 men.

On the 27th August Brigadier Carpenter marched from Kirwi with the troops detailed in the margin, on an expedition into the hills south of Tirohan and Chitrakot, for the purpose of destroying the enemy who were in possession of the towns and villages of Dudri, Tekarria, Dundha, Entowa, Dundhela, Karriah, Koreri, and Dingrahat. The rebels numbered not less than 7,000 men, 500 being mutinous sepoys and troopers, by whom the peace and security of the country was continually disturbed.

Sikh Horse, 30.
Hyderabad Sowars, 23.
Levies of Native Chiefs armed with matchlocks, sword, and shield, 280.
10 Elephants.

As the British column advanced, the insurgents evacuated all the above named villages, but on the evening of the 5th September, when encamped about six miles from Entowa and fifteen from Kothi, Brigadier Carpenter received intelligence that three or four thousand had determined to make a stand at Panghati Pass, where they had driven off a party sent to repair the road.

The column reached the pass at 7 A.M. next day, when the enemy appeared in great numbers, crowning the heights that commanded the pass, where they presented a formidable appearance. Brigadier Carpenter led the advanced guard, consisting of a party of each of the infantry regiments, in skirmishing order to within two hundred yards of the gorge, the main body being in reserve, with a portion protecting the guns. A party of infantry under Captain Rishton was then sent up the thickly wooded hill on the right, running parallel to the pass, the left being protected by a deep, wooded ravine, with instructions to crown the summit and sweep the brow of the hill, right shoulders forward, so as to join the advanced guard in its ascent. This duty was well carried out. The pass was then carried, the guns firing over the heads of the advancing skirmishers, and the enemy fled in all directions into dense jungle, abandoning the pass, which might easily have been defended by 500 resolute men against 10,000.

After a short halt at the top of the pass to bring up the guns, the force again moved on, and in about an hour came in sight of four or five hundred insurgents, who retreated but were charged by the cavalry, and some of them cut up before they could reach the forest.

The column reached Kothi at 6 P.M., and found that the enemy had abandoned the place and their camp. The rebels lost forty or fifty; there were no casualties in the British side.

Action at Sahao, 5th September.

Early in September Brigadier J. MacDuff was in camp near Rajpur with the 2nd Brigade, about a thousand strong, when he received information that the rebels who had been plundering in the district, numbering about 500 mutineer sepoys and some three thousand matchlock men, were strongly posted in the village of Sahao, four miles north of Jalaun. Brigadier MacDuff moved out to attack them on the morning of the 5th September, and as he neared Sahao the rebels, sounding the assembly, appeared in great strength on rising ground, crowned with the ruins of an old fort. Their left was protected by the village, and their right by houses and walled gardens. From the centre of their position they opened fire with their guns at a distance of 500 yards, and appeared determined to dispute fiercely the ground they held.

The Brigade was formed up with the guns in the centre, under Captain Ommaney, R.A., the 43rd under Lieutenant-Colonel Primrose was on the right of the guns, and a party of Metge's Sikh Horse, under Lieutenant Dick, took ground well to the right, to act as opportunity offered; the remainder of the Sikh Horse, under Major Davis, took ground to the extreme left, with orders to sweep round the right of the enemy and cut off their retreat; a party of the 8th Irregular Cavalry, under Risaldar Mir Husain Ali, remained in support of the guns.

The enemy's fire from the centre was answered by that of the four British guns, which soon made the rebels abandon their position, with the loss of a gun. The sepoys of the right wing retired with remarkable steadiness and in close order; but the left wing retreated in great disorder, and were charged in flank by Lieutenant Dick who cut up a great number, but was himself severely wounded by a sabre cut; nevertheless he charged again, receiving two more severe wounds in this encounter, and cut down five men with his own hand. The whole line then advanced, the cavalry charging the rebels repeatedly on both flanks, the guns, supported by the 43rd, being well to the front. The rebels, now closely pressed, took up a second position on a ridge, but retired again before the fire of the guns, taking advantage of all cover, and defending themselves in buildings and gardens on the outskirts of the villages. Major Davis, in command of the Cavalry, continued the pursuit for six miles, and stopped only when his horses were tired out, and the fugitives took refuge in intrenched gardens and groves where cavalry could not follow them. Some mutineers having taken up a position in the village of Rajpura were turned out and all destroyed by the 43rd. Twenty-one rebels were captured and some two to three hundred killed. The British loss amounted to seventeen wounded.

The Hamirpur District.

Madras Artillery, 57, and two 9-pounders.
No. 1 Horse Field Battery.
50th Madras Infantry, 71.
Jalaun Jat Horse, 85.
43rd Light Infantry, 67.

On November 28th a force under Captain G. S. Hilliard, 50th Madras Infantry, detached by General Whitlock to operate against Barjur Singh in the district, marched from Hamirpur. On the 30th they halted at Jalalpur to await the detachment of the 43rd from Kalpi, and then marched south as far as Rath, which the rebels were reported to be threatening. There Captain Hilliard heard that the enemy were encamped near Tola Kanjaran on the right bank of the Dhasan, and pushed on to Naoranga, which was reached on the afternoon of the 3rd December. Early next morning, leaving a camp guard of the 50th Madras Infantry, Captain Hilliard marched against the enemy, and drove them with some loss across the river.

Action at Larcherra, 5th December.

Lieut.-Colonel T. Oakes 2th Lancers.

12th Lancers, 88.
Madras Horse Artillery, two 12-pounder howitzers.
3rd Bengal Irregular Cavalry, 15.

On the night of the 4th December, Brigadier Munsey, commanding a detachment of the Saugor Field Division in camp near Badwaru, despatched the marginally named force against a body of rebels reported to be at the village of Larcherra.

On arriving at Kashipura, two miles from his destination at 9 A.M. on the 5th, Lieutenant-Colonel Oakes heard that the main body of the enemy, about 2,000 strong under Chhatar Singh, was encamped on the left bank of the Dhasan river on the heights above Larcherra. He pushed on rapidly, and on arriving opposite the village opened fire with the guns on the enemy's advanced picquet, and at the same time sent a troop of the

12th Lancers across the river to cut off any who might endeavour to escape into the open country. The village was deserted; and, finding it impossible to act without infantry, Colonel Oakes re-crossed the river and encamped about a mile from the bank. Finding themselves unmolested, a party came down to the waterside, and commenced firing on the grass-cutters and horse-keepers, of whom one was killed.

Early the following morning, being reinforced by a company of the 3rd Madras Europeans under Lieutenant Burge, Colonel Oakes sent a party of them on elephants across the ford, under cover of the guns, the remainder, with the cavalry, at the same time crossing a little higher up. The guns then followed, and the infantry advanced through the jungle in skirmishing order, and soon exchanged shots with the enemy, driving them through the bush with the loss of 60 or 70 killed. The rebels in the vicinity were quite broken up by these operations.

Attack on Kirwi, 25th December.

Royal Artillery,	11
43rd Light Infantry,	46
1st Madras Infantry,	65
5 brass native guns.	

On the 25th December Captain C. Woodland, 1st Madras Infantry, commanding the detachment of the Saugor Field Division at Kirwi, received intelligence that a large body of rebels under Radha Govind and Ranmat Singh, estimated at five to six thousand, including 600 disciplined troops, were advancing to attack Kirwi. He at once paraded the marginally noted troops under his command, and offered shelter within the palace to the inhabitants of the place.

At 2 P.M. numbers of rebels crossed the roads on all sides leading to the palace, and occupied the surrounding houses, from whence they exchanged a heavy and well-directed fire with the garrison until 6 P.M., when they retired, having killed only one matchlockman.

General Whitlock, who was at Mahoba, heard of this attack on the evening of the 23rd, and at once started for Kirwi with a Troop of Horse Artillery, a squadron of the 12th Lancers, and one of the 2nd Cavalry, Hyderabad Contingent. He reached Kirwi, a distance of 83 miles, in 37 hours, and found that the enemy, hearing of his approach, had abandoned their intention of making a second attack, and had retired to the neighbouring hills. The Rewah levies* marched in from Banda, 48 miles, in 38 hours. The detachments of the 3rd Europeans,

* Besides the officers named above, the following were mentioned in despatches—"Major Dorehill, Brigade-Major; Doctor Barclay; Captain Ternan, Deputy Commissioner; Resaidar Mir Husain Ali; Native Doctor Hari Kishn, who received four severe wounds; Risaldars Mena Singh and Raja Pirthi Singh of Kangra, and Naib Duffadar Dawa Singh, all of the Sikh Horse.

The Rewah Levies were under Colonel Hinde, and they and the Nagode troops were badly armed. The troops went into camp on the 14th November 1857, and between then and February 1858, they took the forts of Kanchanpur, Guna, Maihar, Jukehi, Khanwara and Bijeraghogarh, as well as two standards, 42 pieces of ordnance, and a quantity of Government muskets and stores. Little opposition was met with, but many prisoners were taken and 101 were sentenced to death. Colonel Hinde, Lieutenant Mathias, and Lieutenant W. Osborne, Political Agent, (who did so much to maintain order in Rewa State), were mentioned in despatches, besides several native leaders. Sirdar Debi Singh saved the life of Lieutenant W. Osborne, who was attacked by a prisoner who had concealed a sword. Debi Singh was wounded in warding off the blow.

Sappers and Miners, and 50 Madras Infantry, which left Mahoba at the same time as General Whitlock, reached Kirwi on the night of the 27th December.

The enemy had only retired to the heights of Panwari, which, with several villages in the neighbourhood, Radha Govind had occupied in force, from three to four miles distant from Kirwi by the direct road, which was impassable for guns. His troops were also reported to hold the village of Dudri in his rear, thirteen miles from Kirwi by a road over the hills which was scarcely passable for artillery.

Panwari Heights, 29th December.

To have attacked Radha Govind in front would only have produced the same disappointing results as the forces had often experienced—retreat after defeat, where infantry could not have followed. It was, therefore, most desirable to place troops on the probable line of retreat.

The troops assembled on the morning of the 29th, and moved in three columns, as detailed in the margin. The centre column stormed the Panwari Heights, covered by the fire of the Artillery, which was for a time exposed to a heavy flanking fire, and to that of the enemy's battery, which found their range. But the infantry pushed forward and took the guns.

Right Column.

Major Mein.

A Troop, Horse Artillery,	100
12th Royal Lancers,	92
2nd Cavalry, H. C.,	88
3rd Madras Europeans,	63
Sappers and Miners,	40
Total	383

4 guns and 2 howitzers.

Centre Column.

Lieut.-Colonel Hinde.

Royal Artillery,	27
Rewa Artillery,	33
Rewa Cavalry,	123
43rd Light Infantry,	51
50th Madras Infantry,	51
Rewa Contingent,	404
Total	689

2 guns and 2 howitzers.

Left Column.

Captain Southey.

2nd Cavalry, H. C.,	9
4th Battalion, Artillery,	12
5th Madras Europeans,	51
1st Madras Infantry,	99
Sappers and Miners,	13
2 Mortars. Total	184

The left column co-operated with the frontal attack, and compelled the enemy in their retreat to keep to the centre road, driving them back on Major Mein's force, which was posted about the village of Dudri. The enemy was completely surprised by this column, and flying in all directions to the jungles, a party took shelter on a hill close at hand. Here they were all killed, to the number of a hundred and twenty, by a party of the 3rd Europeans and Sappers. The total loss of the rebels amounted to some three hundred killed, including Radha Govind* and his brother, while four guns, four elephants, Radha Govind's silver howdah, and a quantity of arms, accoutrements, and ammunition were taken. The British loss amounted to only 9 wounded. They marched back thirteen miles to camp where they arrived at 9 P.M., having been under arms since 2 A.M. The effect of this action was decisive. The rebels dispersed, and the district generally was cleared of their presence.

It has already been related how there was a recrudescence of disturbance in the region through which Sir Hugh Rose passed during his march from Sehore

* The spot where Radha Govind was killed was of great sanctity, and it was said that he had determined to die there, being wearied with the constant fear of capture, and the clamours of his followers for arrears of pay and for provisions.

to Kalpi, and in those districts which lay on the flanks of General Whitlock's advance. The former commander, with the great objectives he had in view, and the limited means he possessed for their attainment, was unable to leave troops to maintain peace in the country, although he turned aside on many occasions, as at Rahatgarh, Garhakota and Lohari, to destroy rebel strongholds. The disturbances in the Saugor and Narbada District and in Jhansi and Bundelkhand, apart from the irruption of Tantia Topi, continued far into 1859. The operations for the pacification of Jhansi and Bundelkhand during 1858 have already been narrated. It remains to give some account of the measures undertaken for the suppression of rebellion in the Saugor and Narbada territories during that year, and throughout the whole region in 1859.

In August 1858 a large band of rebels plundered Shahpur and the surrounding villages, mutilated some of the inhabitants and police, and then had the temerity to attack the fort of Garhakota, which had been captured by Sir Hugh Rose in February. On the 20th August a force of the strength noted in the margin, under Captain H. Finch, 31st Bengal Light Infantry, made a rapid march of 20 miles across country from Saugor, and reached Garhakota in ten and a half hours. The rebels were completely surprised, as they thought the detachment was going to Shahpur, where supplies had been laid in. From the direction in which Captain Finch approached, they were unable to retreat to the jungle, and obliged to take to the open plain in rear of Hardanagar.

31st Bengal Infantry	180
3rd Irregular Cavalry	65
Najibs, Police (under Lieutenant Dickens	50

Defeat of rebels at Garhakota. 20th August 1858.

On the arrival of the force at 3-30 P.M., the enemy fled precipitately, followed by the troops. The infantry after their long march were unable to catch up the fugitives, but the cavalry led by Woordie-Major Subhan Khan came up with them in the open plain, and killed upwards of 150 on the spot, while 72 prisoners were brought into camp. The Panna Thakur was killed, and among the prisoners were several men of note, a sepoy of the 52nd and one of the Gwalior Contingent. Three hundred matchlocks and swords were taken. On the British side three troopers were slightly wounded.

On the 8th November a detachment under Lieutenant C. R. Clemons marched from Saugor to escort treasure, and reached Narhat on the 13th. Here Lieutenant Clemons found a Field Detachment of the Bombay Army under Lieutenant-Colonel S. H. Partridge, who requested his co-operation to attack 1,500 rebels in the neighbouring hills who were disturbing the country. The combined forces marched on the morning of the 13th against the village of Patna, situated at the foot of a hill surrounded by thick jungle, with a fort above. The rebels had abandoned the village, and posted themselves in the fort and in the rocks surrounding it. Lieutenant Clemons' detachment formed the advanced party, and moved up the hill to the attack under fire from the fort, while the reserve, under Major Lamb, passed through the village and up the other side of the hill. Lieutenant Clemons' men advanced

3rd Madras Europeans,	52
50th Madras Infantry,	51

Action at Narhat, 13th November.

in dashing style, driving the enemy from rock to rock, and in half an hour the fort was in their possession. The rebels retreated into dense jungle, leaving some dead on the ground.

Action at Kenti, 4th March 1859.

On the 3rd March 1859 a column of the Saugor Field Division under Brigadier P. P. Faddy reached Rewah and left the same day for Semaria where they arrived at 9 P. M. Early on the morning of the 4th intelligence was received by Captain W. Osborne, the Political Agent, that the rebels had proceeded towards Nayagarhi. Brigadier Faddy pushed on at once with the cavalry and Horse Artillery, crossed the Tons river, and came up with the enemy a mile from the village of Kenti. The rebels, to the number of 1,500, had taken up a strong position, but moved slowly off on the approach of the pursuing column.

A Troop, Madras Horse Artillery, 2 guns, 1 howitzer (Captain Henegan).
2nd Sikh Cavalry, 168 (Captain Boileau).

The guns were unable to keep up, owing to the difficult country they had to cross, but Brigadier Faddy headed a charge of the cavalry, and dispersed the enemy, of whom 102 were killed and many wounded. The regimental colour of the 30th Bengal Infantry was captured on this occasion. Captain Boileau and one man, Madras Artillery, were wounded; 3 men of the Sikh Cavalry were killed, and Jemadar Gulab Singh and 11 men wounded.*

Columns under Colonel Apthorp, Major Middleton, Major Oakes, and Major Babington were also out in the districts at the same time.

Fight at Marauri, 23

A force under Captain T. Venables, 97th Regiment, marched from Nowgong and reached Rajgarh on the left bank of the Ken river on the 22nd March 1859. Here an application for assistance was received from Captain A. Rishton, 1st Madras Infantry, who arrived the same evening at Rajgarh with 115 rank and file of his regiment and the Madras Rifles, but whose baggage had broken down at the foot of Panna Ghat. At 5 o'clock on the following morning Captain Rishton sent a strong party under two native officers of the Madras Rifles and Light Company, 1st Madras Infantry, † with camels and other cattle to convey the men's kits which were left at the foot of the *ghat*.

97th Regiment	.. .. ..	150
Rewah Contingent	Cavalry ..	80
	Infantry ...	66

On the return of the advanced portion of this party to the village of Marauri on the right bank of the Ken river the enemy came suddenly upon them, killing three sepoys out of five, and capturing the baggage under their escort; the remaining two escaped and rejoined their own party. One of the camp followers, who had witnessed the attack, escaped and gave information. Captain Rishton immediately marched with the rest of his detachment, leaving a guard in a strong

* In his despatch Brigadier Faddy mentioned Captain Howlett, D.A.Q.M.G.; Captain Harrison, Brigade-Major; Lieutenants Ward and Shaw, Orderly Officers; Captain Osborne; Captain Boileau Naib Risaldar Khan Singh, Jemadars Akbar Khan and Gulab Singh; Duffadars Muhammad Khan and Shivji Singh of the 2nd Sikh Cavalry.

† Now the 61st Pioneers.

position on a temple. He then marched on Marauri, having sent for assistance to Captain Venables.

A party of the Rewah Contingent Cavalry under Lieutenant Ireland accordingly overtook Captain Rishton near Marauri, where the bodies of the three sepoys were found stripped and mutilated. Some stragglers were here overtaken and a few killed, while others took to the hills and were pursued by a company of the Madras Infantry under Subadar Parwesh Khan and some Madras Rifles under Lieutenant Cox.

Meanwhile the remainder of Captain Venables' detachment reached Marauri, and the combined forces pursued the enemy, who were following the course of the river. After a march of about fifteen miles through dense jungle, the rebels were overtaken at their encampment at nightfall. Captain Venables at once deployed the force and charged through the camp, capturing camels, horses, arms, and other property. The rebels, who were some 500 in number, retreated across the river, and darkness precluded further pursuit. Among the captured stores were sabres, carbines, and uniform of the 1st Bombay Cavalry, 12th Bombay Infantry, and Bombay Artillery. In this action three men of the Madras Rifles were wounded.

Adil Muhammad attacked, 27th March.

On the 27th March 1859 Brigadier F. Wheler, Commanding the Saugor District, attacked Adil Muhammad,* the Bhopal rebel Nawab of Ambapani, near Udzpur. Having reliable information of the enemy's position, Brigadier Wheler left Basoda at 11 P.M. on the 25th and reached the village of Basoda Sujabad a little after daylight next morning. So complete was the surprise, that when the force reached the village no one was stirring, but in a few minutes many rebels were seen on the edge of the jungle. Four companies of the 43rd at once dashed into the jungle, but the rebels made no stand, and were pursued three miles to the end of the valley, when further pursuit was useless. They lost many killed as well as some of their cattle, arms and plunder.

12th Lancers, 40 (Captain Clinton).
3rd Irregular Cavalry, 118 (Captain Mayne).
43rd Light Infantry, 380 (Major Syage).

Rebels dispersed at Imlipani, 29th March.

In March 1859 Major-General Whitlock sent out a column under Colonel Apthorp, C.B., to disperse the rebels, consisting chiefly of mutineers from Gwalior under Mukund Singh, who had assembled in strong positions on the left bank of the Ken river.

At 4 A.M. of the 29th March the force detailed in the margin, detached by Colonel Apthorp, under command of Captain T. Wright,† 2nd Sikh Irregular Cavalry, marched from Sipur, a village 8 miles west of Kishengarh, situated among the Chhatarpur hills, against a large body of rebels at the village of Imlipani, 12 miles distant.

2nd Sikh Cavalry ..	67
Grenadier Company, 3rd Madras Europeans (Lieutenant Hunt) ..	70
1st Madras Infantry (Lieutenants Johnstone and Taylor) ..	104

*Adil Muhammad had escaped from Rahatgarh when that place was captured by Sir Hugh Rose in January 1858.

† Afterwards General Sir Thomas Wright, K.C.B.

When within two and a half miles of Imlipani, Captain Wright, with the Cavalry, reconnoitred the enemy's position, and found them posted a little beyond the village in a deep hollow near the dry bed of a mountain torrent, surrounded by dense jungle and steep rocks. It was an admirable position, and with a few resolute troops might have been held against vastly superior numbers.

The enemy's vedettes posted in the village gave the alarm, when the whole of the rebels turned out to defend their position, and a number rushed up the steep slopes to the British front and right, and commenced a heavy musketry fire from behind rocks and jungle within eighty yards. Captain Wright therefore retired fifty yards to await the arrival of the infantry. Lieutenant Johnstone, commanding the infantry, hearing the firing brought his men up at the double, and the Europeans, afterwards reinforced by the Madras Light Infantry, formed skirmishing order. These movements were carried out under a sharp fire. After two well-directed rounds from the Enfield Rifles of the 3rd Europeans, the whole of the troops advanced to the attack, when the enemy began a precipitate retreat.

Captain Wright now pursued with the cavalry as rapidly as possible, and in spite of boulders and dense jungle which gave the enemy considerable advantage, numbers were cut up. In all parts of the field the troopers engaged the rebels in desperate hand-to-hand conflicts, and suffered none to escape when they came within their reach. The pursuit was continuous over five miles of this difficult country, and about 50 were killed by the cavalry, in addition to those who fell from the fire of the 3rd Europeans. The jungles in the vicinity of Imlipani were strewed with arms and property of all kinds, and ponies and camels were straying about in every direction.

The enemy numbered about 800, of whom 100 were said to be cavalry belonging formerly to the Lucknow Contingent, while the infantry were chiefly Gwalior and Kotah Contingent mutineers. From one of the bodies lying on the field jewels worth upwards of 2,000 rupees were taken, and it was afterwards ascertained that the owner was Hira Singh, formerly a Subadar in the Kotah Contingent. Eight of the Sikh Cavalry were wounded. In his report Captain Wright said :—"The blow thus struck at the rebels will show them at all events that neither in dense jungles nor in steep rocks are they safe from the attack of British troops. The effect of it on the minds of the people in this neighbourhood is certainly that of instilling confidence, for whereas before the action I could gain little or no information of the movements of the rebels, this is now volunteered on all sides."

In forwarding this and other reports from Nagode on the 12th April, General Whitlock remarked :—"There are and will be for some time small bodies of mutineers scattered throughout the jungles and in the hills. But I trust the arrangements I have made in the location of detachments will be the means of preventing the rebels collecting in any great numbers."

In May, 1859, a small column under Lieutenant F. Roome,* 10th Bombay Infantry, was at Mangraoli, when information was received that Adil Muhammad Khan was collecting a force in the neighbourhood of Richia for the purpose of attacking Basoda. Crossing the Betwa at Bherkhera Lieutenant Roome reached Richia half an hour after daybreak on the 16th May and found that the enemy had left a few hours before. Not being able to get any information from the villagers, he divided the cavalry into three parties to look for tracks; Lieutenants Roome and Bradford, with 40 of Mayne's Horse, soon came on fresh foot prints on a jungle path leading towards Konda.

Action in Basoda District, 16th May.

10th Bombay Infantry	250
Mayne's Horse	200
Camel Corps	250

Proceeding at a canter, they had gone about four miles when they suddenly came on a strong body of rebel cavalry which they at once charged, cutting up many. They fled in the direction of Dumri, pursued for some miles, and 35 were killed and some prisoners taken. Adil Muhammad Khan, Sarfaraz Khan, and other chiefs were with the party, but escaped.

Jemadar Gujar Singh, Mayne's Horse, the only man wounded, was hit by a bullet in the chest, but cut down the rebel who fired at him. Others who distinguished themselves on this occasion were Sir Subha Ram Chander Baji Rao, Risaldar Indar Singh, and Jemadar Laximan Singh.†

Desultory operations, June and July 1859.

Desultory operations continued until July 1859, when the embers of rebellion in Central India were finally quenched. In June some 500 rebels under Barjur Singh, Chattar Singh, and Deshpat left the Gursarai district and crossed the Dhasan into Hamirpur. Marching through Mau Ranipur and Alipura, Lieutenant Hawthorn with 85 of the 24th Bombay Infantry and Major Davies with 140 Military police came up with the insurgents at Gonda on the bank of the Dhasan on the 19th June, and killed about a dozen.

At Indurkhi on the 27th June Daulat Singh and 500 rebels were dispersed by a detachment from Kalpi under Lieutenant Osborn; and Deshpat's band was again attacked by Lieutenant Lewin in the jungle in the vicinity of Jaitpur on the 6th July 1859.

At 1 A.M., on the 23rd June 1859, Lieutenant F. Roome left Garispur with the force detailed in the margin to attack Adil Muhammad on the hills near Gunapura. Proceeding by a jungle track over several ranges of hills, he found the rebel encampment burnt and deserted; but in the bushes two prisoners were taken who said that Adil Muhammad was encamped on the hills with 2,000 men, including 80 mutinied cavalry troops, 700 regular sepoys, and the rest *Walayatis* and *badmashes*.

Fight at Gunapura, 23rd June.

Mayne's Horse	95
10th Bombay Infantry	160
Camel Corps	140

* Afterwards General Roome.

† Besides the officers named above, Captain Wright mentioned Assistant Surgeon J. Brake, 2nd Sikh Cavalry, who attended the wounded under fire; and Naib Risaldar Khan Singh, who was admitted to the Order of Merit for conspicuous gallantry on this occasion.

The enemy's position was found deserted, and Lieutenant Blair started in pursuit with the cavalry, the infantry following in support. After galloping about a mile through thick jungle, the cavalry came up with and charged a large body of regular sepoys and troopers mounted on horses and ponies, and although many of them made a desperate resistance the detachment of Mayne's Horse cut up a number. It was estimated that 100 rebels were killed by the cavalry, while the infantry coming up destroyed some who were escaping. Three troopers were wounded.

As the column approached the village of Gunapura after the pursuit, some rebels hidden in the houses shot a daffadar of the Camel Corps. The infantry was at once formed into three storming parties under Lieutenants Roome, Harris, and Newport. Lieutenant Newport took up a position on a hill at the back of the village, while the other parties drove the rebels towards him, but owing to the dense jungle they escaped with the loss of 10 of their number. Gunapura was found to be full of supplies, as much as possible was taken away, and the remainder destroyed and the village burnt.

CHAPTER XI.

THE CAMPAIGN IN RAJPUTANA.

It has been related how the mutineers of the Jodhpur Legion had established themselves at Awah, and in conjunction with the troops of the rebel Thakur of that place, had defeated an army of Jodhpur State troops on the 8th September.

Brigadier-General Lawrence had in Rajputana at this time only a small force of Europeans, on whom alone he could place full reliance. These, moreover, were mainly required to hold such important places as Ajmer, Nasirabad, and Neemuch, and few could be spared for offensive operations. For although Rajputana generally was quiet, the adjoining districts of Central India were seething with revolt. Considering, however, that it would have an injurious effect on the country to remain quiescent, and allow the nucleus of rebellion at Awah to continue on the high road between Deesa and Nasirabad, the Brigadier-General assembled at Beawar the force detailed in the margin for the purpose of co-operating with the Marwar (Jodhpur) troops. Although he considered his force insufficient for siege operations, he felt that it was necessary to show a bold front, knowing that if he could bring the enemy into the field he was certain of victory, and that the mere fact of moving a force from Ajmer would restore confidence both to the troops and to the people of the country.

Advance against Awah.

Two 12-pounder howitzers.
Three 6-pounder guns.
Two $3\frac{1}{2}$-inch mortars.
200 H. M's 83rd Foot.
200 1st Bombay Cavalry.
200 Merwara Battalion.
40 12th Bombay Infantry.

The force was detained by heavy rain for some days,* which prevented its reaching Awah until the 18th September. After defeating the Marwar troops at Pali, the rebels had retired to Awah, and strengthened the fortifications of that place. It was surrounded by a high wall, the approach being through thick jungle, and when within six hundred yards, only a portion of the Thakur's keep was visible. When the British force approached, the enemy's guns on the bastions and on the batteries outside the town at once commenced a heavy fire, to which the British Artillery replied. But as after three hours Brigadier-General Lawrence found that the enemy would not meet him in the field, and that he could not effect more than oblige them to withdraw their guns into the town, he deemed it

Action at Awah, 18th September.

* To compare great things with small, we may quote Napoleon who said—"It rains, but that does not stop the march of the Grand Army." Wellington, then Major-General Wellesley, considered the rainy season the best time for operations against the Mahrattas in 1803.

expedient to withdraw the troops. On the British side Captain Monck-Mason, Political Agent, Jodhpur, and two men were killed and three wounded. Captain Mason had arrived during the action, and apparently rode by mistake in the enemy's direction, when he was shot down by some men of the Legion.

Retreat of Brigadier-General Lawrence.

The Brigadier-General then retired to a village three miles distant, and encamped there three days, hoping to induce the enemy to attack, but hearing from spies that they had no intention of doing so, and were engaged in strengthening their defences, the troops were withdrawn to Ajmer and Nasirabad.

This abortive attempt against Awah was exaggerated by the rebels into a great victory, and it is obvious that the expedition had better never have been carried out than conducted in this half-hearted fashion. The force may have been too small for an assault on the town, but the annals of the history of India record many instances of much stronger places being taken by British soldiers against greater odds. The history of the British conquest of India proves that bold and aggressive action seldom or never fails against an Asiatic foe, but that timid or undecided tactics frequently result in disaster.

Seizure of Nimbahera, 18th September.

On the 18th September Captain Showers, Political Agent in Meywar, marched the greater part of the Neemuch force against Nimbahera, 20 miles distant, and on the Tonk sepoys refusing to surrender the place and lay down their arms within an hour, the gates were shut by them and the attack began. The Amil and authorities had not only come out to speak with the Agent but had thrown down their arms and tendered their submission in the name of the Nawab. Colonel Jackson, however, who commanded the troops, drove them back at the point of the bayonet. At nightfall, having made no impression on the town, he retired the troops, and next morning the place was found to be evacuated. The British loss amounted to 18 killed and wounded.

The Amil, a man of well-known respectability, proceeded to Tonk, and the military leader to Mandesar, where he joined the rebels, his property being confiscated and himself exiled by the Nawab. It is worthy of note that this very man was the most active in assisting Captain Lloyd to escape at the time of the Neemuch mutiny. Subsequent to his expulsion from Nimbahera he was one of the leaders of the Mandesar force that besieged the fortified square at Neemuch, and is believed to have instigated that undertaking. He was consequently declared a rebel. Many of the Tonk troops had gone off to Delhi at the beginning of the Mutiny, but the Nawab appears to have been loyal, and he was unable to restrain his rebellious soldiery. Neither the policy of the attack on Tonk, nor the manner in which it was conducted, were, in the opinion of Brigadier-General Lawrence, creditable to the British who were responsible.*

* Colonel Jackson was afterwards obliged to retire from the service.

It has already been related that on the arrival of British troops at Neemuch the levies of Kotah, Bundi, and Jhalawar returned to their respective capitals. Major C. Burton, the Political Agent, did not return to Kotah with the troops, as the Maharaja, on hearing of his intention to do so, requested him to defer his journey, as "after seeing the unsettled times, he could not have entire confidence in his troops." On the 5th October, the Maharaja having asked him to return, Major Burton set out for Kotah, accompanied by his two sons, Arthur and Frank, aged 21 and 16, and an escort of 25 Sikhs in the service of the Kotah Government. They halted a day at Nandta, on the south bank of the Chambal river, about three miles from the capital, whilst the Kotah *Vakil* who accompanied them went on to make the necessary arrangements for their reception. On his return he informed Major Burton that the Maharao would not come out to meet him but would visit him at the Agency.

Murder of Major Burton at Kotah, October 15th, 1857.

At 5 P.M. on the 12th Major Burton and his sons reached the Residency, and the same evening a salute was fired by the Maharao in honour of the fall of Delhi. At the suggestion of the Durbar the escort of the Kotah Contingent on duty at the Agency house had been sent back to Deoli, being relieved by a guard of the Raj troops, composed of Nagars and Sikh sowars, the guard being posted under a tree in front of the house.

Next day the Maharao paid the usual State visit to the Agent, which was returned by the latter and his sons, attended by 25 Sikh troopers and 20 Nagars, on the afternoon of the 14th. On this occasion after the public meeting a private conversation took place at which no one was present except the *Vakil*, Nand Kishor, who was afterwards blown from a gun by the Kotah rebels. The Maharao stated that the Agent urged him to punish and dismiss some of his principal officers, who were known to be disaffected, and that probably the *Vakil* communicated this to the Minister Ratan Lal, and thus it became known to the troops.

At 11 A.M. on the 18th October bodies of troops and rabble suddenly approached and surrounded the Residency; the servants and native officials escaped into the ravines close to the house, and Major Burton and his sons were left alone. The Raj guard, composed of Sikhs and Bairagis, appear to have offered no resistance. After murdering Sub-Assistant Surgeon Salder, who was lying ill on his bed, and a native Christian doctor who lived in the compound, the mutineers opened fire on the Residency with round shot.

They then surrounded the Residency, but being fired upon from within, and some of them being wounded, they retreated after setting fire to the house. Major Burton and his sons took refuge in a stone-built room at the top while the house was in flames. The rebels, thinking that they were burnt, approached the house, but were again fired at by the defenders, when they retreated and opened fire with the guns, knocking down a portion of the room in which the Europeans were concealed. The latter continued firing when anyone attempted to approach, and thus kept them at bay. The firing went on until about 4 P. M., when the defenders' fire ceased, probably owing to their ammunition giving out. The rebels then entered the room. Arthur Burton, who was standing at the door, made a cut at them with his sword, but overwhelming numbers poured in and the three were quickly cut down. Major Burton's head was cut off and hoisted on a standard, and afterwards fired from a gun, the bodies being thrown out into the plain, where they remained until they were buried by order of the Maharao.

The Maharao does not appear to have been concerned in this dastardly crime; he expressed his grief to Brigadier-General Lawrence saying that he was quite ignorant of the plot, and was unable to save the victims. The Raj troops that mutinied consisted of four regiments of infantry, ten troops of cavalry, some 300 artillery, and 3,500 police. The two principal leaders were Jai Dyal, a man of low and intemperate habits, who had been removed from his office of *vakil* in attendance on the Political Agent, and Makrab Khan, a Risaldar in the Maharao's service, a man of character and decision. Jai Dyal, said to have been a tool in the other leader's hands, was made Commander-in-Chief by the troops after the murders.

It was long before anything could be done to punish the Kotah rebels, and considering that their continued impunity endangered the peace of Rajputana, Brigadier-General Lawrence urgently called for troops from Bombay.

Jiran occupied by Mandesar rebels.

An account of the gathering of the insurgents under Feroz Shah at Mandesar has been given in a previous chapter.* In October these rebels, rendered bold by long impunity and the inaction of the Malwa Field Force which had arrived at Mhow in August, seized the town of Jiran, ten miles from Neemuch. To have allowed such an insult to pass unnoticed would have been productive of the worst consequences to British prestige and to the peace and loyalty of the district, so, despite the weakness of their force, the civil and military authorities determined on attacking the insurgents.

Attack on Jiran, 23rd October.

2nd Bombay Cavalry, 6 officers, 120 men.
83rd Regiment, 2 officers, 50 men.
12th Bombay Infantry.

On the 23rd October, the force detailed in the margin, under command of Captain Tucker, 2nd Bombay Cavalry, marched to attack the rebels, who were in a strong position, which was well defended. Captain Tucker opened fire with his guns, and then sent the infantry to the attack, but the enemy sallied out in great numbers, drove back the infantry, and captured a mortar. Captain Tucker then charged with the cavalry, drove the insurgents back into the town, and recovered the mortar, but was himself killed. The place being too strong for assault, the force was withdrawn, but the rebels evacuated the town that night, and authority was re-established. The loss in this action, which would have been disastrous but for

* Page 13.

the dash and gallantry of the officers, was—killed, Captain Tucker,* 2nd Bombay Cavalry, Captain Reade, 83rd Regiment, and one sepoy; wounded—Captain Simpson, Lieutenants Blair and LeGeyt, 2nd Bombay Cavalry; Captain Soppitt, 12th Bombay Infantry; and Captain Laure, Line Adjutant.

Events at Neemuch.

2nd Bombay Cavalry, 2 squadrons.
83rd Regiment, 200.
12th Bombay Infantry, 400.
4 Guns.
Meywar Troops.

The garrison of Neemuch in November was composed of the troops detailed in the margin. Captain Simpson, who had been severely wounded, continued to exercise command, although unable to take the field, and this circumstance appears to have been the cause of friction with Captain Showers, Political Agent in Meywar. Captain Simpson, hearing of the approach of the rebels to attack Neemuch, withdrew the garrison left at Nimbahera after the capture of that place. At the same time the next senior officer, Captain Bannister, appears to have been in executive command, and this division of authority was not conducive to efficient action.

Rebel attack on Neemuch, November 8th.

On the 8th November the Mandesar rebels advanced to attack Neemuch, and on hearing of their approach Captain Bannister, with the 2nd Bombay Cavalry, and Captain Showers, with the Meywar Horse, moved out and met them a mile or two from cantonments. The rebels formed up on the approach of the Cavalry at about 4 P.M., to the number of some 2,000, with many standards, and cavalry on the advanced and rear-guard, and opened fire from three guns. In his report Captain Showers wrote :—

"After keeping them in check for an hour, the regular cavalry was retired under general restrictive orders, as it appeared, from Captain Simpson, who had assumed command of the troops while still unable to take the field with them. Perceiving the rebels then moving towards the town of Neemuch, I moved forward with the Meywar Irregulars and headed them. They halted and opened fire again, but with no effect, beyond Lieutenant Stapleton's horse shot under him, and thus they were held in check till dark, when I withdrew the main body of the troops, leaving picquets to protect the rear of the cantonments. Had the bulk of the force been moved out to-day with our guns, a complete success over the rebels would, in my opinion, have attended our operations, that is if they had been conducted without reference to restrictive orders from a commandant not in the field."

In acknowledging this report, Brigadier-General Lawrence wrote that he considered "Captain Simpson used a wise discretion in not risking his handful of infantry against so strong an enemy, as any reverse would in all probability have involved the loss of the fortified square and destruction of all the force."

* Captain Tucker's head was carried off and placed over a gate at Mandesar. It was replaced by the heads of two rebel leaders when Mandesar was taken by the Malwa Field Force.

Certainly the experiences of the mutiny would seem to show that active as opposed to defensive tactics were most effective against the rebels, and on many occasions far greater numbers were defeated by smaller British forces than those composing the garrison of Neemuch.

In his report regarding this affair Brigadier-General Lawrence wrote that the cavalry "made a feeble attempt to charge the enemy, but as the Meywar Horse under Captain Showers rendered them nothing more than passive aid they effected nothing."*

Siege of Neemuch. November 1857.

The infantry now retired into the fortified square,† the cavalry going out into the district as there was no accommodation for them in the restricted space. The rebels took possession of the station and pillaged and destroyed all the houses that had escaped the mutineers. They besieged the place for fifteen days, generally confining their operations to keeping up a vigorous matchlock fire on the besieged, with occasional cannon shots from a ditch or entrenchment recently constructed round the fort, as Brigadier-General Lawrence‡ wrote, "in opposition to the opinions of the other officers, by Captain Showers, as a line of defence, but which served as a most serious means of attack by giving cover to the enemy. The fire of their guns had no serious effect on the walls of the fort, and they were promptly silenced in every fresh position by our shells. Had the enemy possessed any of the latter the square would not have been tenable. Our garrison wisely kept on the defensive and on the alert against night attack."

An hour before dawn on the 21st November the rebels attempted an escalade, but were signally repulsed, and left their ladders and a green standard on the ground. One of the ladders was mounted on four wheels. On one occasion during the siege a fakir, with a mirror fixed on his breast, walked round the fort under fire, having stated that if he succeeded in completing the circle round the walls, the place would fall into the hands of the insurgents.

For a considerable distance the bullets flew harmlessly round him, but at length one brought him down. A bandsman went out and brought his head and the mirror into the fort, where the sepoys had become superstitious of his supposed magical powers.

Relief of Neemuch.

That night, hearing of the advance of the Malwa Field Force,§ the enemy decamped hastily in the direction of Mandesar. They had 4 guns, 4,000 infantry, and 500 cavalry round Neemuch, but very little ammunition. During the siege Lieutenants Williams and Barnes, 2 havildars, and 4 sepoys had been wounded. The rebels lost heavily from the fire of shell, grape, and musketry.

* There was great friction between Brigadier-General Lawrence and Captain (afterwards General) L. Showers, which is commented on, not altogether impartially, in Appendix A., Volume III. of Colonel Malleson's *History of the Indian Mutiny*.

† See page 54.

‡ He was not present, but was at Ajmer.

§ See page 83.

Neemuch and the surrounding country remained undisturbed after this, and after the siege and capture of Kotah in March 1858, it was garrisoned by a brigade of the Rajputana Field Force.

State of Rajputana.

After the murder of Major Burton at Kotah, the mutineers obtained possession of the city and entirely dominated the place. The Raja Ram Singh appears to have been a weak-minded man, of dull and apathetic temperament. He eventually shut himself up in his palace and fort, and was practically besieged by his own mutinous soldiery, consisting mostly of Hindustanis and Musalmans, who committed many excesses and plundered the inhabitants of the town.

The long impunity of the rebels at Kotah and Awah, while the British forces remained in inaction, scattered about the country, had a very bad effect, and it is remarkable that Rajputana was not even more disturbed towards the end of 1857. In the adjacent territory of Malwa also the rebels remained unpunished at Mandesar and elsewhere, for, although the Malwa Field Force arrived at Mhow in August, they were prevented by bad weather* from moving until October, thus leaving the rebels to plunder the country and to attack Neemuch with impunity.

It would probably have been better had the forces in Rajputana been concentrated in the form of a moveable column, instead of being frittered away in detachments which stood on the defensive at isolated stations. This view was held by Colonel Durand, and expressed in a letter to the Secretary to Government, with regard to an application made to him for reinforcements by Colonel Jackson, commanding at Neemuch, on the 10th August 1857.

It was found, throughout the period of insurrection, that a bold and aggressive military policy was more likely to succeed than an attitude of passive resistance.

Reinforcements for Rajputana.

In January 1858, the troops which had been requisitioned from the Bombay Government began to enter Rajputana on their way to Nasirabad, where the Field Force was to be assembled. On their way to Nasirabad the reinforcements attacked and destroyed the forts of Rowah and Awah. The former belonged to a petty Thakur of Sarohi, who was considered by the Political Superintendent of Palanpur to be in open rebellion, as he had made raids on adjacent villages belonging to the Dewan of that State, and of which he considered himself unjustly deprived.

Capture of Rowah, January 1858.

Royal Engineers, 1 officer, 20 men.
95th Regiment, 4 officers, 105 men.
2nd Bombay Cavalry, 1 officer, 20 men.
10th Bombay Infantry, 4 officers, 200 men.
One 24-pounder howitzer.
One 9-pounder gun.

On the 5th January, 1858, the detachment detailed in the margin, under Lieutenant-Colonel Raines, 95th Regiment, attacked Rowah, which was taken by assault after some hours firing. The enemy fought well until the Europeans entered the village, when they fled to the hills. The British loss was one killed and 16 wounded.

* See note on page 193.

Near Awah on the 19th January the troops under Lieutenant-Colonel Raines were joined by a portion of the Nasirabad Force, detailed in the margin, amounting to 700 cavalry and 1,100 infantry, artillery, and engineers, under Lieutenant-Colonel Holmes, 12th Bombay Infantry. The 2nd Sind Horse were posted so as to overawe Rupnagar, a hill fort and village of Meywar, which had sheltered the Thakur of Awah, and to prevent the escape of the latter to the Meywar Hills.

Capture of Awah, January 19th.

83rd Regiment, Lieut.-Colonel Heatly.
95th Regiment, Lieut.-Colonel Raines.
Wing, 1st Bombay Lancers, Capt. Anderson.
1 Troop, 2nd Cavalry, Major Taylor.
2nd Sindh Horse, Major Green.
10th Bombay Infantry.
12th Bombay Infantry.
Two 18-pounder guns, Two 8-inch howitzers, Two 8-inch motars — Major Wray, Commissary of Ordnance.
Four 9-pounder guns, Captain Aitken.
Four 24-pounder howitzers, Captain Brown.

Awah was invested, and after five days' siege operations, during which there was incessant firing on both sides, a breach was pronounced practicable and the assault ordered for next morning. During the night a fearful storm raged, and the noise and darkness were so great that sentries only a few paces apart could neither hear nor see each other. Under cover of this storm the enemy evacuated the place; and although it was completely surrounded by cavalry to stop all means of escape, only one of the Lancer picquets heard the fugitives, and were able to cut up 18 and take 7 prisoners.

The cavalry sent in pursuit next morning brought back 124 prisoners; 24 being sepoys were shot; the remainder were Rajputs of Marwar.

In the town were found six brass and seven iron guns, three tons of powder, and three thousand rounds of gun ammunition. The defences were found to be of great strength, consisting of a double line, the inner one being of strong masonry and the outer an earth-work, both loopholed. After blowing up the keep, bastions, and masonry works, both in Awah and adjoining villages of rebel Thakurs, the force proceeded to Nasirabad.

It was not until March 1858, that a sufficient force could be assembled at Nasirabad to punish the Kotah rebels, whose continued impunity endangered the peace of Rajputana, and to co-operate with Sir Hugh Rose in his advance through Central India. The force then assembled, detailed in the margin, was placed under the command of Major-General H. G. Roberts, who commanded the Northern Division of the Bombay Army. It was subsequently reinforced before Kotah by the 8th Hussars, 450 sabres, and the 2nd Baluch Horse, 400 sabres, which brought its entire fighting strength up to some 5,500 men.

The Rajputana Field Force.

1st Bombay Cavalry (Lancers)	300
2nd Bombay Cavalry	175
1st Sind Horse	200
	675

Second class siege train, six 18-pounders, four 12-pounders, four 8-inch mortars, four 8-inch howitzers.
2nd Troop, Bombay Horse Artillery, four 6-pounders.
3rd Troop, Bombay Horse Artillery.
European Horse Battery.
Native Foot Artillery, 2 guns.
Mountain train, 6 guns manned by native artillerymen.
11th Company, R.E.

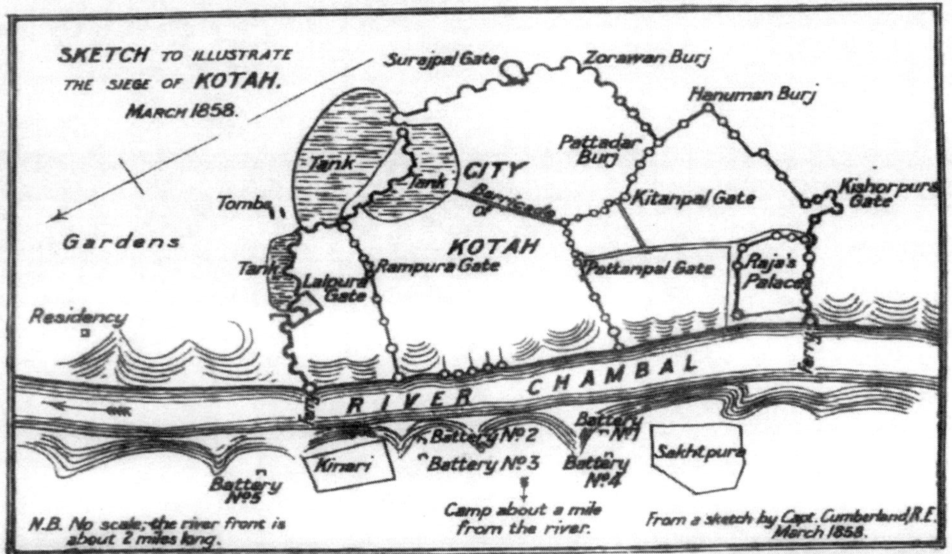

I. B. Topo. Dy. No. 7.076.
Exd. C. J. A., January 1908.

No. 4.245-I., 1908.

A Company, Bombay Sappers.

72nd Highlanders	500
83rd Foot	700
95th Foot	600
10th Bombay Native Infantry	600
12th Bombay Native Infantry	500
13th Bombay Native Infantry	700
Total	3,600

On the morning of the 22nd March Major-General Roberts arrived opposite Kotah with his 1st Brigade, which was under command of Brigadier H. Macan, and encamped to the westward, on the left bank of the Chambal. The 2nd Brigade under Brigadier W. Parke, and the siege train, joined in the evening. The 13th Bombay Infantry had arrived the previous evening, having made forced marches to come up in time.

A reconnaissance having been made, it was determined by the Commanding Engineer that two batteries should be erected on the hither side of the river near the village of Sakhatpur and a third at Kinari, the object being to keep down the fire of some of the enemy's guns, which enfiladed the ferry, and by high elevation threw round shot into the British camp. These batteries were completed and opened fire on the morning of the 24th.

On the 26th General Roberts sent 200 men of the 83rd and the Rifle Company of the 13th Bombay Infantry under Lieutenant-Colonel Heatly, 83rd, into the portion of the town held by the Maharao, whose position, since the arrival of the British force, had on two successive mornings been assaulted by the rebels, who numbered some 6,000, and attempted to carry the place by escalade.

On the 28th the force was joined by the Baluch Horse under Lieutenant Macaulay and by the 8th Hussars under Lieutenant-Colonel DeSalis. The same day the position of the left battery was changed to the left of the village of Kinari. On the 27th and 28th two 12-pounders and six 8-inch mortars were got into position, by the indefatigable labours of the artillery and working parties of the infantry. A slack fire of two shots an hour from each piece at certain points named was opened from these guns, and towards evening a large magazine and some small ones were exploded. Up to this time a heavy fire had been kept up by the enemy on the Raja's quarter of the town.

On the morning of the 30th quick firing was commenced by all the guns and mortars and continued until about half past eleven, and all being reported ready, the firing ceased by signal, and the troops, which had been passed over the river in the morning, and told off into their respective columns of assault, entered the rebel quarter through the Kitanpal gate.

72nd Regiment, 250, Major Thellusson.
13th Bombay Infantry, 250, Captain Adams.
Sappers, Lieutenant Paterson, R.E.

The 1st Column, detailed in the margin, led under Brigadier Parke, and at once wheeled off to the right, and on reaching the Pattadar bastion, wheeled to the left, thus outflanking and turning all the enemy's guns in position, in the various streets leading directly towards the defences occupied by the British. Brigadier Parke then continued his march on the Zorawan Burj, the broad ramp of which was ascended by the 72nd as steadily as if on parade. On the column nearing the top the enemy ran away or let themselves down by ropes, abandoning three guns to the Brigadier, who moved rapidly on, turning again to the left to the Surajpal gate, which, after slight resistance, was occupied with its bastions, on which were more heavy guns.

Brigadier Parke had thus outflanked, and at length taken in reverse the enemy's position in this portion of the city, and, on seeing this, and the advance of the 2nd column under Lieutenant-Colonel Holmes, which followed to the third bastion from the Pattadar Burj, and then turned to the left for the Surajpal gate, and of the 3rd column under Lieutenant-Colonel Raines, the enemy fled in every direction where they could see a chance of escape.

2nd column.
83rd Regiment, 250, Major Steele.
12th Bombay Infantry, 260, Lieut. Howison.
95th Regiment, 250, Major Massey.
10th Bombay Infantry, 250, Lieut. Roome.
Sappers.

Many were shot and bayonetted, many escaped by letting themselves down by ropes from the walls, and others threw themselves over, and were dashed to pieces. Some occupied houses, and fought until they were killed.

Lieutenant-Colonel Holmes, finding that Brigadier Parke had possession of the Surajpal gate and Zorawan bastion, both considered the keys of the place, pushed on and took a number of guns, particularly those in a work called the Fateh Garhi, and entering through the gate from the Rampura division of the town, took the Lalpura gate. The Reserve under Brigadier Macan pushed along to the left until it communicated with Lieutenant-Colonel Holmes' column at the Rampura gate.

Reserve.
83rd Regiment, 250, Lieut.-Colonel Heatly.
13th Bombay Infantry, 250, Captain Stewart.

By half-past two Kotah was completely in the hands of the British. In the afternoon the troops were withdrawn to camp, leaving a force to garrison the city. In his Despatch Major-General Roberts commended the good judgment of the officers in command of the columns, and the gallantry of the troops, European and native, and stated the work of the artillery to have been "almost beyond belief." The Horse and Field Artillery assisted in working the siege guns. Lieutenant Cameron, 72nd Highlanders, was specially mentioned for a conspicuous act of gallantry in having headed an attack up a narrow entrance of a house defended by a party of desperate men, two of whom he killed, and was himself dangerously wounded.*

The cavalry had no opportunity of distinguishing themselves. As the first object of attack was to seize the Zorawan bastion and Surajpal gate, they were posted at a ford 7 miles down the river to watch the only outlet—the Lalpura

* Mentioned in Despatches :—Brigadiers H. Macan and W. Parke, Lieut.-Colonel E. Price, R.A., Lieut.-Colonels Holmes, 12th Native Infantry, Raines, 95th Regiment, Heatly, 83rd Regiment, Blake, 3rd Troop, H. A., Thellusson, 72nd Highlanders; Majors Tremenheere, Engineers; E. Wray, Commissary of Ordnance; Captains Cumberland, R.E., Aitken, Artillery, Petrie, 2nd Troop, H.A., Hardy, 1st Lancers, A.A.G., Ballard, C.B., Engineers, A.Q.M.G., Lucas, 7th Native Infantry, A.C.G.; Lieutenants Newall, A.D.C., Heathcote, 12th Native Infantry, Cameron, 72nd Highlanders, Brown, 12th Native Infantry; Surgeons Burn and Hockin.

gate. But the rebels had in the morning taken their moveable guns out at the Surajpal gate, many accompanying them, and they fled when they saw how the day was going. These two gates, two miles apart, were separated by a belt of thick jungle stretching out for many miles, and impracticable for the action of cavalry.

Over 400 rebels were killed, and numbers of prisoners taken. Of the British 14 were killed, and 46, including two officers, wounded.*

The pursuit was taken up by the Cavalry and Horse Artillery on the 1st April, but, starting so late, they failed to intercept the fugitives, who were followed to the Parbati river, 60 miles distant; but although their track was marked by dead bodies and plundered carts, not a mutineer was overtaken. Seven field guns were found abandoned in the heavy sand of the Parbati.

Kotah, after its capture, presented a desolate appearance; the mutineers had plundered it for many months, and shot and shell had caused considerable damage. The plunder carried off by the rebels must have been great, for since the days of Zalim Shah, who resisted the Mahratta inroads, Kotah had been famed as a secure emporium for treasure, opium, and valuable merchandise. The town was abandoned to plunder by the troops for five days, but the articles collected by the prize committee were of inferior value, and hardly worth the miseries they cost the poorer classes, to whom they mostly belonged.

Thirty-four brass and 22 iron guns were taken. At the ends of the streets were found "infernal machines," consisting of 40 matchlock barrels fixed on frames, moveable on wheels.

The capture of Kotah was not only of importance in re-establishing British prestige in Rajputana, and avenging the atrocious murders of the preceding October, but it enabled Sir Hugh Rose to continue his advance from Jhansi, relieved of all fear of an attack on the latter place by the Kotah rebels.

Distribution of the Rajputana Field Force.

No garrison was left at Kotah, and after the dispersal of the rebels there no further trouble was experienced in Rajputana until the irruptions of Tantia Topi, who, however, received no accession of strength in that part of the country. The Rajputana Field Force was distributed at various important stations, a Brigade being sent to Neemuch, while a Brigade under Brigadier Smith fought the battle of Kotah-ki-Serai in June 1858, and took part in the capture of Gwalior as already related.

In the pursuit of Tantia Topi, the Field Force bore an important part, but apart from the operations related in the next chapter, the only military episode in Rajputana was the capture of Nahargarh in January 1859.

* In addition Captain Bainbridge, 23rd Native Infantry, Brigade-Major, 1st Brigade, and Captain Bazalgette, 95th Regiment, were killed by the explosion of one of the enemy's magazines on the 1st April.

In January, 1859, 62 men of the Highland Light Infantry and 224 of the Gwalior Camel Corps under Captain Lambton arrived at Nahargarh in Kotah territory. Captain Lambton sent in to the town for provisions, which were refused, the Kotwal threatening to shoot the first European who came in. An armed party under a subaltern was sent to seize provisions, when the gates were closed and matchlocks were fired at them.*

Capture of Nahargarh, 21st January, 1859.

The gates were then forced by the detachment, and the outer works of the fort taken with slight resistance. The inner part could not be taken, as the walls were very high and there was only one gate, strongly plated with iron. Captain Lambton retired, and attacked the place next morning. The garrison, numbering some 200, kept up a brisk fire from matchlocks and nine or ten guns.

The gate could not be blown open owing to scarcity and inferior quality of the powder. The garrison maintained fire on the detachment so long as it was within range, and on the 21st abandoned the place and retired into the jungle when the fort was dismantled and the guns were burst. Sir Robert Napier arrived at Nahargarh on the 23rd January, and, in reporting the affair, wrote :—"It is certainly marvellous to see the works attacked by that small detachment. The indomitable pluck of Englishmen is the secret of all their success. The small party, far from support, unacquainted with the strength of the garrison and with the country, did not hesitate to attack a place of considerable strength, and had they had a good petard they would have taken it. The best shots in India, I believe, they went to work systematically, and cleared the parapets ; through a chink in the strong gate they fired and cleared the gateway, and drove from two guns planted to command the entrance, the gunners who were ready to fire on them. They had previously assaulted and taken the two outer gates."

* Nahargarh appears to have been hostile to all comers. Tantia Topi was fired at here during his flight early in January.

CHAPTER XII.

THE PURSUIT OF TANTIA TOPI.

Flight of Tantia Topi.

It has been related in Chapter IX how Tantia Topi was defeated by Napier at Jaura Alipore, after he had been driven from Gwalior, with the loss of his guns. On the 22nd June 1858, accompanied by Rao Sahib and the Nawab of Banda, Tantia Topi fled in a north-westerly direction, but was turned by a force sent from Agra by Brigadier Showers to cover Bharatpur. He then marched on Jaipur, but was forestalled by Major-General Roberts, commanding the Rajputana Field Force, who was at Nasirabad at the end of June with the troops detailed in the margin. A Brigade under Brigadier M. W. Smith* had, as already related, been detached from the Rajputana Field Force to co-operate with Sir Hugh Rose in the attack on Gwalior, and was then posted at Sipri.

March of General Roberts.
Two squadrons, 8th Hussars.
" " 1st Bombay Cavalry.
300 Baluch Horse.
Light Field Battery.
Siege train.
Wing, 72nd Highlanders.
" 83rd Foot.
" 12th Bombay Infantry.†
" 13th Bombay Infantry.‡

On hearing of Tantia Topi's approach, General Roberts marched for Jaipur on the 28th June, and Tantia Topi turned southwards to Tonk. The Nawab of Tonk shut himself up in his fortress, and left outside a portion of his force with four guns to oppose the rebels; but these men welcomed the insurgents and made over their guns to them.

Tantia Topi moved southwards to Madhopur and Indargarh, some forty miles north-east of Kotah, and then marched on Bundi, where the Maharao shut his gates, and the fugitives turned east to a position between Sanganir and Bhilwara on the Neemuch–Nasirabad road.

Colonel Holmes' pursuing column.

During this period the rebels were pursued by a Light Field Force under Lieutenant-Colonel Holmes, and were thus kept on the move, while General Roberts followed with the main body of his force. But the troops had little chance of catching the swift-footed rebel, who carried no tents and no provisions; these he looted as required and when his horses were worn out left them on the road to die, and replaced them, sometimes from the post stations. His light horse could hover round the British columns like shadows, and always get away from overworked irregular, or overweighted regular, cavalry. The sympathy of the people was,

* Colonel M. W. Smith, 3rd Dragoon Guards.
† Now the 112th Infantry.
‡ Now the 113th Infantry.

moreover, with the fugitives, who obtained information and supplies without difficulty. As will be seen, when disencumbered of their guns, they moved with greater celerity and secrecy, and thus more easily eluded their pursuers.*

Lieutenant-Colonel Holmes was detached by General Roberts from the north of Tonk on the 8th July with the force detailed in the margin, and on that evening marched on Seelah, 18 miles distant, which he reached on the morning of the 9th. On the march cannonading was heard, and information was received that the rebels were in possession of the town of Tonk. On the morning of the 10th Colonel Holmes marched to the ford over the Banas river at Kakraj, and there heard that the rebels had fled in the direction of Baneta carrying off 4 guns, 4 tumbrils and spare ammunition belonging to the Nawab of Tonk. On the 12th the column marched 12 miles to Ghas, receiving conflicting reports of Tantia's movements, some saying he was at Baneta, others, at Aligarh Rampura, while again it was said that his force, amounting to 20,000 men, was divided between the two places.

8th Hussars	147
1st Bombay Lancers	123
Baluch Horse	300
2nd Troop, Horse Artillery.	
72nd Highlanders	227
12th Bombay Infantry	486

On the 13th Holmes marched to Suntala, and halted, hearing that the enemy were still on his left flank. In the evening he received intimation that the whole rebel force was at Kasthala and Madhopur, trying to obtain possession of the latter place. At midnight he continued his march for Kasthala, 18 miles distant, and at Pachala some four miles from Kasthala, heard that the rebels were encamped at that place. Leaving his baggage at Pachala, Holmes moved forward in hope of bringing them to action. On the cavalry skirmishers approaching Kasthala, parties of rebel horse and foot were seen in flight through the ravines up to the hills. The Baluch Horse pursued, and killed four men, including a jemadar of the Kotah Contingent.

That night numerous camp fires were seen along the side of hills to the left, front and rear of the force, and Colonel Holmes was informed by a Christian officer commanding the Nagar Battalion at Madhopur that his battalion had gone over to the enemy.

On the morning of the 14th the column marched to Panchaulas, and there halted, the Europeans being much exhausted by the heat. The march to Kasthala had forced many of the rebels into the hills, and Colonel Holmes had information that in flight before him were Tantia Topi, Rao Sahib, the Nawab of Banda, Rahim Ali, and other leaders; two regiments of Sindhia's sepoys; some

* The difficulty of contending with heavy cavalry against light horse has been experienced in many campaigns, before and since, as in the South African War. An officer who took part in the Mahratta and Pindari War of 1817, wrote:—"We could see the Pindaris flying like the wind, at a considerable distance off, our cavalry having no chance with these fellows even on an open plain. The Pindaris, unencumbered with accoutrements and heavy saddle, will gallop round and round the most active of our troopers; and his very horse seems to partake of the master's cunning and dexterity, and to know exactly the moment for a quick and timely retreat."

hundreds of Bengal mutineers, the 5th and 7th Regiments of Irregular Cavalry and three or four thousand other horsemen, in all some 10,000 or 12,000 men.

On the morning of the 15th July he marched six miles to Guli, and in the evening six miles to Augora. The country was very difficult owing to jungle and ravines, and the column was obliged to move by daylight. On the 16th Holmes halted to renew his supplies; all those on the route had been used up by the enemy. Next day he marched 13 miles to Pontara through a difficult pass, and entered a valley formed by hills on the right and the Mej river on the left. This valley to Khatkar was full of ravines and jungle, and unsafe for cavalry or artillery to traverse without the protection of infantry. Information was received that the enemy had halted in front of Khatkar, unable to cross the river.

At daylight on the 18th the column moved on Khatkar, distant 18 miles, and on arrival found that the rebels had mostly passed the ford the day before and their rear-guard had crossed at dawn. A tumbril and some ammunition were found on the road during this march. The ford was deep, and it took all day and the greater part of the night to pass the baggage over.

On the 19th, hearing that the rebels were intrenching and had determined to make a stand at Matunda, Colonel Holmes marched six miles to Naogaon, and halted for the night, the information being that the enemy had moved to Bundi, on which place the column marched at early dawn. Here he heard the rebels had gone to Nimkakhera the day before, and that they were moving through the Kina Pass and intended to go to Johaipur. The road through this pass was extremely difficult, and supplies were not procurable. Colonel Holmes therefore decided to leave the direct line of pursuit, and by marching through the Bundi Pass to Johaipur, to move on in pursuit in the direction of Mandalgarh, and intercept them between the river Banas and the pass they were traversing.

On the 21st he marched to Naogaon and encamped on the bank of the Mej. The river, which was ankle deep when he arrived, rose rapidly, and within an hour was impassable,* and it was not until the morning of the 25th that the column was able to cross over to the village of Mangali. On the morning of the 26th the force marched for Etonda; the cavalry advanced guard, and a detachment of the 72nd crossed a *nala* a short way in front and the artillery was about to follow, when the water rose so rapidly that no further progress could be made, and the portion of the force that had already started re-crossed with difficulty. The river in rear and the *nala* in front rose to so great a height that the column was obliged to halt until the 30th July. During this halt supplies were ob ained with the greatest difficulty, and it was only by the construction of rafts, and by the employment of some men of the 12th Bombay Infantry who were expert swimmers, that subsistence was procured for the troops and horses. During this delay Colonel Holmes received intelligence of the enemy

* It must be remembered that it was the rainy season, when, after a heavy downpour, rivers swell in a very short time.

being at Khera, Jalodra, Manpura, Hora, and Mandalgarh. The force crossed on the 31st and encamped just beyond the *nala*, marching next day four miles to Sherpura, the road being deep in mud.

On the 2nd August the column was only able to make five miles to Tukra, the road being most difficult for artillery; and it was with the greatest exertions that the troop of Horse Artillery reached camp at 8 P.M., while part of the baggage did not arrive until next morning.

On the 3rd August a halt was necessary, as the road ahead was impracticable. On the 4th, having discovered another route, Colonel Holmes marched to Johaipur, where he heard that the rebels were at Mandalgarh, some 27 miles distant. On the 5th he intended to resume the pursuit, but was prevented by want of carriage, great numbers of camels having died on the march. On the morning of the 6th he marched to Kajuru, where information was brought that the enemy were crossing the Banas river at the Tarbani ford, and intended to march to Bhilwara.

On the 7th the column marched to Karhola, and next day crossed the river, a ford having been discovered with difficulty. That day Colonel Holmes received information that General Roberts was at Sanganir and the enemy encamped at Bhilwara. Marching all night, the column reached Bhilwara at 2 P.M., on the 9th August, after a march of 35 miles, only to find that the insurgents had been driven off by General Roberts the previous day. In spite of the difficulties of the march, the troops had covered upwards of 340 miles since leaving head-quarters on the 8th July, and had been obliged to halt eleven days.

Movements of General Roberts.

Meanwhile Major-General Roberts had been moving down the Nasirabad-Neemuch road, and on the 7th August when at Dabla ten miles from Sanganir, he received information that Tantia Topi had taken up a position near the latter place. He reached Banera on the 8th, after a long and very heavy march, and soon found that the rebels were congregated about that place and Bhilwara. He decided to attack them, and as soon as the men had had their breakfasts, marched with the troops detailed in the margin. On nearing Sanganir, some 35 of the Gujrat Irregular Horse, with some Baluch Horse under Risaldar Mir Muhammad Ali, being in advance came on a strong picquet of the enemy, about 100 in number; these retreated, but were pursued to the town, through which they passed, and the pursuers halted, finding the enemy in great force beyond it. They had wounded and taken one man of the 44th Bengal Infantry.

8th Light Field Battery, 3 guns.	
12 Golandazes.	
18th Irregular Horse.	
11th Company, R. E.	
3rd Company, Sappers and Miners.	
83rd Regiment	500
Gujrat Irregular Horse	50
A few Baluch Horse.	
13th Bombay Infantry	200

On approaching at about 5 P.M. General Roberts found that the body of the enemy who were west of the city were crossing to the right bank of the r'ver From further observations the rebels appeared in great force, extending from near the river in a semicircle far to the right and for upwards of two miles, his own front occupying 400 yards. The guns soon brought them to action, and having broken their right and caused much confusion, the infantry was sent across the river, under fire of two of the enemy's guns. Having forced their right to close on their left, the General brought his troops on, left thrown forward, and directed a party of the 83rd to storm and occupy the small hamlet of Rowari on an eminence on his right. This done, the guns advanced and opened fire on the enemy's left. The left was driven in and the rebels were fast retreating on Bhilwara when, as it was getting dark, the General called in his troops and encamped on the high ground. The enemy lost 50 or 60 killed and wounded; there were no casualties on the British side.*

Skirmish at Sanganir, 8th August.

Tantia Topi at once left Bhilwara, and retreated to Kankroli in Udaipur where he lost time in performing religious ceremonies at the shrine of Nathdwara.

On the 13th August, after marching seventy miles in three days, General Roberts arrived within eight miles of the rebels, with the force detailed in the margin. On the approach of the pursuing force next day, the enemy took up a strong position on a rocky ridge of low hills which forms the right bank of the Banas near Mui. The river flowed at the foot of the ridge along the whole front of their position; on the left bank was a perfectly level plain, which was swept by the enemy's guns placed on their right.

The pursuit continued.

2nd Troop, Horse Artillery	6 guns.
Left half, No. 8 Light Field Battery	3 guns.
R. E. and 3rd Company, Sappers and Miners.	
Detachment, 8th Hussars	125
1st Bombay Cavalry (Lancers)	100
72nd Highlanders	270
83rd Regiment	562
12th Bombay Infantry	336
13th Bombay Infantry	330
Gujrat Irregular Horse	50
Lieutenant Macaulay's Baluch Horse.	

The British troops were formed up behind a ridge which concealed them from view; supported by the cavalry on their left, the horse artillery galloped forward to about 400 yards from the rebels' guns, and replied to their fire. The infantry then crossed the plain and waded knee-deep through the river, accompanied by the three guns of the field battery and attacked and drove the enemy from the ridge, taking four guns. The artillery and cavalry

Action at Banas River, August 14th.

* Major-General Roberts acknowledged the services of Captain Eden, Political Agent at Jaipur, who had accompanied his force, and obtained supplies and information.

The Vakil of Jaipur, Maulvi Muhammad Mohiuddin was with Colonel Holmes.

NOTE.—"The method which General Roberts adopted for obtaining information was to have about twenty cavalry in advance close to the rebels. They left connecting links of two or three men every two or three miles, so as to keep up the chain of communication. The advance party was composed half of Baluch Horse, who had no sympathy with the rebels, but could communicate very well with the villagers, and half of horsemen belonging to the Raja of Jaipur who were supposed, as Rajputs, to be on good terms and able easily to communicate with the villagers, but not to be very warm partisans of the British."—*Blackwood's Magazine, August* 1860.

then passed the river, and the latter charged and cut up numbers of the enemy, the infantry advanced in line, killing many. After passing some rocks where one of the rebels mortally wounded Sergeant-Major Holland, 8th Hussars, and where numbers of the enemy were killed by the infantry, the 72nd High landers and two guns were detached to the right to drive back a body of in fantry that had been pursued by a small detachment of the Gujarat Irregular Horse, and stood at bay in some jungle. This body retreated after an exchange of shots at long range.

The main body of the enemy, consisting of cavalry and of some of the more active of the infantry, who had thrown away everything but their muskets, retreated so rapidly across the undulating country that they were soon out of sight. Accordingly the cavalry took up the pursuit, together with four guns of the horse artillery, under Colonel Naylor, 8th Hussars, and killed numbers of the fugitives.

After following about seven miles, the artillery horses were unable to proceed, and about four miles further on Colonel Naylor came up with a large body, and drove in their rear-guard, composed of the late Kotah Contingent and 5th Bengal Irregular Cavalry. Most of the remaining infantry and the badly-mounted men were killed, or threw away their arms and sought refuge in the jungle. Three elephants and a number of camels and other baggage animals were here taken. At length the remains of the rebel infantry, about a hundred strong, took post in a village fifteen miles from the field of battle, with their cavalry formed round them : Colonel Naylor, who had with him only about a hundred regulars and eighty Baluchis, and was now in country unsuited for cavalry, then retired towards camp, killing on the way many insurgents who had concealed themselves during the pursuit. He did not reach camp until 11 o'clock at night, when his men had been eighteen hours in the saddle.

The enemy lost about a thousand men, and were completely disorganised and scattered. On the British side 3 were killed and 19 wounded, the 8th Hussars alone having 1 killed and 9 wounded.

Disposition of the Gwalior Division

After the fall of Gwalior and the reinstallation of the Maharaja Sindhia, Sir Hugh Rose proceeded to Bombay to take up the command of the Poona Division leaving Brigadier-General R. Napier in command of the Gwalior Division and the forces in Central India.

Gwalior.
3 squadrons, 14th Light Dragoons.
Meade's Horse.
Wing, 71st Highlanders.
86th Foot.
25th Bombay Infantry.
1 Company, Bombay Artillery.
Light Field Battery.
Company, R. E.

These forces were at the beginning of July disposed as detailed in the margin, Brigadier Smith's brigade of the Rajputana Field Force, which had fought the battle of Kotah-ki-Serai and taken part in the capture of Gwalior, being at Sipri.

Jhansi.
1 Squadron, 14th Light Dragoons.
Wing, 3rd Bombay Cavalry.
3rd Bombay Europeans.
24th Bombay Infantry.
1 Company, Bombay Sappers and Miners.
3 guns, Bhopal Contingent.
Sipri.
2 squadrons, 8th Hussars.
2 squadrons, 1st Bombay Lancers.
95th Foot.
10th Bombay Infantry.
Troop, Bombay Horse Artillery.
Goona.
Mayne's Horse.

Man Singh.

During the month of July affairs were queiscent in Sindhia's dominions, but early in August Man Singh, Raja of Narwar, who had quarrelled with Sindhia, in whose territory his possessions were situated, having called in his followers seized the strong fort of Paori.

Sindhia appears to have regarded the rich territory of Narwar, which lies 44 miles south of Gwalior, as a Naboth's vineyard, and refused to recognise Man Singh's right to succeed his father in the principality and adjacent country. The Raja therefore took up arms, intimating to Brigadier Smith that he had no cause of quarrel with the British, and no connection with the rebels.* But Smith was responsible for the peace of the country and was therefore obliged to take action against Man Singh.

The fort of Paori.

The fort of Paori, twenty miles north of Sipri, was seized on the 4th August by Man Singh, ex-Raja of Narwar, who was joined by most of the garrison after they had let him into the place. He was reported to have a force of 4,000 men, of whom 700 were rebel sepoys, well armed with flint and percussion muskets. The local authorities made urgent applications for protection to Brigadier Smith as Man Singh was on the point of seizing other valuable towns, and the well-disposed inhabitants of the neighbourhood were alarmed.

The Brigadier therefore moved to Paori on the 6th, but found it too strong to be attempted with field guns, and, encamping at a distance of three miles, applied to Brigadier-General Napier at Gwalior for two 18-pounders, two 8-inch mortars, and reinforcements. The Siege Train left Gwalior on the 11th and arrived at Paori on the 20th, accompanied by Brigadier-General Napier who encamped just out of range of the enemy's guns, with Brigadier Smith's force, the total strength of which was now brought up to the numbers detailed in the margin

European Artillery	14
Native Artillery	119
European Cavalry	166
Native Cavalry	280
Engineers	29
European Infantry	552
Native Infantry	733

Capture of Paori, 22nd August.

A party of 100 infantry, with 200 infantry and 2 guns in support, under command of Major Vialls, immediately seized a temple 400 yards from the main gate, the enemy's picquet retiring into the place, from which a heavy fire of round shot and musketry was opened, and replied to

* Malleson says that this was true; but mutineers of several corps of the Bengal Army were among those killed and captured in the subsequent operations. Tantia Topi in his statement (Appendix) says that Man Singh joined him before the battle of Betwa River.

The fort was then reconnoitred by Brigadier-General Napier ; and at sunset four 8-inch mortars were sent down to the temple, and continued firing all night without intermission ; while a breaching battery for two 18-pounders was commenced at 300 yards from a bastion on the east side, and nearly completed by morning. A battery for the howitzer, to give an oblique fire on the defences of the east side, and cross-fire on the breach, was also commenced at 400 yards.

The mortars continued firing all day on the 21st, but during the night Man Singh and his followers escaped. It had been impossible to invest the fort completely, as it was a mile and a half in circuit, one side resting on an impracticable precipice, flanked by ravines and jungle, and backed by a deep torrent, and a forest extending for many miles. In front of the other side was open ground, with tanks and marshes. The main gateway was very strong, having three gates, and numerous lofty bastions to flank them. The Dhang, or jungle, gateway, had two gates, and opened on ravines and jungle ; a wicket led down by the one side of the precipice, and there was also a path down the other side by which men could escape in single file. The walls, though ancient, and in some places dilapidated, were generally 10 feet thick, of massive stone, and from 25 to 50 feet high, and well protected by the precipice, by deep tanks, and by a wet ditch, except at two or three points. Seventeen guns were found on the walls. The enemy lost 10 killed and 30 wounded. On the British side Lieutenant C. Fisher, 95th Regiment, and 2 men were wounded.

On Man Singh's flight from Paori, the pursuit was taken up by the troops detailed in the margin, under Lieutenant-Colonel G. H. Robertson, 25th Bombay Infantry. The column, which was furnished with 15 days' supplies for Europeans, and elephants and camels to mount about 200 men, marched from Paori on the 27th August. On the 29th they came up with a small party of Man Singh's infantry, some of whom were killed, some captured, and the rest dispersed. The column followed closely on the track of the fugitives, who kept ten or twelve miles ahead. On the 31st Man Singh's force, said to be reduced to 500, split up at Sangi ; 200 going towards Shahabad under Piari Lal, and 300 with Man Singh and his uncle Ajit Singh towards Rai.

Pursuit of Man Singh.

1 Troop, 2nd Division, Bombay Horse Artillery.	
1 Division, 4-2 Bombay Fort Artillery.	
1 Squadron, 8th Hussars.	
Meade's Horse	250
Royal Engineers	7
86th Regiment	93
95th Regiment	118
10th Bombay Infantry	392
25th Bombay Infantry	250

The column reached Rai on the 2nd and Barhampur on the 3rd September. At 2 A.M., next day, Colonel Robertson pushed on ahead with the detachment noted in the margin ; arrived at Jagar at 10 A.M., marched again at 5 P.M., and, bivouacking when it became dark, moved off at midnight, arriving just before daybreak on the 5th September within a short distance of Bijapur on the Chupet river.

8th Hussars	47
Meade's Horse	150
86th Regiment	79
95th Regiment	59
10th Bombay Infantry ..	100
25th Bombay Infantry	100

The village of Bijapur lay between the column and the enemy, who were encamped on the bank of the river. At daybreak the cavalry was sent round the village by the right, to attack the enemy on their left flank, while the infantry went through the village straight at them. They were posted in great numbers on the high ground with a smaller body lower down, about seven or eight hundred infantry and 150 cavalry. Their appearance was imposing for a few minutes; but the infantry rushed forward and shot and drove before them those who were on the lower ground, while the cavalry charged across the lower ground, using their sabres most effectively, 37 bodies being afterwards counted on the spot.

Action at Bijapur, 5th September.

The action commenced at a quarter past 5 and was over by 7 o'clock. The enemy were shot and bayonetted along both banks of the river, and while crossing the river, and in the thickly-wooded ravines in its neighbourhood, the cavalry getting among them wherever the ground admitted of their acting, and at least 450 mutineers were destroyed. They belonged to the 1st, 2nd, 3rd, and 4th Regiments of the Gwalior Contingent, Sindhia's Ali Jah Bahadur Regiment, 1st Kotah Contingent, 40th, 50th and 52nd Bengal Infantry.

On the British side Lieutenant Fawcett, 95th Regiment, and 5 men were killed; Captain Poore and Lieutenant Hanbury, 8th Hussars, Lieutenants Stewart and Page, Meade's Horse and 14 men wounded. With one halt only the column had made long and harassing marches, averaging 16 miles daily, in rainy weather, across ploughed and muddy fields of blacksoil and dense forests, where frequently there was no track whatever; through rivers whose rough and stony beds and banks injured the gun-carriages; and over rocky mountain passes. Most of the country traversed was at one time under Man Singh's charge, and many villages belonged to him, so there was great difficulty in obtaining information. After this action, Colonel Robertson marched with his force to Goona.

After his defeat at Banas River, Tantia Topi fled eastwards towards the Chambal, followed by General Roberts, who met Brigadier Parke, commanding the Neemuch Brigade, on the 18th August at Puna, not far from the Neemuch-Nasirabad road. Reinforced by the 8th Hussars and Baluch Horse, Parke took up the pursuit, and proceeded to Neemuch to obtain remounts for the Hussars. Here he heard that the Chambal was unfordable, and marched to Morasa, 15 miles distant, hoping to cut off Tantia Topi on his way to the south. But the latter meanwhile was making the passage of the Chambal, and Parke followed on his tracks, only to find a few disabled ponies standing on the left bank of the river, and the rebels disappearing among some mango trees on the horizon.

Parke's pursuit of Tantia Topi.

Parke returned to Neemuch, while Tantia Topi made for Jhalra Patan, thirty miles distant, a town of Jhalawar State, ninety miles east of Neemuch. The Rana of the State was loyal, but his troops sided with the rebels, and Tantia took possession of his guns, some thirty in number, ammunition and horses, and surrounded the palace. The Rana fled to Mhow, having been forced to make a contribution of fifteen lakhs of rupees to the rebels, who halted five days at Jhalra Patan, secured from pursuit by the rising of the Chambal. Reinforced by the Jhalawar levies, Tantia Topi then marched south-east to Rajgarh, intending to try and reach Indore and raise Holkar's troops in rebellion. But Major-General Michel, who was commanding in Malwa, had already foreseen this movement, and despatched the force detailed in the margin under Colonel Lockhart to cover Ujjain. Lockhart moved northwards to Susner, thirty miles west of Rajgarh, and there awaited a reinforcement from Mhow under Colonel Hope, not considering himself strong enough to attack the rebels.

Tantia at Rajgarh.

92nd Highlanders	350
3rd Bombay Cavalry, 1 squadron.	
Bengal Artillery, 2 guns.	
19th Bombay Infantry*	450

At the end of August Major-General Michel succeeded General Roberts in command of the Rajputana Field Force, and on the 14th September, having joined the forces of Parke and Hope at Nalkhera, ten miles south-east of Susner, he marched on Rajgarh and reconnoitred the enemy's positions, which were on both sides of the river at that place. Next morning‡ he moved against the rebels, but found that they had marched during the night to a very strong position on the road to Biaora. They moved on four or five miles before a cavalry reconnaissance, and there was a skirmish with the rear-guard, in which the 3rd Cavalry behaved very gallantly. Eventually their guns were found in position commanding the British line of march. The cavalry were compelled to retire, and the enemy's artillery opened fire on the troops as they came up. General Michel endeavoured to check this fire with his 9-pounders, but the range was too great, and he partially retired his force, while the rebels advanced. On the arrival of the European Infantry the whole line advanced, covered by the skirmishers of the Rifles and 92nd.

General Michel takes up the pursuit.

Major-General Michel.

17th Lancers	80
3rd Bombay Cavalry	180
No. 8 Bengal Light Field Battery, 4 guns.	
71st Highlanders .. .. }	600
92nd Highlanders .. .. }	
4th Bombay Rifles † .. .. }	1,100
19th Bombay Infantry .. .. }	

During the advance the enemy kept up a well-sustained fire from some 8 heavy guns, but without effect, and on the British approaching their position, they began to retreat and crowds of fugitives were seen hurrying to the rear. Although within range, the General did not allow his soldiers to fire a round from their Minie rifles, as it would

Action near Biaora, 15th September.

Note.—Captain Bolton, A.Q.M.G., Lieutenant Williams, Commissariat; Captain Poore, 8th Hussars; Captain Foster, 95th; Captain Rice, 25th; Lieutenant Stewart, Meade's Horse; Lieutenant Roome, 10th; were mentioned in despatches; also Havildar Ram Lal, 10th; and Daulat Singh, 25th, who acted as spies and risked their lives in procuring information.

* Now 119th Infantry (The Mooltan Regiment).

† Now 104th Wellesley's Rifles.

‡ Owing to the excessive heat and consequent exhaustion of his troops, he found it impossible to attack the same evening.

have checked the advance. Having proceeded in this order for two or three miles, two guns were rapidly brought into action in front of the skirmishers, and their fire soon threw the rebels into extreme confusion. Another advance and another dash forward of the artillery completed their defeat. Every minute guns, material, and baggage were falling into the hands of the pursuers, and the 17th Lancers under Captain Sir W. Gordon, who had been advancing on the British right, now charged, dispersing the remaining organized bodies of the enemy, and continuing the pursuit for four or five miles until men and horses were exhausted.

The rebel army, estimated at 10,000 men, was entirely dispersed, losing some two or three hundred killed, 27 guns, 5 ammunition wagons, 152 gun bullocks, and a quantity of camp equipage. On the British side 3 men died of sunstroke and 3 were wounded.*

Rebel movements.

After this action, Tantia fled eastwards to the valley of the Betwa river, marching through the densely wooded district of Maksudnagar, followed by General Michel. At Sironj he found 4 guns and rested a week, then marched northwards to Isagarh, which he stormed and plundered, taking five more guns. Here his force split up, Tantia marching on Chanderi, while the Rao Sahib with six guns and a portion of the force made for Talbahat and Lalitpur. Chanderi held out against the rebel attacks, and after three days there Tantia Topi and the Nawab of Banda moved twenty miles southwards to Mangraoli on the left bank of the Betwa river. Here they were headed off on the north by Brigadier Smith and on the north-east by Colonel Liddell with the Jhansi force, while Brigadier Parke from Neemuch covered Indore and Bhopal.

Action at Mangraoli, 10th October.

On the night of the 8th October, while at Bahadurpur, General Michel heard that the insurgents had reached a village near Mangraoli late that night. He accordingly marched before daybreak with the force detailed in the margin, and on reaching Mangraoli was informed by his scouts that the enemy, to the number of about 5,000, was advancing some two miles off. The rebel advanced guard, 1,000 strong, was found close to the village of Barulpur, out of which a few shells drove them on to their main body, posted at the elevated village of Shahjehan Mau. The surrounding country was covered with high scrub, in which the infantry could not see the enemy until close to them. The force then advanced, each regiment covered by skirmishers.

Bengal Artillery, 4 guns	62
17th Lancers	90
71st Regiment	210
92nd Highlanders	300
19th Regiment, Bombay Infantry ..	429

* Mentioned in Despatches:—Captain Champion, A. A. G.; Lieutenant Holland, A. Q. M. G.; Lieutenant Shewell, D. A. C. G.; Major Elkington, A. D. C.; Captain Sir W. Gordon, 17th Lancers; Lieutenant-Colonel Hope, Captain Parker, 71st; Lieutenant-Colonel Lockhart; Captain St. John, 92nd Captain Oldfield, 3rd Cavalry; Lieutenant Le Marchant, Bengal Artillery; Lieutenant Malcolm, Bombay Engineers; Major Manson, 4th Rifles; Captain Barrow, 19th Bombay Infantry; Captain Hutchinson, Political; Lieutenant Cummings, Bhil Agent.

Captain Mayne, with his regiment of Irregular Horse from Goona, joined at Biaora.

The jungle was so thick that a column of the rebels got unperceived in rear of the support, when they were charged and cut to pieces by the 17th Lancers. The enemy stood to their six guns, which were taken by the infantry, and then dispersed, having lost some 300 killed.* About 2,500 crossed the Betwa that night by a ford 8 miles off near the Chanderi road. The British lost only 1 killed and 1 wounded.†

Tantia fled across the Betwa through Jakhlaun to Lalitpur, where he joined Rao Sahib. The latter and the Nawab of Banda next day marched south-east some 15 miles to Sindwaha.

Meanwhile General Michel had marched on the 18th October from Balabhat to Narhat, for the purpose of covering Tehri, and at midnight received information that the enemy were at Sindwah and the neighbouring villages, evidently with the intention of turning the protected fords of the Jamni river, and passing to the east. At 4 o'clock next morning General Michel marched for Sindwaha with the force detailed in the margin, and at about half-past 8 found the rebels drawn up on a hill beyond Sindwaha on the road to Marauni. They numbered some 10,000, including a great many sepoys and regulars of Contingents, with four guns.

Battle of Sindwaha, October 19th.

1st column.	
3rd Troop, Horse Artillery	60
8th Hussars	118
17th Lancers	90
1st Bombay Lancers	93
3rd Bombay Cavalry	98
95th Regiment	20
Mayne's Horse	50
2nd column.	
3rd Bombay Cavalry	50
2-6th Bengal Battery	80
71st Regiment	210
92nd Highlanders	320
19th Bombay Infantry	500

General Michel, to prevent them from proceeding eastwards, advanced rapidly with a portion of his cavalry parallel to their extreme left. The enemy came down in strength, and boldly attacked the cavalry (8th Hussars and 1st Bombay Lancers), but were driven back by those regiments and the 17th Lancers. The Horse Artillery, having now arrived with the rest of the cavalry, opened fire on the enemy's guns. At this moment the 71st and 92nd Highlanders came up in line on the British left, with the Bengal battery, followed by the 19th Bombay Infantry on their left rear, and drove the enemy up the hill. The rebels then tried to turn both flanks, and the Horse Artillery and Cavalry were so hard pressed on the right by the enemy posted in a field of high corn, that the 19th Bombay Infantry had to be brought up; they were eventually driven back by grape. The 92nd had also to wheel to their left to meet a flank attack. The 71st still advanced steadily to the front up the hill, and drove the rebels back, and the guns were captured by the combined movement of the two Highland regiments. The enemy now retreated at all points, constantly rallying or

* Few would have escaped but for the paucity of the British Cavalry, General Michel having detached most of his cavalry to join Brigadier Smith near Chanderi.

† Mentioned in Despatches :—Colonel Hope, Captain Parker, 71st; Colonel Lockhart, Captain Bethune, 92nd; Sir W. Gordon, 17th Lancers; Captain Barrow, 19th; Lieutenant Hope Johnstone, A. D. C.; Captain Champion, A. A. G.; Captain St. John, A. Q. M. G.; Major Elkington, A. D. C.; Captain Gordon, Political Agent. The man killed was a wounded soldier of the 71st who was attacked while being carried in a *dooli*.

massing before the pursuit, which was slowing to heavy ground, and as often dispersed by the fire of the guns. The pursuit was continued for about nine miles, and was eventually checked by the difficult nature of the country, and the division of the rebels into small parties.

In recording the general good conduct of the troops, General Michel wrote—"I may state that as on the cavalry the whole loss of the day fell, so they did their duty well and gallantly. But I cannot refrain from expressing my admiration of that spirit of chivalrous endurance, which during a rapid march of at least twenty miles, enabled our infantry to keep almost up to the cavalry, nor from recording a fact which shows the spirit of the British soldier, that, notwithstanding the heat, when the firing commenced all the sick of the 71st and 92nd Regiments could not be restrained but fell into the ranks and so remained until the close of the day." Among many officers mentioned in the Despatch*, was Lieutenant Wood,† 17th Lancers, who, having from paucity of officers in the 3rd Cavalry, volunteered during the campaign to command a troop of that regiment, on this occasion came up to and almost single-handed attacked a body of the enemy.

The result of the day's operations was the capture of 4 guns, and 500 of the enemy left dead on the field. The Nawab of Banda's *palki*, bloody and evidently just evacuated, was captured during the pursuit. The British loss amounted to 4 killed and 19 (including 5 officers) wounded.

After this action Rao Sahib rejoined Tantia at Lalitpur, whence they marched to Kajuria, with the intention of crossing the Betwa there, and then moving southwards. But they were turned by Colonel Liddell at the Sairas Ghat, and retraced their footsteps to Jakhlaun and from thence to Itawah and Kurai.

General Michel arrived at Lalitpur on the 22nd October, and heard of this movement. Without guns or wheeled carriage the rebels were able to move through the mountains and dense jungle, proceeding *viâ* Pali, Narhat, and Balabahat to Kanjia. General Michel was, however, obliged to proceed by Malthone and Duji by forced marches. On the night of the 24th he heard

Fight at Kurai, 25th October.

that the rebels were at Khimlasa, and knowing they would move during the night, he marched on Kurai at 2 A.M. on the 25th, and at dawn discovered the enem crossing his front just beyond that place.

* Mentioned in Despatches:—Colonel Hope, Captain Parker, 71st; Captains Cameron and St. John, 92nd; Captain Champion, A.A.G.; Major Elkington, A. D. C.; Captain Le-Marchant, R. A.; Colonel DeSalis, Major Chetwode, Lieutenant Jenkins, 8th Hussars; Captain Sir W. Gordon, 17th Lancers; Lieutenant-Colonel Blake, Bombay H. A.; Lieutenant-Colonel Curtis, 1st Cavalry; Captain Oldfield, 3rd Cavalry; Captain Mayne, Mayne's Horse; Captain Barrow, 19th; Captain Maude, Lieutenant Shewell, Staff; Captain Gordon Cumming, Political Agent.

† Afterwards Field Marshal Sir Evelyn Wood, V.C., G.C.B., etc.

He had with him the force detailed in the margin. As he was desirous of bringing his infantry into action, he had ordered their march one hour ahead of the cavalry; consequently the cavalry had only just come up in rear when the infantry, under Colonel Lockhart, having cut the enemy's line of march in half, had wheeled to the right, and was advancing in skirmishing order. The infantry had already dispersed the enemy, who had not formed up in order of battle when the cavalry arrived.

1st column.	
3rd Troop, Bombay Horse Artillery	60
8th Hussars	118
17th Lancers	90
1st Bombay Lancers	93
3rd Bombay Caval y	98
95th R.giment	20
Mayne's Horse	150
2nd column.	
3rd Bombay Cavalry	50
2-6 Bengal Artillery	80
71st Regiment	210
92nd Highlanders	320
19th Bombay Infantry	550

The pursuit was taken up in three different directions, after three separate bodies of rebels, a difficult task owing to the broken nature of the country Colonel Curtis on the right did not come up with the enemy, who were principally cavalry on his side, and he could not advance far, as they threatened the baggage; Captain Sir W. Gordon with the 17th Lancers and 3rd Cavalry pursued for about six miles, and cut up numbers. Captain Mayne, with about 60 of his horse, pursued nine or ten miles, and killed 150. The infantry followed for five miles, clearing the villages. The result of the day's action was the cutting off and driving to the north some 3,000 rebels, of whom 350 were killed; half the remainder threw down their arms, and the rest were dispersed over the country. The only casualties on the British side were 2 men of Mayne's Horse wounded

Tantia crosses the Narbada.

Tantia Topi, with the main body, passed Kurai two or three hours afterwards to the south, losing on the way 40 men who were cut up by Colonel Becher with a body of newly raised cavalry of the Central India Horse. Tantia passed through Rajgarh, crossed the Narbada some forty miles above Hoshangabad, and proceeded in the direction of Nagpur, as far as Multai.* Turned at this point by the Nagpur force, he fled westwards through the Tapti Valley, hoping to pass to the south through the wild country of the Melghat Forest.† Here, however, his way was barred by the Berar Field Force of the Hyderabad Contingent under Brigadier Hill, and he turned north-west into Holkar's dominions, making for Baroda. On the 19th November he arrived at Kargaon in Nimar, where there was a detachment of Holkar's army, consisting of two troops of cavalry, a company of infantry, and two guns, which he forced to join him.

* The rebels entered Multai with great pomp, proclaiming that they were the advanced guard of the Peshwa's army advancing to take possession of the Deccan after numerous victories in Central India.

† Some of the rebels appear to have left Tantia and taken refuge in the Gawilgarh Hills, where a party was cut up by the Berar Field Force under Brigadier Hill on the 8th and 9th December. Among these rebels were men of the Gwalior Contingent, 14th Irregular Cavalry, and 70th Bengal Infantry. In the pursuit of this party Captain Clogstoun, 2nd Cavalry, Hyderabad Contingent, behaved with distinction. This officer was soon after awarded the Victoria Cross for valour in the fight at Chichamba near Hingoli on the 15th January 1859.

Meanwhile General Michel, following on the track of the rebels after defeating them at Kurai, reached Hoshangabad on the 7th November, where he was joined by Brigadier Parke. Michel crossed into Betul, while Parke passed the Narbada at Hoshangabad and marched to Charwa, eighty miles south-east of Indore. Michel also moved in the same direction, while the troops at Asirgarh barred the way to the south across the Tapti river. Meanwhile detachments were sent out from Mhow to watch the fords over the Narbada in that direction.

Movements of pursuing columns.

One of the columns, under Major Sutherland, 92nd Highlanders, arrived at Tekri on the 23rd November; there information was received that the rebels under Tantia Topi and the Rao Sahib were at Khargon, west of Khandwa, about twenty miles east of the Grand Trunk Road, and thirty miles from the Sendhwa Ghat. On the following morning Sutherland moved to Gwana, sixteen miles from Sendhwa, so as to cut the rebels off if they made for Khandesh, or move rapidly back along the main road if they tried to turn his left flank.

Sutherland's operations.

On the morning of the 24th he was joined by 50 men of the 71st Highlanders, who had been brought from Mhow by Barras' Camel Corps, 70 miles in thirty hours, 20 Sikhs and 100 of Holkar's Horse. During the forenoon the rebels sent a patrol of 200 horse towards Sendhwa, and another of the same strength towards Than, six miles north of Sutherland's position along the road, making it doubtful which route the main body would take. The latter party cut the telegraph wire to Indore and plundered some carts, and were at Than at night-fall. The reports brought in by scouts led to the supposition that the rebels would not attempt the Sendhwa Ghat but move north-west, crossing the main road at Than. Sutherland, therefore, on the morning of the 25th November, took the party detailed in the margin to clear the road in that direction, intending, if the rebels had not moved, to attack them next day at Khargon. The remainder of his force, a subaltern and 60 rank and file, were left to guard the encampment.

71st Highlanders	41
92nd Highlanders	92
4th Bombay Rifles	61
Holkar's Horse	101
Agent's Escort	20
Camel Corps	150

On arrival at Than, Sutherland found that the whole of the rebels had passed that place during the night, going westward towards Rajpur and Barwani, and he determined to pursue at once, following the tracks of their gun-wheels and elephants. After eight miles' rapid marching he overtook the rebel rear-guard streaming out of Rajpur, and allowed them five minutes to clear the town, as, if they attempted to hold it, his small force could never have dislodged them. He then pursued at a rapid trot with the Camel Corps and horsemen, directing the infantry to follow as quickly as possible. The road lay through jungle in which the camels could not move, but Sutherland pushed on, disregarding stragglers, and passing quantities of abandoned stores, bullocks, and baggage. After about five miles

Action at Rajpur, 25th November.

of this pursuit, during which some of the fugitives were cut down by the Sikh Horse and shot by the Highlanders, the rebels formed up on the further bank of a watercourse which crossed the road at right angles. When five hundred yards from this spot the infantry on the camels were dismounted, and proceeded to attack, when Major Sutherland was surprised to see the remainder of his men, who were on foot, appear a few hundred yards in rear, having kept up with the camels at more than five miles an hour.

The rebels hardly waited to exchange shots, and the pursuit was continued for a couple of miles, when they again formed up in a strong position where the road ascended the slope, lined on both sides by thick jungle, and overlooked by a rocky ridge, which they held, placing their two guns in the centre of the road. Here they opened fire on the skirmishers with grape and musketry, but the pursuers charged straight along the road and carried the guns, and the rebels lost heart and fled, leaving some 70 killed and wounded. The men being exhausted, the pursuit ended, and the British column returned to Rajpur. In this action Lieutenant Humpreys, 92nd, and three men were wounded and three missing.*

The flight towards Baroda.

Relieved of his guns, Tantia Topi was able to retreat with greater celerity, and when Sutherland, following on his tracks, arrived next evening on the bank of the Narbada, he beheld the rebels encamped on the opposite side. Deeming it impossible to cross five hundred yards of water in the face of an enemy so superior in numbers, Sutherland halted south of the Narbada.

That night Tantia moved on in the direction of Baroda, hoping to reach that place and attach the Gaekwar's troops to his cause, and halted at Rajpur, twenty miles short of Chota Udepur. But other columns were on his track. General Michel and Brigadier Parke had moved to Charwa, south of the Narbada, as already related. From this place, on receiving information of the movements of the fugitives, Michel marched to Mhow, and sent Parke in pursuit.

After marching 240 miles in ten days, Brigadier Parke,† with the force detailed in the margin, came up with Tantia Topi and Rao Sahib on the 1st December, opposite Udepur on the river Or. The town is situated on the right bank of the river, surrounded by dense jungle and mountains, with the exception of a small clear space, leading up to the town, on which the rebels had been encamped. Udepur is on the direct road to Baroda from Kuksi and the east.

Two 9-pounders, Bombay Artillery	50
8th Hussars	47
2nd Bombay Cavalry	51
72nd Highlanders	24
Gujrat Irregular Horse	164
Gaekwar's Horse	304
2nd Southern Mahratta Horse ..	161
Aden Troop, Scinde Horse ‡ ...	66
	837

* Mentioned in Despatches:—Captain Helbert; Captain Langston, 4th Bombay Rifles; Captain Newall, Lieutenant Humpreys, 92nd; Lieutenant Lewis, 71st; Lieutenant Bonnor, 9th Bombay Infantry; Lieutenant Montriou, 25th Bombay Infantry; Assistant Surgeon Don; Commandant "Bheengir," Holkar's Horse, Woordie-Major; Jodh Singh, Agent's escort.

† Lieutenant-Colonel W. Parke, 72nd Highlanders, Commanding 2nd Brigade, Rajputana Field Force.

‡ Now the 35th Scinde Horse.

On the 30th November Brigadier Parke reached the village of Chandpur, 45 miles west of Kuksi, and learnt that the rebel army had marched that morning to Udepur, *en route* to Baroda and Gujarat. The force marched that night through dense jungle for 22 miles, at the end of which the narrow road debouched into a less thickly wooded plain, which gradually opened out as they advanced. Shortly afterwards the advanced guard of the Aden Troop sabred some of the men of the enemy's outlying picquets, which gave the alarm. Brigadier Parke moved rapidly forward, throwing out skirmishers of the 72nd Highlanders. The cavalry was formed in two lines in rear of the artillery and infantry support; the Irregular Cavalry in the first and the 8th Hussars and 2nd Bombay Cavalry in the second line.

Parke defeats Tantia at Udepur, 1st December.

The enemy, mostly well-mounted cavalry, soon appeared in front and on both flanks, with the evident intention of opposing the advance. To clear the right flank first, the Southern Mahratta Horse under Lieutenant Kerr made a brilliant charge, and captured a standard. The artillery now moved forward with the Highlanders skirmishing on both flanks; the enemy's trumpets sounded the "Advance," and they came on with a bold front, but were turned by the artillery and Enfield rifles; at the same time another body threatened the British left. Front was changed, the Gujrat Horse at the same time charging to the original front, led by Lieutenant Newton, driving the enemy before them through the town of Udepur, across the river and into the mountains. The artillery was now brought up rapidly into new positions and opened fire with canister. The ground in the immediate front was much broken; and several small huts on the right were held by matchlockmen.. These were cleared by a party of Highlanders under Lieutenant Champion, and the rebels fled past the right, giving the opportunity for a charge by the 8th Hussars under Captain Clowes, 2nd Bombay Cavalry, under Captain Smith, and a Troop of Mahratta Horse under Lieutenant Bannerman, who distinguished himself, and had his horse wounded.

The enemy were now driven across the river, which runs almost in a semicircle round the town; the opposite side and a small island were held by their infantry, of whom a considerable number were killed, including many dressed in British uniforms and accoutrements. The cavalry pursued, killing many, until the remainder were scattered in the jungles and mountains.

The loss of the enemy, who were three or four thousand strong, amounted to some 300 men; of the British force 10 were killed and 15 wounded. In his Despatch Brigadier Parke brought to notice the services of that portion of the 2nd Brigade which was not present in the action, "but which has marched upwards of fifteen hundred miles during the hot, as also during the rainy season in the pursuit of rebels throughout the greater part of Rajputana, through Malwa, and has crossed eight principal rivers on this side of India, some at great risk and with much difficulty."*

Tantia Topi re-enters Rajputana.

Thus turned from Baroda, Tantia Topi fled north into the jungles of Banswara, which place he entered on the 10th December; he was accompanied by Rao Sahib; the Nawab of Banda had surrendered in November under the terms† of the Royal Proclamation.

From this place he intended to march on Udaipur, but was met by a column under Major Roche at Bhansror, and turning north-east he made for Partabgarh, intending to effect a junction with Man Singh and with Feroz Shah, who, crossing the Ganges and the Jumna, was coming south to meet him. Emerging from the forest near Partabgarh, he was met by Major Roche on the 25th December, but the latter was not strong enough to break up the rebel force, and Tantia moved on to the neighbourhood of Mandesar, and thence to Zirapur, a hundred miles east-south-east of Neemuch, near which place he was caught up by Colonel Benson.

Colonel Benson's pursuit.
Royal Horse Artillery, 37 men, 2 guns.
17th Lancers, 16 officers, 210 men.

On the 29th December, after a pursuit of 148 miles in 120 hours, Colonel H. R. Benson, commanding the 2nd Cavalry Column, detailed in the margin, came up with some 4,000 rebels under Tantia Topi and Rao Sahib, three miles from Zirapur.

On the 24th December at Ninoz, having carefully ascertained that the passes leading out by Raipur had been blocked by felled trees, by Lieutenant Coglan, 4th Native Infantry, who had been detached to Raipur with 100 men for the purpose, Colonel Benson struck his camp and marched to Nawagon. Next day he made a reconnaissance with a small body of cavalry and Highlanders, and found that the rebels, after an attack on Partabgarh, had marched the previous evening towards Mandesar.

Colonel Benson immediately returned to camp, and made a forced march to protect Mandesar, where he arrived that evening and heard that the rebels were encamped four miles distant. Next day, taking two days' supplies and leaving the infantry and baggage to follow, he started towards Sita Mau, but changed the direction to Khempur, where tracks of the rebels were found. As most of the villages had been plundered, it was difficult to obtain guides, and the column halted that night on the left bank of the Chambal.

Marching at daybreak, as the track could not be followed by moonlight, Colonel Benson came up with the rebel force encamped at Dag at 5-40 P.M., drove in their advanced posts, and bivouacked for the night in sight of their fires.

*Mentioned in Despatches:—Captain Buckle, 3rd Bombay Cavalry; Captain Clowes, 8th Hussars; Captain Smith, 2nd Bombay Cavalry; Lieutenant Kerr (afterwards, V. C.), Southern Mahratta Horse; Captain Rice, Lieutenant Vesey, 72nd Highlanders; Captain Stewart, Brigade-Major; Lieutenant Heathorn, Bombay Artillery; Assistant Surgeons Rutter and Bell; Lieutenant Burton, Assistant Superintendent, Neemuch.

† A free pardon to those who laid down their arms, not having been concerned in murder.

Advancing at 4 A.M., the column halted in the plains of Dag until daylight, when it was found that the main body of the enemy had struck camp the previous evening, but had left a strong mounted piquet which remained until 3 A.M., and then followed the main body across the Kolisind river.

At 3 A.M. on the 29th December Colonel Benson marched from the right bank of the Kolisind, and after going 8 miles came in sight of the fires of the rebel camp at Zirapur. Advancing over ploughed land to deaden sound, he waited for daylight, and then found that the rebel main body had moved and was two miles ahead. He immediately trotted after them, and on emerging from a wooded lane found them drawn up in line of battle on rising ground, with jungle and a ravine in their rear.

Benson disperses the rebels.

The cavalry advanced, formed into columns of division, and the rebels opened fire. Colonel Benson then moved his leading column to the right, and, uncovering his guns, brought them rapidly to the front, when they opened fire with grape and shell at about 400 yards. The rebels, after a great deal of shouting, retired, and the cavalry attacked their right and drove them into the jungle. Having reformed, the cavalry advanced in two columns through the jungle and across the ravine, driving the enemy before them. On the other side of the strip of jungle it was found that the rebels had changed their position left back, and reformed on rising ground on the British left. The columns formed line and advanced with the guns in the centre to within 400 yards of the rebel line, when an effective fire of grape and shell was opened. The rebels then made an attempt to advance in line, and failing that tried to turn the British left, but Sir George Leith moved up with the left squadron, and they retired, whereupon Sir William Gordon charged with the right squadron, and cut up numbers, the rebels flying through the jungle and across the ravine. The pursuit was taken up for about five miles across stony and hilly country towards Manowar Sara, when it was abandoned, the horses being dead beat and the rebels dispersed. Four elephants were captured at the end of the action. The casualties on the British side were one man of the Horse Artillery wounded; one trumpeter wounded; and a Corporal and three privates of the 17th Lancers missing.*

Brigadier Somerset attacks Tantia Topi, 31st December.

Meanwhile Brigadier Somerset was on the track of the rebels, and reached Zirapur the morning after they left. Marching rapidly, Brigadier Somerset overtook Tantia Topi near Chapra Baraud, with the force detailed in the margin, soon after daylight on the 31st December. He had marched from Sarthal, 10 miles off at 11-30 the previous night, having sent on spies to watch the enemy. His spies not returning, he waited four miles off, fearing to disturb the enemy in the dark,

17th Lancers	100
Royal Horse Artillery	4 guns
92nd Highlanders on camels ..	100

* Colonel Benson's Despatch was dated the day of the action, and these men may have rejoined afterwards. The following were mentioned in the Despatch:—Major Learmouth; Lieutenants Gonne and Nolan, 17th Lancers; Lieutenant Reeve, 6th Native Infantry; Captain Hutchinson, Political Agent, Sergeant-Major Butler, R. H. A., who was highly praised for the manner in which he brought the guns into action over difficult country.

and did not meet his spies until near Chapra Baraud, when the rebels had moved. Pursuing at a rapid trot for about seven miles, he overtook three large bodies of cavalry, some 3,000 strong, drawn up just beyond the village of Tancha. The Horse Artillery were immediately brought into action, and their fire was so rapid and effective that although the rebels endeavoured to carry out a charge before the infantry were brought up and dismounted, they could not effect it, but retired, pursued by the Cavalry and Horse Artillery. The enemy scattered, and the pursuit, having been continued some twelve miles, Brigadier Somerset fell back on Chapra Baraud where his supports, 300 of the 9th Bombay Infantry, arrived in the afternoon.

Owing to their rapid flight the loss of the rebels was not severe, but some were seen to fall under the fire of the guns, and some were cut up by the Lancers in the pursuit. One man of the 17th Lancers was wounded. The force had marched 50 miles between 12 noon of the 30th December and 6 A.M. on the 1st January, not resting more than two hours at a time, having made forced marches for five days without tents or European supplies.*

The flight continued northwards

After his defeat at Baraud, Tantia Topi fled to Nahargarh† in Kotah territory where he halted, and was joined by Man Singh. The rebels then pushed on to Paron, and from there to Indargarh, leaving Man Singh on the banks of the Chambal. It is now necessary to follow the fortunes of this chieftain, and of Feroz Shah, who, with the mutinied 12th Irregular Cavalry, joined Tantia Topi at Indargarh early in January.

Brigadier Smith and Man Singh

On the 10th November Brigadier Smith, who had been protecting Chanderi from Tantia Topi, marched to Gadaoli to cover Mangraoli and the fort of Nahargarh, which were threatened by the rebels under Man Singh. On the night of the 12th he ascertained that the enemy, three thousand strong, composed of Bengal troops, the late Gwalior Contingent, and Man Singh's followers had recrossed the Betwa and reached the small fort of Gurpera.

Action at Kundri, 14th November.

On the night of the 13th Brigadier Smith heard that the rebels were at Kundri, and marching at 3-30 A.M. on the 14th he came to that place just as day was breaking, and halted with his force just in rear of the village and some *jowari* fields which served to conceal them from the rebels. Here he formed the 95th in column of sections, one company a hundred yards distant protecting their right flank; the 10th Bombay Infantry in quarter distance columns in echelon to the left

3rd Troop, Bombay Horse Artillery (Lieutenant-Colonel Blake).	90
8th Hussars (Colonel De Salis) ..	85
1st Bombay Lancers (Lieutenant-Colonel Curtis.)	42
95th Regiment, Lieut.-Col. Raines.	
10th Bombay Infantry, Captain Pelly.	
Meade's Horse	12

**Note.*—Mentioned in the Despatch—Major White, Lieutenant Wood, 17th Lancers; Captain Paget, Royal Horse Artillery; Captain Bethune, 92nd; Captain Baugh, 9th Bombay Infantry; Lieutenant Barras, Camel Corps.

† Tantia was fired on at Nahargarh, where a British force later also met with hostilities. See page 204.

rear of the 95th, leaving the road between the two regiments clear for the guns to advance, as the ground on either side was bad and unsuited for their passage. The 1st Lancers had orders to form in rear of the right flank of the 95th, and the 8th Hussars in rear of the left flank of the 10th when the infantry formed to the front.

In this order the force moved forward, the advanced guard, consisting of a company of the 95th and two companies of the 10th under Major Vialls (95th) in skirmishing order, advancing on the right through some *jowari* fields. When within a hundred yards of the enemy, the advanced guard was reinforced by a company of the 95th, and as they came in view of the rebel camp and the ground opened, the infantry deployed, the 10th being in short echelon with the 95th.

The artillery galloped to the front by the road, formed line, and came into action on the left of the 95th, commencing with a few round shot and then with shrapnel at 500 or 600 yards, fired into the largest masses which had collected after their sudden surprise. Meanwhile the 1st Lancers had conformed to the movements of the infantry, by advancing in column of troops, and on approaching the enemy, formed line to the right flank; the 8th Hussars formed front to the left of the line. A rapid flight now began, the cavalry and a division of the guns pursuing at the gallop. The artillery opened fire with case at short range, followed by shrapnel, and continued in pursuit with the cavalry, coming into action whenever opportunity offered.

The pursuit continued six or seven miles, some 600 of the rebels being shot or sabred. The casualties on the British side amounted to 12 wounded. After the pursuit was over, Brigadier Smith* assembled his force at the village of Rajpur. From this time Man Singh appears to have remained inactive until, as already related, he joined Tantia Topi at the end of December.

We had last to do with Feroz Shah, one of the Delhi princes, at Mandesar.

Feroz Shah.

After the defeat of the rebels by the Malwa Field Force at that place in November 1857, Feroz Shah went to Rahatgarh, which he left the day before its investment by Sir Hugh Rose in January 1858, and then proceeded to Rohilkhand. From there he was expelled by Sir Colin Campbell, and we find him in December repulsed near Etawah by Mr. A. O. Hume, the Collector, and pursued by Brigadier Herbert across the Jumna, which he passed at the Uriya Ghat on the 9th December.

Pursuit of Feroz Shah.

On the morning of the 12th December, Brigadier-General Sir R. Napier received intimation from Captain McMahon, 14th Dragoons, commanding a small force near the confluence of the

* Besides all Commanding Officers, the following were mentioned in the Despatch:—Cornet Goldsworthy, 8th Hussars, Brigade Major; Lieutenant Hanbury, 8th Hussars; Lieutenant Rawlins, 95th; Captain Bolton, A. Q. M. G.; Lieutenant Mayne; Jemadar Chattar Singh; Havildars Mata Bakhsh, Chithu Singh, Havildar-Major Shaikh Abdulla, Naiks Roghar Khan, Shaikh Khuda Bakhsh, 1st Bombay Lancers; Jemadar Ramlal Upadia, Sepoy Parsad Pande, 10th Bombay Infantry. The Native ranks were mentioned for their services in obtaining intelligence.

Jumna, Chambal, and Sindh rivers, that the rebels under Feroz Shah had passed into the Lohar Pargana of Kachwaja. Believing that their course would be up the jungles of the Sindh river, Sir R. Napier marched from Gwalior at 2 P.M. on the 12th, with the force detailed in the margin, intending to proceed to Dabrha on the Jhansi road, and intercept the enemy.

No. 4 Bombay Light Field Battery, 2 guns, (Captain G. G. Brown).	
14th Light Dragoons (Major R. B. Prettijohn).	150
* 2nd Gwalior Mahratta Horse (Captain F. H. Smith).	100
71st Highlanders (Major J. W. T. Rich)	117
25th Bombay Infantry (Lieutenant J. F. Forbes).	50
Gwalior Camel Corps (Captain H Templer).	40

At Antri, where the force rested during part of the night, he received at 2 A.M. on the 13th an express from the Political Agent of Gwalior to the effect that his information led him to believe that the rebels would pass by Gohad to the north of Gwalior. But this information proved to be erroneous. At 10-30 A.M., the Tehsildar of Antri reported that he had just ridden in from Dabrha, and had seen the smoke of the staging bungalow, which the rebels were then burning, and that they were proceeding in a south-westerly direction. General Napier immediately marched south in pursuit, and at Bitiwar, where he arrived at 1-30 A.M., on the 14th, he was informed that the enemy were eight or nine miles distant. The force had been on the move thirteen and a half hours, and required a rest. Owing to delay in getting grass and disposing of a rear party of the rebel infantry, in which some of the Mahratta Horse, under fire for the first time, greatly distinguished themselves, the troops did not move until 10 A.M.

Sir Robert Napier continued the pursuit through Narwar, where he left the greater portion of the 71st and the artillery, which could not keep up, and took on the cavalry, 38 Highlanders on camels, and 25 Balandshahr Horse that were halted at Narwar on their way to Keria, and after a long chase the rebels were overtaken at Ranod on the morning of the 17th December. Their course had been south of Narwar through the Amolo Pass, and their direction appeared to be along the right bank of the Sindh.

Twice the British were encamped within a few miles of them, but owing to the darkness and their ignorance of the country, and to its wild and hilly character, they could not take advantage of this. The rebels chose the most difficult and unfrequented paths, evidently guided by some one well acquainted with them. Once or twice the pursuers were close on their traces and stragglers were cut off and their horses taken, the riders darting off into the dense thickets which almost closed up the paths. At one moment the General believed they were driven into the hands of Colonel Scudamore, 14th Dragoons, who had posted his detachment on the right bank of the Sindh below Kolaras to intercept them. But on getting into more open country, it was found that they were leaving the river and going towards Ranod. They took a circuitous and difficult road through the jungles, while the pursuing column marched by an easier, more direct route. The people of Ranod were found to be in great excitement, as

* Now the 18th Prince of Wales' Own Tiwana Lancers.

they said the enemy were close at hand and in full march to attack them, guided by Bhairu Singh of Tehria, a rebel landowner whose fort a few miles off had recently been destroyed by Sindhia. The rebels, whose numbers had increased since they crossed the Jumna, advanced in an irregular mass, extending on a front of nearly a mile. They had been promised by Bhairu Singh plenty of plunder and an easy prey.

Action at Ranod, 17th December.

There was barely time to form up the 14th Dragoons when the enemy were within a few hundred yards. The Mahratta Horse were impeded by the riding camels in crossing a deep ravine, and were a little behind. The force actually engaged consisted of 113 of the 14th Dragoons, 60 Mahratta Horse, and 38 Highlanders, guided by Captain Templer. It was a complete surprise. The 14th Dragoons dashed at once into the centre of the enemy, who never attempted to stand as a body, although individuals died fighting desperately. Major Prettijohn having received a severe wound, the command devolved on Captain Need, who, with much energy and judgment, continued the pursuit for nearly eight miles, cutting up great numbers, particularly at the end, where the fugitives were stopped by a ravine, those who could cross it taking refuge in jungle impracticable for cavalry.

The enemy's loss amounted to 150 counted at Ranod, and some 300 killed in the pursuit, among them many of the 12th Irregulars. Among the killed were several persons of distinction, including Maulvi Fazal Haq and Risaldar Zohur Ali of the 12th. Six elephants were taken, and numbers of horses and arms. The enemy were completely scattered. The British loss amounted to 1 killed and 15 wounded. Besides the other troops, the General in his Despatch made special mention of the spirited conduct of the Mahratta Horse, who had only been recently enrolled. He mentioned among others * Malik Sahib Khan Tiwana, who being on a visit to him on leave volunteered his services; and Jemadar Jehan Khan, Tiwana Horse, attached to the Mahratta Horse, who received six wounds while singly engaged with several of the enemy, of whom he killed one and wounded others.

Flight of Feroz Shah.

Feroz Shah fled towards Chanderi, but forces under Brigadier Ainslie from Jhansi and Colonel Liddell from Lalitpur, moving respectively in the direction of Ranod and Chanderi, obliged him to turn, and he made for the jungles of Aroni, passing south of Isagarh and Pachhar. When near Rampur, between Goona and Sironj, the rebels accidentally came upon Lieutenant Stack's detachment of 40 men of the 1st Bombay Lancers, escorting remounts and clothing to Brigadier Smith. They captured the clothing and one trooper, but Lieutenant Stack brought up the remainder of his men, and skirmishing with the enemy, carried the rest of his charge back in safety to Goona.

* Brevet-Major Prettijohn, Captain Need, Captain Todd, Lieutenant Giles, Apothecary Waite, Regimental Sergeant-Major Clarke, Corporal G. Best, 14th Dragoons; Captain Lumsden, A. Q. M. G., Captain F. H. Smith, Lieutenant Gough, Mahratta Horse; Lieutenant Anderson, 1st Bombay Lancers, A D.C.; Captain C. F. Smith, 71st; Captain Templer.

A force of the strength noted in the margin had been detached from Goona under Captain Rice to intercept the fugitives. On the morning of the 22nd Captain Rice* marched from Barod ten miles to Aroni, where a man who had been robbed of his horses by the rebels during their retreat past that place reported that they were encamped in a deep glen, to the number of 2,000, chiefly cavalry, in thick jungle near Sarpur village, about 11 miles south-west of Aroni. This man, who had been beaten and abused, furnished the only information Captain Rice was able to obtain from the people of the neighbourhood. Leaving the camp standing in charge of 42 men, the column marched at 6 P.M., and favoured by bright moon-light, arrived at the place indicated at 11 P.M., moving latterly through very dense jungle.

The Goona column.

Two 9-pounders, 4-2 Bombay Artillery.	
Royal Engineer	20
86th Foot	55
25th Bombay Infantry	150
Meade's Horse	140

The enemy's camp, situated in a deep ravine in the forest, was at once attacked. Owing to the narrow rocky path the two guns could not keep up, so Captain Rice pushed forward with the Infantry only, under Lieutenants Festing and Waller. They shot down the rebel picquet, and charged completely through their long winding camp, causing them to seek shelter in the surrounding jungle. Owing to the haste with which they fled, few were killed, but nearly a hundred horses, several camels, much clothing and many arms were captured. The enemy made no stand and scarcely returned the fire of the attacking party, which suffered no loss. The column passed the night in their camp. In the morning 100 Meade's Horse under Captain Cochrane started in pursuit but apparently did not come up with the fugitives. Sir R. Napier recommended to notice the officers and troops of this column, "for this very dashing and difficult enterprise, which has taught the enemy to distrust the security even of the deepest jungles that have so often favoured their escape."

Night attack on Feroz Shah, 22nd December.

Feroz Shah then fled to Rajgarh, and eventually made his way to Indargarh, where he joined Tantia Topi early in January. After his defeat at Baraud, Tantia Topi fled to Indargarh, south-east of Tonk, on which place Brigadier Smith moved from Sironj in pursuit of Feroz Shah. General Michel was at Chapra, 12 miles north of Baraud, and had directed Brigadier Honner, Commanding the Nasirabad Brigade, to march towards Indargarh, watching the fords over the Chambal between that place and Kotah. Brigadier Showers, meanwhile, had advanced from Agra and taken up a position at Kushalgarh, north of the Banas river. Tantia Topi, trying to escape to the north marched to Dausa, a town some thirty miles east of Jaipur on the Bharatpur road. This was the situation early in January 1859.

The rebels surrounded by British columns.

* Captain Rice was a noted tiger-hunter. This successful attack shows the value of a hunter in conducting such enterprises.

On the 4th January Brigadier Showers marched for Hindaun with the troops detailed in the margin, to oppose the rebels who, by their position, threatened Jaipur and Bharatpur. From Hindaun he advanced to Malarna, where he learnt on the 11th that the rebels were moving northwards between his position and Tonk, evidently marching on Jaipur. He immediately threw forward a strong advanced guard to Ripliwara, 18 miles distant, to intercept stragglers, and followed with the main body during the night. The rebels had passed the village only a few hours before, and Brigadier Showers took up the pursuit, and, following close on their heels, came up with them at Dausa at 3 A.M. on the 14th January.

Brigadier Showers' march.

Artillery 4 guns	61
3rd Europeans	220
Alexander's Horse	138
Agra Mounted Police	127

Dausa is situated on the western slope of a rocky hill, bounded to the west by fields with high banks, among which the rebels took up their position. The approach to it was difficult, as there were only two roads leading out of the town in this direction. Having no guide on whom he could rely, Brigadier Showers proceeded with his column for some distance down one of these roads, in hope of finding an opening to lead him to the rebel camp. Failing in this, and day beginning to break, he determined to begin the attack with the cavalry, leaving the artillery to follow, with the infantry as escort. He countermarched the cavalry, threaded the streets of the town at a sharp trot, and came to the second road which debouched nearer to the enemy's position. He pushed up one of the banks on the right, and formed the cavalry on the high ground, the Agra Mounted Police on the left, the squadron of Alexander's Horse on the right, and then, advancing at a charging pace across the intervening fields, came upon the rebels preparing to march.

Action at Dausa, 14th January

They were taken by surprise. The cavalry dashed at once amongst them. Being unable to escape from the enclosures, numbers were killed. They, however, soon recovered, and opened a sharp musketry fire. The charge was continued through a second field, when all who remained were cut up; the cavalry then emerged on to the plain, where the pursuit was continued.

The attack was made on the centre of the enemy's position, and separated their force into three parties; one went off to the right, another to the left, while a considerable body were driven to the front and vigorously followed up by Alexander's Horse and the Agra Mounted Police under Lieutenants H. Chapman and H. T. Oldfield. The artillery and infantry now came up after a harassing march.

In the last 25 hours the column had followed the enemy continuously for 57 miles. Men and horses had been accoutred and harnessed the whole time, and had no rest but what short bivouacs afforded. But the guns were brought up by Lieutenant R. S. Robinson to within 1,200 yards of the party of rebels who had fled with Feroz Shah to the right, although at that long range they were unable to inflict much damage. The party under Tantia Topi disappeared to the left early in the action. The pursuit was kept up for five miles, when men and horses were exhausted.

The rebels had some 3,000 fighting men, and lost 300 killed. Three elephants, 8 camels, several horses, and 300 muskets and swords were captured. On the British side 7 men were killed and 22 wounded.

In his Despatch Brigadier Showers acknowledged the assistance he received from the Contingent of Cavalry of the Bharatpur State under Captain Nixon, Political Agent.*

Movements of Colonel Holmes' Column from Nasirabad.

While Brigadier Showers was following the rebels, Lieutenant-Colonel Holmes, 12th Bombay Infantry, had moved out from Nasirabad on the 8th January with the field force detailed in the margin, for the protection of Tonk and Jaipur. Marching through Barra Samba, Dighi, and Jarrana, he received information at the latter place on the 10th that the rebels were in camp at Aligarh Rampura, 24 miles distant, threatening Tonk. Next day Colonel Holmes marched through Tonk to Bambaur, thus effectually covering the former place. At Tonk he heard that the rebels were on the march from Bhagwantgarh towards Jaipur, and on the morning of the 12th he marched through Nathdwara to Jhalai, hoping to intercept them. Arriving at Jhalai at 3-30 P.M., he found the enemy had moved on to Chaksu, and that Brigadier Showers had passed through the place in pursuit, and was encamped some ten miles ahead. Moving on at 9 P.M., Colonel Holmes marched through Brigadier Showers' camp (interviewing the latter on the way), and reached Chaksu at daylight on the 13th, having marched 44 miles in 24 hours. The rebels had left Chaksu, and after a halt of five hours, it having been arranged that the Agra and Nasirabad columns should pursue different routes, Colonel Holmes marched six miles to Gatwassi, in the direction of Lalsot, and encamped there for the night. On the morning of the 15th he received permission of Brigadier Honner, Commanding the Rajputana Force, who marched into Lalsot that morning, to move in the direction of Jaipur,† and marched at 4 P.M.

No. 8 Light Field Battery (Captain Shekleton).	103
83rd Regiment (Lieutenant Colonel Austen).	347
12th Bombay Infantry (Lieutenant-Colonel Holmes).	291
11th Company, R. E.	16
Bombay Sappers and Miners ..	27
Sikh Horse (Lieutenant Nowall) ..	89
Mayne's Horse (Lieutenant Hawkins)	173

* This important action is dismissed by Colonel Malleson[1] in a few words, and he assigns to it a wrong date, the 16th January.

Mentioned in Despatches, besides those whose names are given above:—Captain R. Stevenson, and Lieutenant A. Money, 3rd Europeans; Captain A. L. McMullin; Lieutenant G. F. G. Graham.

Ressaidar Shaikh Aminud-din (severely wounded), Sowars Meg Singh (Jat), Meg Singh (Sikh), and Kurtab Singh, Alexander's Horse; Risaldar Shadi Ramana, Jemadar Sobha Singh, Sowar Kanhiya Singh, Agra Mounted Police

† There seems to have been a want of co-operation between Brigadier Showers and Colonel Holmes, such as has been heard of in the case of column commanders in other campaigns. The enemy was moving on Jaipur; Brigadier Honner barred their retreat in the direction of Lalsot; and there appears to be no reason why Colonel Holmes should have turned off to Lalsot; by doing so he left the way clear for Brigadier Showers, and as Holmes at once made for Jaipur on obtaining permission from Brigadier Honner, it looks as if he had turned aside to obtain orders from the later officer, having had orders from Brigadier Showers not to march on Jaipur.

to Tonga arriving there at 1 A.M. on the 16th. At 4 P.M., Colonel Holmes marched for Jaipur, encamped six hours on the road, and reached it at 11 A.M. on the 17th; here he received a reinforcement of 172 Mayne's Horse (new levy) under Lieutenant Hawkins, and obtained information that the enemy, having been defeated three days earlier by Brigadier Showers, were at Bairat. Marching north, he reached Chamu on the 18th, Kujrauli on the 19th, and Khandela on the 20th. Here he heard that they had moved to Sikar, 28 miles to the west; and marching at 6 P.M., the force reached the vicinity of the rebel camp at a quarter past four on the morning of the 21st January, having covered upwards of 290 miles in 13 days without a single halt, and marched 54 miles in the last 24 hours.

The rebels surprised at Sikar, 21st January.

The surprise was complete, the rebels having no intimation of the approach of the pursuing column until their outlying picquets were driven in. Confusion followed, the rebel horsemen galloping off in every direction, without attempting to make a stand and numbers without saddling their horses. Colonel Holmes immediately attacked, sending 4 guns to the front at a gallop, with all his cavalry, the infantry in line moving in support. The artillery got quickly into action, but not much execution was done as it was not daylight (there was bright moon-light). The cavalry charged and completed the rout, continuing the pursuit for some hours, but unfortunately missed the road taken by Tantia Topi, Rao Sahib, and Feroz Shah. The cavalry killed over 50, and brought in 51 prisoners, besides a number of women. A greater number might have been killed, but all those who had thrown away their arms were spared, and the anxiety to capture the leaders did not admit of time being lost in securing worthless followers.

Brigadier Honner's march.

Captain Carnegy, A. A. G.
Captain Heathcote, A.Q.M.
Captain Malcolmson, Orderly Officer.
8th Hussars, 146 (Captain Phillips).
1st Bombay Lancers, 105 (Captain Dennis).
83rd Regiment, 137 (Lieutenant-Colonel Heatly).
12th Bombay Infantry, 57 (Lieutenant Forteath).
Sikh Horse, 57 (Risaldar Mitka Singh).
Camel Corps, 70 (Lieutenant Stevenson).

It has been mentioned that Colonel Holmes met Brigadier Honner at Lalsot on the 15th January. The latter had left Nasirabad on the 18th December, with the force detailed in the margin, and had marched over a great part of Rajputana.*

On the day of the surprise at Sikar, Feroz Shah and the 12th Irregulars left Tantia Topi, who next day quarrelled with the Rao Sahib. The latter with some 3,000 followers moved towards the west, and then turned southwards to Kushana west of Ajmer, where he arrived on the 10th February. Brigadier Honner, following on his track, having marched over 800 miles, including 130 in the last four days, arrived at Kushana at 5 o'clock the same evening. When he was about 8 miles distant, the rebels heard of his approach, and instantly broke up and fled in two large

* For route followed by the Nasirabad Field Force under Brigadier R. W. Honner, C. B., see Appendix XVI. On entering the Bikaner desert he had been obliged to leave his Horse Artillery behind, as the horses could not draw the guns through the sand.

bodies, going south-west and south-east respectively, one under Feroz Shah and the other under Rao Sahib.

The rebels dispersed at Kushana, 10th February.

Within three miles of Kushana the force was formed up, the Hussars in column of divisions on the right, the 1st Bombay Lancers in the same formation in the centre, at squadron distance, the Sikh Horse on the left considerably in advance in echelon, the 83rd and the 12th Bombay Infantry mounted on camels in line in front. In this formation they advanced at a sharp canter, the camels keeping their place in excellent order, until they came close to Kushana when, seeing that the rebels had taken off to the left, the front was changed in that direction, and a pursuit at the gallop commenced. After going about two miles, the infantry returned to hold the village and the rebels' camp, but the Hussars and Lancers went on at a dashing pace for eight or ten miles, long into the moonlight, cutting up many of the insurgents and not returning to camp until 10 P.M. The patrols sent out next morning counted 226 of the rebel dead. Seventy horses and ten camels were taken. On the British side 2 were killed, 2 wounded and 5 of the Sikh Horse reported missing.*

Fate of Tantia Topi, 1859.

After the defeat at Sikar, the rebels dispersed. Six hundred surrendered to the Raja of Bikaner, and Tantia Topi proceeded in the direction of Paron, with only three or four followers, where he met Man Singh. The forests of Paron were in Narwar, the territory of the latter, and here Tantia Topi was safe so long as his ally afforded him protection. But Major Meade of Meade's Horse entered into negotiations with Man Singh for the betrayal of the fugitive. On the night of the 7th April 1859, Man Singh guided a party of the 9th Bombay Infantry to the place where Tantia Topi was concealed, and the rebel was seized and taken to Meade's camp next morning. From there he was marched to Sipri, and tried by court-martial on the charge of having waged war against the British Government. He was found guilty and hanged at Sipri on the 18th April.

Tantia Topi was one of the most blood-thirsty advisers of Nana Sahib and assisted in the massacre of the Cawnpore garrison. But, presumably for want of evidence, which, although it did not then exist, was afterwards elicited at Cawnpore, he was not tried on this charge. At the same time it is difficult to agree with Colonel Malleson, who compares Tantia with Hofer, the hero of the Tyrol, that posterity will not confirm the sentence on the former. A rebel appears to be no less a rebel because he was the servant of one who was once an independent prince. Tantia Topi was brought up in the household of Baji Rao, *ex*-Peshwa, and adoptive father of Nana Sahib, whose servant he was. But the *ex*-Peshwa was not an independent prince; he resided on an estate granted to him by the British Government on his deposition forty years before the outbreak of the mutiny. Nor in

* Brigadier Honner's report is dated 11th February, and these men probably rejoined later. Among others mentioned in the Despatch were Corporal Landly, 8th Hussars, and Troop Havildar-Major Ram Singh, and Trooper Ajudhiya Parsad, 1st Lancers. Also Captains Phillips and Paget, 8th Hussars, and the officers of the Staff.

any case did his title or his pension descend to his adopted son. If the right to take up arms against the Government is conceded to every holder of an estate on such terms, large numbers of landowners in India might rebel with impunity, except that involved in the ordinary risks of war, and the same impunity would extend to their followers.

In any case it is not probable that posterity will waste sympathy on a blood-thirsty ruffian whose least crime was that he was a rebel; who was concerned in the perpetration of the most cruel and atrocious deeds recorded in the history of the world; and for whom a thousand deaths would have been a light punishment.

Feroz Shah and Rao Sahib.

After the operations narrated, there remained no organised body of rebels to act against, but the Seronj jungles, forming a zone of about 40 miles' radius, were infested with several considerable bands, acting apparently independently, yet not entirely without concert. It was in these jungles that Feroz Shah took refuge. The pursuing columns of General Michel had taken up positions at Manawar Thana, Pachaori, and Bersia, and Brigadier Wheler had moved out from Saugor towards the Betwa, ready to take up the pursuit should the rebels break cover. Sir Robert Napier had at his disposal a remnant of Smith's Brigade forming a column under Colonel DeSalis, with which he made arrangements to sweep these jungles. A strong detachment under Major Chetwode formed a cordon between Seronj and Bersia, and thus cut off a portion of this extensive jungle and reduced the field operations considerably. The columns of Colonels Rich and DeSalis, and a detachment of the 92nd Highlanders on their way to Jhansi under Colonel Lockhart, swept the northern portion of the jungle, but without success, the enemy evading their pursuers in the dense thickets.

Colonel Lockhart then pursued his march, while the other columns returned to the southern part of the jungle.

Combined movements through the forest.

On the 2nd April Colonel DeSalis was at Maksudnagar and Colonel Rich at Lateri, when arrangements were made for a movement of the columns to the south to sweep the jungles. They accordingly marched on the 3rd, but the rebels escaped to the west, crossing the Parbati river, and a body of their cavalry cut through the long column of the baggage which had been sent by the level road skirting the forest. The rebels killed the bandmaster of the 10th Bombay Infantry and severely wounded two sepoys, taking some rifles and camels. That night Colonel DeSalis camped at Ganjari, 12 miles south of Maksudnagar, and Colonel Rich at Deogarh, about 8 miles to the east of Ganjari, but on the other side of the belt of jungle. Colonel DeSalis had reason to believe that the rebels who had crossed the Parbati would endeavour to return, and having few cavalry he could not spare them for pursuit. He knew that other rebels under Feroz Shah had been left behind, and on the 4th April information of their position was obtained, and Colonel DeSalis arranged with Lieutenant-Colonel Rich to make long marches to the north that night and attack them simultaneously from different sides.

Colonel DeSalis marched at 7 P.M., with the force detailed in the margin, leaving the remainder in camp and his tents standing in order to deceive the enemy's scouts. The column marched 13 miles beyond Maksudnagar, to a point north of the jungle village of Burdah, 10 miles north-north-east of Maksudnagar, sending a detachment to Tinsiah, a village in the heart of the jungle about five miles south of Burdah.

Colonel deSalis' operations, 5th April.	
8th Hussars	75
95th Regiment, on camels ..	90
and on foot	60
10th Bombay Infantry on camels ..	60
and on foot	60

The plan was to attack Burdah, where the rebels were encamped, from the north, and endeavour to drive them east towards Lieutenant-Colonel Rich, who was to be at Isarwas, whilst the detachment at Tinsiah was to show itself and prevent any attempt to break south. Colonel DeSalis was a little north of Burdah by daybreak on the 5th, and, forming one-third of the infantry in skirmishing order and the rest in four supports, advanced quietly through the thick jungle in the direction where the enemy's camp was said to be. On nearing the camp they at once charged with a cheer and the sound of trumpets and bugles. Here a good many of the rebel infantry were killed, but the cavalry, who were encamped on the other side, escaped, their horses being always ready saddled. Colonel DeSalis at once pushed on with 40 Hussars and some infantry in the direction of Isarwas, but finding no enemy he went on with the cavalry alone, and after going a couple of miles found the rebel horsemen moving on a parallel line. These were attacked, and 40 killed, while their camels and baggage, turning back, fell into the hands of the infantry. Colonel DeSalis had only one sepoy of the 10th wounded. The rebels, who were commanded by Feroz Shah, numbered some 1,500. It was estimated that 300 were killed, among them Subadar Chattar Singh, a General in the rebel force, and formerly of the Gwalior Contingent.

At Tinsiah—	
Hussars	20
95th	30
10th Bombay Infantry	30

Meanwhile Lieutenant-Colonel Rich had marched at 8 P.M. on the 4th to Kotra, detaching in passing a Jemadar and 30 sepoys of the 9th Bombay Infantry to Tinsiah. As there was no water between Kotra and Burdah, he concluded that the rebels would either come to Kotra for water, or try to escape by way of Tinsiah, their favourite resort. Many of the rebels flying from Colonel DeSalis went towards Kotra and made for some villages on the edge of the jungle, favourable to their cause. Fifteen sepoys were cut down in the forest and then, moving his force outside, Colonel Rich discovered a numerous body near the village of Ninawas, half a mile distant, and some running to Isarwas. The cavalry at once surrounded the village and cut down all those in open country; the infantry entered the village and found rebels in every tenable house and in the grass stacks outside; all these were killed. These were sepoys of the Gwalior

Operations of Colonel Rich, 5th April.

Lieutenant-Colonel G. W. Rich, 71st Highlanders.
14th Light Dragoons, 50, Lieut. Gowan.
Mayne's Horse, 50, Lieut. Bradford.
71st Highlanders, 80, Capt. Dalgleish.
9th Bombay Infantry, 70, Capt. Tubbs.
Gwalior Camel Corps, 170, Capt. Templer.

Contingent, Sindhia's army, and a few of different regiments. About a hundred were killed. The British casualties were 3 men of the 71st and 1 of the 9th Bombay Infantry killed; 2 of Mayne's Horse and 1 of the Camel Corps wounded. The party under Jemadar Ramji Kadam also killed some 35 rebels near Tinsiah.

Fate of Feroz Shah and Rao Sahib.

This was practically the final dispersal of the rebels under Feroz Shah whose following was again broken up by Brigadier Showers,* with a force from Goona, near Patan on the 15th April. Feroz Shah, disguised as a pilgrim, made his way to Kurbela, where he lived many years afterwards.

Rao Sahib wandered about until the year 1862, when he was arrested in the hills to the north of the Punjab, and sent to Cawnpore. There he was tried and found guilty of having been concerned in the murder of Europeans, and was hanged on the 20th August, 1862.

Lessons of the pursuit.

The pursuit of Tantia Topi affords valuable lessons in regard to the measures, such as the co-operation of various columns, that have to be undertaken in such circumstances. It may be aptly compared with other similar operations recorded in history—the pursuit of Mithridates; of Baji Rao Peshwa, and of Chitu Pindari in the same country in 1817-18, and of DeWet in South Africa; when converging columns were employed with more or less success. All these pursuits inculcate one great lesson, the necessity for whole-hearted co-operation on the part of column commanders, who should be actuated by patriotic and not by selfish motives—a measure apparently very difficult of attainment. An officer who took part in the pursuit of Tantia Topi wrote—"Each fresh commandant who took the field fancied he could catch Tantia; prodigious marches were made, officers and men threw aside all baggage, even their tents, and accomplished upwards of forty miles daily—the rebels did fifty. The end was, all our horses were sore-backed, and the halt of a week or ten days rendered absolutely necessary. Then came a new aspirant for a C.B. and Tantia's head, who brought fresh troops and camels into the field. He, perhaps, had not only to chase Tantia, but to keep clear of other forces commanded by a senior in rank to himself. It was wonderful the amount of energy that was thrown into the pursuit, and the hundreds of dead camels strewn over every jungle track: roads were no object, or rivers either, to pursued or pursuers. On they went until dead beaten. Occasionally someone more fortunate than the rest had the luck to catch up the fugitives and cut up stragglers; but it was always in heavy jungle; they had the very best of information and never trusted themselves to the open country when any force was near. We had the very worst of information, even in the territories of professedly friendly Rajas. The sympathy of the people was on their side."

* Brigadier Showers, Commanding Agra District, was awaiting orders at Goona.

THE END.

APPENDIX I.

Substance of a letter from His Highness Maharaja Holkar to the Agent for Central India, 4th July 1857.

It is a matter of deep regret that the detachment of State troops that had under your orders been stationed for the protection of the Residency, joining with the British forces, adopted a course of direct mutiny, and led on by their unfortunate fate did, on the 1st instant, raise a great disturbance, and having commenced firing guns, killed some innocent beings. But thanks to the Almighty that yourself and all British officers were safe and escaped the hands of these miscreants doomed to destruction.

Subsequently the whole Residency was plundered, and the Muhammadans raised the standard of religion. A total disorganisation followed; none of my troops would listen to orders, and, quite confused, I had nothing left but to regret. I immediately sent out a mission to Mhow asking for aid; but my people could get no admission to the Colonel.* About the same time the Mhow troops, also mutinying, killed some officers, and having burnt some houses marched to Indore where they joined the mutinous, and disaffected here. It is impossible to describe the excitement, plunder, and bloodshed that continued here for the two following days. I had no troops left to think of fighting with the troops of the line from Mhow, who under the excuse of supplies and carriage sent their men in to the town and were joined by hundreds of bad characters to plunder the people.

Although I sent my people to persuade them, yet the mutineers of the Durbar troops that had joined them would not desist from plundering.

At length a message was sent by the mutineers to send them the heads of the few Europeans and Christian women that had found shelter in my own palace, and that if this were not done the plundering would not cease. I replied that the murder of these Christians would not be suffered as long as I live, even if the town were destroyed. The mutineers insisting in their demands, I was obliged in the absence of even a few hundred faithful and trustworthy troops, to go to the mutineers, followed by a few personal attendants, and told them that they would one day be recompensed for what they had done, and wished them to leave Indore. The mutineers had forcibly taken carriage from the town, and with that and some that was supplied them in order to have them removed and the town saved. The mutineers marched off from Indore towards Dewas last night, having plundered the Government Treasury and taken as much of the treasure as they could load, and followed by about 500 of the real mutineers from Durbar troops and 6 Durbar guns that had joined them. I am now quite unprotected and unassisted. How far shall I describe my regret at what has taken place. I trust you have heard of these misfortunes from independent sources. I am heartily loyal to the British Government and alive to the thousands of obligations I owe to that Government. I am quite ashamed at my inability, but the epidemic of disaffection of troops had left nothing in my hands. No doubt at the proper time sufficient punishment will be given to the criminals, but the parties really guilty of this crime have marched with the Mhow troops to save their lives.

The preservation of the honour of this State now lies only in your hands. Myself and the whole State, save the disloyal troops above alluded to, are quite innocent in the matter, and this circumstance can be solemnly witnessed to by the Christians that were eye-witnesses to the affairs here. I trust to the justice of the British Government in the hope that without full enquiry into all circumstances you will not give up your usual and long-cherished kindness in an angry moment. In the disturbed state of my mind I have sent Rao Ram Chandar to describe to you all the particulars, and I have every hope that, having listened to him, you will be pleased at your earliest convenience to console me with a favourable reply.

* The letter to Colonel Platt is on record.

APPENDIX II.

List of Europeans and East Indians murdered at Jhansi.

Captain Alexander Skene, Superintendent, Mrs. Skene, and two female children.
Mrs. Browne, wife of Captain Browne, Deputy Commissioner of Jalaun, and Miss Browne, his sister.
Captain F. D. Gordon, 10th Madras Infantry, Deputy Commissioner of Jhansi.
Lieutenant Burgess, Revenue Surveyor, Bundelkhand.
Lieutenant Turnbull, Assistant Revenue Surveyor.
Lieutenant Powis, Assistant Surveyor, Irrigation, Mrs. Powis, and one female child.
Dr. and Mrs. McEgan.
Mr. T. Andrews, Principal Sadar Amin, Jhansi.
Mr. R. Andrews, Deputy Collector and Magistrate, Mrs. Andrews, two male and two female children
Mr. W. Carshore, Collector of Customs, Mrs. Carshore, and four children.
Mr. D. C. Wilton, Mrs. Wilton, one child, and two sisters of Mrs. Wilton.
Mr. D. D. Blyth, Assistant Revenue Surveyor, Mrs. Blyth, and her mother and four children.
Sergeant Millard, Sub-Assistant Revenue Surveyor, Mrs. Millard, and three children.
Mr. Bennett, Sub-Assistant Revenue Surveyor.
Mr. J. Young, Sub-Assistant Revenue Surveyor, and Mrs. Young.
Messrs. G. Young and Palfreyman, Apprentices.
Mr. Munrow, Sub-Assistant Revenue Surveyor.
Mr. A. Scott, Head Clerk, Deputy Commissioner's Office.
Mr. C. Purcell, Head Clerk, Superintendent's Office.
Mr. J. Purcell, Clerk, Deputy Commissioner's Office.
Mr. Mutlow, Clerk, Superintendent's Office.
Mr. Mutlow (2nd), unemployed.
Mr. D. G. Elliot, Clerk, Deputy Commissioner's Office.
Mr. and Mrs. Elliot, parents of above.
Messrs. Flemming and Crawford.
Captain Dunlop, 12th Bengal Infantry, commanding at Jhansi.
Lieutenant Taylor, 12th Bengal Infantry.
Lieutenant Campbell, commanding Detachment, 14th Irregular Cavalry.
Quarter Master-Sergeant Newton, Mrs. Newton, and two children.

Total murdered—Men 30, women 16, children 20.

APPENDIX III.

Abstract of the Statement of Muhammad Bakhsh, son of Shaikh Lutf Ali, Sepoy, 52nd Regiment, Bengal Native Infantry.

My regiment and the 74th remained together for 7 months at Cawnpore. Then we were sent to Oudh, which, when being completely annexed, my regiment came to Jubbulpore, where we remained until the late troubles.

We were much vexed and annoyed when we heard that forces were coming to Jubbulpore to disarm us, but Captain Jameson gave us assurances and directed us to keep our arms with us. This we did for one and a half months, when one day we were ordered to put our arms in the Quarter Guard. Some obeyed the orders, while others did not part with their arms. We were at the same time told that we would hear the sound of two guns; but that there was no cause for alarm. It turned out that the Raja of Gadha and his son were blown from the guns. As we had not been previously informed of what was to take place and were not ordered to do any service, except our ordinary duties, this gave cause for alarm. The Subadar-Major of the Madras Regiment the same night having informed Lal Tribedi that we were going to be disarmed that night, about 11 o'clock the whole of the regiment deserted Jubbulpore, taking what baggage they could carry. We reached Patan and brought with us Captain Macgregor, who was arrested by Subadar Dayal Singh, to Koni, a place situated at the foot of the hills. It was settled that Captain Macgregor should be released, but the Raja of Tejgarh sent word that, as there was another European prisoner with him, Captain Macgregor should also be sent to him. Lal Tribedi, our Commandant, went to Tejgarh, and finding no European Officer at that place Captain Macgregor was not sent to the Chief. In the meantime we got information that two companies of our regiment were disarmed at Damoh and that the Commissioner was moving down with them. It was settled to move to Damoh and to release them. Accordingly we left Koni about 4 o'clock, and, travelling the whole night, we reached Katangi, where Captain Macgregor was first fired at by a sepoy probably by the order of Lal Tribedi, our Commandant, and then attacked by others who came close to him.

From Katangi we went to Gubra where we met the Commissioner and had a regular fight with him for six hours. The regiment then returned to the hills and the Commissioner went to Katangi whence he proceeded to Jubbulpore.

Debi Singh Gond, Thakur of Kor, a place near Sagrampur, sent his men to different places in the hills and collected all the men of my regiment. For two days he provided us with provisions.

We remained with him for 20 or 22 days. In the meantime we got hold of a gun from the house of a blacksmith and put it in order. Bhore Sukal, the Agent of the Shahgarh Chief, came and requested us to go and take service with the Chief. We followed him to Shahgarh. Debi Singh Thakur, leaving his village, came with us with his family, and is still with the regiment. On our reaching Damoh the Panna authorities refused to give us supplies. This led to an action in which the Panna forces were defeated; their guns, four in number, came into our possession. We remained here for about ten or twelve days, then by order of the Shahgarh Chief, who paid us for three months, we came to Garhakota and remained here until yesterday. The Chief had told us to remain here until our services were required by him. Dawa and Pahar Singh directed us to attack Rehli, which we did, but failing in our attempt we returned to this place after 8 days. The Chief sent us word not to go out, but to remain at our post. On the morning of the 10th instant, being informed that we were going to be attacked on the side of

Rehli, we went out to a distance of two *koss*, but finding no one we came back and were informed that the British forces had come in from Saugor. The regiment got under arms and came out to the intrenchment. The action commenced. All our camp followers and sick men went into the fort, where with the latter I remained for 24 hours. Yesterday evening Lal Tribedi sent word to the camp followers to come out of the fort. They did so, and were out by 7 o'clock. The march of the camp followers commenced at 8 P. M. for the hills. The regiment might have followed us. My bearers mistook the road, and left me where I was found. The regiment might have passed me. There were about 500 men of my regiment at this place with about 200 men newly levied. There were men from no other regiment at this place. The pay of the sepoys was raised to 12 rupees. Lal Tribedi, besides his other allowances as a Havildar, got Rs. 500 a month and commanded the whole regiment. Tika Ram served under him. The Subadars drew their pay. The intrenchment was constructed at the time when the regiment first came in here. The guns were brought from Damoh, and ten men from each company, that were formerly instructed, worked the guns. Dawa always rode upon an elephant and was with us in the fort until we came out of it. Lal Tribedi being a huge man cannot ride. Pahar Singh was never seen by me riding. Two men were killed, one by a musket, the other by a cannon shot. We remained in our own lines which were constructed when the regiment came in here. My hut was near the hospital close to the river. Debi Singh Thakur lived near the temple. There were two native doctors with us, Elahi Bakhsh and Yad Ali; Hospital stores from Damoh were brought in here. We all lived in the lines with guns. Some bullocks were brought from Damoh and some were furnished by Debi Singh. Being sick in the hospital I could not see our parade ground and the quarter-guard. Only a few of us had our families with us. The deserters have gone to the hills and they will ultimately go to Shahgarh. Gunpowder was made by the people here. Lal Tribedi might know whether some treasure was brought from Damoh. There were about 175 Musalmans in the regiment, out of these about 80 or 90 were at Garhakota.

The Bundelas in the fort might amount to about 1,000 men. The *bunniahs* supplied us with provisions and settled their accounts. Only two men returned from leave, one a naik, brother of Lal Tribedi, and the other a sepoy. I being sick could not see who put up the flags.

There was one Baldeo Tiwari among us, but he died of fever when the regiment came in here. I cannot explain how his medal was found on the body of the sepoy whose head was taken off by a cannon shot. There were only about 15 or 20 sowars of the Shahgarh Chief at this station. I never heard that Tikaram wrote to the 31st that the 52nd and 74th were united to promote the cause of religion.

CAMP GARHAKOTA
12th February, 1858.

APPENDIX IV.

Malwa Field Force.

Staff.

[*] Brigadier C. S. Stuart, 1st Bombay Europeans, Commanding.
Captain Macdonald, Deputy Assistant Quarter Master General.
Captain Coley, Brigade-Major.
Captain Hungerford, Commanding Royal Artillery.
Major Boileau, Field Engineer.
Captain H. O. Mayne, Intelligence Department.
Lieutenant Thain, Sub-Assistant Commissary General.
Surgeon Mackenzie, Staff Surgeon.

Troops.

[1] 14th Light Dragoons (Left Wing), Major Gall.
No. 4 Light Field Battery, Bombay Artillery, Captain J. D. Woolcombe.[†]
[2] 3rd Cavalry, Hyderabad Contingent, Captain S. G. G. Orr.
[3] 25th Bombay Infantry, Major G. H. Robertson.
B Company, Madras Sappers and Miners, Captain Brown.
[4] Four Companies, 86th Regiment, Major Keane.

The Hyderabad Contingent Field Force.

Major W. A. Orr, 1st Company Artillery, Commanding.
Lieutenant F. Samwell, 4th Cavalry, Staff Officer.
Lieutenant Hastings Fraser, 4th Cavalry, Staff Officer (succeeded Lieutenant Samwell, wounded at Rawal).

1st Cavalry, Captain H. D Abbott (succeeded by Lieutenant H. Dowker).
[6] 3rd Cavalry, Captain S. G. G. Orr (invalided at Indore; succeeded by Captain H. D. Abbott).
[7] 4th Cavalry, Captain W. Murray.
[8] 1st Company, Artillery.
[8] 2nd Company, Artillery.
[8] 4th Company, Artillery, Captain J. D. C. Sinclair.
[9] 3rd Infantry (Wing), Captain J. Sinclair (killed at Jhansi).
[10] 5th Infantry (Wing), Captain G. Hare.

* Made C. B., March 24th, 1858. Afterwards K. C. B.
† Brevet-Major, March 1858.
1 Now 14th (King's) Hussars.
2 Broken up in 1903.
3 Now 125th Napier's Rifles.
4 2nd Battalion, Royal Irish Rifles.
5 Now 20th Deccan Horse.
6 Broken up in 1903.
7 Now 30th Lancers (Gordon's Horse).
8 Disbanded in 1904.
9 Now 96th Berar Infantry.
10 Now 98th Infantry.

APPENDIX V.

Route of the Malwa Field Force from Ahmadnagar to Aurangabad and Mhow.

Date. 1857.	Stages.	Miles.	Flngs.	REMARKS.
20th June ...	Imampur ..	12	3	
21st " ...	Wadalla	14	..	
22nd " ...	Toka	14	...	North bank of Godavery. General Wellesley (Duke of Wellington) encamped here during the Mahratta War on August 22nd, 1803.
23rd " ..	Aurangabad ...	26	...	A station of the Hyderabad Contingent. The force halted here to suppress an incipient mutiny in the 1st Cavalry. A small force was detached to Buldana during this halt.
12th July ..	Chauk	11	...	
13th " ..	Patri	13	...	
14th " ...	Bonegaon ..	14	..	
15th " ...	Pahlud	6	...	
16th " ...	Ajanta	12	...	
17th " ...	Samrod	20	...	
18th " ...	Bodar	14	..	
19th " ...	Edalabad ...	15	1	
20th " ...	Anturli	13	...	Major Follett, 25th Bombay Infantry, and many men died here of cholera.
21st " ...	Burhanpur ...	13	...	Encamped a mile beyond the town. Crossed the Tapti by the Hatma ford. A company of Gwalior Contingent Infantry disarmed here.
22nd " ...	Asirgarh ...	2	...	Halt. Camp in the Ram Bagh. Brigadier C. S. Stuart assumed command. Gwalior Infantry disarmed here and some tried and executed. The fort was taken by a British force under Colonel Stevenson in 1803, and again by General Doveton in 1819.
	Carried over ...	...	...	

Date. 1857.	Stages.	Miles.	Flngs.	Remarks.
	Brought forward ..	..	..	
24th July ..	Borgaon	13	..	
25th „ ..	Desgaon	24	..	
26th „ ..	Dhangaon ..	13	..	
27th „ ..	Barwai	11	..	Halt.
30th „ ..	Balwara	11	..	
31st „ ..	Simrol	15	..	Halt. Colonel H. M. Durand, Officiating Agent to the Governor-General in Central India, joined here.
2nd August..	Mhow	12	..	Captain Hungerford's Bengal European Artillery had held the fort since the outbreak of the mutiny.
	Total ..	308	4	

APPENDIX VI.

Casualties in the Campaign in Malwa.

Corps.	Dhar.		Rawal.		Mandesar.		REMARKS.
	Killed.	Wounded.	Killed.	Wounded.	Killed.	Wounded.	
14th Light Dragoons	..	..	..	..	1	10	
No. 4 Light Field Battery ..	..	..	..	..	..	1	
Bengal Artillery	..	..	..	..	..	2	
86th Regiment	..	..	..	..	2	9	
25th Bombay Infantry	..	..	..	..	..	4	
Hyderabad Contingent.							
1st Cavalry	..	..	..	..	..	..	No return can be found of the casualties at Rawal, which are said to have numbered 100. Only the Hyderabad Contingent took part in the action.
3rd Cavalry	2	5	..	..	1	9	
4th Cavalry	..	..	..	..	..	..	
1st Company, Artillery	..	..	..	..	..	..	
2nd Company, Artillery	1	..	..	..	..	..	
4th Company, Artillery	..	..	..	..	..	..	
3rd Infantry	..	2	..	..	1	6	
5th Infantry	..	..	..	..	1	5	
Total ..	3	7	..	..	6	46	

Rawal.—Lieutenant F. Samwell, Hyderabad Contingent, was dangerously wounded in the abdomen.

Mandesar.—Staff. Lieutenant-Prendergast, Madras Engineers, severely wounded (afterwards General Sir H. Prendergast V.C.).

14th Light Dragoons.—Lieutenant W. L. Redmayne, killed; Lieutenants J. Leith, L. Gowan, and C. Martin, wounded.

25th Bombay Infantry.—Major G. H. Robertson, Lieutenants C. Jameson, J. F. Forbes, and D. B. Young, wounded.

Bombay Artillery.—Captain Christie (who was afterwards killed by a tiger) was dangerously wounded.

One Sergeant, 86th Regiment, and 3 privates, 25th Bombay Infantry, died of wounds.

APPENDIX VII.

The Central India Field Force.

Major-General Sir Hugh Rose, K.C.B., Commanding.
Captain Rose, A.D.C.
Captain Wood, A.A.G.
Captain Macdonald, A.Q.M.G.
Major Boileau, Commanding Royal Engineers.
Captain Ommaney, Commanding Royal Artillery.
Lieutenant Haggard, Commissary of Ordnance.
Lieutenant Lyster, Interpreter.
Surgeon Arnott.
Surgeon Vaughan.

1st Brigade.

Brigadier C. S. Stuart.
One Squadron, 14th Light Dragoons (now the 14th (King's) Hussars), Captain Gall.
One troop, 3rd Bombay Light Cavalry (now the 33rd Queen's Own Light Cavalry)
86th Regiment (2nd Royal Irish Rifles), Lieutenant-Colonel Lowth.
21st Company, R.E.
25th Bombay Infantry (now 125th Napier's Rifles), Major G. H. Robertson.
No. 4 Battery, European Artillery, Captain Woolcombe.
" " " Captain Ommaney.
Bombay Sappers and Miners.

2nd Brigade.

Brigadier C. Steuart, C.B., 14th Light Dragoons.
Head Quarters, 14th Light Dragoons, Major Scudamore.
Head Quarters, 3rd Bombay Light Cavalry, Major Forbes, C.B.
3rd Cavalry, Hyderabad Contingent, Captain H. D. Abbott (succeeded Captain S. G. Orr, invalided from Indore).
3rd Bombay European Regiment, Lieutenant-Colonel Liddell.
24th Bombay Infantry (now the 124th Baluchistan Infantry).
No. 1 Troop, Horse Artillery, Captain Lightfoot.*
Field Battery.
Madras Sappers and Miners.
Siege train.

* Took command after Lieutenant-Colonel S. Turnbull was killed at Jhansi.

72 I. B. 2

APPENDIX VIII.

Route from Aurangabad to Hoshangabad and Sehore of the Force under Brigadier C. Stewart.

Date. 1857.	Stage.	Miles.	Flngs.	Remarks.
1st November	Sangvi	8	2	
2nd ,,	Pulmari	10	5	Halt. General Wellesley (Duke of Wellington) encamped here with his army during the Mahratta War in October, 1803.
4th ,,	Nygaon	10	2	
5th ,, ...	Pahlud	18	...	General Wellesley encamped here in 1803.
6th ,, ...	Ajanta	13	...	General Wellesley encamped here on October 30th, 1803, after the battle of Assaye.
7th ,, ...	Fardapur ...	4	5	Road down the pass.
8th ,, ...	Samrod	15	4	
9th ,, ...	Bodar	14	2¼	
10th ,, ...	Edalabad ...	14	1	The Hyderabad Contingent Field Force was encamped here for some time.
11th ,, ...	Anturli	13	...	
12th ,, ...	Burhanpur ...	14	1¼	Ford over the Tapti River.
13th ,, ..	Asirgarh	16	...	Halt.
15th ,, ...	Rustampur ...	19	4	Halt.
21st ,, ...	Khandwa... ...	12	...	
22nd ,, ...	Keirgaon ...	18	...	
23rd ,, ...	Ghisur	14	...	
24th ,, ...	Chepabara ...	16	6	
25th ,, ...	Harda	21	4	
26th ,, ...	Dattia	15	5	
27th ,, ...	Seoni	9	7	
	Carried over ...	...	...	

Date. 1857.	Stage.	Miles.	Flngs.	REMARKS.
	Brought forward ..	..	..	
28th November	Doloria	15	..	
29th " ..	Hoshangabad ..	16	..	Halt.
8th December	Nazzarganj ..	3	1	Crossing the Narbada on 7th and 8th. Few boats available, and camels and horses crossed at Ghundri Ghaut, 5 miles above Hoshangabad.
9th ..	Piprani	11	2	Halt. Crossed a track over the ghaut. Carts did not arrive until midnight of 2nd day.
12th " ..	Bishenkhera ..	9	2	
13th " ..	Dipu	7	1	
14th " ..	Bhopal	15	2	Halt.
16th " ..	Panda	13	1	
17th " ..	Sehore	8	5	
	Total ..	377	7	

APPENDIX IX.

Route from Sehore to Jhansi of Head Quarters and 2nd Brigade, Central India Field Force, under command of Major-General Sir Hugh Rose, K.C.B.

Date. 1858.	Stage.	Miles.	Flngs.	REMARKS.
16th January	Kajuria	11	..	
17th " ..	Bhopal	10	6	
18th " ..	Balampur ..	13	4	
19th " ..	Gulgaon	12	1	
20th " ..	Bhilsa	9	5	
21st " ..	Karri	10	6	
22nd " ..	Garispur	12	6	
23rd " ..	Bagrod	9	6	
24th " ..	Rahatgarh ..	12	1	Country covered with jungle. Halt for siege of fort.
2nd February	Sehura	13	..	
3rd " ..	Saugor	11	6	Halt.
9th " ..	Sanoda	10	..	Halted 2 hours at Shahpur.
10th " ..	Garhakota ..	18	..	Halt for siege of fort. Encamped at Bupari, 2 miles west.
14th " ..	Magrone	10	..	
15th " ..	Saugor	18	..	Halt.
27th " ..	Ranipura ..	8	..	
28th " ..	Bandri	9	..	
1st March ..	Rajwas	9	..	Passed the villages of Chauki and Jigni. Encamped close to the Malthone road. Halt.
3rd " ..	Papria	18	..	Battle of Madanpur Pass
5th " ..	Maraura	7	..	Halt and fort taken.
9th " ..	Kumhari	14	..	
	Carried over ..	..	..	

Date. 1858.	Stage.	Miles.	Flngs.	REMARKS.
	Brought foward ..	..	..	
10th March ..	Banpur	15	4	Fort and residence of the Banpur Raja. Halt.
12th „ ..	Belori	12	..	
13th „ ..	Jamalpur ..	13	..	
14th „ ..	Tal Bahat ..	11	..	Halt.
17th „ ..	Sirasgaon ..	7	..	Left bank of Betwa River. Halt.
20th „ ..	Simra	18	..	
	Total ..	324	5	

APPENDIX X.

Route of the 1st Brigade, Central India Field Force, from Mhow to Jhansi, under command of Major-General Sir Hugh Rose, K.C.B.

Date. 1858.	Stage.	Miles	Flngs.	REMARKS.
6th February	Indore Residency ...	13	2¼	Halt. Crossed 4 large nullahs and Katki river, bridged. Encamping ground on the Agra road.
8th " ...	Dakachia	12	7	The Royal Artillery returned to Mhow to receive 4 guns, under Captain Ommaney.
9th " ...	Dewas	10	1	Halt. A moderate sized town, the residence of a Raja.
11th " ...	Tonk	11	3	
12th " ...	Maksi	10	2¾	
13th " ...	Tintori ...	6	1½	
14th " ...	Sunera	14	6	Halt.
16th " ...	Sarangpur ...	10	...	Halt to enable the Royal Artillery to rejoin the Brigade.
19th " ...	Udenkhera ...	12	...	
20th " ...	Damli	10	5	
21st " ...	Biaora	14	4½	Halt.
23rd " ...	Amargarh ...	12	7¼	
24th " ...	Barsad	16	3	Hilly and jungle country began.
25th " ...	Raghogarh ...	12	2½	
26th " ...	Goona	16	4	Halt for instructions from Sir Hugh Rose. Received orders to proceed to Isagarh.
1st March ...	Pinighati ...	12	3½	Orders received to change the route to Chanderi.
2nd " ...	Shadaura ...	6	2	
3rd " ...	Pachar	9	...	The siege train and escort, which had been one march behind, joined the Force.
	Carried over ...	...	...	

Date. 1858.	Stage.	Miles.	Flngs.	REMARKS.
	Brought forwad ..	..	..	
4th March ..	Amrod	9	..	Difficulty in crossing ford from Amrod across *nala*.
5th „ ..	Kurwassa ..	11	1	
6th „ ..	Fatiabad ..	7	6	
7th „ ..	Ramnagar ..	2	..	Camp moved to this small village for the siege of Chanderi, which was besieged and taken by assault on the 17th March.
19th „ ..	Paranpura ..	3	..	1¼ miles north-east of Chanderi on the Jhansi road. Halt for repacking siege train stores and demolition of fort. Orders received to send left Wing, 14th Light Dragoons, in advance to Jhansi.
21st „ ..	Left bank of Or River	9	4	116 yards broad.
22nd „ ..	Akroni	14	3¼	
23rd „ ..	Left bank of Budan River.	9	1¼	15 yards broad.
24th „ ..	Nagda	10	4	
25th „ ..	Jhansi	19	4½	Made a forced march, leaving the siege train and escort to do the distance in two marches. Joined the Head Quarters and encamped in an open plain near the 2nd Brigade.
	Total ..	308	¼	

APPENDIX XI.

Route of the 1st Brigade, Central India Field Force, from Jhan to Kalpi, under command of Major-General Sir Hugh Rose, K.C.B.

Date. 1858	Stage.	Miles.	Flngs.	REMARKS.
26th April ..	Baragaon ..	9	..	Head Quarters and 1st Brigade marched *en route* to Kalpi. Halt.
28th " ..	Chirgaon	12	..	Country flat and cultivated.
29th " ..	Simri	7	..	
30th " ..	Moth	9	..	
1st May ..	Punch	9	..	Halt to await arrival of 2nd Brigade.
6th " ..	Lohari	10	..	Diverged from high road to Kalpi.
7th " ..	Kunch	11	..	Battle of Kunch. Halt.
9th " ..	Hardoi	9	..	
10th " ..	Orai	9	..	
11th " ..	Sandi	8	..	
13th " ..	Itaura	9	..	Halt to enable 2nd Brigade to join.
15th " ..	Golauli	12	..	On southern bank of the Jumna. A small village 4½ miles east of Kalpi. Engaged in operations until 23rd May.
23rd " ..	Kalpi	4	4	Halt. A moderate sized town. The road lies through ravines.
	Total ..	118	4	

APPENDIX XII.

Casualties in the Campaign in Central India.

Corps.	Barodia. 31-1-1858.		Garhakota. 12-2-1858.		Madanpur Pass. 3-3-1858.		Chanderi. 17-3-1858.		Betwa River. 31-3-1858.		Jhansi. 3-4-1858.		Lohari. 2-5-1858.		Kunch. 7-5-1858.		Kalpi. 22-5-1858.		Bilayan. 31-5-1858.		Total.
	Killed.	Wounded.	Killed.	Wounded.	Killed.	Wounded.	Killed.	Wounded.	Killed.	Wounded.	Killed.	Wounded.	Killed.	Wounded.	Killed.	Wounded.	Killed.	Wounded.	Killed.	Wounded.	
Staff	..	3	..	..	..	..	..	1	..	..	..	..	..	..	1	1	1	4	..	..	11
14th Light Dragoons ..	..	..	..	..	..	3	..	..	5	24	..	3	..	..	4	19	2	..	..	..	60
3rd Bombay Light Cavalry.	..	4	..	..	..	1	..	..	..	..	..	..	..	..	..	..	4	3	..	..	8
1st Troop, Horse Artillery.	..	2	..	1	..	2	..	..	1	4	..	1	..	..	..	..	..	1	..	..	10
No. 6 Field Battery, R. A.	..	..	..	..	..	..	1	..	..	..	..	..	..	..	..	..	3	2	..	..	5
European Artillery ..	..	..	..	2	..	..	..	..	..	..	..	2	..	..	..	..	..	..	..	..	4
Siege Train	1	..	..	..	..	..	..	2	..	..	..	..	..	..	..	..	..	..	..	..	3
21st Company, R. E.	..	..	..	..	..	..	..	2	..	..	..	6	..	..	..	..	..	..	..	..	8
71st Highlanders ..	..	..	..	..	..	..	..	..	..	..	..	..	..	..	..	1	..	..	..	..	1
86th Regiment ..	..	..	..	..	..	..	2	17	..	2	8	60	..	..	..	1	..	13	..	..	103
Carried over ..	..	..	..	..	..	..	..	..	..	..	..	..	..	..	..	..	..	..	..	..	..

Casualties in the campaign in Central India—contd.

Corps.	BARODIA. 31-1-1858.		GARHAKOTA. 12-2-1858.		MADANPUR PASS. 3-3-1858.		CHANDERI. 17-3-1858.		BETWA RIVER. 31-3-1858.		JHANSI. 3-4-1858.		LOHARI. 2-5-1858.		KUNCH. 7-5-1858.		KALPI. 22-5-1858.		BILAYAN. 31-5-1858.		Total.
	Killed.	Wounded.	Killed.	Wounded.	Killed.	Wounded.	Killed.	Wounded.	Killed.	Wounded.	Killed.	Wounded.	Killed.	Wounded.	Killed.	Wounded.	Killed.	Wounded.	Killed.	Wounded.	
Brought forward ..	..	..	..	..	..	..	..	..	..	..	..	..	..	..	..	..	..	..	..	..	..
Camel C rps ..	..	5	..	..	..	..	..	..	..	..	..	..	..	..	..	..	..	3	..	..	3
3rd Bombay Europeans	..	..	..	1	..	4	..	..	2	3	7	47	1	17	..	2	2	..	..	..	86
24th Bombay Infantry	..	..	..	..	..	..	..	..	1	8	5	10	..	..	..	..	4	4	..	..	32
25th Bombay Infantry .	..	..	..	..	..	..	..	3	2	3	5	25	..	5	..	..	9	10	..	..	62
Madras Sappers and Miners.	..	..	..	..	..	..	..	..	..	..	3	10	..	..	..	..	..	..	..	..	13
Bombay Sappers and Miners. ..	..	..	..	..	..	..	..	..	..	..	2	6	..	..	..	..	..	..	..	..	8
Hyderabad Contingent.																					
1st Cavalry	..	7	..	..	..	2	..	..	1	4	1	10	..	..	1	8	1	1	..	2	38
3rd Cavalry	1	..	..	..	..	..	..	..	2	4	..	..	..	..	1	2	1	2	..	..	12
4th Cavalry	..	..	..	..	..	..	..	..	2	2	3	8	..	..	1	5	4	3	..	2	30
1st Company, Artillery	..	..	..	..	..	..	..	..	..	..	..	1	..	..	1	2	..	..	..	..	4
2nd Company, Artillery	..	..	..	..	..	..	..	..	..	..	2	1	..	..	..	1	..	..	..	..	4
4th Company, Artillery	..	..	..	..	..	..	..	..	..	..	..	..	..	..	..	..	..	..	..	..	..
3rd Infantry ..	..	..	..	..	..	..	..	..	..	4	5	8	..	..	..	..	1	11	7	4	40
5th Infantry ..	..	..	..	..	..	..	..	..	1	5	1	13	..	..	..	5	..	..	..	..	25
Total ..	2	21	..	4	..	12	3	2[illegible]	17	63	42	211	1	22	9	47	31	57	7	8	560

Officers Killed and Wounded.

Rahatgarh.—Subadar Bahadur Singh, 24th Bombay Infantry, wounded.

Barodia.—Captain Neville, R. E., Jemadar Ahmad Husain Khan, 3rd Cavalry, Hyderabad Contingent, killed.

Captains J. Macdonald and E. Campbell and Lieutenant H. H. Lyster, Staff, Lieutenant R. Pitman, 1st Troop Horse Artillery; Lieutenant R. Westmacott, 1st Cavalry, Hyderabad Contingent; Jemadar Ghulam Husain Khan, wounded.

Chanderi.—Lieutenant Moresby, R. A., killed.

Captain Keatinge, Political Agent; Lieutenants Lewis and Cochrane, 86th, wounded.

Betwa River.—Lieutenant-Colonel S. Turnbull, 1st Troop Horse Artillery; Captain J. G. Lightfoot, 2nd Company, Reserve Artillery; Lieutenant H. Clark, Ressaidar Sikandar Ali Beg, 3rd Cavalry, Hyderabad Contingent; Jemadar Sayyid Nur Ali, 4th Cavalry, Hyderabad Contingent, wounded.

Jhansi.—Lieutenant-Colonel S. Turnbull, mortally wounded.

Lieutenants W. G. D. Dick, Bombay Sappers and Miners, and Meiklejohn; Captain Sinclair, 3rd Infantry, Hyderabad Contingent; Lieutenant Park, 24th Bombay Infantry; Surgeon Stock, killed.

Assistant Surgeon J. Cruickshank, R. E.; Lieutenant G. Simpson, 4-2nd Artillery; Captain C. Darby, Lieutenants J. G. Dartnell, W. R. M. Holroyd, R. F. Lewis; Ensigns S. W. Sewell and G. Fowler, 86th Regiment; Captain Sandwith and Assistant Surgeon Miller, 3rd Europeans; Lieutenant F. R. Fox and Jemadar Ali Khan, Madras Sappers and Miners; 2nd-Lieutenant J. Bonus, Bombay Sappers and Miners: Subadar Samaji Abaji. 24th Bombay Infantry; Lieutenant J. J. Fenwick, Subadar Kishen Singh, Jemadar Raghoji Powar, 25th Bombay Infantry; Captain H. D. Abbott, Lieutenant H. C. Bowker, and Jemadar Muhammad Din Khan, 1st Cavalry, Hyderabad Contingent; Captain W. Murray. Jemadars Hanuman Singh, and Sayyid Nur Ali, 4th Cavalry, Hyderabad Contingent, Sergeant Major Dixon, Subadar Husain Bakhsh, Jemadar Ganga Singh, 5th Infantry, Hyderabad Contingent, wounded.

Lohari.—Lieutenants Armstrong and W. A. Donne, and Ensign W. H. Newport, 3rd Europeans; Lieutenant W. Rose, 25th Bombay Infantry, wounded.

Kunch.—Ressaidar Safdar Ali Beg, 3rd Cavalry, Hyderabad Contingent, killed.

Captain W. MacMahon, 14th Light Dragoons; Lieutenant Baigrie, D. A. Q. M. G.; Risaldar Zulfikar Ali Beg, 3rd Cavalry, Hyderabad Contingent; Jemadar Chobi Singh, 2nd Company, Artillery, Hyderabad Contingent, wounded.

Kalpi.—Lieutenant Baigrie, D. A. Q. M. G., killed.

Sir H. Rose, Colonel Wetherall, Chief of the Staff, Captains Cockburn and Lyster, A. D. C.; Subadar Bhairu Singh, 3rd Infantry, Hyderabad Contingent, wounded.

Bilayan.—Lieutenant Westmacott, 4th Cavalry, Hyderabad Contingent; Subadar Shaikh Ahmad Ali, 3rd Infantry, Hyderabad Contingent, wounded.

APPENDIX XIII.

Route of the 1st Brigade, Central India Field Force, from Kalpi to Gwalior, under command of Major-General Sir Hugh Rose, K.C.B.

Date. 1858.	Stage.	Miles.	Flngs.	REMARKS.
2nd June ...	Sarsela	7	...	1st Brigade marched *en route* to Gwalior; country flat.
3rd " ...	Ataria	10	...	Water brackish; road partly through ravines.
4th " ...	Jalaun	12	...	
5th " ...	Bangra	9	...	
6th " ...	Mohana	9	...	Left bank of Pahuj River.
7th " ...	Jetpura	11	...	Water very brackish.
8th " ...	Indurkhi	7	...	Small village with strong mud fort on right bank of Sind River. Encamped on left bank of river. Halt.
11th " ...	Amain	11	...	
12th " ...	Dagaon	13	...	Water scarce, but abundant, 1½ miles south at Bilauni.
14th " ...	Supaoli	10	...	Halt.
16th " ...	Morar Cantonment ...	10	...	Cantonments on right bank of river Morar and 5 miles from the Lashkar country begins to get hilly.
	Total	109	...	

APPENDIX XIV.

CASUALTIES IN THE GWALIOR CAMPAIGN.

In the Operations before Gwalior.

———	Killed.	Wounded.	REMARKS.
8th Hussars	8	8	Lieutenant J. Reilly died of sun-stroke; Lieutenant R. Jenkins and Assistant Surgeon Sherlock wounded. One man mortally wounded.
14th Light Dragoons ...	...	4	
1st Bombay Light Cavalry ...	1	6	Cornet W. Mills killed. Captain W. Anderson wounded.
3rd Cavalry Hyderabad Contingent.	2	3	
3rd Troop, Horse Artillery ...	...	4	
4th Company, 2nd Battalion, Artillery.	1	2	One mortally wounded.
71st Highland Light Infantry..	6	7	Lieutenant Wyndham Neave, killed.
95th Regiment	1	16	Lieutenant-Colonel J. A. R. Raines, Lieutenants J. W. Crealock and J. M. Sexton wounded. One man mortally wounded.
Artillery	1	2	One man mortally wounded.
10th Bombay Infantry ...	...	3	
25th Bombay Infantry ...	2	7	Lieutenant W. Rose killed.
Total ...	22	62	

At Jaora-Alipur.

—	Killed.	Wounded.	REMARKS.
14th Light Dragoons ...	...	1	
1st Troop, Horse Artillery ...	2	...	
3rd Troop, Horse Artillery ...	1	...	
3rd Cavalry, Hyderabad Contingent.	1	3	
Meade's Horse	...	4	
Total ...	4	8	

APPENDIX XV.

Saugor Field Division.

Major-General G. C. Whitlock, Commanding.
Lieutenant Homan, 50th Madras Infantry, A. D. C.
Major R. Hamilton, A. A. G.
Captain Lawder, A. Q. M. G.
Major Ludlow, Field Engineer.
Major Barrow, Commissary of Ordnance.
Surgeon Davidson, Superintending Surgeon.

Cavalry Brigade.

Major T. Oakes, Commanding.
Lieutenant Roe, 12th Lancers, Brigade-Major.
Left Wing, 12th Lancers, Captain Prior.
Squadron, 2nd Cavalry, Hyderabad Contingent, Captain A. W. Macintire.

Artillery.

Brigadier W. H. Miller, Commanding.
A Troop, European Horse Artillery, Major Mein.
F. Troop, Native Horse Artillery, Major Brice.
Detachment, Royal Artillery, Captain Palmer.
Detachment, Madras Foot Artillery, Major Lavie.
No. 1 Horse Battery, Lieutenant Pope.

Engineers.

Detachment, Madras Sappers and Miners.

1st Infantry Brigade.

Brigadier Carpenter, Commanding.
Major Hodson, Brigade-Major.
* 3rd Madras Europeans, Colonel E. Apthorp.
1st Madras Infantry.
Detachment, 50th Madras Infantry.

2nd Brigade.

Brigadier J. MacDuff.
Major Dorehill, Brigade-Major.
Dr. Barclay, Senior Surgeon, Cavalry.
Major W. Davis, Commanding.
8th Irregular Cavalry, Mir Hussain Ali.
Metge's Sikh Horse, Lieutenant Dick.
Jhansi Mounted Police, Lieutenant Sawers
No. 6 Battery, Royal Artillery, Captain F. Ommaney.
Detachment, H. M.'s 43rd Regiment, Lieut.-Colonel Primrose.
Jhansi Foot Police.

---

* Now 2nd Battalion, Royal Inniskilling Fusiliers.

APPENDIX XVI.

Route of the Nasirabad Brigade, Rajputana Field Force, under the command of Brigadier R. Honner, C. B., from 18th December, 1858, to 1st March, 1859.

Date. 1858.	Stages.	Miles.	Flngs.	Remarks.
	From Nasirabad.			
18th December	Kumaria ..	8	6	
19th „	Binai ..	10	4	
20th „	Agucha	15	2	
21st „	Chota Lamba 18-1 }	31	7	Arrived 9-20 A.M.
	Sanganir .. 13-6 }			Arrived 9-45 P.M.
24th „	Hamirgarh ..	14	6	
25th „	Chittor	21	..	
31st „	Bassi	14	¼	
1859.				
1st January	Barandi	16	7	
2nd „	Mandalgarh ..	10	6¼	
5th „	Dhamni	13	5½	
6th „	Johagpur ..	13	7¾	
7th „	Kuchawara ..	13	5¾	
8th „	Duni	15	3½	
9th „	Nagar	14	4½	
10th „	Karwar	25	2	
11th „	Uniara	14	7	
12th „	Burwara	13	3¾	
3th „	Isarda .. 12-1¾ }	28	3½	Arrived 8-30 A.M.
	Jallai .. 16-1¾ }			Arrived 5-30 P.M.
14th „	Dattuli	18	4	
	Carried over ..	..	..	

Date. 1859.	Stage.		Miles.	Flngs.	Remarks.
	Brought forward ..		..	..	
15th January	Lalsot		12	4	
16th "	Manpura ..	18-1	25	...	Arrived 8-45 A.M.; left 11-30 A.M.
	Diusa ..	6-7			Arrived 2-15 P.M.
19th "	Sankotra		19	6	
20th "	Gatwara		18	1	
21st "	Raipura		20	2	
22nd "	Dhui		11	1	
23rd "	Ringas		20	7	
24th "	Astia		10	..	
25th "	Kishengarh ...		11	5	
27th "	Sambar		19	2	
28th "	Harmara		24	2	
29th "	Ajmere		25	5	
31st "	Govindgarh ...		23	5½	
1st February	Barra Padu ...		14	1½	
2nd "	Chandaran ...		24	1	
3rd "	Tosina		22	6½	
4th "	Kattoli		17	2½	
5th "	Duguli		11	5	
7th "	Surpalia ..	11-6	25	1	Arrived at 8-15 A.M.; left at 10-30 A.M.
	Dai ...	11-3			Arrived at 3-30 P.M.
8th "	Garerha ...	16-4	32	2	Arrived 9-15 A.M.; left 11-45 A.M.
	Alai ...	15-6			Arrived 5-30 P.M., 3 wells 200 feet deep, great difficulty in obtaining water.
9th "	Baswani ...	16-4	29	5	Arrived 7-40 A.M.; left 10 A.M.
	Gowar ...	13-1			Arrived 3-20 P.M.
	Carried over ..		...	...	

Date. 1859.	Stage.		Miles.	Flngs.	Remarks.
	Brought forward		...	..	
10th February	Bhani ...	17-7	42	4	Arrived 7-15 A.M.; left 10-45 A.M.
	Kussana ...	24-5			Arrived 5-30 P.M., 11th and 12th attacked the rebels and killed 226.
13th „	Bhanwi ...	..	16	3¼	
14th „	Sujat ...	...	21	7¾	
15th „	Rajgiya ...	...	15	3¾	
16th „	Awah ...	...			
	Siwas ...	...	23	½	
19th „	Khirwa ...	...	15	7½	
24th „	Muwawas	...	14	7	
25th „	Chandrawal	...	19	6¼	
26th „	Birr ...	...	17	4¾	
27th „	Beawar ...	...	19	2	
28th „	Liri ...	...	17	...	
1st March ...	Nasirabad	...	14	2	
	Total ...		984	5½	

APPENDIX XVII.

Statement of Tantia Topi taken at Camp Mushairi, 10th April, 1859, in presence of Major Meade, Commanding Field Force.

My name is Tantia Topi; my father's name is Pandurang, inhabitant of Jola-Pargana, Patoda Zilla, Nagar. I am a resident of Bithur. I am about forty-five years of age, in the service of Nana Sahib, in the grade of companion or aide-de-camp.

In the month of May, 1857, the Collector of Cawnpore sent a note to the Nana Sahib at Bithur, asking him to forward his wife and children to England. The Nana consented to do so, and four days later the Collector wrote to him to bring his troops in from Bithur. I went with the Nana and about one hundred sepoys and three hundred matchlockmen and two guns to the Collector's house at Cawnpore. The Collector was then in the intrenchment and not in his house. He sent us word to remain, and we stopped for the night at his house. The Collector came in the morning and told the Nana to occupy his own house which was in Cawnpore. We remained there four days, and the gentleman said it was fortunate we had come to his aid, as the sepoys were disobedient, and that he would apply to the General on our behalf. The General wrote to Agra, whence word came that arrangements would be made for the pay of our men. Two days afterwards the three regiments of infantry and the 2nd Light Cavalry surrounded us and imprisoned the Nana and myself in the Treasury, and plundered the magazine and Treasury of everything they contained, leaving nothing in either. The Sepoys made over two lakhs and eleven thousand rupees to the Nana, keeping their own sentries over it. The Nana was also under charge of these sentries and the Sepoys who were with us joined the rebels. After this the whole army marched from that place, and the rebels took the Nana Sahib and myself and all our attendants with them, and said, "Come to Delhi." Having gone six miles from Cawnpore, the Nana Sahib said that as the day was far spent, it was better to halt, and march next day. They agreed and halted. In the morning the whole army told the Nana to go with them towards Delhi. He refused, and they then said "Come with us to Cawnpore, and fight there." The Nana objected to this, but they would not listen to him, and so, taking him as a prisoner, they marched towards Cawnpore, and began to fight there. The fighting continued for twenty-four days, and on the twenty-fourth day the General raised the flag of peace, and the fighting ceased. The Nana got a female who had been captured before to write a note to General Wheeler, that the Sepoys would not obey his orders, and that if he wished he would get boats and convey him and those with him in the intrenchment as far as Allahabad. An answer came from the General that he approved of this arrangement, and the same evening the General sent the Nana something over one lakh of rupees, and authorised him to keep the amount. The following day I went and got ready forty boats, and having caused all the gentlemen, ladies, and children to get into the boats, I started them off to Allahabad. In the meantime the whole army, artillery included, having got ready, arrived at the river Ganges. The Sepoys jumped into the water and commenced a massacre of all the men, women, and children, and set the boats on fire. They destroyed thirty-nine boats. One, however, escaped as far as Kola Kankar, but was there caught and brought back to Cawnpore, and all on board of it destroyed. Four days after this the Nana said he was going to Bithur to keep the anniversary of his mother's death; the Sepoys allowed him to go, some of them accompanying him. Having kept the anniversary, they brought him back to Cawnpore, and took for their pay the money they had first made over to the Nana's charge, and made arrangements to fight against Hasan Fatehpur, where they heard some Europeans had arrived from Allahabad, and they told the Nana to accompany them. The Nana refused. The Nana and I remained at Cawnpore, and sent Jawala Persad, the Nana's Agent, with them to Fatehpur. Being defeated there, they retreated to Cawnpore and the European force pressed them the whole way to Cawnpore, when there was a battle for about two hours, and the rebel army was again defeated, and ran away from Cawnpore. Under these circumstances the Nana and I fled to Bithur, arriving there at midnight, and the rebel army followed us. Next morning the Nana, taking some money with him, went to Fatehpur. The rebel army followed and looted the place. The Nana, Bala Sahib, Rao Sahib, and I, with all our wives, crossed the Ganges in boats, and arrived at Fatehpur in the Lucknow territory, and put up with the Chaudri Bhopal Singh. Some days passed, when the 42nd Native Infantry arrived at Sheorajpur, and wrote to the Nana to send them some one to take them to him.

I went and told them that the Nana had sent for them. In the meantime the English army had arrived, and the 42nd went to Bithur and fought there. I accompanied them, and having been defeated we fled, crossed the Ganges, and came to the Nana. Some days later I received orders from the Nana to go to Gwalior, and bring back to fight the English such of the Contingent as were at Morar. I went to Morar, and brought back the Contingent to Kalpi. The Nana had sent his brother, the Bala Sahib, to Kalpi, and according to his order I went with the army to fight against Cawnpore, leaving a small force and magazine at Kalpi. At Cawnpore there was a battle which lasted eleven days, when the rebel army was defeated, and we all ran away. Next day we fought at Sheorajpur, and, having been defeated, we ran away, taking fifteen guns with us. I and the Bala Sahib and the Rao Sahib, who had been sent by the Nana to Cawnpore, crossed the Ganges at Nana Mau-ki-Ghat. We remained at Khera for the night. I got orders from the Rao Sahib to go and take charge of the small force and magazine left at Kalpi, in obedience to which I went there. After my arrival at Kalpi I received orders from the Nana to go and attack Charkhari, and that the Rao Sahib would be sent after me. I accordingly went to Charkhari with 900 sepoys, 200 cavalry, and 4 guns, and fighting began. Four days afterwards the Rao Sahib came to Kalpi. I fought at Charkhari for eleven days, and took it. I took 24 guns and three lakhs of rupees from the Raja. The Rajas of Banpur and Shahgarh and Divan Deshpat and Daulat Singh, the Kuchwaya Kharwala, and a great gathering of people joined me there at this time. I received a note from the Rani of Jhansi to the effect that she was waging war with the Europeans, and begging me to come to her aid. I reported this to the Rao Sahib at Kalpi. The Rao came to Jaipur and gave me permission to go to the assistance of the Rani. Accordingly I went to Jhansi and halted at Barwa Sagar. There Raja Man Singh came and joined me. The next day about a mile from Jhansi our army had a fight with the English Army. At this time we had 22,000 men and 28 guns. In this battle we were defeated. Part of the rebel army with 4 or 5 guns fled to Kalpi, and I went to the same place by way of Bhander and Kunch, with 200 sepoys. The Rani arrived at Kalpi the same evening as myself, and begged the Rao Sahib to give her an army that she might go and fight. The following morning the Rao Sahib ordered a parade of all the troops, and told me to accompany the Rani to battle. Accordingly I accompanied her with an army, and there was a battle at Kunch which lasted until noon. We were again defeated, and I fled to Chirki, which is about four miles from Jalaun, where my people were. The Rao had a battle afterwards at Kalpi, and was defeated, and he and his whole army arrived at Gopalpur; we all marched thence towards Gwalior. We had one day's fight with Maharaja Sindhia and defeated him. Three days afterwards all Sindhia's army joined the Rao Sahib, and having procured from the Gwalior treasury through Amarchand Batia, the treasurer, sufficient funds, pay was distributed to the army. Ram Rao Govind was also with us. Some days after the English army arrived at Gwalior from Kalpi, and a force also came from Sirpur. Fighting again took place and continued for four or five days, during which the Rani of Jhansi was killed. Ram Rao Govind had her corpse burnt and we were all defeated and fled, taking 25 guns with us. We reached Jaora-Alipur, and remained there during the night. Next morning we were attacked, and fought for an hour and a half. We fired five shots, the English army fired four shots, and we then ran off, leaving all our guns. We crossed the Chambal and reached Tonk. The Nawab of Tonk fought with us, and we took four guns from him. With these guns we proceeded to Bhilwara by way of Madhopur and Indargarh. We were there attacked by the English force, and I fled during the night, accompanied by my army and guns. At that time I had 8,000 or 9,000 men and 4 guns. We halted a night at Kotra, four miles from Nathdwara. Next morning we marched towards Patan, and, after proceeding about a mile, the English army arrived. We left our guns and fled, reaching Patan as fugitives. The Nawab of Banda, who had come with us from Kalpi, and the Nawab of Kumona, who had joined us at Indurkhi, were both with us. On our arrival at Patan we conquered the Raja, got possession of his guns and magazines, and surrounded the palace. Next day I told the Raja to give me some money to pay the expenses of my army. He said he could give me only five lakhs of rupees. I returned and told the Rao Sahib this. Next day the Rao Sahib sent for the Raja and demanded 25 lakhs. The Raja declared that he could not give more than five lakhs; but after some discussion it was settled that he should pay fifteen. The Raja said he would go to his palace and send this sum. He went accordingly, and sent two and a quarter lakhs in cash, and promised that the rest should follow. By next day he had paid up five lakhs.

Imam Ali, Woordie-Major, 5th Irregular Cavalry, ill-treated the Raja, who fled during the night. We remained there five days, and issued three months' pay to our troops at the monthly rate of thirty rupees to each sowar and twelve rupees to each foot soldier. We then marched for Sironj, taking eighteen guns with us. On reaching Rajgarh the English army came up and attacked us. We left our guns and fled, reaching Sironj by way of Nija Kila. We halted at Sironj eight days, and proceeded thence to Isagarh. On arrival we demanded supplies, but the people woud not give them. We, therefore, attacked and plundered the place. We halted the following day, and the Rao Sahib told me to go to Chanderi while he went round by Talbahat. I accordingly went to Chanderi and the Rao Sahib to Lalitpur. On reaching Chanderi, four shots were first fired on us from the fort, which we attacked and fought with Sindhia's Agent. After three days we marched from Chanderi towards Mangraoli, taking eleven guns, seven of which we got from Isagarh and four from Sironj. On our march to Mangraoli we met the English army. Shots were fired for a short time, when we left all our guns and fled.

I reached Jakhlaun, and next day went to Sultanpur, where the Rao Sahib also arrived. After three days the English force arrived, and the Rao Sahib took his army to Jakhlaun, and some firing took place there. I was not present in this fight. The Rao Sahib returned to Lalitpur, and the following day proceeded to Kajuria and halted there. Next day the English army came up just as we were going to march, and an action began which lasted an hour and a half. We then left all our guns and fled, and reached Talbahat. We halted there, and the following day went to Jakhlaun, and then to Etawah, 12 miles distant, where we stopped. We there heard that the English army was coming to surround us, and marched at night. The English force came up in the morning, and our army became separated. I accompanied the Rao Sahib, and we proceeded *viâ* Rajgarh, and crossed the Narbada and got to Khargon. The troops with us burned the Government *thana* (station) and bungalow at Kandula. This was about four months ago. At Khargon there were some of Holkar's troops—one hundred and forty troopers, a company of infantry, and two guns. These we forced to join us and took with us the following day when we marched towards Gujrat, crossing the high road where the telegraph wire ran. The Sepoys broke the wire and plundered seven carts which were on the road proceeding with Government property towards Gwalior, and seized the *chaprasis* and *chaukidars* who were with the carts, and took them with them. Some of the Chaukidars were hanged by them. We there left the high road and proceeded westward. Next day we were surprised by the English force, and leaving our two guns we fled and reached the Narbada. An officer with a hundred men was on the opposite bank. Our force began to cross and the officer and troopers ran off. We plundered the village of Chikla, and marched thence at midnight. After proceeding 34 miles we halted at Rajpur. Next day we took 3,900 rupees and three horses from the Raja of that place, and went on to Chota Udepur. The following day the English force surprised us, some of them were killed and some of ours. From Chota Udepur we went to Deogarh Bari, and our army became separated. There was jungle at that plac , and I halted there two days Our troops having been assembled again, we went to Banswara. There our men plundered sixteen or seventeen camel loads of cloth belonging to a merchant. We went thence to Salomar, and I called on Kaisar Singh, Agent to the Udaipur Raja, to furnish us with supplies. He sent us some, and we started the following day with the intention of going to Udaipur. However, on the way we received news of the English force, and retraced our steps to Bhilwara. We remained there two days and then proceeded to Partabgarh where we fought for two hours with a body of English troops from Neemuch. About 8 o'clock in the evening we ran off, and halted six miles east of Mandesar. We then went by three stages to Zirapur. An English force surprised us there, and we were again surprised by another force at Chapra Baraud. We fled thence to Nahargarh, at which place nine shots were fired at us from guns. We moved out of range, and halted for the night, and the Rao Sahib sent Risaldar Nannu Khan to call Raja Man Singh. The Raja came and accompanied us to a place about two miles from Paron, where we halted. We remained there two days and on the third went on to a place about 8 miles beyond Kilwari. Raja Man Singh accompanied us as far as a river which we crossed on the way, and then left us. We made two stages thence to Indargarh, where Feroz Shah met us with the body-guard and 12th Irregulars. Next day we made two stages to Dausa. The English force surprised us there; some men on both sides were killed, and flying thence towards Marwar we reached a village about sixty miles from Marwar, whose name I forget. At 4 o'clock that night we were surprised by the English force, and the 12th Irregular Cavalry separated from the Rao Sahib's army. Next day Thakur Narayan Singh, Ajit Singh, uncle of Raja Man Sing, and Thakur Ganga Singh joined us. They were coming in this direction. I had been quarrelling with the Rao Sahib all the way from Deogarh Bari, and told him I could flee no longer, and that I should leave him on the first opportunity. The opportunity occurred here, and I left him and accompanied the above named parties in this direction. When I left the Rao Sahib he had about six thousand men with him. I was accompanied by three men, two to cook my food and one groom, three horses and a pony. The two *pandits* were Ram Rao and Narayan. The groom Gobind left me and ran off after coming two stages. We reached the Paron jungle, and met Raja Man Singh. Ajit Singh took leave of Raja Man Singh and went home. Narayan Singh and I remained with Raja Man Singh. The Raja said, "Why did you leave your force? You have not acted rightly in so doing." I replied that I was tired of running away, and would remain with him whether I had done right or wrong. I heard after this that the Rao Sahib's army had gone to Patan and thence towards Sironj. I told Raja Man Singh I would send a man to obtain news of them, and he approved of my doing so. I sent accordingly, and got information that the Rao Sahib was not there, but Imam Ali, Woordie-Major, Feroz Shah, and Adil Muhammad, Nawab of Ambapani, were there with eight or nine thousand men. Imam Ali, Woordie-Major of the 5th Irregular Cavalry, wrote to me to come and join them. I had lost my master's (the Nana's) seal, and had another made up at Paron.

When I heard as above from the Woordie-Major, I sent a man to Raja Man Singh, who was at Mahudia in Major Meade's Camp, to inform him that I had received a note of this purport, and to ask him if I should go or remain. Raja Man Singh had consulted me before giving himself up to Major Meade, and had left one of his men with me, saying "Stop wherever this man takes you." Raja Man Singh replied to my message that he would come in three days to see me, and we should then decide what to do.

He came accordingly on the night of the third day, and spoke a great deal to me, and told me that he had met Major Meade and that his disposition was good. When I asked him what he advised—whether I should go or remain—he said he would reply in the morning. I then went to sleep, and during the night some of the sepoys of the Government came and seized me and took me to Major Meade's camp.

Signed by TANTIA TOPI.

Question by Major Meade.—Have you made this statement of your own free will and without compulsion ? and has any promise been made or hope held out to you to induce you to make it ?

Answer.—I have of my own free will caused this statement to be written, and no one has force me, or held out hope or promise of any sort to induce me to do so.

Signed by TANTIA TOPI, Agent of Nana Sahib, and two witnesses.

The above deposition or statement was made by the prisoner Tantia Topi in my presence on the 10th of April, 1859, at Camp Mushairi, of his own voluntary act and without compulsion of any sort, or promise made or hope held out to him as inducement to make it.

(Sd.) R. J. MEADE, *Major,*
Commanding Field Force.